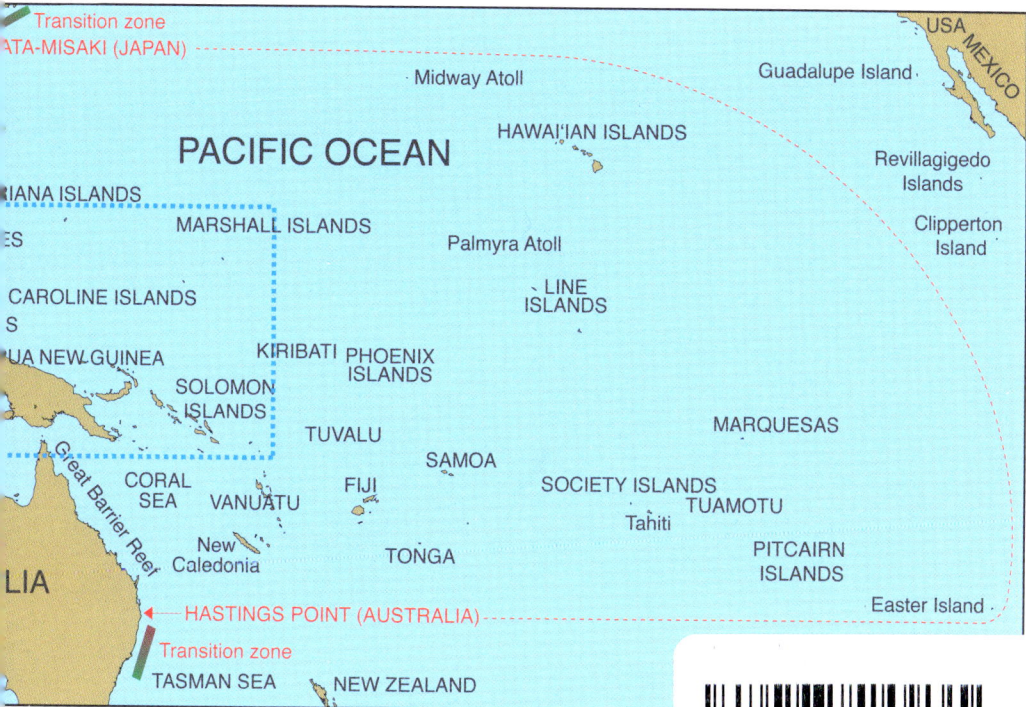

Midway Atoll

Guadalupe Island

USA
MEXICO

PACIFIC OCEAN

HAWAIIAN ISLANDS

Revillagigedo
Islands

RIANA ISLANDS

MARSHALL ISLANDS

Palmyra Atoll

Clipperton
Island

CAROLINE ISLANDS

LINE
ISLANDS

UA NEW GUINEA

KIRIBATI PHOENIX
ISLANDS

SOLOMON
ISLANDS

MARQUESAS

TUVALU

SAMOA

CORAL
SEA   VANUATU

FIJI

SOCIETY ISLANDS

TUAMOTU

Tahiti

New
Caledonia

TONGA

PITCAIRN
ISLANDS

Easter Island

Great Barrier Reef

LIA

HASTINGS POINT (AUSTRALIA)

Transition zone

TASMAN SEA   NEW ZEALAND

MARIANA ISLANDS

Guam

MARSHALL ISLANDS

Enewatak

Palau

Pohnpei

CAROLINE ISLANDS

PAPUA NEW GUINEA

New Guinea

Latangai

New
Britain Bougainville

SOLOMON
ISLANDS

ulauan
aru

Santa Isabel
Malaita

Guadalcanal

San Cristobal   Lord Howe Is.

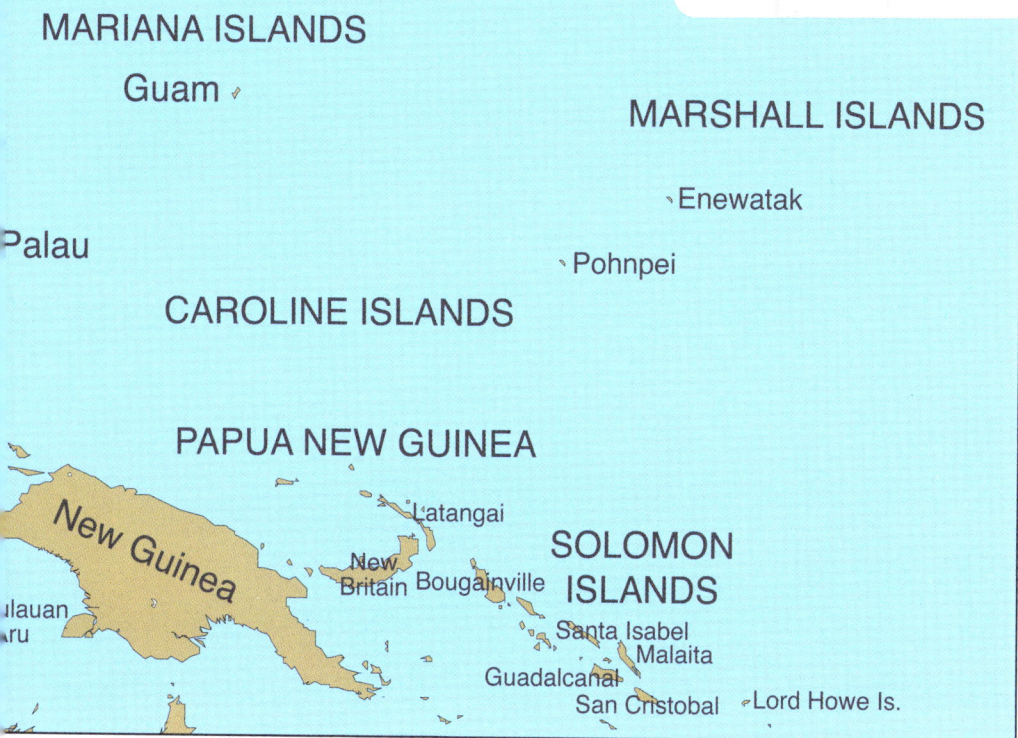

o-Pacific indicated in red; the blue broken rectangle delineates the central Indo-Pa-
Indo-Pacific region where most of the diversity of sea slugs is concentrated.

Nudibranch & Sea Slug Identification

INDO-PACIFIC

Second Edition

Terrence M. Gosliner
Ángel Valdés
David W. Behrens

New World Publications, Inc.
Jacksonville, Florida USA

ACKNOWLEDGMENTS

We especially thank many individuals who have enabled us to advance our knowledge of opisthobranchs since the publication of *Indo-Pacific Nudibranchs and Sea Slugs* in 2008. The increased understanding of species distributions and records of new species come from a large and dedicated network of individuals from throughout the Indo-Pacific. We thank all of these individuals who are too numerous to name specifically.

Support for our work in the Philippines, particular thanks go to Margaret and Will Hearst, without whose generosity the various expeditions would not have occurred. All of the friends and partners who helped make this work a success are literally too numerous to mention here, but special acknowledgment must be given to: Secretary of Agriculture Proceso J. Alcala; former Philippine Consul General Marciano Paynor, Consul General Henry Bensurto, and the Consular staff in San Francisco; BFAR Directors Dr. Malcom I. Sarmiento and Attorney Asis G. Perez; BFAR colleagues, especially Attorney Analiza Vitug, Ludivina Labe, Alma Dickson, Captain Ernaldo T. Cawaling, Rafael Ramiscal, and Loida Cainglit, PAWB Director Dr. Mundita Lim, the U.S. Embassy staff, especially Heath Bailey, Maria Theresa N. Villa and Dovas Saulys; staff of the Department of Foreign Affairs; UP administrators and colleagues including UP Presidents Emerlinda Roman and Alfredo Pasqual, Vice President Giselle Concepción, Dr. Malou McGlone, Dr. Annette Meñez; staff of the National Museum of the Philippines, especially, Dr. Jeremy Barns and Marivene Manuel Santos; Jessie de los Reyes; Marites Pastorfide; Sol Solleza; Boy Venus; Joy Napeñas; Peri Paleracio; Alexis Principe; Ditto de la Rosa; Darwin Raymundo; May Pagsinohin; Susan Po-Rufino; Ipat Luna; Enrnique Nuñez; Jen Edrial; Anne Hazel Javier; Jay-o Castilla, Arvel Malubag; Malou Babilonia; Mada Rivera; and certainly not least of all, Mary Lou Salcedo.

We also thank Michael Berumen and his colleagues at the King Abdullah University of Science and Technology for enabling the expedition that allowed us to find many of the new species and records from Saudi Arabia.

Extensive field observations and photos were made by Christiane Waldrich and her many friends and colleagues in Indonesia added remarkable observations from poorly known areas in the Coral Triangle. Alicia Hermosillo, Kevin Lee, Jim Black, Mike Miller, Jim Anderson, and others continued to make huge contributions to understanding of Indo-Pacific opisthobranchs from Indonesia, the Philippines and Papua New Guinea. While the Coral Triangle continues to provide the richest fauna in the Indo-Pacific, major advances in our knowledge of more isolate parts of the Indo-Pacific such as the remote islands of the western Indian Ocean, largely through the study by Philibert Bidgrain and colleagues. Other major new observations were made by Scott and Jeanette Johnson from the Marshall islands and other localities. Anthony Berberian, Fabien Michenet, Jean Marc Levy and several other keen observers shared their amazing observations and discoveries from throughout French Polynesia. Special appreciation is extended to Cory Pittman for his collection of specimens of from the Hawai'ian Islands. His detailed notes and collection records greatly added to the description of many species. Sincere thanks are also extended to Philippe Bouchet and his colleagues at the Muséum national d'Histoire naturelle, Paris for making possible the collections from southern Madagascar and Papua New Guinea. Philippe's continuing zeal for collecting new material from remote parts of the world is greatly appreciated. Richard Willan and Nathalie Yonow pointed out a number of errors in the 2008 book that were corrected in this edition. Last but not least, we would like to recognize five very important contributors who are no longer with us: Mary Jane Adams, Neville Coleman, Allen Connell, Denise Tackett, Steve Drogin, Leslie Newman, and Leanne Atkinson provided numerous photographs and important data on the natural history of many species; they will be greatly missed.

Systematics research producing results reflected in this book was sponsored by the U.S. National Science Foundation (NSF) through grants DEB-9978155 and DEB-0329054 to Gosliner and Valdés, DEB-1257630 to Gosliner, Mooi, Williams and Rocha that permitted work to be undertaken in the Philippines and collaborative grants DEB-1355190 and DEB-1355177 to Krug and Valdés respectively. Scanning electron microscope photographs were taken at the Natural History Museum of Los Angeles County SEM purchased with NSF grant DBI-0216506 to Valdés *et al.*

SCIENTIFIC COLLABORATORS

The following individuals provided data from their research: Patrick Krug (various sacoglossan groups), John Berriman (*Oxynoe*), Vanessa Knutson (*Gymnodoris*), Jessica Goodheart (*Pleurobranchus*), Sabrina Medrano (*Polybranchia*), Jennifer McCarthy (Juliidae, *Placida*), Carissa Shipman (Dotidae), Rebecca F. Johnson (Chromodorididae), Shayle Matsuda (*Glossodoris* and *Doriprismatica*), Kara Layton and Nerida Wilson (*Chromodoris*), Yara Tibiriçá (*Halgerda*, *Chromodoris*), Leila Carmona (Aeolidiidae), Marta Pola (Proctonotidae), Kelly Larkin (*Dermatobranchus*), Brenna Green (Flabelliidae), Jennifer Austin and Manuel Malaquias (*Phanerophthalmus*).

CREDITS

PHOTO CREDITS

Graham Abbott, 110ml, 113ml, 169lr, 197t, 300llr, 404tr; *Mary Jane Adams*, 11[Fig12]ml, 30tr, 39tl, 44lr, 46tl, 68mr,lr 69ll, 70tr, 78tr, 138ml, 140tl, 151ml, 153lr, 155tr, 172mr, 192lr, 194mr, 202ltr, 210lr, 213tl,lr, 219lr, 300mr, 374tr; *Charles Anderson*, 88tl; *Jim Anderson*, 37ll, 69m, 121mr, 210tr, 220ll, 252tr, 269lr, 270tl, 275ml, 276ll, 322ml, 37ll; *Ryanskiy Anrey*, 83mr; *Dharma Antonio*, 365ml; *Justine Arnold*, 134ll; *Leanne & David Atkinson*, 172lr, 230tl; *Mike Bartick*, 60lr, 255tr; *Be Ike*, 410ml; *Scott Bennett*, 40mr; *Anthony Berberian*, 21tr, 23tr, 27lll, 34lr, 55ll, 56tl, 106mr, 143tr, 144ll, 145mr, 148lr, 156ml,ll, 173tl, 181mr, 183ml, 216ll, 222tr, 233mr, 235lr, 252lr, 275mr, 293lr, 328m, 340ll, 386ll,lr,mr, 387tr,ll, 390lmr, 396tl, 410tl, 413tr, 419mr, 421ll, 424tr, 432ll; *Vishal Bhave*, 55tr,ml, 159tl; *Philibert Bidgrain*, 84mr, 110tl, 149lr, 162ml, 164tl, 411lr, 430ll; *Kerstin Binoth*, 53mr; *Jim Black*, 11[Fig12]tr, 24tl, 31mr, 35lr, 37tl, 65lr, 86lr, 104lr, 110mr, 143tl, 152tl, 183lr, 188mr, 192tl, 196ll, 208ml, 238lr, 242mr,ll, 249tr, 252tl, 255lr,mr, 265tl, 273tr, 304tmlr, 321ml, 337lr, 338mr, 341t, 376tr, 377tr, 400mr,l, 404tr, 409ll; *Ed & Laura Blackshaw*, 303lr; *Bob Bolland*, 53tr, 54lr, 67tr, 89tr, 106lr, 108tr, 131lr, 143mr, 145ll, 158lr, 166tr, 169ll, 172ml, 236tl,mtl, 237tl, 247mr, 248ml, 254tl, 256m, 269tl, 320lr, 372lr, 388tl, 395mr, 414mr, 428ll; *Pauline Bosserelle*, 420mr; *Philippe Bouchet*, 197tr, 242lr; *Kevin Bourdon*, 423lr; *Clay Bryce*, 87tl,tr, 125tr, 183tr; *Carol Buchanan*, 139tl; *David Burdick*, 20ml, 107ll; *Debra Burnsworth*, 139lr, 352tl; *Ferda Büyükbaykal*, 33mr; *Christophe Cadet*, 62ml, 129tl, 203tl, 340t, 427tr; *Yolanda Camacho-García*, 18mr, 25tr, 46lr, 51ml, 70ml, 73ll, 80tl, 92ll, 125tl, 130tr, 140mr, 141ml, 152mmr, 158tl, 160tl, 162tl,tr, 176ml, 181tr, 182ll, 188tl, 209mll, 230lr, 231ml,mr, 313tr, 331lmr, 389tr, 390lml, 403mr, 412tr, 423ll, 426tr; *Clay Carlson*, 173mr, 216ml, 285lr, 312mr, 322tr, 342m, 388ll; *Mark Chamberlain*, 13[Fig15]tr, 40tr,mr, 63ml, 135tl, 196tl, 199tr, 322ll, 374ml, 432lr; *Sneha Chandran B. K.*, 203ll; *Chay Hoon*, 74tl; *Steve Childs*, 324mr; *Ivan Choong*, 37ml, 297ml; *Stewart Clarke*, 150tl,tr,ml,mr, 288tl; *Les Clear*, 88ml; *Gary Cobb*, 79ll, 164ml, 168ll, 330l; *Neville Coleman*, 178tr, 255tl; *Pat Colin*, 92mr,mr, 162ll, 240mr; *Allan Connell*, 166tl; *David Cowdery*, 21ll, 28ml, 203lr; *Christopher Crowley*, 39tr, 111mr, 137lr, 146ll, 169ml, 200ml, 300tr; *Chris Cunnold*, 231tr; *Sophie Darnis*, 145lr; *Jeffrey Davies*, 37mr, 289ml, 407ll, 414ll; *Tom Davis*, 60tr; *Angelo de Faveri*, 234ml, 318ll, 365tr; *Lorenzo de Ponti*, 286tr; *Lorenzo de Ponti*, 307mr; *Helmut Debelius*, 256tr; *Henk Dekker*, 208tl; *Darlene DeLancey*, 262mr; *Ned DeLoach*, 376ll; *Francesco DeMarchi*, 291tl; *Maureen Dengah*, 248tr; *Noah DesRosiers*, 136lr; *Marta Dominguez*, 220mr; *Steve Drogin*, 45tr, 225ll; *Philipp Eschweiller*, 121ml; *Mabel Fang*, 7[Fig3]tl, 114lr, 157lr, 304ml; *Pauline Fiene*, 17mr, 18tl,ml, 46mr, 50tl, 91mr, 160tr, 216mr, 232ll, 243t, 245ll, 249tl, 250lr, 257ml, 263mr, 268tr,mr, 273mr, 313tl, 321lr, 340ml, 354ll, 371mr, 391tr, 393tr; *Eric Fly*, 20tr; *Valda Fraser*, 19ll, 44ll, 89mr, 97mr, 178ml, 230tr,ml, 246mr, 258l, 263lr; *Lynn Funkhauser*, 104ml; *Jessica Goodheart*, 249ml, 353ll, 354tr; *Michael Gosliner*, 220tr; *John Greenamyer*, 26tl, 36mr, 41tr, 104mr, 148tl, 196ml, 252m, 276tr; *Jeff Hamann*, 9[Fig8]bl, 9[Fig8]bm, 45tl,ll, 57mr, 69tr, 109ll, 129ml, 135tr, 174ml, 177tl, 185lr, 186mr, 260m, 261tl, 266mr, 271m, 280mr, 289ll, 306mr, 320mr, 375tl; *Carole Harris*, 13[Fig15]ml, 41tl, 44mr, 158ml, 159tr, 193tr, 228ll, 229tl, 231ll, 247ml, 264tl,m 339mr; *Alicia Hermosillo*, 7[Fig3]bl,br, 9[Fig7]ml,mtr,bl, 11[Fig12]bl, 12[Fig14]tl,bl, 21ml,mr,lr, 23tl, 29mr, 31ml, 32ml, 35ll, 36tr, 41tl, 43tl,tr, 46tr, 49tl,lr, 51mr,ll, 52tl, 53ll, 60ll, 61mr, 64ml, 67tl, 68tl, 69tl,ml, 70lr, 71tl, 74ml, 79tr, 83tr,ml, 84ml, 94tl,ml, 98tl, 100tl, 103mr, 105ml,tl, 108ml,mll, 111ll, 115mr, 116tl,tr, 118tl, 119tl, 122tl,tr, 145tr, 169tl, 178mr, 201tl,tr,tml,mr,tll, 206lml,ll, 211lr, 212tr, 228tr, 237ll, 241tr, 248tl, 257tl, 277tr, 279mr, 280lr, 286tl, 295ll, 297tl, 298mr, 303tl, 305tl, 307ml, 319tl, 323lr, 326mr, 371lr, 376tl,mr, 377lr, 383lr, 384tr, 388lr, 391tl, 402tr, 413ml, 421mr, 425tr, 429tml,tr, 432ml, 434mr; *Jean-François Hervé*, 110tr, 113tl, 178tl; *Heide Hoesel*, 434ml; *Anthony Holley*, 55lr, 377mr, 410lr, 420lr; *Wofgang Holz*, 402mr; *Anouk Houben*, 167tr, 385mr; *Paul Humann*, 317tl, 401t; *Stuart Hutchison*, 57l; *Kaoru Imagawa*, 273ml; *Jun Imamoto*, 175ml, 177mr, 276ml, 321mr, 335ll, 434ll; *Fabia Inhof*, 299lr; *Yury Ivanov*, 64tr, 269ll, 327tl, 379tr; *Jo Jamieson*, 246tr, 256tl; *Jeanette Johnson*, 34ml, 58mr, 61ml, 84ll, 120mr, 122ll, 123tr, 155lr, 177ll, 206tr, 208mr,ll, 237lr, 244ll, 246ll, 268ml, 282ll, 287tr, 306tr, 312tl, 314tl, 318ml, 336tl, 398lr, 402lr, 404mr, 426ml,mr; *Scott Johnson*, 18ll, 30ml, 48tr,mr, 66tr, 72tl, 76lr, 85mr, 88lr,ml, 89lr, 90ml, 99tl, 103ll, 109ml, 127tr, 130mr, 139tr, 143ml, 144mr, 153tl,mr, 160ml,ll, 171tl,tr, 174t, 175lr, 179tr, 180tr, 181lr, 190tl, 195tl, 199ll, 200tl, 208tr, 214lr, 244ml, 246ml, 250ll, 286mr,lr, 290ll, 291tr, 294mr, 306tl, 324tl, 329ml, 358tr, 374tl, 396tr, 401tl, 422ml; *Burt Jones & Maurine Shimlock*, 198mr, 256lr, 373ml; *Georgina Jones*, 310tr; *Sven Kahlbrock*, 272tl; *Yuri Kawahara*, 292lr; *Martha Kiser*, 146mr; *Vanessa Knutson*, 76tr,mr, 77lr, 79mr, 101tr, 191tl,lr; *Binyamin Koretz*, 225tr, 270mr; *Patrick Krug*, 397lr, 398m, 399mr,lr, 404tl, 404mr, 405tr; *Pierre Laboute*, 112tl,lr, 133tl, 196tr,mr, 217mr, 224mr,tl, 224tr; *Kara Layton & Nerida Wilson*, 134lr; *Oren Lederman*, 141l; 350ll; *Kevin Lee*, 23mr, 29lr, 41ll, 62tl, 64lr, 65mr, 93tr,mr, 111lr, 138tl, 158ll, 168mr, 173tr, 186tr, 192mr, 194mr, 223mr, 229lr, 234tr, 251ll, 255ml, 258mr, 259tr, 260mr, 313ml, 317tr, 370ml, 378tl, 382mr, 383mr, 384tl, 385tr, 405lr, 415tl; *Jean-Mark Levy*, 54ml, 99ml, 171ll, 184lr, 285ll, 294tr, 302lr, 304tr, 307lr, 312ml, 328ll, 330t, 332m,lr, 348tl, 399tr, 421tl, 431lr; *Philippe Maestrati*, 234tl, 343tr,mr, 346ll, 347ml,mr, 348mr,ll,lr, 349mr, 350lr, 351lr, 352tl, 359ll,lr; *Manuel Malaquias*, 355tl, 358tl; *Julie Marshall*, 62ll, 244tl, 390tr; *Nishina Masayoshi*, 45lr, 158tr, 168tl, 226ll, 242tr, 259ml, 271l, 341lr,ll, 420tl; *Brian Mayes*, 239tr; *Fabien Michenet*, 137tr, 139ml, 149tl,ll, 183mr, 250tr,tl, 338tr, 386ml, 387tl,ml,lr,mr, 410tr, 413tl, 417mr; *Mike Miller*, 22tl, 23ml, 33ll, 41mll,mr, 60ml, 82tr, 95ml, 96lr, 100ll, 104tl, 105lr, 118ml, 119ll, 123lr, 126tl,ll, 134ml, 137ll, 151tr, 154lr, 163lr, 168ml, 170l,ml, 179mr, 187ll, 190ll, 192tl, 194tl, 202ttr,mr, 206tml,lmr, 224ll, 227ll, 251tl, 253mr, 263tr, 264ttr, 266tl, 300tl, 309ml, 338ml,lr, 369mr, 401mr, 429lml; *David Mullins*, 63mr, 139ll, 141tr, 284ll, 365mr; *Emilia Lydia Murcott*, 325ml; *Rie Nakano*, 187lr, 378ml; *Susumu Nakayama*, 174ll, 175mr; *Lawrence Neal*, 154tl, 181ll, 192ml, 207l, 223lr, 225tl, 251lr, 385ml, 430mr; *Leslie Newman*, 257ll; *Chicako Nishina*, 153ll; *Kazuko Ojima*, 276tl; *Atsushi Ono*, 129tr, 159mr, 292tl, 325mr, 364lr, 378tr, 381mr, 417lr; *Peri Paleracio*, 228tl, 265tr; *Vie Panyarachun*, 247tl, 298ll; *Dishant Parasharya*, 301ll, 319mr; *Gustav Paulay*, 150l, 187tl, 190ml, 193ml, 269ml, 353mr, 420ml; *Francis & Pirjo Pellet*, 50ml, 142ll, 239ll, 378lr, 430mr; *Constantinos Petrinos*, 8[Fig6]l,r, 9[Fig7]tl, 10[Fig9]bl, 11[Fig11]lr, 11[Fig12]tbl, 12[Fig14]tr,br, 13[Fig15]tl, 24mr, 25tl,ml, 26mr, 27ml, 32ll, 35tr, 40tl,ll, 43mrl, 45mlt, 72tl, 102tl, 109tr, 122mr, 124m, 132lr, 135lr,ml, 137ml, 140ml, 148trt,ll, 152lr, 161tl,tr, 164ll, 165lr, 168lr, 171mr,mr, 183ll, 187mr, 190tmr, 195lr, 197tm, 199tl, 202ml,ll, 207mr, 210tl, 225mr, 232ml, 236l, 238mr, 262lr, 284tr, 287lr, 306ll,lr, 323tl, 334tl, 336lr, 368tml,mr, 369mr; *Cory Pitman*, 344mr, 348lr, 349ml, 358ll,lr, 363mr, 368t, 396ll,lr, 397ml,ll,tr, 398tl; *Christiane Plate*, 165ll; *Marina Poddubetskaia*, 16mr, 17ml,tr, 19tr, 79lr, 106ll, 108lr, 136tl,tr, 167tl, 170tr, 185ll, 221lr, 234mr, 249mr, 263ll, 264tmr, 270ll, 299tr, 351ml, 360t, 364tl,tr, 369ml, 378tl, 397tl, 400t, 430lr, 435t,ll; *Marta Pola*, 40lr, 45mrl; *Wolfgang Pölzer*, 60ml; *Bruce Potter*, 101tl; *Veronique Pretorius*, 305lr; *Duncan Pritchard*, 334ml; *Jack Randall*, 241lr; *Alain Benoit Rassat*, 93ll,lr, 117mr,ml, 217ml; *Jeff Rosenfeld*, 167mr, 265ml, 418lr; *Bill Rudman*, 11[Fig12]ttl, 17lr, 57ml, 59mr, 64mr, 164lr, 167l,ml, 178lr, 180mr, 324tr; *Carine Schrurs*, 27mr, 243lr; *Terry Schuler*, 13[Fig17]b, 24tr; *Wolfgang Seifarth*, 215tl; *Brian Sellick*, 56tr, 205lmr, 313tr,ml; *Mike Severns*, 20lr, 189t, 200mr, 337tr; *Yasuhiro Shirai*, 381tr; *Roger Steene*, 70mr, 95mr, 135ll, 229ml, 262tr, 399tl; *Keoki Stender*, 180tl, 223ll; *Mark Strickland*, 13[Fig15]br, 24ml, 73mr, 87m, 108tl, 111tl, 143ll, 147tl,mr, 149mr, 157ml, 169lr, 184tl, 198tl, 207tl, 213tr,mr, 225ml, 247ll, 300ml, 304lmr, 331ll, 374ll, 416ml,lmr,ll; *Wonowidjojo Swari*, 294tl, 377ll; *Cornelis Swennen*, 79ml; *Denise Tackett*, 36ml, 132ll, 254lr; *William Tan*, 231tl, 432mr; *Kotaro Tanaka*, 19lr, 385lr; *Marcel Tanke*, 36lr, 193tl, 324ll; *Doris Teufel*, 140tr, 141tl; *Yves Thévenet*, 71tr, 88tr, 89lr; *Hans Tibboel*, 149tr,ml, 151tl, 173ll, 219mr, 232tr,mr; *Yara Tibiriçá*, 88mr, 113ll,lr, 114tl, 137tl, 284ml, 354ml, 384mr; *Gordon Tillen*, 29ll, 271tr, 289mr, 297mr, 388mr, 409ml,lr; *John Todt*, 64tl, 313lr; *Martha Tressler*, 42mr, 61tr, 182tl, 199lr, 267ml, 276mr, 279tl, 288ll, 295tr, 310tl, 329mr, 332ll, 410ll, 423tl; *Bob VanSyoc*, 13[Fig16]b; *Yann von Arnim*, 241ll; *Heike Wägele*, 12[Fig13]b, 411ml; *Christiane Waldrich*, 9[Fig7]mr, 11[Fig12]mr,br, 31ll,lr, 32tl, 36tl, 37tr, 44ml, 47ll, 49tr, 53ml, 54tl,tr, 56ll,mr, 62lr, 63tl,tr, 64ll, 66ml, 67tl, 68tr, 91ll, 92tr, 94mr, 96ml, 98mr,ll, 123ml, 127tl,ml, 160mr, 180ll, 188ml, 238ml, 246tl,lr, 249ll,lr, 261tr, 268ll,lr, 273ll, 274tml,tmr, 275tl, 277tl,mr, 279ml,lr, 280tr,ml,ml, 281tr,mr,lr, 282tl, 283tr, 284tl,lr, 290mr, 291lr, 293tl, 294ll, 296tl, 309mr, 311mr,tl,lr, 318mr, 319lr, 321ll, 322lr, 324lr, 325tl, 328lr, 329lr, 334lr, 338ll,lr, 340lr,mr, 356ll, 367ml,mr, 413mr, 415tr, 424tl, 433lr; *Lindsay Warren*, 239lr, 290tl, 336tr; *Bob Widman*, 43l, 46mr, 47tl, 51lr, 80tr, 105tr, 144ml, 148tl, 241m, 247tlr, 248mr, 275ll, 289tr, 290ml, 315tl, 370tl,tr, 383tl, 390ll, 400ml, 417ml, 424ml, 427tl; *Bruce Wight*, 13[Fig17]t, 27tr, 194tr, 272tr, 429ttl; *Richard Willan*, 38tl, 273tl; *Gary Williams*, 26lr; *Nerida Wilson & Greg Rouse*, 134mr; *Leena Wong*, 407lr; *Steven Wong*, 57tl, 109tl, 142lr, 146tr; *Nathalie Yonow*, 39ml, 222mr; *Paul Zahl*, 158mr. All other photos taken by the authors.

ABOUT THE AUTHORS

Terrence M. Gosliner (center) – Senior Curator at the Department of Invertebrate Zoology and Geology of the California Academy of Sciences. Terry has devoted his 50 year-long research career to the scientific study of opisthobranchs and has published many papers and several books. Over the last 23 years, his research has focused on building an understanding of the biodiversity of the Philippines and working with local communities to develop more effective conservation strategies. The foundation of this book is the information and specimens collected during his many scientific expeditions to the tropical Indo-Pacific.

Ángel Valdés (left) – Professor of Biology at the California State Polytechnic University, Pomona and Research Associate at the Natural History Museum of Los Angeles County and the California Academy of Sciences. Ángel's research career focuses on the study of the biodiversity, phylogeny and biogeography of nudibranchs and other sea slugs and has published more than 140 scientific papers on these topics as well as several field guides. Ángel would like to dedicate this book to his daughter Lucía, the light of his life.

David W. Behrens (right) – Lecturer of Physiology, Marine Biology and Oceanography at Central Washington University and Research Associate at the California Academy of Sciences. Dave has a prolific career as an opisthobranch researcher and he is best known as the author of field guides and other books on opisthobranchs. He has also described many new species to science, and published over 75 referred journal publications and 80 popular articles on marine science topics. David would like to dedicate this book to Peggy Prudell, partner, lover and friend.

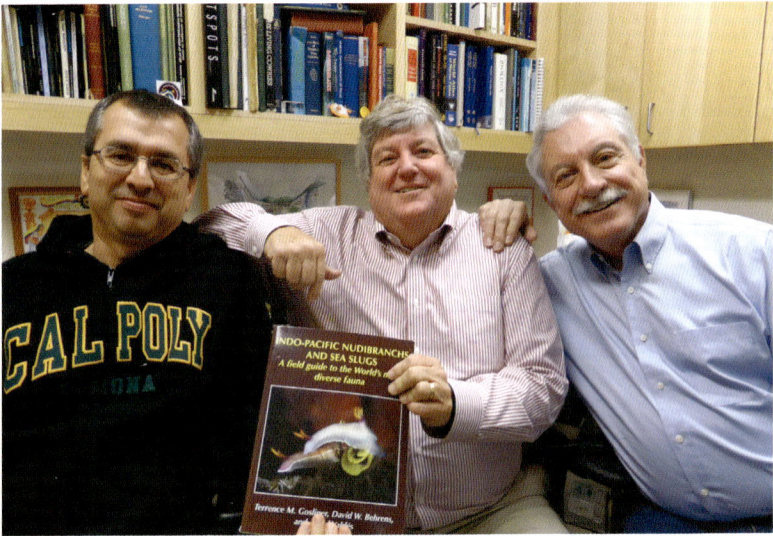

The three authors have collaborated in many projects together including a previous edition of this book. The present edition has been significantly improved, including an updated classification and more than 100 additional photos and species. The photo above was taken at the California Academy of Sciences in San Francisco, California in 2014.

INTRODUCTION

Where are the Indo-Pacific tropics?

Several recent books on opisthobranchs have dealt with animals from the Indo-Pacific (Debelius, 1996; Debelius & Kuiter, 2008; Coleman, 2001, 2008; Yonow, 2008), but these works also include species from adjacent temperate regions or focus in one region. In the case of Debelius' (1996), for instance, there are species from the tropical eastern Pacific of the Galápagos Islands, the California coast, and British Columbia. British Columbia is hardly tropical; the species found there are not just different, but do not share their closest relatives with species found in the Indo-Pacific region. So then, what is the Indo-Pacific region and what makes it unique? The Indo-Pacific represents the largest expanse of tropical ocean in the world, stretching from the Indian Ocean coast of southern Africa to the Red Sea to the central Pacific of the Hawai'ian Islands, Easter Island and the Marquesas. The eastern boundary of this region is not sharp, but we do know that the majority of the biota found along the tropical coast of the Americas is dramatically different from that of the Indo-Pacific. This major break in distributions is called the East Pacific Barrier and has been recognized by biogeographers (biologists who study the distribution patterns of organisms) for more than 150 years. The tropical eastern Pacific is isolated from the tropical Indo-Pacific by the shear size of the Pacific Ocean (most species are unable to disperse across the Pacific Ocean due to the fact that their larvae cannot stay alive long enough to endure the journey). Does this mean there are no Indo-Pacific species present in the tropical eastern Pacific? To the contrary, about 10% of the species found in the eastern Pacific are Indo-Pacific species that "leaked" into the Americas. Examples from this book include species like *Philinopsis cyanea*, *Dendrodoris elongata*, and *Phestilla melanobrachia*. However, the vast majority of species in the eastern Pacific is found nowhere else in the world and are endemic to this region. Their closest relatives, determined by genetic and phylogenetic studies, are most commonly found in the more temperate portions of the Americas or in the Caribbean. Thus, they have very different evolutionary histories that have been separated from those of Indo-Pacific species for about ten million years.

Just as there is no sharp east-west boundary of the Indo-Pacific, there are similarly no sharp southern and northern boundaries. While the tropics are strictly defined as the region between the Tropic of Cancer and the Topic of Capricorn, individual species each have their own distributional limits. Some species are more tolerant of cooler, sub-topical temperatures and can survive in these areas. The areas of the Indo-Pacific where the most ambiguity exists (as to where the boundaries of the Indo-Pacific are), include the Indian Ocean coast of South Africa, the east and west coasts of Australia and Japan. In southern Africa, the waters of Algoa Bay near Port Elizabeth is the area where tropical species no longer dominate and are instead replaced by a warm temperate endemic fauna. Along the coast of Western Australia the area south of Shark Bay represents this transition zone. In the east coast the border between southern Queensland and northern New South Wales represents the area where the endemic temperate fauna begins to dominate and we use Hastings Point as the southern boundary for eastern Australia. Similarly, the North Island of New Zealand also supports many Indo-Pacific species. In Japan, the Ryūkyū and Kerama Islands are inhabited by largely Indo-Pacific species while the main islands support largely warm-temperate and cold temperate species. We have used Sata-Misaki, at the end of the Osumi-Hanto Peninsula on the southernmost end of Kyūshū Island as the boundary for this book. However, Hachijo Island is a more northerly offshore island that still has a large number of tropical species and is influenced by offshore warmer water currents. We have used these convenient boundaries to determine the geographical scope of this book while being mindful that these boundaries are simply a necessary way to circumscribe what is actually a continuum of change. We should also point out, with global climate change, distributional patterns of all

the world's plants and animals are changing and we can fully expect that the tropical species will further extend their ranges into what are currently temperate regions. Numerous examples of species moving into previously colder waters have already been observed along the California coast, such as *Phidiana hiltoni*, which has moved north across the Golden Gate and is now the dominant nudibranch in this region. This will certainly happen also along the Japanese, Australian, and South African coasts.

Indo-Pacific Biodiversity: The most diverse marine biota of the world

The Indo-Pacific tropics support the richest marine fauna of any place in the world for most groups of organisms. The opisthobranchs (nudibranchs and sea slugs) are no exception to this rule. There are about 3,000 described species of opisthobranchs and at least 40% of these have been found exclusively in the Indo-Pacific tropics. When we examine how that diversity is distributed around the Indo-Pacific (Table 1), we find that the western Indian Ocean and the central Pacific have relatively fewer species than the western Pacific. The region bordered by the Philippines, Indonesia, and Papua New Guinea is known to have the greatest richness for most marine species and is known as the Coral Triangle.

Table 1. Diversity distribution around the Indo-Pacific.

Locality	Number of species known	Percent undescribed
Tanzania	258	16%
Madagascar	278	28%
Philippines	1200	54%
Papua New Guinea	646	52%
Guam	474	47%
Hawai'ian Islands	513	44%
French Polynesia	504	56%

Within the Coral Triangle recent studies (Carpenter & Springer, 2005) have demonstrated the greatest diversity of shore-fishes has been found in the area known as the Verde Island Passage (the waters between southern Luzon and Mindoro Islands, in the northern Philippine Archipelago). The same is true for nudibranchs and their relatives. In the "Anilao" area which includes the municipality of Mabini, the offshore communities of Tingloy and the area around Puerto Galera in northern Mindoro we have now found more than 1050 species of opisthobranchs! This area is truly the Center of the Center of Marine Diversity or the Apex of the Coral Triangle.

What is also surprising is that this region is not only so rich, but that more than half of the species found here are newly

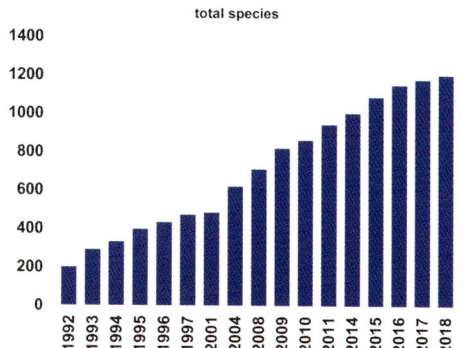

Figure 1. Cumulative total number of species found during successive expeditions to the Philippines.

Introduction

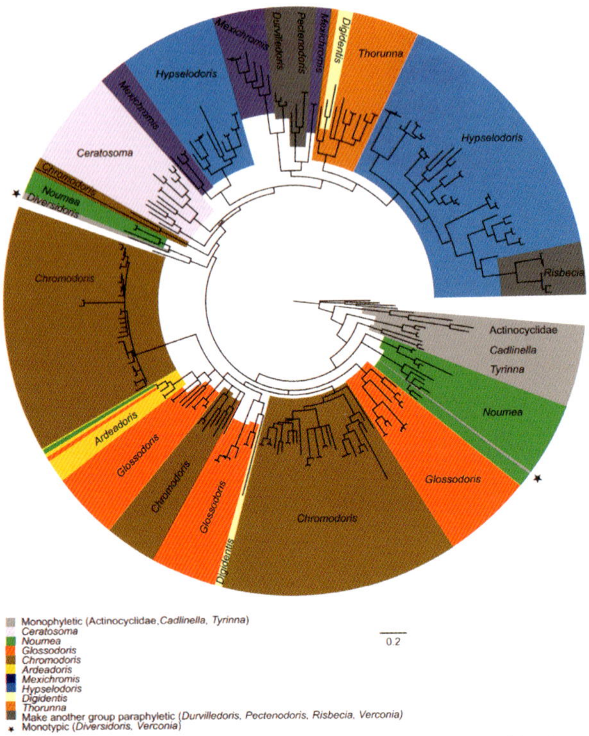

Figure 2. Molecular phylogenetic tree of the Chromodoridae with the traditional genera highlighted in different colors (see legend). Reprinted from R. Johnson & Gosliner (2012).

discovered, undescribed species. This is one reason why this area has received so much of our attention and research focus since 1992.

Since we began our studies in the Philippines, we have been tabulating the cumulative total number of species we have found. (Figure 1). In 2001, it looked like the species accumulation curve was about to level off, but successive trips in 2004 and 2008 have shown that clearly was not the case. We are still far from finding the total number of species that inhabit this region. For example, in 2008, we found 97 species not previously known from the Philippines and at least 50 of these species were new species. That is an amazing average of one new species per dive!

While the shallow waters of the Indo-Pacific are great places to search for new species, the deeper waters of this region are also relatively unexplored. Recent deep-water collections made by our colleagues at the *Museum National d'Histoire Naturelle*, in Paris have found specimens from New Caledonia, Vanuatu, Fiji, and the Philippines. Almost 90% of the material they have collected represent new species. Other frontiers of diversity in the Indo-Pacific include collection of microscopic opisthobranchs found between sand grains in shallow water and in fresh water streams that empty into the ocean. These efforts have also discovered many new species.

Recently, teams of scientists from the California Academy of Sciences and the Bishop Museum in Hawai'i have been exploring the twilight zone (from 60-150 m) of the Indo-Pacific using rebreathers to make these deep dives. These early explorations have already yielded several remarkable new species that are included in the present edition of this book.

Another measure of how much still remains to be discovered is in the percentage of undescribed species in the total fauna (Table 1). Several years ago our studies in both Madagascar and the Philippines indicated that respectively 19% and 42% of the species we had found there were undescribed. With additional study, those numbers have now risen to 28% and 54%, indicating that more of the species that we have found more recently are undescribed versus described ones. This is particularly surprising given that we have described more than 175 new species from the Coral Triangle and Western Indian Ocean since 1995.

Phylogeny of opisthobranchs and its impact on systematics and classification

Systematic biology, the naming and classification of organisms, is at the foundation of all fields of biology, because it provides the names that the rest of our science is founded upon. In other words, systematics provides the language by which all biologists communicate. Until relatively recently, systematics was as much art as science. Species were included in genera depending on how different or how similar they might be. This was a subjective interpretation of an individual systematic biologist or taxonomist, and systematists being people, they did not always agree.

All of that began to change in the 1960's with the advent of what is called phylogenetic systematics or cladistics. These ideas were introduced by a German systematist named Willi Hennig. He advocated a new philosophy that stated that names should be based on evolutionary relationships. These relationships should be determined by derived features (evolutionary novelties) that organisms share. Once those relationships are determined only groups that are monophyletic (include an ancestor and all of its descendants) should be formally named.

How do these philosophical ideas translate into practice? In the first place, a phylogenetic tree must be produced which incorporates as much information as possible about the group of organisms including characteristics of their anatomy and genetic information from DNA sequences, if that is available. All of those characteristics are then analyzed using computer programs that look for the evolutionary trees that have the shortest length. These tools operate using probability programs which function on the principle that the shortest trees that require the fewest steps are the most likely explanation of what really happened in the evolution of groups of living organisms.

The direction of evolutionary change is determined by comparing the condition of each character in a sample of species that are not in the group that one is studying, but are likely close relatives of that group. The species that are representatives of taxa not being studied are collectively called the outgroup. The taxa being studied are called the ingroup. If a specific character is found in only one form in the outgroup (but varies in the ingroup) we assume that the primitive condition for the ingroup is that which is found in the species forming the outgroup. Thus, the species with the more advanced condition have a derived feature they share, and the more derived features that they share the more likely that they are more closely related to each other than to other species.

The concept becomes real when we look at actual opisthobranchs. For many years there was debate as to whether the shelled sea hare, *Akera*, should be classified

Figure 3. Head shots of dorid nudibranchs showing oral tentacle and anterior edge of the foot morphology, tl: *Jorunna funebris* with a notched anterior border of the foot and digitiform oral tentacles ; tr: *Phyllidiopsis annae* with partially fussed tentacles and entire anterior border of the foot; bl: *Dendrodoris denisoni* with fussed oral tentacles; br: *Goniobranchus coi* with an entire border of the foot and digitiform oral tentacles.

the name *Risbecia* since members of this group have behavioral similarities in that they exhibit following behavior and they vibrate their gill, we are striving to create a classification system that is based on evolutionary principles and one where these principles are consistently applied. The same logic is why names like *Coryphella* is no longer separated from *Flabellina*, *Notodoris* is now included in *Aegires* and *Hopkinsia* is not separated from *Okenia*. While not all systematists agree with these decisions, it is largely because they have not accepted the phylogenetic principles that are now commonly practiced by the vast majority of systematic biologists. Modern phylogenetic studies have also provided much new information that has allowed us to revise the classification of major groups such as the dorid nudibranchs. We now know that many dorid groups are monophyletic, while others may not be. For example, dorids have been divided traditionally into two major groups, the Cryptobranchia (species where the gill can be retracted into a pocket) and Phanerobranchia (species where the gill is non-retractile). Most studies show that Cryptobranchia is possibly monophyletic while Phanerobranchia is clearly paraphyletic (Fahey & Gosliner, 2004).

These studies also show that the highly diverse Discodorididae are very distinct from members of the Dorididae and are differentiated in having a notched foot and digitiform oral tentacles (Figure 3). Within the Discodorididae, the presence of unique notal papillae called caryophyllidia (Figure 4), which are sensory in nature, unites many of the species of genera like *Platydoris*, *Rostanga*, and *Jorunna*.

Some of the other surprising findings of these phylogenetic studies have shown that the externally primitive shelled group, Acteonacea, have many characteristics that indicate they should not be included in the Cephalaspidea. This conclusion is supported by both morphological and molecular data. The Arminina, which have been traditionally united as a major nudibranch group, based on the presence of an oral veil. All evidence now suggests that this is not a monophyletic group and that taxa like *Janolus* are very different from Arminidae. The same is true for the Notaspidea, where *Umbraculum* and *Tylodina* do not appear to be closely related to the Pleurobranchidae.

Even opisthobranchs themselves may not be a monophyletic group. Some opisthobranchs appear to be more closely related to pulmonate snails and slugs than they are to other opisthobranchs. We are still sorting out the deeper relationships, but the evidence so far suggests that many groups traditionally included in the Opisthobranchia like the Cephalaspidea, Anaspidea, Nudibranchia and Pteropoda are probably all monophyletic. Sacoglossa is monophyletic, but

within the bubble snails or sea hares, since it has characteristics of both groups. For example, it has a bulloid external shell like most bubble snails but has a radula and reproductive system like most sea hares. Phylogenetic systematics here provides an easy and unequivocal solution. All of the characteristics that *Akera* shares with bubble snails are primitive features while all those it shares with sea hares are advanced features. Since relationships are determined by shared advanced features, not the retention of primitive ones, *Akera* is clearly a sea hare. Case closed.

A phylogenetic tree allows us to determine how species in a group are related to each other (Figure 2) and has major implications to the names and classification we use. For example, *Chromodoris* was once considered one of the largest genera of nudibranchs with more than 120 named species. A study undertaken by R. Johnson & Gosliner (2012) showed a very different understanding of the evolutionary relationships of this group. The species traditionally included in *Chromodoris* were not each other's closest relatives and they were more closely related to species in other genera. The solution we proposed was to divide the species traditionally included into three major groups: *Chromodoris*, *Goniobranchus* and *Felimida* that represented monophyletic groups that contained the ancestor of the group plus all of the descendants of that ancestor. The same problem was also present in *Glossodoris*, where there were actually three distinct groups: *Glossodoris*, *Doriprismatica* and *Ardeadoris*. The name *Risbecia* has been used for several species, but *Risbecia* is not a monophyletic group as seen in the figure, because it does not include all of the descendants of the common ancestor of the group to which it belongs; most of the species of *Risbecia* fell within *Hypselodoris*. Continuing to use the name *Risbecia* creates a problem, however. *Hypselodoris* is then no longer a monophyletic group since only some of the descendants of the common ancestor of *Hypselodoris* and *Risbecia* are included in the group *Hypselodoris*. This is then a paraphyletic group which cannot be named. R. Johnson & Gosliner (2012) decided it made more sense to consider all *Risbecia* as *Hypselodoris*, which is a monophyletic group when the two are combined. While we all feel badly losing

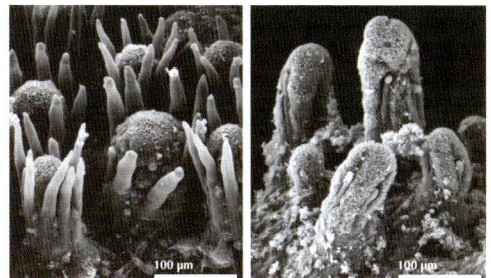

Figure 4. Scanning electron microscope photographs of caryophyllidia.

Introduction

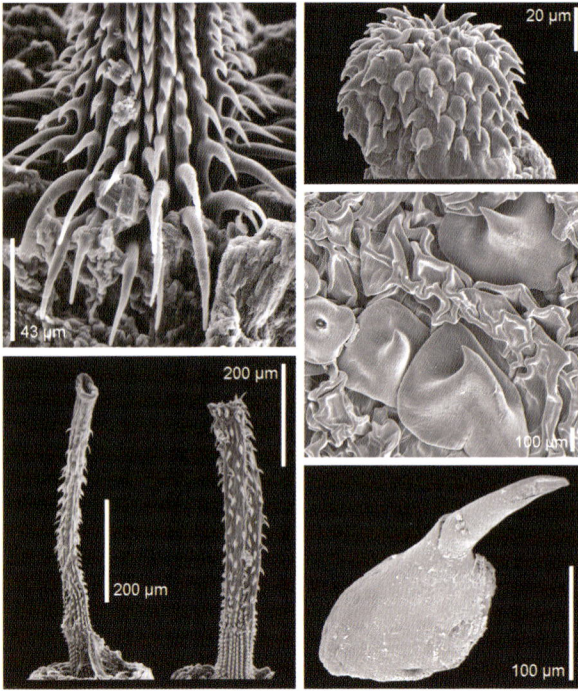

Figure 5. Scanning electron microscope photographs of copulatory organs in several species of opisthobranchs, tl: Close up of the penis of *Nembrotha mullineri*; tr: Penis of *Thordisa albomacula*; mr: Vaginal spines of *Platydoris*; bl: Penises of species of *Nembrotha*; br: penial spine of *Glaucus*.

the amazing variety of body forms making them remarkable subjects for photography and evolutionary studies. Based on evolutionary studies, it is evident that opisthobranchs lost their shells on at least seven separate occasions.

With the loss of the shell, opisthobranchs have been able to modify their body form in many ways. Even the name opisthobranch reflects this trend. Opisthobranch means "hindend gill" since the gill has moved from its anterior position to a more posterior one, once the shell was reduced or discarded. Opisthobranchs also exhibit "detorsion" or an untwisting of the typical coiled snail body. This is another result of the freedom acquired when the shell was lost.

Also, within the opisthobranchs we find that in more advanced forms, like nudibranchs, the nervous system is more highly concentrated into a distinct brain, while the ganglia are more diffuse around the body in less derived forms. The presence of large individual nerve cells in the brains of opisthobranchs has made them ideal subjects for neurophysiological studies of how less complex brains function. Species of sea hares and the nudibranchs *Tritonia* and *Hermissenda*, have been critical in this biomedical research.

Almost all opisthobranchs are hermaphroditic with both male and female reproductive organs in the same individual. Most opisthobranchs can function as males prior to the maturation of the female organs. The reproductive system of opisthobranchs also shows considerable variation from primitive to advanced forms. In the more primitive opisthobranchs, all of the reproductive products flow through a single duct. More advanced forms have the eggs and sperm separated in distinct ducts. The most advanced opisthobranchs have three ducts, one for outgoing sperm, one for outgoing eggs and a third for incoming sperm. They also have elaborate sperm storage organs and can store the sperm of their partner for weeks or even months until eggs are mature and ready for fertilization. Opisthobranchs also have elaborate structures to facilitate mating. Penial spines, spines in vestibular glands, and vaginal spines (Figure 5) that also produce elaborate structures for anchoring mating individuals during copulation.

Why all the fantastic colors?
With the evolution of chemical defenses (Figure 6) and loss of the shell, came the evolution of bright color patterns that are the signature of nudibranch diversity. Some species

it may not be most closely related to other "opisthobranchs" but rather to pulmonates. There are still many things about the evolution of these amazing slugs that require further refinement, but our understanding seems to be improving almost daily.

Modern molecular tools also allow us to recognize greater diversity than we thought existed based on morphology alone. For example, a recent study of Carmona *et al.* (2014a) showed that several species that had all been considered as the circumtropical species *Antaeolidiella indica*, just a few years ago, actually represented seven distinct species worldwide, including three species that are found exclusively in the Indo-Pacific.

While all these changes seem very disruptive, which they are, they represent small steps in achieving a new overall classification that will ultimately be more stable and one that accurately represents our understanding of the evolution of these amazing animals. The new insights are exciting to those of us who study evolution and much progress is being made in understanding the complex evolution of opisthobranchs and how they are classified. In the mean time, hold on to your hats and enjoy the ride.

Major trends in the evolution of opisthobranchs
Beginning with the earliest shelled opisthobranchs, these animals embarked on a journey that took them in vastly different evolutionary directions. With the evolution of storage of toxic chemical compounds from their prey, opisthobranchs no longer required a shell for their primary defense, having developed real weapons of mass destruction. Producing a shell is expensive in an energetic sense and constrains the movements of most mollusks. With the freedom from the cumbersome shell, adult opisthobranchs have evolved

Figure 6. Chemical secretions in two species of dorid nudibranchs, l: *Glossodoris hikuerensis*; r: *Paradoris liturata*.

8

went down the track of being cryptic, blending in with their surroundings and some adapted amazing strategies of resembling their specific prey (Figure 7). In other cases, vivid colors advertise the presence of toxicity or distastefulness. Specific color patterns characterize individual species and many species exhibit little variability while others are highly variable. Within various species groups that are closely related, such as the black-lined group of *Chromodoris* species all have common elements of their color pattern inherited from a common ancestor of all of these. These species also have a characteristic flat egg mass, which separates them from other chromodorids. Molecular studies (Wilson & Lee, 2005) confirm that this represents a monophyletic group of chromodorids. Also, within *Hypselodoris* (Gosliner & R. Johnson, 1999), a group of five species found Hawai'ian islands is distinguished by having a pink body, white or purple longitudinal lines and purple markings on the front and rear of the notum (Figure 8). Are these species most closely related to each other or are their color pattern similarities due to convergent evolution where closest relatives have different color patterns? Again, phylogenetic studies provide answers. Four of the Hawai'ian species, *H. insulana*, *H. peasei*, *H. violabranchiata*, and *H. alboterminata*, are most closely related to each other and to another species with white lines, while the fifth, *H. bertschi*, is most closely related to *H. kanga* and *H. nigrostriata*, which lack longitudinal lines. This suggests that the color pattern of *H. bertschi* has converged with the others and is a case of Müllerian mimicry.

Müllerian mimicry, where a group of distasteful species has evolved similar color patterns, has been widely reported in opisthobranchs (Figure 9) (Gosliner & Behrens, 1990; Rudman, 1991; Gosliner, 2001; Behrens 2005). Numerous examples exist between different opisthobranchs, opisthobranchs and flatworms, and opisthobranchs and sea cucumbers; many of these are found in the Indo-Pacific tropics.

How are opisthobranchs distributed around the Indo-Pacific tropics?

Some of the species found in the Indo-Pacific are extremely widely distributed from the East coast

Figure 7. Examples of species of sea slugs that are cryptic on their prey, tl: *Phyllodesmium rudmani* feeding on a *Xenia* soft coral; tr: *Phyllaplysia* sp. on a seagrass blade; ml: *Rostanga* sp. 8 on a sponge; mtr: *Pinufius rebus* on a *Porites* stony coral; mbr: *Favorinus japonicus* on sea slug eggs; bl: *Okenia plana* on encrusting bryozoans; br: unknown sea slug on *Caulerpa* seaweed.

of Africa to at least the Hawai'ian Islands; species like *Phestilla lugubris* and *P. melanobrachia* are found all the way to the eastern Pacific of Mexico and Central America. Other species are far more restricted in their ranges. In some cases, the apparent restriction of those species is simply a sampling artifact, since so many areas of this vast region are poorly known. For many years, it was thought that *Peltodoris fellowsi*, was restricted to the Hawai'ian Islands, but Bill Rudman has recently documented specimens from New Caledonia. In other cases, species are genuinely found nowhere else but from very restricted areas. For example, many species are endemic to the Hawai'ian Islands, such as *Bulla peasiana*, *Halgerda terramtuentis*, and *Thorunna kahuna*. In some cases, members of clades (monophyletic groups) are endemic to restricted regions.

Of the white and purple-lined species clade of *Hypselodoris*, four species are endemic to the Hawai'ian Islands and this represents one of the first documented cases of adaptive radiation of marine island endemics. These nudibranchs are the marine equivalent of Darwin's finches. Even more striking is that the two sister species, *H. insulana* and *H. peasei* are even geographically separated within the islands. *H. insulana* is found only in the northwest Hawai'ian Islands such as Midway and

Figure 8. Hawai'ian species of *Hypselodoris*, tl: *H. bertschi*; tr: *H. peasei*; bl: *H. violabranchiata*; bc: *H. alboterminata*; br: *H. insulana*.

9

Introduction

French Frigate Shoals, while its closest relative, *H. peasei* is found only on the high Hawai'ian Islands. These are great examples of vicariance biogeography, where populations become geographically isolated. In the absence of gene flow between these populations and in the presence of different ecological conditions, the populations differentiate and eventually can be recognized as distinct species. This is further evidence that the process of evolution is occurring before our very eyes!

The Coral Triangle contains the greatest diversity of sea slugs anywhere in the world. Within the Coral Triangle, there appear to be few species of opisthobranchs that are endemic to individual islands or archipelagos, but there are many species that are found only in this region of the Indo-Pacific. There has been a debate among people who study biogeography as to whether this region is a center of origin of new species or whether it is an area where lots of species have accumulated, arriving from different regions. There really is no contradiction between these two points of view. The fact that many sister species are found only in this region, such as most of the members of the *Hypselodoris bullockii* complex suggests that this area is a hotbed of speciation. It may also mean that additional species may have had larvae brought here from other regions. When we look at the relatively recent geological history of the region, it is not surprising that a great deal of geographical isolation or vicariance biogeography has occurred here. During the last glacial maximum, the sea level in this region was much lower and present straits and channels were much more restricted than they are today. Also new islands are continually popping up and dropping down in this area of volcanic and tectonic activity. All of these factors have likely contributed to the spectacular biodiversity that characterizes this region.

Basic biology and amazing adaptations

A great deal has been published on the behavior of nudibranchs and their ecological diversification (Behrens, 2005; Rudman & Bergquist, 2007). The diversification of feeding types has resulted in the evolution of many types of radular teeth to facilitate feeding on a particular prey (Figure 10). While opisthobranchs exhibit a tremendous variety of prey specializations on algae, sponges, cnidarians,

Figure 9. Examples of mimicry among species of sea slugs and other organisms, tl: three species of *Phyllidia* [*P. picta* (top left), *P. varicosa* (right), *P. coelestis* (bottom)] and a juvenile sea cucumber *Bohadschia graeffei*; tr: *Dermatobranchus caeruleomaculatus* (bottom) and *Goniobranchus rufomaculatus* (top); mtr: *Goniobranchus preciosaus* (right) and an unidentified flatworm (left); ml: *Phyllidiella pustulosa* (left) and the flatworm *Pseudoceros imitatus* (right); middle: *Paradoris liturata*; mlr: *Goniobranchus geometricus*; bl: ovulid snail *Ovula ovum*; br: *Phyllidia carlsonhoffi*.

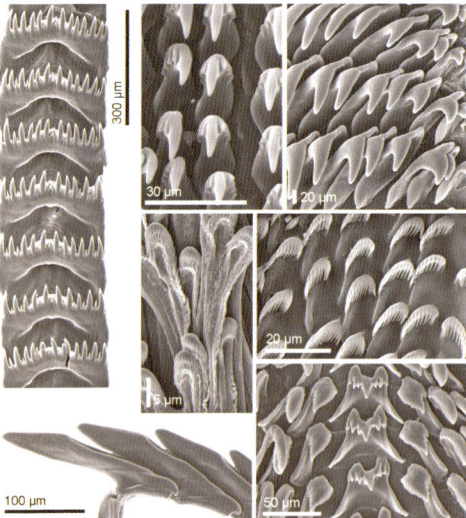

Figure 10. Examples of radula variation within sea slugs, tl: aeolid nudibranch of the genus *Cerberilla*; tm: dorid nudibranch of the genus *Glossodoris*; tr: dorid nudibranch of the genus *Hexabranchus*; m: dorid nudibranch of the genus *Aldisa*; mr: Acteonidae; bl: sacoglossan of the genus *Elysia*; br: sea hare of the genus *Akera*.

bryozoans and tunicates, some of the feeding adaptations of opisthobranchs require special mention.

Among the herbivorous taxa, the sacoglossans are among the most remarkable. Many species retain chloroplasts (Figure 11) from the algae upon which they feed. These chloroplasts are retained in the slug's tissues and continue to undergo photosynthesis, providing additional nutrition to the slug. In species of *Plakobranchus*, these chloroplasts are retained indefinitely and animals kept in captivity on sterile sand continue to grow and reproduce. This means that *Plakobranchus* gains sufficient nutrition solely from chloroplasts to complete its life cycle. Members of this genus are essentially crawling plants.

Some groups of nudibranchs retain zooxanthellae (Figure 11) a type of dinoflagellate with chlorophyll. These zooxanthellae are the primary source of nutrition for most reef-building corals and giant clams. In nudibranchs such as *Melibe*, *Phyllodesmium* and *Baeolidia*, there are species that lack zooxanthellae but they are present in others. All of the Indo-Pacific species of *Melibe* have zooxanthellae. In *Phyllodesmium*, which is restricted to the Indo-Pacific and adjacent temperate regions, virtually all conditions, from no symbionts, through species that gain most of their nutrition from zooxanthellae are present, making them magnificent subjects for the study of the evolution of symbiosis.

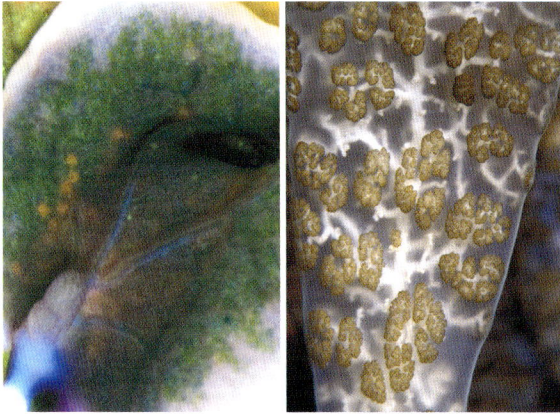

Figure 11. Solar-powered sea slugs, l: chloroplast aggregations in *Thuridilla albopustulosa*; r: zooxanthellae accumulations in *Phyllodesmium longicirrum*.

Figure 12. Various feeding behaviors of sea slugs; ttl: *Glaucus* feeding on a Portuguese Man-of-War on the ocean surface; tbl: *Gymnodoris rubropapulosa* feeding on *Mexichromis mariei*; tr: *Nembrotha chamberlaini* feeding on a tunicate; ml: *Gymnodoris nigricolor* feeding on the soft tissues of a goby; mr: *Fiona pinnata* feeding on goosenecked barnacles of a floating rope; bl: *Thecacera picta* feeding on arborescent bryozoans; br: *Doto greenamyeri* feeding on plumularid hydroids.

Among carnivorous species there is a large variation in prey organisms, including tunicates, sponges, bryozoans, hydroids and others (Figure 12). Some extreme cases include *Glaucus*, a group of aeolids that feeds on the Portuguese Man-of-War and other pelagic colonial organisms. Members of the dorid genus *Gymnodoris* are specialized predators, generally feeding on other opisthobranchs. One species has taken its specialization to the extreme. *Gymnodoris nigricolor* no longer feeds on opisthobranchs but feeds on the soft tissue of gobies that live in sandy burrows together with commensal snapping shrimp. The nudibranch crawls on to a goby and slowly eats its way down the fin spine consuming the fleshy part of the fin. This is one of the few opisthobranchs that functions as a parasite.

Another remarkable adaptation is found in species of *Favorinus*, which are specialized predators on the eggs of other opisthobranchs. One species, *Favorinus* sp. 10, takes this to a new level (Figure 13). It lives within the egg masses of *Diniatys dubius*. It tucks its rhinophores and cerata close to the body and virtually swims through the mucus of the egg mass consuming the individual developing embryos. Similarly, members of the herbivorous sacoglossan species *Ercolania kencolesi* spend their entire lives inside of the giant cells of the lobed green alga *Boergesenia forbesii* feeding on them from the inside.

Reproduction in opisthobranchs also shows great diversity. Mating slugs most often line up right side to right side where both individuals exchange sperm (Figure 14), but cepahalspideans such as species of *Chelidonura* line up head to tail with the slug in the rear being the functional male. Sea hares take this to the extreme and form daisy chains of mating individuals.

Following mating, opisthobranchs produce a mucous mass that contains individual eggs or clusters of eggs. Each species produces its own characteristic egg mass shape (Figure 15).

Saving Coral Reefs: A wake up call for emergency action and hope in the face of mass extinction

Coral reefs are among the most threatened ecosystems on the face of the planet and global climate change is only going to make that situation even more dire. Already, it is estimated that 70-80% of the world's coral reefs face serious threats (Figure 18). The dominant corals in the Caribbean have already been replaced by other species of corals in a historically unprecedented environmental change that has not been observed in more that 4,000 years of reef history.

Traditionally, reefs have been threatened by pollution and non-sustainable fishing practices, such as dynamiting and cyanide fishing. Within the Coral Triangle these practices are prevalent. Overfishing has decimated predator communities where apex predators such as Napoleon wrasses and sharks that have all but been eliminated.

Many communities, local and national governments have taken drastic action to reverse these trends. Some of the greatest successes have taken place in the "Anilao" region of southern Luzon, Philippines. When we first started visiting this area in 1992, dynamiting was prevalent. It was not uncommon to hear deafening underwater explosions and see dying fish right next to us while diving.

Introduction

Since then, a transformation has begun to take place. Marine protected areas have been set up and are being strictly enforced. Recreational divers are charged a modest fee for diving on reefs and those funds are supporting conservation efforts within the municipality of Mabini. Community groups work together to make informed decisions as to how to administer funds and enforce regulations. Often their regulations are stricter than national regulations. Within some areas, such as Tingloy, community groups are taking the initiative themselves. The reef of Red Palm (Pulangbuli) was made a marine sanctuary largely through the efforts of community leader, Princess Aldovino. The regulations have forbidden any fishing or diving on the reef for more than 6 years. Local conservation leaders received threats from irate fishermen, but firmly held their ground. When we dove on this reef 15 years ago it was pretty well decimated with dead coral rubble and hardly any fish. As part of a joint Philippine Bureau of Fisheries and Aquatic Resources and California Academy of Sciences expedition, we were granted the privilege of being some of the first divers to observe the reef. This once dead reef has made a remarkable comeback and young coral heads and healthy populations of diverse reef fishes now abound. Thanks to the heroic efforts of enlightened local people who understand that short-term sacrifice is worth the long-term benefit of conserving resources for future generations, many Philippine reefs are now healthier than when we first started working there. Local communities and conservation organizations like Pusod, World Wildlife Fund, Conservation International, Wildlife Conservation Society and the Coral Reef Alliance are making a huge difference in turning the tide of reef destruction. Supporting these organizations is one of the most important things any of us can do to make a difference.

Figure 13. Extreme feeding behaviors, tl: general view of an egg mass of *Diniatys dubius* being eaten by *Favorinus* sp. 10; tr: detail of *Favorinus* sp.10 specimens feeding on the eggs; b, giant cells of the lobed green alga *Boergesenia forbesii* being eaten from the inside by specimens of *Ercolania kencolesi.*

Figure 14 Diversity of mating strategies and behaviors in several species of sea slugs, tl: reproductive aggregation of *Chromodoris lochi*; tr: reproductive aggregation of *Chelidonura amoena*, showing the species typical mating behavior, lining up head to tail with the slug in the rear being the functional male; ml: a mating pair of *Haminoea ovalis*; bl: everted sexual organs of *Nembrotha lineolata*; br: a mating pair of *Nembrotha* sp. 2.

Other environmental problems, especially the effects of global climate change, are more difficult to address quickly. Corals are bleaching and dying all around the world from increased sea temperatures from anthropogenic carbon dioxide being produced in industrialized nations half a world away. Local people cannot control their own fate since these conditions are produced on a global scale. In recent years, inhabitants of the western Indian Ocean have seen entire reefs die. For example, a thriving reef that we visited in 1985 at Aldabra Atoll was nothing but dead coral in 1999. A year later, some new coral heads were beginning to take hold. A group of scientists from the California Academy of Sciences participated in a joint expedition with the Wildlife Conservation Society to the isolated Radama Islands in northwestern Madagascar in 2005. WCS had asked us to assess the success of the establishment of a marine reserve system in the region. Fishing was not the most serious threat. What we found were reefs where corals were bleached or dead that were being overgrown by a scum of cyanobacteria (blue-green algae) (Figure 16). This was a much more serious problem where establishment of a marine protected areas could not help deal with the root problem, human-caused climate change.

In July of 2010 we saw a large and devastating bleaching event that effected large areas on both sides of the Malay Peninsula. Shallow reefs were largely dead around Phuket, Thailand and the effects extended all the way to parts of Indonesia and the Philippines. We had been making observations on the reefs of the Verde Island Passage of the reef for more than two decades beginning in 1992 and had seen little evidence of coral bleaching. In October 2010, the impact of the bleaching event that began on the Malay Peninsula spread to the Verde Island Passage and about 30% of corals, sea anemones and other reef organisms exhibited extensive bleaching. When we returned in January 2011, there was a lot of good

Introduction

Figure 15. Egg masses of different species of opisthobranchs, tl: *Pleurobranchaea brockii* laying an egg mass; tr: *Chelidonura hirundinina* laying eggs; ml: *Favorinus* egg mass on a *Haminoea* egg mass; bl: *Doto* sp. 12 with the egg mass attached to a hydroid; br: *Goniobranchus annulatus* with egg mass.

news. Most of the impacted corals were beginning to regain pigment by acquiring new zooxanthellae. Four months later in May, all the impacted corals had completely regained their pigment and there was no evidence of bleaching or dead corals. The Verde Island Passage appears to be an area of natural resilience by virtue of the facts that the passage has deep water, swift currents and lots of upwelling. To make certain that these areas of natural resilience can replenish other areas that are not so fortunate, we must make certain that we especially protect these areas!

The increase in sea surface temperature is directly related to global warming. Another looming impact of global climate change is ocean acidification. Decrease in the pH of the world's ocean is placing additional stress on all organisms that produce calcium carbonate skeletons, including all corals and most mollusks. This decrease in pH will likely reduce the ability of these organisms to produce protective skeletons. The consequences to coral reefs could be catastrophic.

Never in the history of our planet has any single species placed the fate of so many other species in such serious jeopardy. The good news is that we have the intellect, skills and resources to begin to change this. As individuals we can take steps to reduce our individual carbon footprints, but we also need to convince our policy makers that we must make the rapid transition to non-carbon producing sources of energy. Just as Princess Aldovino figured out in Tingloy, we must make changes in our behavior to preserve the world for future generations and to make certain that they can enjoy and reap the benefits of the glorious biodiversity that has evolved on Earth (Figure 17). The future is in our hands, and we must act now.

Figure 16. Damaged reefs, t: Pulau Gut reef (Malaysia) destroyed by crown of thorns sea stars; b: Radama Island reef overgrown by a scum of Cyanobacteria

Figure 17. Healthy coral reefs contain large amounts of biological diversity.

13

Introduction

TABLE OF CONTENTS

VISUAL GUIDE TO COMMON DESCRIPTIVE TERMS

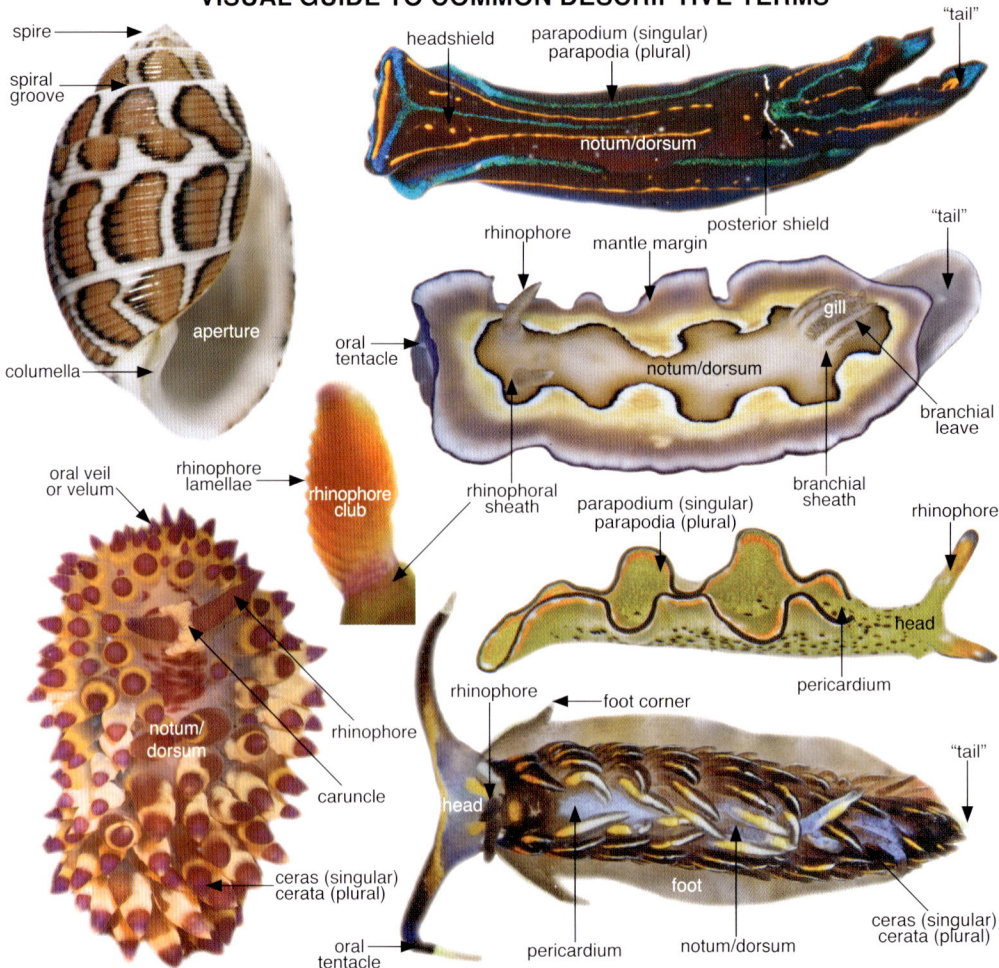

spire · spiral groove · aperture · columella · headshield · parapodium (singular) parapodia (plural) · notum/dorsum · "tail" · posterior shield · rhinophore · mantle margin · "tail" · gill · oral tentacle · notum/dorsum · branchial leave · branchial sheath · rhinophore · oral veil or velum · rhinophore lamellae · rhinophore club · rhinophoral sheath · parapodium (singular) parapodia (plural) · pericardium · head · notum/dorsum · rhinophore · caruncle · rhinophore · foot corner · "tail" · head · ceras (singular) cerata (plural) · oral tentacle · pericardium · foot · notum/dorsum · ceras (singular) cerata (plural)

IDENTIFICATION KEY

Identification key to the major groups of sea slugs, for illustrations of anatomical traits see page 14. To use this identification key, follow the steps below using the habitat and body shape/characteristics on your unknown species to help narrow down your search. Once you are in the correct section review the photos to identify your species.

1. Pelagic life style (found floating in open water, swimming freely or in association with other free-floating organisms) .... go to step 2
• Benthic life style (found on the bottom or on solid floating objects)... go to step 3

2. Found in association with drifting brown seaweeds, color yellow, brown or green – **Stylocheilus longicaudus** (p. 391), **Scyllaeidae** (p. 252).
• Swimming freely in the open ocean or in association with sea jellies or other floating animals such as the Portuguese man-of-war. Can be found washed out on the beach after storms. Color bright blue or translucent – **Phylliroidae** (p. 250), **Glaucus** (p. 330), **Pteropoda** (p. 386).

3. Found in unusual habitats, mainly interstitial (living between sand grains), but also in fresh water (rivers) or on mangrove roots – **Acochlidia** (p. 435), **Philinoglossidae** (p. 386).
• Found in usual benthic marine habitats such as rocky reefs, coral, soft bottoms (mud, sand), sometimes buried in the substrate, or on algae and sea grasses.. go to step 4

4. Headshield present: **Cephalaspidea**, **Acteonidae**, **Ringiculidae**, **Akera**, **Ascobulla**, **Cylindrobulla**, **Runcinidae**.. go to step 5
• Headshield absent: **other Nudibranchia, Pleurobrachidae, Umbraculidae, Aplysidae, other sacoglossans** .... go to step 9

5. Headshield with two elongate posterior appendages, covering a portion of the shell. Shell spirally coiled, with or without a spire .... go to step 6
• Headshield lacking two elongate posterior appendages. If two short posterior appendages are present, the shell is bulloid, lacking a spire or with a short, conical spire .... go to step 7

6. Shell external white, with thickened folds on the columella (inner margin of the aperture) – **Ringiculidae** (p. 16).
• Shell external, typically colored, with or without small folds on columella – **Acteonidae** (p. 17).

7. Headshield deeply notched, cleaved into two distinct sections, one on each side of the head. Shell bulloid (lacking a spire), and fragile. Found in close association with green algae, color typically green or white – **Ascobulla** (p. 394), **Cylindrobulla** (p. 393).
• Headshield not notched or shallowly notched, but not divided into two distinct sections. Sometimes with two antero-lateral appendages or a single central appendage .... go to step 8

8. Headshield simple; animal cylindrical, with a worm-like appearance. Body very small (typically less than 5 mm), tail clearly differentiated, wide, triangular and elongate, shell internal and reduced – **Runcinidae** (p. 388).
• Body typically larger, and more complex, with or without an external shell – **Cephalaspidea** (p. 342), **Akeridae** (p. 389).

9. Gill on the right side of the body .... go to step 10
• Gill dorsal, ventral, posterior or absent, never on the right side of the body..................................... go to step 11

10. Shell external, dorsal, flattened, similar to a limpet shell – **Umbraculidae** (p. 341).
• Shell absent or internal – **Pleurobranchidae** (p. 22).

11. Head with two pairs of tentacles (rhinophores and oral tentacles) clearly visible, two parapodia on the sides of the body and often an internal shell between them. Animals typically large or very large, often produce purple ink – **Aplysiidae** (p. 389).
• Head with a single pair of tentacles (rhinophores), or if two pairs of tentacles are present (rhinophores and oral tentacles) there are no parapodia on the sides of the body.. go to step 12

12. Body with leaf-like appendages and/or an external shell (bulloid or composed of two valves) or parapodia on the sides of the body. Rhinophores often enrolled and devoid of lamellae. Color typically green or greenish, but sometimes with a bright pattern. Normally found in close association with algae – **other Sacoglossa** (p. 393)
• Shell absent, with or without dorsal appendages but not leaf-shaped. Found crawling around freely or in close association with other animals (sponges, cnidarians, bryozoans) – **other Nudibranchia**................ go to step 13

13. Anus located dorsally or ventrally, but not laterally, near the posterior end of the animal, often surrounded by a circlet of several branchial leaves. One pair of tentacles on the head (rhinophores) – **Doridoidea** (p. 27).
• Anus located on the side of the animal, typically with numerous dorsal appendages (cerata) or with dorsal longitudinal ridges, never with a dorsal circlet of branchial leaves. One or two pairs of tentacles on the head (rhinophores and oral tentacles) – **Cladobranchia** (p. 227).

Basal shelled heterobranch sea slugs

These groups have been considered traditionally as cephalaspideans, but molecular and morphological studies (Mikkelsen, 1996; Wägele & Klussmann-Kolb, 2005; Malaquias *et al.*, 2009) show they have diverged early. Ringipleura and Acteonimorpha are closely related but distinct evolutionary lineages. The families Acteonidae, Bullinidae, and Aplustridae are included in Acteonimorpha and the single family Ringiculidae in Ringipleura (Kano et al. 2017).

Ringipleura

Ringiculidae Philippi, 1853

Members of this family have an inflated, well-developed shell, with a series of thickened columellar folds along the inner margin of the aperture. They have a narrow radula and lack gizzard plates. Variations in the sculpture and folds have been used to differentiate species, but very few studies have described anatomical differences. Very little is known on the biology and habits of these organisms, they live burrowed in sandy areas and seem to feed on small animals.

Ringicula mariei Morlet, 1880
Size: 4 mm   Western Indian Ocean
ID: Body and shell white; shell with a faint sculpture and large columellar folds; similar to *Ringicula doliaris* from the western Pacific but detailed studies of species known only from shells are needed to clarify their identity. Burrows in fine clean sand in 20-30 m.

Ringicula sp. 1
Size: 4 mm   Philippines
ID: Body and shell white; shell with a thick lip, far less globose than in *Ringicula mariei*; white defensive glands visible. Burrows in fine clean sand in 10-20 m.

Ringicula sp. 2
Size: 5 mm   Papua New Guinea
ID: Body white with opaque white defensive glands and an orange siphon tip; shell shiny, white; apex short, brownish grey. Coarse sandy slopes where it feeds on polychaetes in 2-6 m.

Ringicula sp. 3
Size: 7 mm   Papua New Guinea
ID: Body white with orange spots over the head surface; shell white with deeply incised spiral grooves, spire elongate. Coarse sandy slopes in 8 m; feeds on polychaetes.

Acteonimorpha

Acteonidae d'Orbigny, 1843

The Acteonidae represent a family consisting of many different genera. The most common shallow-water genus in the Indo-Pacific tropics is *Pupa*. Genera are generally distinguished by internal differences such as the shape, number, and arrangement of radular teeth. All the species in this family that have been studied are predators on polychaete annelid worms. There is a rich diversity of deep-sea species that remains poorly known.

***Japonacteon suturalis* (A. Adams, 1855)**
Size: 15 mm   Indian and western Pacific oceans
ID: Body translucent white; shell white with black spots and channeled sutures between the whorls. Externally very similar to several species of *Pupa*, but has distinct radular teeth. Burrows in clean sand in 3-10 m.

***Japonacteon* sp.**
Size: 15 mm   Philippines
ID: Body translucent white; uniform white shell with channeled sutures between the whorls. Burrows in clean sand in 3-10 m.

***Maxacteon flammeus* (Bruguière, 1789)**
Size: 20 mm   Indian and western Pacific oceans
ID: Body white; shell white with red, crescent-shaped spots, sometimes bordered in black. Likely feeds on polychaete worms.

***Pupa alveola* (Souverbie, 1863)**
Size: 15 mm   Widespread in the Indo-Pacific
ID: Body translucent white with opaque white spots; shell white with large checkered brown markings. Under clean coarse sands; presumably feeds on polychaetes.

***Pupa nitidula* (Lamarck, 1816)**
Size: 15 mm   Indian and western Pacific oceans
ID: Body opaque white; shell variable from pure white to orange, lacking checkered markings. Coarse white sandy substrates on reef flats and sand slopes, 15 m.

Pupa coccinata (Reeve, 1842)
Size: 20 mm   Indian and western Pacific oceans
ID: Body white; shell white with red-orange checkered markings on the surface. Burrows in sandy substrates; likely feeds on polychaete worms.

Pupa solidula (Linnaeus, 1758)
Size: 30 mm   Indian and western Pacific oceans
ID: Body white; shell white with large dark brown or black checkered markings. Shallow subtidal sandy slopes.

Pupa tessellata (Reeve, 1842)
Size: 11 mm   Widespread in the Indo-Pacific
ID: Body white; shell white with relatively large, irregular brownish markings on the shell. Shallow subtidal sand banks and algal turf.

Pupa sulcata (Gmelin, 1791)
Size: 15 mm   Western Pacific Ocean
ID: Body white with opaque white dots; shell white, elongate, with small dark quadrangular checks. Coarse sandy slopes where it feeds on polychaetes in 5-15 m.

Acteon virgatus (Reeve, 1842)
Size: 20 mm   Western Pacific Ocean
ID: Body white; shell white, elongate, with dark brown blotches in some specimens, others with large, dark quadrangular checks and some with black undulating lines.

Specimens with lines on the shell are considered a color variant of *Acteon virgatus*, but this requires confirmation. Clean sandy slopes in 5-15 m; feeds on polychaetes.

Acteon sp. 1
Size: 9 mm   Vanuatu
ID: Body translucent white; shell uniform white with a yellowish apex; sculpture with strong spiral bands of deep punctuations. Dredged from relatively shallow water.

Acteon sp. 2
Size: 9 mm   Philippines
ID: Body white; shell similar to the preceding species except that is evenly sloping between whorls rather than being sharply stepped. On mud in 10-26 m.

Bullinidae J. E. Gray, 1850

Members of this family have a more inflated shell than the typical shell found in other Acteonidae. The shell is often brightly ornamented with red or black lines or spots, forming a distinctive pattern. Other minor internal differences also distinguish the bullinids from other acteonoideans. Additional taxonomic studies are necessary to determine the validity of this family.

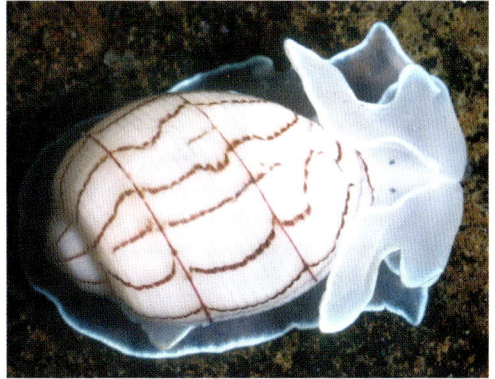

Bullina lineata (J. E. Gray, 1825)
Size: 20 mm   Indian and western Pacific oceans
ID: Body translucent white with an opaque white edge; shell white with two thin spiral red lines and curved lines in between. From the intertidal zone to 20 m; feeds on cirratulid polychaetes.

Bullina oblonga Sowerby III, 1897
Size: 12 mm   South Africa
ID: Body translucent with a bluish edge; shell white, more elongate than in Bullina lineata with more numerous fine red lines. Coarse sand in 15 m; likely feeds on cirratulid polychaetes.

Bullina vitrea Pease, 1860
Size: 25 mm   Western Pacific
ID: Body white with concentrations of opaque white dots; shell white, more elongate than in Bullina lineata, with only two brownish lines. In 12-15 m; likely feeds on cirratulid polychaetes.

19

Bullina sp. 1
Size: 8 mm   Philippines
ID: Body white with opaque white dots; shell pinkish, with fine spiral striations. Coarse sand in 5 m; feeds on polychaetes.

Bullina sp. 2
Size: 25 mm   Guam, American Samoa
ID: Body light pink with opaque white dots; shell deep rose pink, with fine spiral striations. Coarse sand in 0-1 m; most likely feeds on polychaetes.

Bullina sp. 3
Size: 20 mm   Guam
ID: Body translucent white with opaque white dots; shell white with a yellow spire and fine spiral striations. Coarse sand in 0-1 m; feeds on polychaetes as shown on the photo.

Aplustridae J. E. Gray, 1847

Members of this family are distinguished from Acteonidae and Bullinidae by having a shell with a bulloid spire. As in Bullinidae, the shell is ornamented with distinctive patters of lines, in some species forming a complex network. All species are predators upon cirratulid polychaetes from which they sequester secondarily derived toxins for their own protection.

Hydatina physis (Linnaeus, 1758)
Size: 60 mm   Possibly circumtropical
ID: Bright reddish pink body with ruffled white edges; shell white with numerous black spiral lines. Shallow water; feeds on cirratulid polychaetes and incorporates toxins from its prey for its own defense.

Hydatina zonata (Lightfoot, 1786)
Size: 50 mm   Widespread in the Indo-Pacific
ID: Bright reddish body with ruffled white edges; shell brown with numerous elongate lines and with one or more white spiral bands. Shallow water; feeds on cirratulid polychaetes and incorporates toxins from its prey for its own defense.

Hydatina amplustre (Linnaeus, 1758)
Size: 30 mm   Widespread in the Indo-Pacific
ID: Body white; shell whitish, normally with 2-3 pink spiral bands outlined in black; some specimens with just a few

black bands. Intertidal reef flats to 10 m; feeds on polychaete worms.

Micromelo undatus (Brugière, 1792)
Size: 30 mm   Possibly circumtropical
ID: Body bluish green to yellow, with opaque white spots; shell white with dark brown undulating bands. *Micromelo*

guamensis is a synonym. Rocky habitats from the intertidal zone to 5 m; feeds on cirratulid polychaetes and incorporates their toxins.

Pleurobranchoidea - "side-gilled slugs"

Members of this group are carnivores and closely related to nudibranchs (Wägele & Willan, 2000). Most species have a reduced, internal shell, while species of *Pleurobranchaea* and *Euselenops* lack shells as adults. The systematics of this group, as well as the Umbraculoidea, was studied by Willan (1987). More recently a molecular phylogeny and a revision of the systematics of *Pleurobranchus* was published by Goodheart *et al.* (2015).

Pleurobranchidae J. E. Gray, 1827

Pleurobranchids are soft-bodied animals with a small internal shell or no shell at all. Their gill is normally clearly visible on the right side of the body, although it may be covered by the mantle in living animals. Some species reach a very large size and are normally active at night. Many produce acidic defensive secretions.

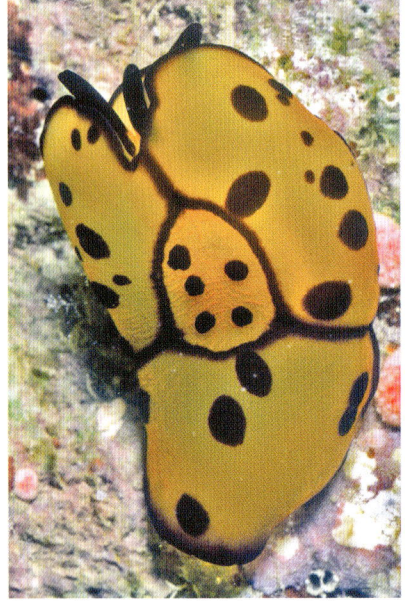

Berthella martensi (Pilsbry, 1896)
Size: 60 mm   Indo-Pacific and eastern Pacific
ID: Color extremely variable, white, yellow, brown or black, with or without mottling of a different colors. Feeds on sponges; when disturbed sheds the mantle along three distinct fracture zones.

Berthella stellata (Risso, 1826)
Size: 25 mm   Possibly circumtropical
ID: Translucent white with an opaque white star-shaped mark. Feeds on sponges on the underside of small rocks and coral rubble. Unpublished molecular evidence suggest it could constitute a species complex

Berthella sp. 1
Size: 60 mm   Western and central Pacific Ocean
ID: Uniformly tan with opaque white spots and a large centrally situated brown spot. The similarity of this species with *Berthella africana* has been noted. Under rocks on reefs in 5-20 m.

Berthella sp. 2
Size: 40 mm   Philippines
ID: Brown, with the dorsal surface having opaque white patches forming a radiating pattern; rhinophores pinkish, relatively short. Shallow rocky patch reefs.

Berthella sp. 3
Size: 30 mm   French Polynesia
ID: Uniformly reddish-orange with some lighter mottling and a darker central spot on the back; rhinophores short. Shallow rocky reefs.

Berthellina delicata (Pease, 1861)
Size: 40 mm   Widespread in the Indo-Pacific
ID: Light to deep orange, rarely with white spots on the notum. Several Indo-Pacific species of Berthellina included

here are not readily distinguishable by external anatomy. Under coral heads during the day, active at night.

Berthellina citrina (Rüppell & Leuckart, 1828)
Size: 30 mm   Red Sea
ID: Uniformly reddish-orange. Under coral heads during the day, emerges at night.

Berthellina sp.
Size: 40 mm   Western Indian Ocean
ID: Orange, sometimes with opaque white spots on the notum. At night crawling in tide pools, during the day under rocks.

23

Pleurobranchoidea - "side-gilled slugs"

Pleurobranchus grandis Pease, 1868
Size: 200 mm   Western and central Pacific Ocean
ID: Color variable, usually with different proportions of white, red, yellow and black pigment; tubercles arranged in distinct clusters. Nocturnal, crawls over the surface of living reefs at night; presumably feeds on tunicates, but has not been observed feeding.

Pleurobranchus mamillatus Quoy & Gaimard, 1832
Size: 500 mm   Indian and western Pacific oceans
ID: Color variable, tan, orange, dark reddish or black; a series of elevated tubercles along the surface of the notum; smaller tubercles arranged in clusters; juveniles of *Pleurobranchus forskalii* are sometimes misidentified as this species. In the open during the day and at night, in 20-50 m.

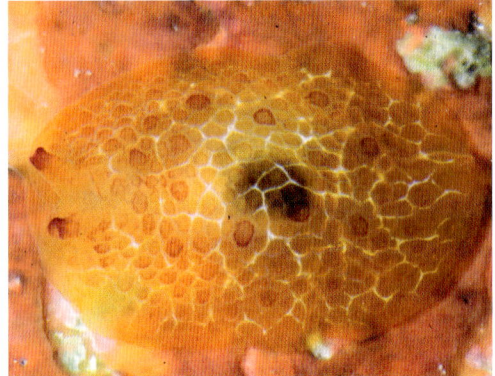

Pleurobranchus peronii Cuvier, 1804
Size: 60 mm   Widespread in the Indo-Pacific
ID: Reddish purple or orange; dorsum with simple tubercles; some specimens with dark reticulating pigment around some tubercles. In shallow rock pools and reef flats at night, otherwise under coral heads and rocks during the day.

24

Pleurobranchus forskalii (Rüppell & Leuckart, 1828)
Size: 300 mm   Indian and western Pacific oceans
ID: Brownish to dark maroon to almost black; opaque white or black circles or semicircles frequently present on the dorsal surface; tubercles arranged in clusters; mantle with an elongate posterior extension. Nocturnal, frequently observed crawling on sandy and rubble bottoms.

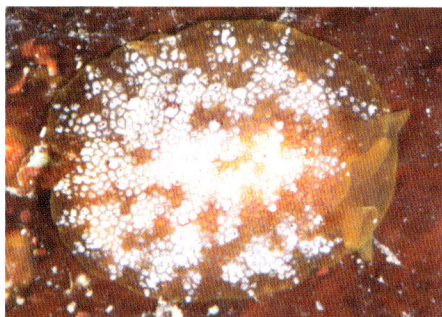

Pleurobranchus varians Pease, 1860
Size: 60 mm   Western and central Pacific
ID: Color variable, typically with an orange-red background; some specimens with abundant opaque white pigment scattered over the notum; dorsum covered with quadrangular tubercles. Often confused with *Pleurobranchus albiguttatus* but is genetically distinct. Under coral slabs during the day and crawling about on reef flats at night.

Pleurobranchoidea - "side-gilled slugs"

Pleurobranchus albiguttatus (Bergh, 1905)
Size: 65 mm   Indian and western Pacific oceans
ID: Color variable, cream, orange or reddish-brown; dorsum covered with uniform conical tubercles, some tubercles much longer than the rest and opaque white. Under coral slabs during the day and crawling about on reef flats at night.

Pleurobranchus weberi (Bergh, 1905)
Size: 200 mm   Western Pacific Ocean
ID: Dark reddish with opaque white "double bullseyes" on the notum; some specimens with reticulate white pigment. At night on reef flats in 10-30 m.

Pleurehdera haraldi (Ev. Marcus & Er. Marcus, 1970)
Size: 40 mm   Western and central Pacific Ocean
ID: Uniformly pinkish-white to reddish-brown with numerous reticulations on the notum. Feeds on crustose sponges on the underside of coral rubble in 1-10 m.

Euselenops luniceps (Cuvier, 1816)
Size: 70 mm   Widespread in the Indo-Pacific
ID: White with brown spots; front of the animal with a large fringed oral veil; shell absent in adults. This bizarre looking opisthobranch initially looks more like a cephalopod than a side-gilled slug. Sandy and silty habitats; capable of swimming.

Pleurobranchaea brockii Bergh, 1897
Size: 120 mm   Indian and western Pacific oceans
ID: Tan with opaque white spots; brownish reticulate markings covering the notum; broad oral hood with elongate papillae. Feeds on other opisthobranchs as well as on cerianthid anemones.

Pleurobranchella alba (Lin Guangyu & Tchang Si, 1965)
Size: 300 mm   South China Sea
ID: White, with golden brown mottling; some specimens entirely lack mottling; broad rounded body with elongate rhinophores extending laterally, and a broad frontal veil. Fish traps in 135-541 m.

Nudibranchia - "nudibranchs"

With more than 6,000 species this is the most diverse group of sea slugs. Nudibranchs have colonized all marine environments and include some pelagic species. They are all characterized by lacking a shell in the adult state.

Clade 1: Doridoidea - "dorid nudibranchs"

Most dorid nudibranchs feed upon sponges and use their broad radula to scrape tissue. Other groups of dorids feed upon tunicates, bryozoans and other opisthobranchs. Most dorids are distinguished by having a dorsal circle of gill branches surrounding the anus.

Phanerobranchia - "phanerobranch dorids"

These dorids tend to have an elongated body and the gill cannot be retracted into a distinct pocket. Recent morphological and molecular studies support the idea that "phanerobranchs" do not represent a natural group and the lack of a retractile gill is a primitive feature (Vallès, 2002; Fahey & Gosliner, 2004; Hallas, Chichvarkhin & Gosliner, 2017). Members of this group usually feed upon bryozoans, tunicates or other opisthobranchs.

Hexabranchidae Bergh, 1891

Members of this family feed on sponges and are exclusively found in the tropical Indo-Pacific and the Caribbean. When disturbed, they may display a flashing behavior by suddenly exposing brightly colored areas of the dorsum, which are normally covered by folds of the mantle margin; this can be accompanied by a vigorous swimming escaping behavior. There appears to be only one, highly-variable Indo-Pacific species of this group. *Hexabranchus* was thought to be a cryptobranch, possibly related to chromodorids, but more recent studies (Valdés, 2002a) show that it is more closely related to some basal "phanerobranch" groups.

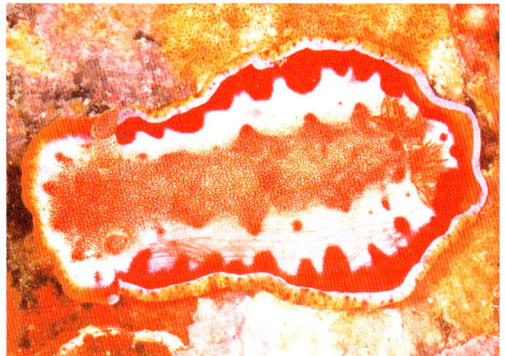

Hexabranchus sanguineus (Rüppell & Leuckart, 1830)
Size: 600 mm   Widespread in the Indo-Pacific
ID: Color variable reddish to orange with markings and spots of different colors; mantle margins inrolled; six distinct gill branches that emerge from the mantle separately. Commonly seen swimming in relatively shallow water where it propels itself by unfurling its mantle margins and undulating through the water; often has the commensal shrimp, *Perclimines imperator* associated with it.

Polyceridae Alder & Hancock, 1845

Members of this group are varied in their body form but usually have a series of velar tentacles along the anterior margin, one or more pairs of extrabranchial appendages, and other lateral appendages. They are divided into three subgroups: Polycerinae, Triophinae and Nembrothinae. Polyceridae is more closely related to cryptobranchs than other "phanerobranchs."

Polycerinae Alder & Hancock, 1845

Members of this subgroup of polycerids have well developed velar tentacles and extrabranchial processes, but lack other lateral processes.

Polycera abei (Baba, 1960)
Size: 20 mm   Widespread in the Indo-Pacific
ID: Orange with black spots and dark pigment on the velar tentacles, rhinophores and gill. On the underside of coral rubble generally in association with arborescent bryozoans.

Polycera sp. 1
Size: 12 mm   Indonesia
ID: White with black interrupted lines and yellow pigment on the velar tentacles, rhinophores, gill, and foot. On shallow sandy bottoms where it feeds on arborescent bryozoans.

Polycera sp. 2
Size: 25 mm   Kwazulu Natal (South Africa)
ID: Translucent white with numerous black longitudinal lines and yellow spots on the notum, gill, and subapically on the velar and extrabranchial appendages. On arborescent bryozoans on shallow subtidal reef flats.

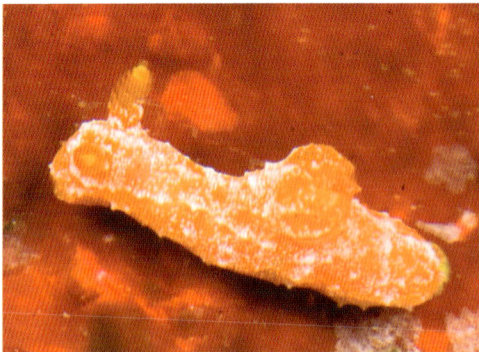

Polycera sp. 3
Size: 9 mm   Philippines, Japan, Hawai'ian Is.
ID: Orange with numerous white spots, most dense along the margins of the notum; bright orange pigment on the tips of the rhinophores and gill and along the margin of the foot. On arborescent bryozoans growing on the surface of coral rubble.

Polycera japonica Baba, 1949
Size: 6 mm   Widespread in the Indo-Pacific
ID: Brownish with dark rings on the velar tentacles and a black line on the dorsal side of the foot; tubercles rounded with a short filamentous apex. On the underside of coral rubble on shallow reefs; feeds on arborescent bryozoans.

Polycera risbeci Odhner, 1941
Size: 8 mm — Indian and western Pacific oceans
ID: Brownish with a series of fine dark brown transverse lines across the body surface; tubercles smaller than in the preceding species. Feeds on arborescent bryozoans.

Polycera sp. 4
Size: 15 mm — Papua New Guinea, Japan
ID: Light brown with dark brown spots and opaque white pigment on the rounded tubercles. Feeds on arborescent bryozoans in shallow reefs.

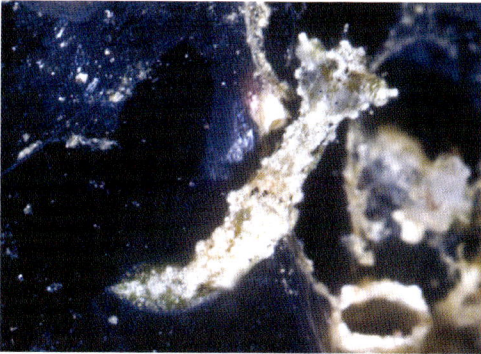

Polycera sp. 5
Size: 7 mm — Western Pacific Ocean
ID: Opaque brownish white with clear areas around the eyes and minute black spotting scattered over the body surface. On the underside of coral rubble on shallow reefs.

Polycera sp. 6
Size: 12 mm — Western Pacific Ocean
ID: Dark green with a complex pattern of black spots, thin opaque white lines and opaque white pustules; notal ridge with a line of pustules; rhinophores darker than the body. Feeds on bryozoans.

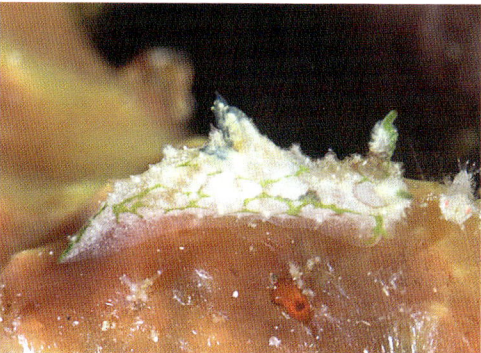

Polycera sp. 7
Size: 4 mm — Philippines
ID: Whitish body with pattern of orange reticulations on notum; gill with bluish grey apices on branches.

Polycera sp. 8
Size: 8 mm — Philippines
ID: White body with yellowish brown peppering of spots; notal ridge prominent and gill large for size of animal.

Triophinae Odhner, 1941

Most members of this subgroup of polycerids have well developed lateral appendages and often lack extrabranchial processes. They have a radula with one or two granular central plates. The systematics of *Plocamopherus* and *Kaloplocamus* has been reviewed with descriptions of several new species by Vallès & Gosliner (2006). *Kalinga* is often included in its own subgroup, Kalinginae Pruvot-Fol, 1956, but the actual position of this group remains unknown.

Kalinga ornata Alder & Hancock, 1864
Size: 130 mm   Indo-Pacific
ID: Translucent white with numerous rounded tubercles and bright red pigmented areas; oral veil broad with elongate tentacles. From shallow to deep water (at least 182 m) on soft sediment where burrows into sand; feeds on brittle stars.

Kaloplocamus ramosus (Cantraine, 1835)
Size: 25 mm   Eastern Atlantic, Mediterranean, Indo-Pacific
ID: Whitish with scattered orange spots over the surface; lateral and velar appendages relatively short and moderately branched. Further study is needed to determine whether it is a complex of several distinct species. Feeds on bryozoans in 5-100 m.

Kaloplocamus acutus Baba, 1949
Size: 20 mm   Western Pacific Ocean
ID: Color variable, from red to orange, with scattered opaque white spots and white markings on the gill and lateral appendages. On the underside of coral rubble in 10-15 m; presumably feeds on bryozoans.

Kaloplocamus sp. 1
Size: 15 mm   Madagascar
ID: Red-orange; appendages elongate, translucent white, tipped with yellow and red pigment. On coral rubble in 15 m. Similar to *Kaloplocamus acutus* but probably undescribed.

Kaloplocamus sp. 2
Size: 10 mm   Philippines
ID: Mottled orange with moderately long, slightly branched lateral appendages; body short. Shallow sandy slopes with rocky patches, in 10 m.

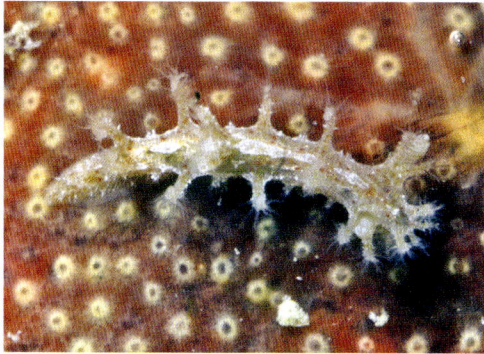

Kaloplocamus peludo Vallès & Gosliner, 2006
Size: 15 mm   Indian and western Pacific oceans
ID: Brownish with opaque white markings; notal appendages highly ramified, looking like bryozoan zooids. On arborescent bryozoans on reef walls in 10-20 m.

Kaloplocamus maru Vallès & Gosliner, 2006
Size: 15 mm   Palau
ID: Brownish with darker brown spots on the notum and gill; mid-dorsal ridge with lighter pigment; notal appendages highly ramified, resembling bryozoan zooids. On arborescent bryozoans on reef walls in 15 m.

Kaloplocamus sp. 3
Size: 10 mm   Philippines
ID: Smooth dorsal surface with mottled orange patches; lateral appendages elongate with scattered elongate papillae; 3-5 gill branches. Shallow silty sand flats, 5 m.

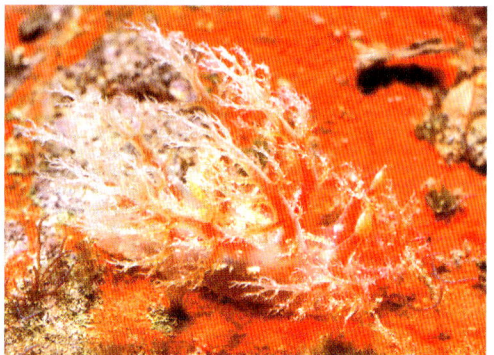

Kaloplocamus sp. 4
Size: 25 mm   Philippines, Indonesia
ID: Translucent white with scattered opaque white spots; red orange digestive gland visible through the notum and into the lateral appendages; lateral appendages elongate, highly ramified with secondary branching. Shallow rocky reefs.

Kaloplocamus sp. 5
Size: 30 mm   Indonesia
ID: Translucent orange with scattered opaque white and dark brown spots; lateral appendages elongate, highly ramified with secondary branching. Shallow rocky reefs.

Kaloplocamus sp. 6
Size: 30 mm   Indonesia
ID: Uniformly orange with opaque white patches; lateral appendages long with a few elongate papillae, curved at the apex; low tubercles covering the body. Shallow rocky reefs.

Nudibranchia - "nudibranchs"

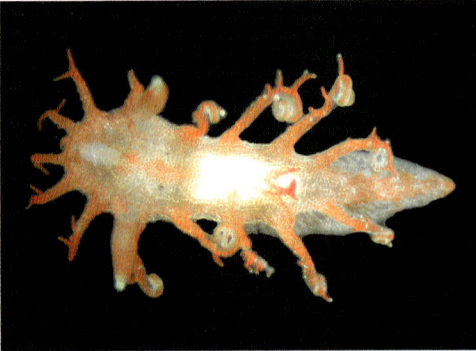

Kaloplocamus sp. 7
Size: 10 mm   Papua New Guinea, Indonesia
ID: Translucent white with fine orange punctuations over the dorsal surface and isolated white patches; lateral appendages elongate, slightly branched with curled apices. Shallow rocky reefs.

Kaloplocamus dokte Vallès & Gosliner, 2006
Size: 12 mm   Western and central Pacific Ocean
ID: Opaque white with a red gill; velar and notal processes moderately ramified. On the underside of dead coral slabs; appears to be associated with unidentified arborescent bryozoans.

Kaloplocamus sp. 8
Size: 10 mm   Papua New Guinea
ID: Light orange with areas of whitish pigment; lateral appendages relatively short tips of the lateral appendages bearing fine branched filaments resembling hydroid polyps. On bryozoans on shallow reefs.

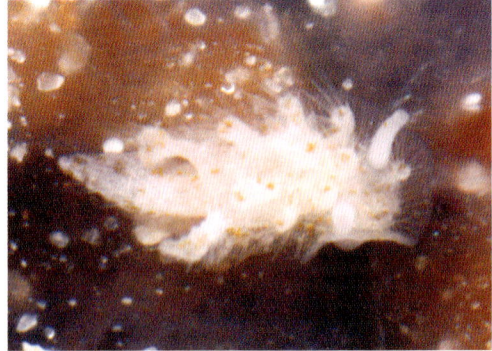

Kaloplocamus sp. 9
Size: 4 mm   Philippines
ID: Uniformly opaque white with orange spots on the lateral appendages; lateral appendages short with filamentous branches at the tips; rhinophores smooth. Shallow rocky reefs in 8 m.

Plocamopherus margaritae Vallès & Gosliner, 2006
Size: 75 mm   Indian and western Pacific oceans
ID: Pink or red with large white spots; black spots surrounded by opaque white rings; margins of the foot, oral veil and keel with yellow-orange lines; three pairs of rounded lateral appendages, forming pinkish yellow globular structures.

Plocamopherus imperialis Angas, 1864
Size: 100 mm   Eastern Australia, northern New Zealand
ID: Yellow-brown with irregular brown dots all over the body; a single pair of pink globular structures on the most posterior lateral appendages. In the open on intertidal rocky benches. Records from Japan may represent a distinct species.

Plocamopherus tilesii Bergh, 1877
Size: 60 mm   Western Pacific Ocean
ID: Translucent yellowish, speckled with black and white spots; oral veil margin yellow; oral tentacles black; three pairs of short lateral appendages, the last two pairs having prominent white globular structures. In relatively deep water.

Plocamopherus maculatus (Pease, 1860)
Size: 30 mm   Widespread in the Indo-Pacific
ID: Translucent white, lightly speckled with minute brown-orange dots; only one pair of lateral appendages situated behind the gill that bear white or yellow globular structures. From the intertidal zone to 20 m in association with arborescent bryozoans.

Plocamopherus ocellatus Rüppell & Leuckart, 1828
Size: 60 mm   Red Sea
ID: Dark brown to black with large yellow spots. The name derives from these large spots. On relatively shallow submerged reefs in 10-30 m. Migrated into the eastern Mediterranean through the Suez Canal.

Plocamopherus maculapodium Vallès & Gosliner, 2006
Size: 25 mm   Widespread in the Indo-Pacific
ID: Red, speckled with minute white dots; three pairs of short lateral appendages, with the last pair having white or pinkish prominent rounded globular structures. On relatively shallow submerged reefs in 5-20 m.

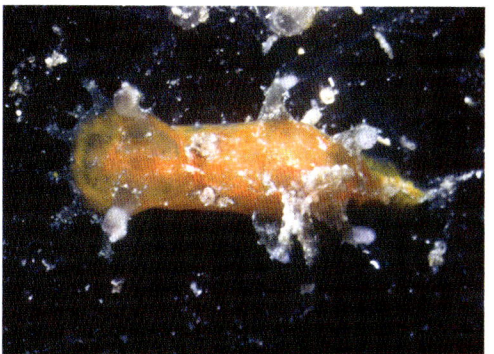

Plocamopherus pecoso Vallès & Gosliner, 2006
Size: 20 mm   Western Pacific
ID: Translucent white, densely speckled with small orange dots; three pairs of short lateral appendages, the two posterior ones with prominent, brown globular structures; gill with distinctive opaque white lines. In association with arborescent bryozoans.

***Plocamopherus lemur* Vallès & Gosliner, 2006**
Size: 9 mm   Madagascar
ID: Brownish, densely speckled with minute brown dots; orange dots clustered to form orange patches; white pigment along the body side margin, oral veil, tips of gill, and rhinophores; three pairs of lateral appendages, with only the last pair forming brown globular structures.

***Plocamopherus* sp. 1**
Size: 15 mm   Aldabra Atoll
ID: Pale orange body with opaque white markings on the notum; the single pair of globular structures are opaque white. Under rocks in rubble in less than 1 m.

***Plocamopherus* sp. 2**
Size: 25 mm   Indonesia
ID: Orange with minute opaque white spots forming a network on the dorsum; more diffuse elsewhere; lateral appendages branched at their tips; posteriormost appendages forming single pairs of rounded white light organs. Shallow rocky reefs.

***Plocamopherus* sp. 3**
Size: 7 mm   South Africa
ID: Brown with scattered opaque white spots; lateral appendages branched at their tips. In intertidal rocky pools at night.

***Plocamopherus ceylonicus* (Kelaart, 1858)**
Size: 20 mm   Widespread in the Indo-Pacific
ID: White with scattered brown blotches and yellow spots; two pairs of lateral projections immediately anterior and posterior to the gill with white knobs at the tips. On the underside of coral rubble in 10-15 m.

***Plocamopherus* sp. 4**
Size: 29 mm   French Polynesia
ID: Orange with opaque white patches with brown spots at the base of each lateral appendage and along the edge of the notum; lateral appendages branched at the tip; posteriormost appendages forming single pair of rounded orange light organs. Shallow rocky reefs.

34

***Limacia* sp.**
Size: 7 mm   Indian Ocean
ID: Translucent white with about 9-10 globular appendages on each side; appendages with an orange core and purplish apices; numerous smaller papillae in the center of the notum with a similar color pattern. Under small coral rubble in 1-3 m.

***Thecacera pacifica* (Bergh, 1884)**
Size: 50 mm   Widespread in the Indo-Pacific
ID: Orange and black with blue markings; two elongate extrabranchial appendages. Relatively uncommon, in shallow water down to 20 m. Recently recorded from the Gulf of Mexico.

***Thecacera picta* Baba, 1972**
Size: 20 mm   Indian and western Pacific oceans
ID: White with black, orange and opaque white pigment. Distinguished from *Thecacera pacifica* by its smaller body size and color pattern. On arborescent bryozoans in areas with strong currents.

***Thecacera* sp. 1**
Size: 15 mm   South Africa
ID: Opaque white with orange lines and black apices on the extrarhinophoral and extrabranchial appendages. In 1-2 m on bryozoans on rocky reefs.

***Thecacera* sp. 2**
Size: 18 mm   Philippines
ID: White with a pattern of parallel longitudinal orange lines along the length of body; extrabranchial appendages elongate, orange with white tips; rhinophores with purple markings and apices. Deep sand and rock slope on bryozoans, in 35 m.

***Thecacera* sp. 3**
Size: 15 mm   Philippines
ID: Uniformly orange with rounded black tubercles; black also present on the extrarhinophoral, extrabranchial lobes, rhinophoral apices and gill tips; extrabranchial lobes short. Shallow rocky reefs.

35

Thecacera sp. 4
Size: 7 mm   Indonesia
ID: White with dense covering of minute brown spots and scattered opaque white patches; extrabranchial and extrarhinophoral appendages short, flat on top, with concentric rings of yellow and purple and a central white spot. Deep sand and rock slopes on bryozoans.

Thecacera sp. 5
Size: 25 mm   Indonesia
ID: Uniformly cream to salmon-pink with black spots over the surface of the body; black pigment on the extrabranchial, extrarhinophoral appendages, rhinophores and foot; extrabranchial processes elongate; inner surface of the extrarhinophoral processes fimbriate. Sandy flats.

Thecacera sp. 6
Size: 25 mm   Indonesia
ID: Beige with black longitudinal lines; extrarhinophoral processes fimbriate, outlined in black; extrabranchial processes long and acute, mostly black; rhinophores and gill with black pigment.

Thecacera sp. 7
Size: 40 mm   Malaysia, Indonesia, Japan
ID: Cream to orange with large black spots and black markings on the large extrabranchial processes; extrarhinophoral processes fimbriate. On arborescent bryozoans on shallow reefs.

Thecacera sp. 8
Size: 40 mm   Malaysia, Indonesia, Philippines, Japan
ID: Orange with purple to black markings; extrarhinophoral processes fimbriate. It differs from the previous species by consistently having rhinophores with black tips and a different arrangement of the spots. On shallow reefs in 20 m.

Thecacera sp. 9
Size: 70 mm   Maldives, Myanmar, Thailand
ID: Cream to orange with large black spots and markings on the large extrabranchial processes; extrarhinophoral processes fimbriate. Feeds on arborescent bryozoans on shallow reefs.

Thecacera sp. 10
Size: 30 mm   Indonesia
ID: Uniformly translucent white with orange spots over the body surface; dark blue and opaque white pigment on the extrabranchial and extrarhinophoral appendages; rhinophores dark blue. Sandy flats.

Thecacera sp. 11
Size: 40 mm   Indonesia
ID: Deep maroon purple with yellow rings and white apices on the various processes along the body surface.

Thecacera sp. 12
Size: 15 mm   Indonesia
ID: Uniformly translucent white with yellow and black spots over the body surface; red and opaque white pigment on the extrabranchial and extrarhinophoral appendages, rhinophores and velar tentacles with red tips. Sandy flats.

Thecacera sp. 13
Size: 18 mm   Thailand
ID: Uniformly translucent white with orange spots over the body surface; dark blue and yellow pigment on the extrabranchial processes; extrarhinophoral appendages elongate with yellow bases and blue apices; rhinophores white. Feeds on arborescent bryozoans.

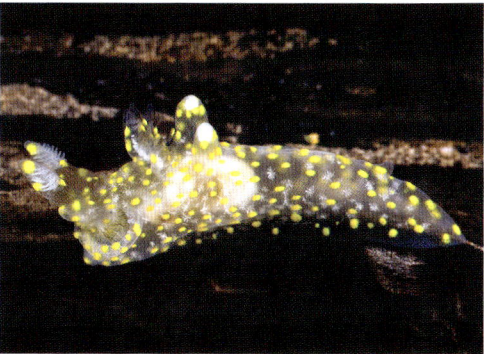

Thecacera sp. 14
Size: 5 mm   Philippines
ID: White with yellowish brown peppering of spots; notal ridge prominent and gill large for size of animal.

Thecacera sp. 15
Size: 10 mm   Philippines
ID: Light orange to white with purple spots and white lines. extending into the gill and extrabranchial processes; rhinophores, gill, extrarhinophoral and extrabranchial processes with orange blotches.

Thecacera boyla Willan, 1989
Size: 10 mm   Queensland (Australia)
ID: Pale cream with brownish mottling; relatively short extrabranchial and elongate extrarhinophoral processes. On shallow water reefs.

Crimora lutea Baba, 1949
Size: 15 mm   Widespread in the Indo-Pacific
ID: Orange with black pigment on the velar appendages and dorsal papillae. Feeds upon arborescent bryozoans on shallow reefs in 1-20 m.

Nembrothinae Burn, 1967
Members of group lack velar and extrabranchial as well as other lateral processes, and the oral tentacles are usually relatively small compared to those of other polycerids. This group has been recently reviewed by Pola *et al.* (2005a, 2005b, 2006a, 2006b, 2007, 2008a), and several new species have been described. Willan & Chang (2017) added the names *Martadoris* and *Tyrannodoris* for some members of this subfamily, but these taxa do not constitute monophyletic groups and therefore those names are not used here.

Nembrotha Bergh, 1877
Species of *Nembrotha* are specialized predators on tunicates. They fall into two natural groups, one including species with raised tubercles or lines and the other with a white background color and longitudinal brown to red lines.

Nembrotha milleri Gosliner & Behrens, 1997
Size: 100 mm   Indian and western Pacific oceans
ID: Greenish-black with black pigment on the rhinophores and gill; body may be relatively smooth with longitudinal folds or with elevated pustules. Feeds on solitary and colonial tunicates, especially *Sigillina signifera* and less frequently *Clavellina moluccensis*; on shallow reefs in 3-10 m.

Nembrotha kubaryana Bergh, 1877
Size: 120 mm   Widespread in the Indo-Pacific
ID: Black with bright green spots or lines; orange pigment on the rhinophores, rhinophoral sheaths, gill, and margin of the foot. *Nembrotha nigerrima* is a synonym. Feeds upon colonial and solitary tunicates such as *Clavellina moluccensis* and *Sigillina signifera* on the sides of reef walls, in 15-40 m.

Nembrotha yonowae Goethel & Debelius, 1992
Size: 100 mm   Indian and western Pacific oceans
ID: Black with orange spots surrounded by green circles and orange pigment on the rhinophores, rhinophoral sheath, gill and foot margin.

Nembrotha cristata Bergh, 1877
Size: 120 mm   Indian and western Pacific oceans
ID: Black with green pigment on the large, rounded tubercles, gill and base of the rhinophoral sheath. Feeds on colonial tunicates such as *Eudistoma* sp. on shallow reefs and slopes to at least 40 m.

Nembrotha sp. 1
Size: 30 mm   Papua New Guinea
ID: Uniformly black or dark reddish with orange spots, some lighter mottling and a darker central spot on the back; rhinophores and gill branches white with dark brown; velar tentacles purple. Rocky reefs, in 12 m on colonial tunicates.

Nudibranchia - "nudibranchs"

Nembrotha chamberlaini Gosliner & Behrens, 1997
Size: 60 mm   Indonesia, Philippines, Japan
ID: White with a dark red-brown or brown saddle; notum with yellow markings and yellow and purple lines; gill and rhinophores bright red, lacking purple pigment. Often misidentified as *Nembrotha rutilans*, which is a synonym of *N. livingstonei* and has purple on the gill and rhinophores. Common on shallow reefs in 5-20 m; feeds upon tunicates including *Rhopalaea*, *Clavelina* and *Oxycorynia*.

Nembrotha megalocera Yonow, 1990
Size: 80 mm   Red Sea
ID: Yellowish-orange with black pigment on the notum and white areas; gill branches dark red with purple bases; rhinophores black; oral tentacles and rhinophoral sheaths purple; foot outlined in purple.

Nembrotha sp. 2
Size: 40 mm   Indonesia, Philippines, Japan
ID: White with a few black lines dorsally and yellow pigment, which extends on to the gill and more posteriorly.

Nembrotha purpureolineata O'Donoghue, 1924
Size: 120 mm   Mozambique, Australia
ID: Color variable, but all specimens have a large red brown or dark brown patch that covers most of the notum; rhinophores and gill red with purple and yellow bases.

Nembrotha rosannulata Pola, Cervera & Gosliner, 2008
Size: 70 mm   Eastern Australia, New Caledonia
ID: Dark green with pink circles surrounding black spots; gill with a pink base and black pinnate branches; pink pigment also on the top of the rhinophoral sheaths. In association with stalked tunicates on shallow reefs in 10-20 m.

***Nembrotha* sp. 3**
Size: 60 mm   Western Pacific Ocean
ID: Black with orange spots; a yellow cruciform mark on the head yellow; yellow pigment at the base of the gill; rhinophores and gill brownish-red with purple bases; oral tentacles purple.

Nembrotha mullineri Gosliner & Behrens, 1997
Size: 100 mm   Australia, Indonesia, Philippines
ID: Cream with brown spots and blotches; rhinophores and gill dark brown; tubercles pointed, low, scattered between creases in the brown blotches. On shallow reefs, feeding on colonial tunicates such as *Oxycorynia fascicularis*.

Nembrotha lineolata Bergh, 1905
Size: 40 mm   Indian and western Pacific oceans
ID: Cream with numerous, narrow brown lines and faint red and purple markings on the gill and rhinophores. Feeds on compound or solitary tunicates, such as *Clavelina* sp., *Rhopalaea* sp. and *Oxycorynia fascicularis* in 7-20 m.

Nembrotha sp. 4
Size: 30 mm   Philippines
ID: Cream-white with an irregular pattern of reddish-brown patches; rhinophoral sheath margins, edge of the foot and bases of the gill branches purple; rhinophore and gill branch bases white with red apices. Shallow rocky reefs; in 7 m on colonial tunicates.

Nembrotha livingstonei Allan, 1933
Size: 40 mm   Eastern Indian and western Pacific oceans
ID: White with orange spots on the head that may extend all over the body; longitudinal greenish lines along the sides may be present; head with a white cruciform mark; gill and rim of the rhinophoral sheaths with orange pigment. On reefs in 10-15 m.

Nembrotha aurea Pola, Cervera & Gosliner, 2008
Size: 40 mm   Western Indian Ocean
ID: Yellow between a series of black longitudinal lines; sides white with black lines; red pigment on rhinophores and gill, both with a purple base. On colonial tunicates on shallow water reefs in 10-15 m.

Nembrotha sp. 5
Size: 30 mm   Indonesia
ID: Uniformly greenish with longitudinal rows of opaque spots and lines; white patches on the head and at the base of the gill; gill and rhinophoral bases purple with red apices. Shallow rocky reefs.

Tambja Burn, 1962
This group has more species than any of the Nembrothinae, but does not appear to represent a single natural group, rather a collection of several distinct clades of species. More work is needed to sort out the higher systematics of the group, but the species are now well understood due to the recent studies of Pola et al. (2005b, 2006a, 2006b). Many have a sensory organ on the side of the head.

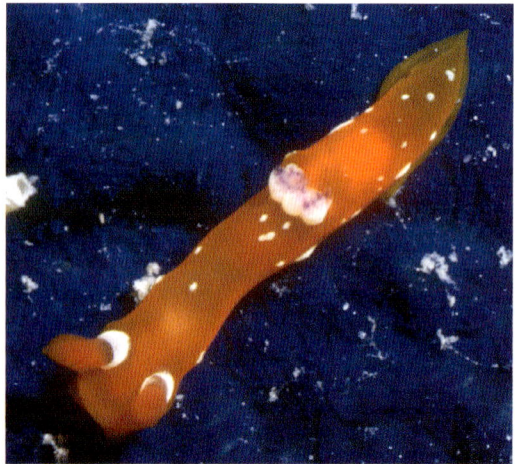

Tambja limaciformis (Eliot, 1908)
Size: 15 mm   Indian and western Pacific oceans
ID: Red with a series of opaque white or yellowish spots on the notum; gill white with bluish tips to the branches; rhinophores red. On shallow water reefs under coral rubble in 5-15 m.

Tambja sp. 1
Size: 30 mm   Papua New Guinea
ID: Green with a few large blue spots, each surrounded by a black ring; gill branches black with a central green line; rhinophores black with blue bases. Shallow reefs, on bryozoans.

Tambja sp. 2
Size: 10 mm   Philippines, Indonesia
ID: Orange with a row of opaque white pustules with yellowish rings and light purple centers along the notal margin; additional pustules on the body; rhinophores and gill branches orange; broad frontal veil. On arborescent bryozoans.

Tambja morosa (Bergh, 1877)
Size: 100 mm   Widespread in the Indo-Pacific
ID: Dark green, blue or more commonly black with blue markings on the head, notum and foot; rhinophores and gill black, greenish pigment may be present on the anterior side of the gill. Common inhabitant of steep slopes and drop-offs, on arborescent bryozoans.

Tambja sp. 3
Size: 30 mm   Indonesia
ID: Dark bluish green with yellow-green longitudinal lines; rhinophores with blue bases and apices and green central areas; gill branches bluish green, each with a yellow green central line. Rocky and sandy areas; shallow water.

Nudibranchia - "nudibranchs"

Tambja affinis (Eliot, 1904)
Size: 50 mm   Red Sea and Indian Ocean
ID: Indigo to dark bluish black with a series of longitudinal yellow-green lines on the notum and sides; a lighter spot between the rhinophores, on the rhinophoral sheaths, and at the anterior base of the gill; rhinophores and gill black; gill outlined in green. On reef slopes and walls in 10-25 m.

Tambja victoriae Pola, Cervera & Gosliner, 2005
Size: 30 mm   Western Pacific Ocean
ID: Bright purple with yellow-orange lines surrounded by black. Similar to *Tambja affinis*, but has consistent differences in its color pattern and in its reproductive anatomy. Feeds on arborescent bryozoans on reef walls in 15-25 m.

Tambja sp. 4
Size: 40 mm   Indonesia
ID: Bluish green with bright yellow lines and a lighter bluish mark behind the rhinophores; a second patch on the anterior face of the gill base.

Tambja tenuilineata Miller & Haagh, 2005
Size: 30 mm   New Zealand, Queensland (Australia)
ID: Greenish with a series of fine black lines on the notum and sides of body; gill and rhinophores tipped with bluish pigment. Feeds on arborescent bryozoans.

Tambja zulu Pola, Cervera & Gosliner, 2005
Size: 40 mm   Mozambique, Kwazulu Natal (South Africa)
ID: Black with a series of longitudinal yellow lines; gill black with yellow lines on the branches; rhinophores also black. On shallow reefs in 5-20 m.

Tambja sp. 5
Size: 100 mm   Papua New Guinea
ID: Green with numerous longitudinal black lines and blue lines and dashes on the sides of the body and head. Feeds on arborescent bryozoans of the genus *Bugula* in 12-16 m.

***Tambja blacki* Pola, Cervera & Gosliner, 2006**
Size: 130 mm   Queensland (Australia), Papua New Guinea
ID: Yellow-green with an orange marginal band on the notum and a series of black spots on the notum and sides of the body. Feeds on the bryozoan, *Amastina rudi*.

***Tambja gabrielae* Pola, Cervera & Gosliner, 2005**
Size: 65 mm   Western Pacific Ocean
ID: Dark green with large yellow or orange spots and a notal marginal band; rhinophores black with an orange apex; gill with light green pigment. On arborescent bryozoans on steep walls and drop-offs.

***Tambja olivaria* Yonow, 1994**
Size: 80 mm   Indian and western Pacific oceans
ID: Olive green with yellow-green pigment on the head, anterior portion of the gill and sometimes on the posterior end of the body; black pigment on the anterior end of the head and behind the light green markings. On the surface of coral rubble in 2-15 m.

***Tambja amakusana* Baba, 1987**
Size: 15 mm   Western Pacific
ID: Uniformly light green with blue pigment on the rhinophores and the tips of the gill branches; rhinophores with blue bases and apices and green central areas; gill branches bluish green, each with yellow green central line. Rocky reefs; shallow water.

***Tambja kava* Pola, Padula, Gosliner & Cervera, 2014**
Size: 20 mm   Western and central Pacific Ocean
ID: Color highly variable from red to green and dark brown, often with lighter spots and lines; it can be recognized by the bluish tips on the gill branches and rhinophores. On the underside of coral rubble in 4-12 m.

Tambja sp. 6
Size: 30 mm   Vanuatu, Papua New Guinea
ID: Indigo to dark bluish black with few orange longitudinal lines and large green spots between the lines.

Tambja sp. 7
Size: 60 mm   Malaysia, Indonesia
ID: Dark green with bright yellow lines; light yellow markings on the gill and rhinophoral lamellae. Similar to *Roboastra tentaculata*, except that the oral tentacles are not as well developed. On shallow reefs in 10-20 m.

Roboastra Bergh, 1877

This is a small subgroup of *Tambja*, including predators that feed on other polycerid nudibranchs. These species have long oral tentacles and a unique radular configuration. Pola *et al.* (2005a) most recently reviewed this group.

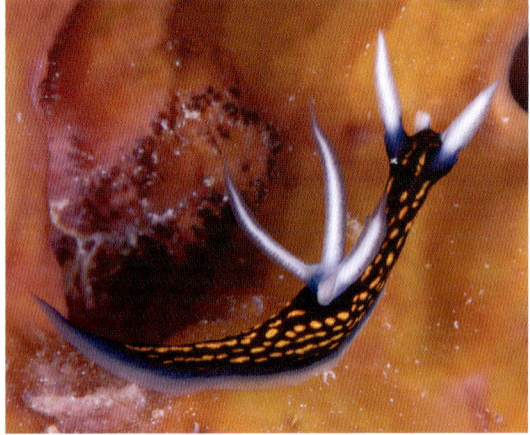

Roboastra gracilis (Bergh, 1877)
Size: 30 mm   Widespread in the Indo-Pacific
ID: Black with yellow lines or spots; white gill, rhinophores, and oral tentacles with black pigment or not; notum with distinct pits and wrinkles; a few long gill branches. On reefs in 3-20 m; presumed to feed on other polycerids but no direct feeding observations have been made.

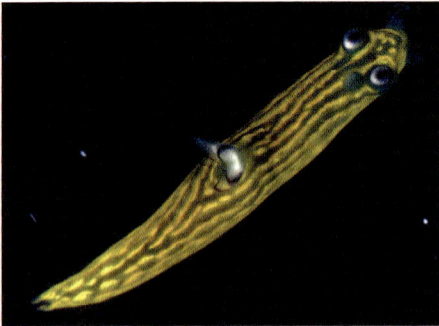

Roboastra luteolineata (Baba, 1936)
Size: 60 mm   Indian and western Pacific oceans
ID: Black with yellow lines. Similar to *Roboastra gracilis*, but has more gill branches that are more highly pinnate. On reefs in 3-20 m; it has been observed feeding on *Nembrotha kubaryana*, *Tambja verconis* (in temperate Australia) and *T. morosa*.

***Roboastra tentaculata* (Pola, Cervera, & Gosliner, 2005)**
Size: 30 mm   Western Pacific Ocean
ID: Yellowish brown with bluish green pigment and several black longitudinal yellow lines; rhinophores and gill black, oral tentacles black and elongate. In 0-21 m where it feeds on bryozoans.

***Roboastra nikolasi* Pola, Padula, Gosliner & Cervera, 2014**
Size: 15 mm   Western Pacific Ocean
ID: Bluish green with numerous longitudinal lighter lines. Similar to *Roboastra tentaculata*, except that the oral tentacles and rhinophores are black with blue pigment more basally. On arborescent bryozoans in 10-30 m.

Okadaiidae Baba, 1930

Members of this group are tiny and have reduced external features. They have small, simple rhinophores and lack a gill. Morphologically there appears to be only a single species, but unpublished molecular evidence suggest it could constitute a species complex.

***Vayssierea felis* (Collingwood, 1881)**
Size: 5 mm   Indo-Pacific and adjacent temperate seas
ID: Uniformly bright orange body; rhinophores simple; gill absent. From the intertidal zone to 20 m; it feeds on the polychaete *Spirorbis* sp., which builds small white calcareous tubes. Not commonly encountered owing to its small body size. It has direct development.

Goniodorididae H. Adams & A. Adams, 1854

Members of this family are very different morphologically from polycerids. Their bodies are more oblong, often with a prominent notal margin. The radular morphology and the presence of a buccal pump demonstrate that these dorids are more closely related to the Onchidorididae than to polycerids. Both the Onchidorididae and Goniodorididae are more closely related to cryptobranchs than to other phanerobranchs.

Goniodoris Forbes & Goodsir, 1839

Members of this group have a well-developed notal edge and lack prominent appendages on the notum.

***Goniodoris felis* Baba, 1949**
Size: 10 mm   Western Pacific Ocean
ID: Opaque white; gill white with brown lines on the rachises. On colonial tunicates under coral rubble.

***Goniodoris* sp. 1**
Size: 6 mm   Indonesia
ID: Uniformly yellow with a brown notal margin and a line on the posterior end of the foot; rhinophoral tips dark brown; gill branches with white tips. Shallow rocky reefs.

Nudibranchia - "nudibranchs"

Goniodoris joubini Risbec, 1928
Size: 12 mm   Widespread in the Indo-Pacific
ID: Brown and white with varying amounts of yellow pigment; notal margin conspicuous. *Goniodoris glabra* Baba, 1937, is a synonym. On colonial tunicates under coral rubble.

Goniodoris sp. 2
Size: 18 mm   Marshall Is.
ID: Mottled white and yellow with dark brown spots on the notal margin and edge of foot; rhinophoral tips dark brown; gill branches with a few brown spots. Shallow rocky reefs.

Goniodoris sp. 3
Size: 8 mm   Papua New Guinea
ID: Brown and white. Similar to *Goniodoris joubini* but lacks mottled pigment on the notal margin; notal margin wider posteriorly while in *G. joubini* is evenly wide throughout. Feeds on colonial tunicates.

Goniodoris sp. 4
Size: 12 mm   Marshall Is.
ID: Mottled grey with a greenish notal margin; rhinophores short, opaque white; posterior end of the foot extending well behind the notum. Shallow rocky reefs on colonial tunicates.

Goniodoris sp. 5
Size: 12 mm   Papua New Guinea
ID: Brown and white. Similar to *Goniodoris joubini* but has more elongate rhinophoral lamellae and a thinner notal margin. Feeds on colonial tunicates under coral rubble on shallow reef crests of barrier reefs.

Goniodoris sp. 6
Size: 7 mm   Indian and western Pacific oceans
ID: Opaque white with burnt orange marginal and yellow submarginal bands around the foot and the oral tentacles. Feeds on colonial tunicates under coral rubble.

Goniodoris sp. 7
Size: 6 mm   Philippines
ID: Uniformly white with a white notal margin; yellow and orange lines around the margin of the foot; gill white; rhinophores light brown with opaque white markings. Shallow rocky reefs.

Goniodoris sp. 8
Size: 7 mm   Indonesia
ID: White with black spots and large dorsal tubercles. Similar to *Goniodoris felis* but it lacks brown pigment on the gill and has mid dorsal tubercles on the notum.

Goniodoris sp. 9
Size: 5 mm   Western and central Pacific ocean
ID: Opaque white with four areas of transparency where the opaque white is absent; rhinophores with orange apices; notal margin with curved lobes anteriorly and posteriorly. On colonial tunicates under coral rubble in 5-23 m.

Goniodoris sp. 10
Size: 6 mm   Philippines
ID: White body with mottled yellow and brown pigment; fine brown reticulations scattered over body surface; rhinophores opaque white; gill with brown lines on branches.

Goniodoris sp. 11
Size: 12 mm   Philippines
ID: White with small black dots; rhinophores uniformly dark brown; distinct medial ridge behind the gill on the notum and foot.

Goniodoris sp. 12
Size: 5 mm   Indonesia
ID: Flat body with opaque white network of lines and scattered bluish patches; shown on its colonial ascidian prey on which it is cryptically colored.

Nudibranchia - "nudibranchs"

Goniodoris sp. 13
Size: 10 mm   Indonesia
ID: Uniformly orange with scattered opaque white spots at the apices of small tubercles.

***Goniodoridella* Pruvot-Fol, 1933**
Species of this group have elongate extrabranchial appendages, smooth rhinophores, and very reduced gill branches. There appear to be many small, undescribed species.

***Goniodoridella savignyi* Pruvot-Fol, 1933**
Size: 11 mm   Indian and western Pacific, Russia, Japan
ID: Opaque white with an orange medial line and marginal band; white, elongate extrabranchial processes, sometimes with orange apices. Under coral rubble on reefs of 5-10 m.

Goniodoridella sp. 1
Size: 7 mm   Western and central Pacific Ocean
ID: Translucent white with opaque white spots on the notum and extrabranchial processes; rhinophores and extrabranchial appendages elongate; small black spots concentrated on the head and in two lines more posteriorly. Under coral rubble on reefs in 5-10 m.

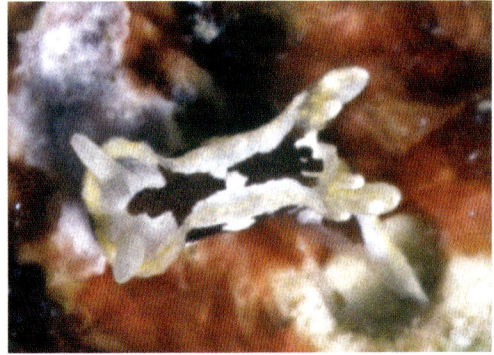

Goniodoridella sp. 2
Size: 5 mm   Papua New Guinea, Philippines
ID: Opaque white with a light yellow anterior margin and a dark green patch on the notum between the rhinophores and the gill and on the sides; a pair of extrabranchial processes rounded and tipped with light yellow. Under coral rubble on shallow reefs in 5-12 m.

Goniodoridella sp. 3
Size: 5 mm   Papua New Guinea, Philippines
ID: Opaque white with green on the sides of the body and a few green spots on the rhinophores; lacks dark green pigment on the notum; extrabranchial processes flattened.

Goniodoridella sp. 4
Size: 4 mm   Papua New Guinea, Japan
ID: Uniformly opaque white with red tips on the rhinophores; extrabranchial processes elongate and angled from their middle. On the underside coral rubble in 12 m.

Goniodoridella sp. 5
Size: 6 mm   Malaysia, Philippines
ID: Uniformly white with short white extrabranchial processes; rhinophores translucent with opaque white and brown pigment. Under basaltic stones in 10 m.

Goniodoridella sp. 6
Size: 7 mm   Madagascar, Philippines
ID: Dark brown with areas of cream and minute white dots; body more quadrangular than in other species, with very large tuberculate extrabranchial processes. Under coral rubble in 1-2 m; feeds on compound tunicates.

Goniodoridella sp. 7
Size: 6 mm   Vanuatu
ID: White with a black crescent just behind the rhinophores and scattered black spots on the notum and head; Gill leaves branched.

Goniodoridella sp. 8
Size: 6 mm   Indian and Western Pacific oceans
ID: Uniformly white with a dark brown to black transverse band on the head behind rhinophores; a second transverse band may be present behind the gill; gill appendages elongate, paddle-shaped; rhinophores smooth. Shallow sandy slopes among coral rubble in 15 m.

Goniodoridella sp. 9
Size: 5 mm   Papua New Guinea, Indonesia
ID: Uniformly white with orange pigment on the head and on the tips of the long, pointed gill appendages; rhinophores perfoliate, white, with orange apices; body extremely long. Shallow sandy slopes among coral rubble.

Goniodoridella sp. 10
Size: 6 mm   Indonesia
ID: Uniformly translucent white with opaque white markings; notal margin well developed with a faint orange line; gill appendages elongate, finger-shaped; rhinophores smooth. Shallow sandy slopes among coral rubble.

Nudibranchia - "nudibranchs"

Okenia Menke, 1830

Species of *Okenia* feed on bryozoans or tunicates and are characterized by having a series of appendages on the sides of the body, and in many cases on the dorsum. This is a diverse group in the Indo-Pacific. Papers by Gosliner (2004) and Rudman (2004; 2007) have described 13 new species.

Okenia plana Baba, 1960

Size: 10 mm   Western Pacific
ID: Brown with numerous black spots; body flat. Similar to *Okenia pilosa* but has two rows of dorsal papillae near the margin and only one mid-dorsal papilla; it also has fewer, more highly ramified gill branches. Under rocks with encrusting bryozoans in shallow water. It has been introduced to California.

Okenia pilosa (Bouchet & Ortea, 1983)

Size: 9 mm   Western Pacific Ocean
ID: Greyish white with black spots; body flat, with numerous dorsal papillae and a circle of small gill branches. On the underside of coral rubble in shallow water, less than 10 m.

Okenia rhinorma Rudman, 2007

Size: 10 mm   Widespread in the Indo-Pacific
ID: White with grey mottling and large orange spots; rhinophores situated far posteriorly, immediately in front of the gill. On sandy substrate with lots of algae in 6 m.

Okenia kendi Gosliner, 2004

Size: 25 mm   Philippines, Indonesia
ID: White with brown and purple pigment on the back; appendages slender. On the underside of the large leafy

sponge, *Phyllospongia lamellosa* and other similar species, where it feeds on crustose bryozoans in 5-15 m.

Okenia brunneomaculata Gosliner, 2004
Size: 10 mm   Indonesia, Philippines
ID: White with dark brown to black spots; numerous small dorsal papillae scattered over the notum. On the underside of foliose sponges were ctenostomatous bryozoan colonies are present.

Okenia purpureolineata Gosliner, 2004
Size: 15 mm   Ryūkyū Is. (Japan), Philippines
ID: White with a network of purple lines and red to orange rhinophores; it also has two mid-dorsal papillae. On arborescent bryozoans in deep water from 40-50 m.

Okenia sp. 1
Size: 7 mm   Indonesia
ID: White with a yellowish center of the dorsum; a brown V-shaped line that extends from the rhinophores to behind the gill; a few elongate papillae in front of the gill; lateral appendages elongate.

Okenia sp. 2
Size: 5 mm   United Arab Emirates
ID: White with dark brown to black lines. Similar to *Okenia brunneomaculata* and *O.* sp. 1 but with burnt orange rhinophores with black tips; gill with a black line on each gill branch.

Okenia sp. 3
Size: 6 mm   Indonesia
ID: Uniformly translucent white elongate body with brown speckling and larger brown spots; elongate papillae in front of the gill; gill and rhinophores brown basally with white tips. Rocky reefs, in coral rubble.

Okenia pellucida Burn, 1957
Size: 20 mm   Widespread in the Indo-Pacific
ID: White with brown reticulate markings. Feeds on the elongate, transparent bryozoan *Zoobotryon* sp., which often forms large mats that are frequently seen drifting in shallow water.

Nudibranchia - "nudibranchs"

Okenia sp. 4
Size: 6 mm   Indonesia
ID: Opaque white with a bright orange patch on the dorsum extending from the head to the gill; an orange line along

the margin of notum, 3 short papillae on the notum, lateral appendages white, moderately elongate; rhinophores orange, elongate. Shallow sandy slopes among coral rubble.

Okenia sp. 5
Size: 8 mm   Marquesas Is.
ID: Brownish with a network of opaque white lines; lateral appendages brown with white spots, elongate, curved, with rounded tips. Feeds on encrusting bryozoans, in 6 m.

Okenia virginiae Gosliner, 2004
Size: 10 mm   Western Indian Ocean
ID: Brown with a white network on the notum and purple markings on the papillae. Under rocks in relatively shallow water.

Okenia lambat Gosliner, 2004
Size: 7 mm   Philippines
ID: Brown on the notum with a white network. It differs from *Okenia virginiae* in having maroon spots and a larger gill. Under rocks in 10 m.

Okenia japonica Baba, 1949
Size: 15 mm   Japan, Hong Kong (China)
ID: Uniform grey-white with a single mid-dorsal papilla. On arborescent bryozoans in deep water from 40-50 m.

***Okenia* sp. 6**
Size: 10 mm   Northern Hawai'ian Is., Midway Atoll
ID: Orange with opaque white longitudinal lines. On the underside of coral rubble in less than 10 m.

***Okenia* cf. *plebeia* Bergh, 1902**
Size: 12 mm   India, Thailand
ID: Uniformly translucent white with a pinkish cast; rhinophores with dark brown lines at the bases and tips; gill with brown tips; a single elongate mid-dorsal papilla, lateral appendages elongate. Intertidal rock pools.

***Okenia* sp. 7**
Size: 15 mm   India
ID: Uniformly lemon-yellow with scattered dark brown spots; a single elongate mid-dorsal papilla, lateral appendages elongate, white with black spots; rhinophores and gill yellow with black markings.

***Okenia* sp. 8**
Size: 10 mm   Philippines, Papua New Guinea
ID: Opaque white with orange tips on the rhinophores and dorsal papillae. On the underside of coral slabs in 6-10 m.

***Okenia* sp. 9**
Size: 7 mm   Marquesas Is.
ID: Uniformly opaque white with yellow-orange blotches and an additional orange line below the notum; two dorsal appendages between the rhinophores and gill; lateral appendages moderately short, rounded; rhinophores orange basally and white apically; gill white. Rocky reefs, in 4 m.

***Okenia* sp 10**
Size: 4 mm   Philippines
ID: Yellowish with white appendages, rhinophoral tips and gill leafs. Similar to *Okenia* sp. 4, but with opaque white tip to rhinophores and more uniform orange pigment. On encrusting bryozoans in 15 m.

Nudibranchia - "nudibranchs"

Okenia sp. 11
Size: 3 mm   Tuamotu Archipelago
ID: Uniformly opaque white with two dorsal orange lines that meet behind the gill, and an additional orange line below the notum; lateral appendages moderately long; rhinophores orange basally and white apically; gill white. On green algae on coral, 1 m.

Okenia sp. 12
Size: 20 mm   Madagascar, South Africa
ID: Uniformly opaque white with yellow or red spots between the rhinophores and the gill; lateral appendages long, white with yellow subapical rings and red tips; rhinophores and gill with yellow and red pigment. Mixed sand and rock; tidal pools to 28 m.

Okenia sp. 13
Size: 6 mm   Philippines, Indonesia
ID: Uniformly opaque white with a yellow margin and a medial longitudinal line; lateral appendages short, triangular with yellow tips; anterior appendages dark brown to black, more elongate; rhinophores white basally and brown to black apically; gill white. On coral rubble on sandy slopes, 15-18 m.

Okenia sp. 14
Size: 20 mm   Papua New Guinea, Indonesia
ID: Uniformly orange with purple tips of the rhinophores and appendages; two dorsal appendages between the rhinophores and the gill; gill branches with opaque white pigment; lateral appendages long. On reefs of mixed sand and coral.

Okenia purpurata Rudman, 2004
Size: 9 mm   Singapore, Indonesia, Australia
ID: Uniformly purple with light yellow on the appendages; rhinophores and gill deeper purple; 2-4 dorsal appendages between the rhinophores and the gill; lateral appendages long. On reefs of mixed sand and coral.

Okenia liklik Gosliner, 2004
Size: 7 mm   Philippines, Papua New Guinea
ID: Purple with opaque white patches on the dorsum; papillae orange with brown apices; gill white; rhinophores purple with orange and white pigment. On the underside of small stones in 8 m.

Okenia nakamotoensis (Hamatani, 2001)
Size: 20 mm   Indian and western Pacific oceans
ID: Flame red with white pigment on the base of the five pairs of elongate, club-shaped papillae; it appears more like an aeolid nudibranch than a dorid. On the arborescent bryozoan *Tropidozoum cellariiforme*, which inhabits open reef walls at 10-30 m.

Okenia kondoi (Hamatani, 2001)
Size: 15 mm   Western Pacific Ocean
ID: Flame red with white pigment on the base of the four pairs of elongate, club-shaped processes; head more elongate than in *Okenia nakamotoensis*. Same habitat and food as *O. nakamotoensis*.

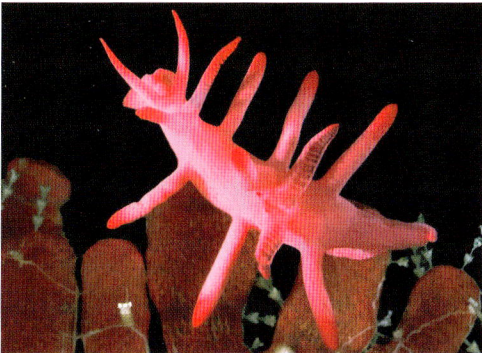

Okenia hallucigenia Rudman, 2004
Size: 15 mm   Tropical and temperate Australia
ID: Light pink with darker reddish apices on the appendages and rhinophores. On the arborescent bryozoan *Pleurotoichus clathratus* in 6-22 m.

Okenia stellata Rudman, 2004
Size: 18 mm   Tropical and temperate Australia
ID: Light pink. Similar to *Okenia hallucigenia*, but the body is much broader and has additional dark lines on the notum. Same habitat and diet as *O. hallucigenia*.

Trapania Pruvot-Fol, 1931

Species of this genus are characterized by having an elongate body and a pair of curved extrarhinophoral and extrabranchial appendages. Gosliner & Fahey (2008) reviewed this genus and described 12 new species. Members of this group are often found on red sponges but are likely feeding on the entoprocts (small colonial organisms) that are commensal with these sponges.

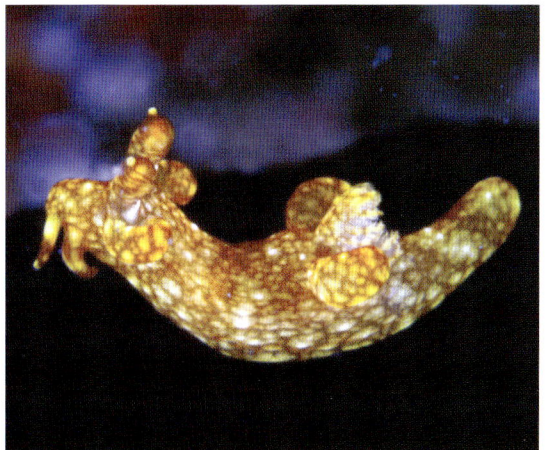

Trapania reticulata Rudman, 1987
Size: 18 mm   Great Barrier Reef (Australia)
ID: Translucent brown with darker brown reticulations that surround yellow spots and opaque white areas; oral tentacles, extrarhinophoral and extrabranchial processes with the same color; rhinophores with yellow tips. On deeper reefs in 30 m.

Trapania tora Gosliner & Fahey, 2008
Size: 15 mm   Indonesia
ID: Translucent white with a network of white lines on areas of brown of pigment; dorsum with conspicuous yellow tubercles; extrabranchial and extrarhinophoral appendages white with yellow lines; gill translucent brown with opaque white spots. On red sponges in 1-15 m.

Trapania squama Gosliner & Fahey, 2008
Size: 10 mm   Papua New Guinea, Marshall Is.
ID: Cream outlined by chocolate brown; scattered brown and white markings on the oral tentacles, rhinophores, extrarhinophoral and extrabranchial appendages, gill and posterior end of the foot. Under coral rubble in shallow water patch reefs.

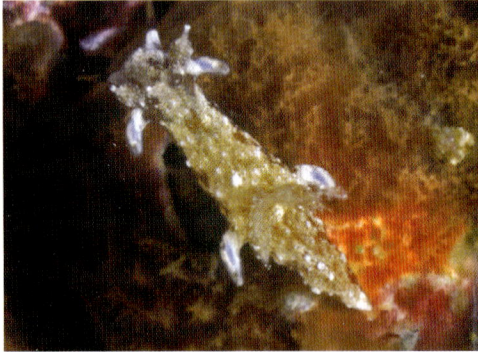

Trapania palmula Gosliner & Fahey, 2008
Size: 8 mm   Philippines, Indonesia, central Japan
ID: Light brown with small opaque white tubercles; diagonal purple markings on the extrarhinophoral and extrabranchial appendages. Under coral rubble in shallow water patch reefs.

Trapania circinata Gosliner & Fahey, 2008
Size: 10 mm   Marshall Is.
ID: Solid white including the oral tentacles; extrarhinophoral appendages black with white bases; extrabranchial appendages grey with black specks; rhinophoral stalks, clubs and gill black.

***Trapania* sp. 1**
Size: 7 mm   Philippines
ID: Creamy white with black along the notal margin; rhinophoral bases and gill red, with red outlines to the rhinophoral lamellae; head with a black line; oral tentacles red; extrarhinophoral and extrabranchial appendages white. On sloping reef faces, in 25 m.

Trapania caerulea Gosliner & Fahey, 2008
Size: 7 mm   Indonesia
ID: Cream yellow with two lines of brown pigment extending from the rhinophoral sheaths; anterior surface of the foot with a mid-dorsal light blue line; rhinophores and oral tentacles reddish-brown; extrarhinophoral appendages creamy yellow. On red sponges.

Trapania vitta Gosliner & Fahey, 2008
Size: 12 mm   Western Pacific
ID: White with orange lines on the rhinophores and gill. Similar to *Trapania aurata*, but lacks orange pigment on the extrarhinophoral and extrabranchial appendages. In 10-20 m on isolated ridges of rubble.

Trapania sp. 2
Size: 4 mm   Philippines
ID: Uniformly opaque whitish over entire body. In association with soft corals on which it is very cryptically colored.

Trapania gibbera Gosliner & Fahey, 2008
Size: 8 mm   Western Pacific Ocean
ID: Opaque white with a black transverse bar across the anterior margin of the head; red pigment on the rhinophores, oral tentacles and gill. Shallow water habitats in 10-15 m.

Trapania aurata Rudman, 1987
Size: 10 mm   New Caledonia, Hong Kong (China)
ID: Solid white with orange pigment on the oral tentacles, extrarhinophoral appendages, extrabranchial appendages, rhinophoral tips, and gill branches. On entoprocts growing on aplysillid sponges in 14 m.

Trapania darvelli Rudman, 1987
Size: 13 mm   Western Pacific Ocean
ID: Solid white with brown on the oral tentacles, rhinophoral tips, extrarhinophoral appendages, extrabranchial appendages, and gill branches. In shallow water, 7-16 m.

Trapania sp. 3
Size: 6 mm   Philippines
ID: Brown with minute white spots; extrarhinophoral and extrabranchial appendages white with black tips. Similar to *Trapania euryeia* but with a much longer gill and dark brown rhinophores.

Nudibranchia - "nudibranchs"

Trapania melaina Gosliner & Fahey, 2008
Size: 12 mm   Kwazulu Natal (South Africa)
ID: Brown with minute white spots and yellow on the oral tentacles, gill, extrarhinophoral and extrabranchial appendages. In a tide pool at night.

Trapania safracornia Fahey, 2004
Size: 8 mm   Western Australia
ID: Dark brown with three areas of opaque white pigment; rhinophores and gill white with pinkish-brown pigment; extrarhinophoral and extrabranchial appendages white. In relatively deep water, 28 m.

Trapania miltabrancha Gosliner & Fahey, 2008
Size: 10 mm   Indonesia, Marshall Is.
ID: Black with complex pattern of brick red patches and white dots; oral tentacles brown with red-flecks; extrarhinophoral and extrabranchial appendages white with pale pink apices; rhinophores with white stalks and blotchy black clubs. In 8 m on rubble slopes.

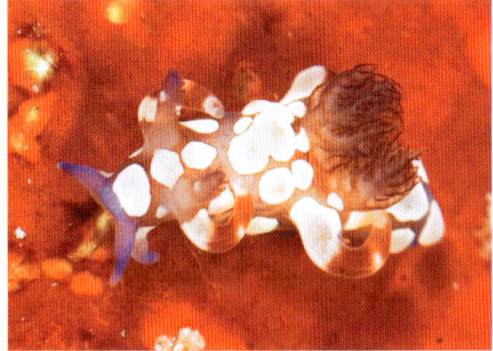

Trapania scurra Gosliner & Fahey, 2008
Size: 15 mm   Philippines, Indonesia, Malaysia
ID: Purple with opaque cream patches; extrarhinophoral and extrabranchial appendages especially large. On the underside of coral rubble in 10 m.

Trapania sp. 4
Size: 7 mm   Western Pacific Ocean
ID: Uniformly maroon, or with opaque white irregular markings variable in size; rhinophores white tipped; large extrarhinophoral and extrabranchial appendages. On sandy slopes in about 15-21 m.

Trapania sp. 5
Size: 5 mm   Indonesia
ID: White with brown spots; rhinophores translucent grey with mottled white pigment; gill extremely large in proportion to the body size, same color as the body.

60

***Trapania armilla* Gosliner & Fahey, 2008**
Size: 7 mm   Indonesia
ID: Uniformly white with a conspicuous dark ring on each oral tentacle; body tuberculate. On shallow slopes in 15 m. Shown here with its egg mass.

***Trapania* sp. 6**
Size: 5 mm   Indonesia
ID: Uniformly opaque white with irregular papillae over the entire body surface and a few small dark spots; extrarhinophoral and extrabranchial appendages the same color as the rest of the body; a dark band on each oral tentacle. On reefs of mixed sand and coral.

***Trapania* sp. 7**
Size: 6 mm   Indonesia
ID: Uniformly pale tan with isolated opaque white tips at the apices of the rounded tubercles; extrarhinophoral and extrabranchial appendages same color as the body but each with a red orange marking in the outer portion. On fine volcanic sand.

***Trapania* sp. 8**
Size: 12 mm   Philippines
ID: Mottled pale tan with darker brown patches and a few small opaque white spots over the entire surface of the body; extrarhinophoral and extrabranchial appendages same color as the body. On reefs of mixed sand and coral.

***Trapania* sp. 9**
Size: 5 mm   Philippines
ID: Uniformly orange; a dorsal black longitudinal line on the "tail"; rhinophores white basally and black apically; oral tentacles and gill black; extrarhinophoral and extrabranchial white. On orange encrusting bryozoans on mixed sand and rock, 15 m.

***Trapania euryeia* Gosliner & Fahey, 2008**
Size: 10 mm   Widespread in the Indo-Pacific
ID: Brown with minute cream spots and white patches. Often confused with the temperate Australian species, *Trapania brunnea*. Under coral rubble in less than 10 m.

Trapania sp. 10
Size: 6 mm   Kenya, Indonesia
ID: Mottled white with irregular dark brown patches over the entire surface of the body; extrarhinophoral and extrabranchial appendages same color as the body. On reefs of mixed sand and coral.

Trapania sp. 11
Size: 15 mm   Philippines
ID: White with a dark brown area; opaque white spots covering most of the body surface; extrarhinophoral and extrabranchial appendages white with brown pigment; rhinophores and gill brown with white spots; lateral appendages long. Active at night crawling on silty sand in 5 m.

Trapania sp. 12
Size: 10 mm   Reunion Island
ID: Creamy white with patches or purple brown surrounded by black lines; rhinophores, gill, extrarhinophoral and extrabranchial appendages brown with cream white spots. On shallow reefs and fringing lagoons.

Trapania sp. 13
Size: 4 mm   Philippines
ID: Creamy white with patches or purple brown. Similar to *Trapania* sp. 12 but without peppering of brown spots on the rhinophores, gills and extrabranchia appendages. On shallow reefs under rocks.

Trapania toddi Rudman, 1987
Size: 10 mm   Red Sea, Australia, Hong Kong (China)
ID: White with dark brown reticulated pigment and often with yellow pigment on the rhinophores and gill and on the extrarhinophoral and extrabranchial appendages. In shallow water, 3-20 m.

Trapania sp. 14
Size: 7 mm   Great Barrier Reef (Australia), Indonesia
ID: White with purplish-black pigment on the oral tentacles, rhinophores, gill and sides of the body; gill and rhinophores tipped with yellow-orange.

Trapania sp. 15
Size: 5 mm   Indonesia
ID: White with dark brown to black patches over the surface of the body and oral tentacles; rhinophores with black on the inner side; gill with black and yellow pigment; extrarhinophoral and extrabranchial appendages yellow. Reefs of mixed sand and coral.

Trapania sp. 16
Size: 10 mm   Indonesia
ID: White with black patches over the surface of the body and oral tentacles; rhinophores each with a black band and apex; gill black with white tips; extrarhinophoral and extrabranchial appendages white basally with black tips. Shallow reefs of mixed sand and coral.

Trapania naeva Gosliner & Fahey, 2008
Size: 7 mm   Japan, Western Australia
ID: White with a few, large, round to oval black spots; rhinophores, gill, oral tentacles, extrarhinophoral and extrabranchial appendages black; gill large in proportion to the body size.

Trapania japonica (Baba, 1935)
Size: 3 mm   Widespread in the Indo-Pacific
ID: White body with black spots, and black rhinohoral tips and oral tentacles; yellow extrarhinophoral and extrabranchial appendages. *Trapania norakhalafae* Khalaf, 2017 is likely a synonym.

Trapania sp. 17
Size: 5 mm   Philippines
ID: Opaque white with a dark brown to black patch on the notum and lines of the same color on the sides of the body behind the gill; head, rhinophores and oral tentacles black; gill white; extrarhinophoral and extrabranchial appendages orange. On shallow patch reef, in 7 m.

Trapania nebula Gosliner & Fahey, 2008
Size: 7 mm   Papua New Guinea
ID: Mottled white with plum pigment on the body and red on the oral tentacles, rhinophores and gill. Under coral rubble in shallow water patch reefs.

Trapania sp. 18
Size: 5 mm   Indonesia
ID: Grey with irregular white pustules; rhinophores white with golden-yellow tips; gill grey tipped with golden-yellow; oral tentacles golden-yellow with white pigment.

Trapania sp. 19
Size: 5 mm   Indonesia
ID: Pale yellowish with small black spots with white circle surrounding each spot; spots also present on rhinophores, gill and extrarhinophoral appendages.

Trapania sp. 20
Size: 4 mm   Indonesia
ID: White body with dusting of small honey brown spots; oral tentacles with yellow and brown pigment.

Onchidorididae J. E. Gray, 1827

Members of this group have a more rounded body than those of the Goniodorididae. The also have numerous tubercles or elongate papillae on the notum. Most species are temperate or boreal, there are just a few tropical species.

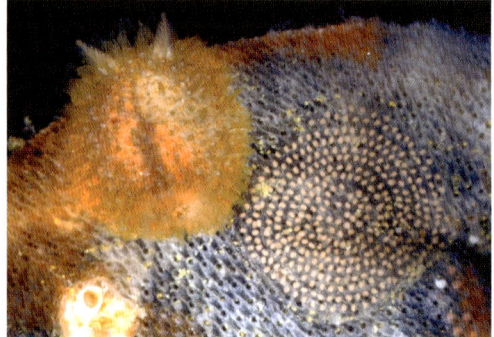

Onchidoris sp.
Size: 9 mm   Southern Australia, New Caledonia
ID: Uniformly brown; body oval, flat, covered with elongate tubercles. Similar to *Onchidoris depressa* from Europe, but molecular studies confirmed its distinctness. On encrusting bryozoans.

Diaphorodoris sp. 1
Size: 9 mm   Philippines, Indonesia
ID: Uniformly opaque white; dorsum with low papillae having light yellow at their base; mantle edge cream with brown spots; rhinophores and gill white with brown; a yellow ridge on the foot. On reef slopes of mixed sand and coral.

Diaphorodoris mitsuii (Baba, 1938)
Size: 12 mm   Indian and western Pacific oceans
ID: Opaque white or yellow with a marginal orange line; rhinophores with orange tips; dorsum tuberculate with a orange crest along the middle of the foot. On patch reefs in 2-10 m.

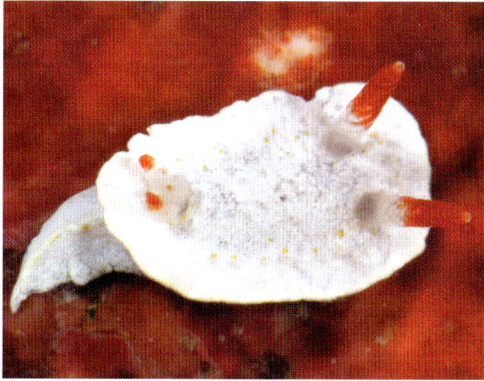

Diaphorodoris sp. 2
Size: 9 mm   Philippines
ID: Uniformly opaque white; dorsum covered with low papillae having light yellow at their base; mantle edge yellow; rhinophores and gill white with red tips; a yellow ridge on the foot. On reef flat under dead coral head, in 7 m.

Aegires villosus Farran, 1905
Size: 12 mm   Indian and western Pacific oceans
ID: Light pink to purple with darker purple and orange spots and tubercles; exhibits considerable variation in color pattern. On shallow reefs under coral rubble; feeds on calcareous sponges.

Aegires pruvotfolae Fahey & Gosliner, 2004
Size: 8 mm   Widespread in the Indo-Pacific
ID: Yellow with short flattened tubercles and brown spots. Feeds on yellow filamentous calcareous sponges from the intertidal zone to 15 m.

Aegiridae P. Fischer, 1883

Aegiridae is the sister group to the cryptobranchs plus the Goniodorididae and Onchidorididae. Aegirids are more closely related to these taxa than to members of the Polyceridae. Members of this group have smooth rather than perfoliate rhinophores. Fahey & Gosliner (2004) reviewed this group and described eight new species, and also shown that *Notodoris* is not distinct from *Aegires*.

Aegires sp. 1
Size: 15 mm   Saudi Arabia
ID: Uniformly yellow with black oval markings; rhinophores and gill yellow; body elongate with large, rounded tubercles. Shallow reefs on yellow calcareous sponges.

Aegires sp. 2
Size: 12 mm   Indonesia
ID: Uniformly yellow with brown spots; rhinophores burnt orange; gill yellow; body elongate with large, rounded tubercles. Patch reefs.

Aegires sp. 3
Size: 20 mm   Philippines
ID: Yellow with brown spots. Similar to *Aegires pruvotfolae*, but has a far more elongate body. In 20 m crawling over the surface of coral rubble.

Aegires sp. 4
Size: 10 mm   Marshall Is.
ID: Uniformly deep purple with deep blue circles; body moderately short with small, irregular tubercles, often with white spots on the apices, rhinophores and gill purple. Shallow rocky reefs.

Aegires sp. 5
Size: 8 mm   Indonesia
ID: Uniformly light greenish with small opaque white spots; rhinophores and gill with the same color as the body; body relatively short with low rounded tubercles. Rocky reefs.

Aegires lemoncello Fahey & Gosliner, 2004
Size: 10 mm   Widespread in the Indo-Pacific
ID: Light yellow with a few elongate darker yellow papillae; each papilla with a yellow-orange ring well below the apex. On shallow water reefs under coral rubble in 9 m.

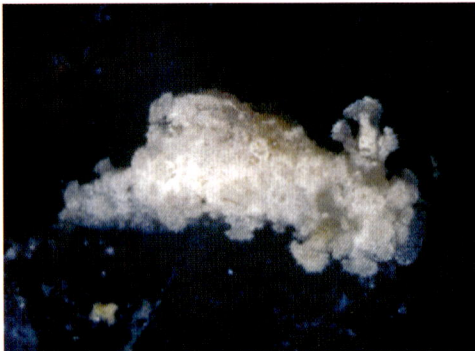

Aegires petalis Fahey & Gosliner, 2004
Size: 5 mm   Papua New Guinea
ID: White; body with large tubercles having a flat apex, especially well-developed around the rhinophoral sheaths. On a shallow reef in 11 m.

Aegires incusus Fahey & Gosliner, 2004
Size: 5 mm   Indian and western Pacific oceans
ID: Greyish white with a few large round tan spots on the notum; tubercles relatively large with flat tops. Shallow water under rubble in 1-3 m.

Nudibranchia - "nudibranchs"

Aegires exeches Fahey & Gosliner, 2004
Size: 7 mm   Western and central Pacific Ocean
ID: White with bright blue spots; dorsum with compound flattened tubercles. Previously known from the Indo-Pacific as *Aegires punctilucens*. On coral rubble on shallow water reefs in 5-7 m.

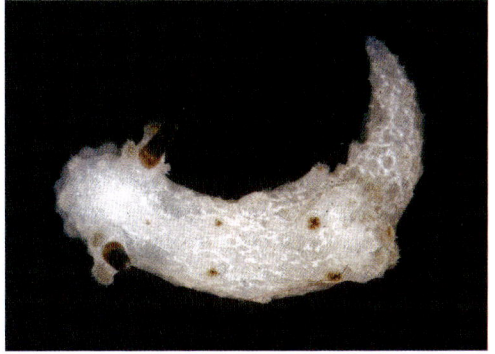

Aegires hapsis Fahey & Gosliner, 2004
Size: 6 mm   Southern Japan
ID: Opaque white with a few large dark brown spots and a network of opaque white lines; rhinophores dark brown; notum relatively smooth. Shallow water under rubble in 3 m.

Aegires flores Fahey & Gosliner, 2004
Size: 15 mm   Western Pacific Ocean
ID: Color highly variable, ranges from white to wine red, with numerous reddish or yellow flat-topped tubercles; appendages

surrounding the gill flat and rounded apically and appear as petals of a flower, giving the species name. On shallow reefs from 3-30 m; feeds on calcareous sponges.

Aegires sp. 6
Size: 15 mm   Philippines
ID: Translucent white with bright orange pigment and purple rhinophores; black pigment on the rounded tubercles, gill branches and rhinophoral apices. On shallow reefs in 15 m on the under surface of coral rubble.

Aegires sp. 7
Size: 6 mm   Philippines, Papua New Guinea
ID: Pinkish purple with large rounded tubercles; tips of the extrabranchial lobes orange; rhinophores deep purplish red. Shallow water under rubble. Feeds on the tubular calcareous sponge, *Pericharax* sp.

67

Aegires sp. 8
Size: 3 mm   Philippines, Indonesia
ID: Uniform pink; notum smooth; extrabranchial processes very large, obscuring the gill. On small calcareous sponges among colonial tunicates.

Aegires sp. 9
Size: 6 mm   Indonesia
ID: Uniformly light brown with small opaque white spots; rhinophores and gill with the same color as the body; body relatively short, with a well elevated gill and elongate rhinophoral sheaths. Rocky reefs.

Aegires malinus Fahey & Gosliner, 2004
Size: 15 mm   Philippines
ID: Brown with apple green rhinophoral sheaths; rhinophores spotted, with short bifid apices; tubercles with branched appendages resembling algae. On reefs among coral rubble in 12 m.

Large species with yellow or grey pigment

The following four species were formerly placed in a separate genus and family: *Notodoris* Bergh, 1875 and Notodorididae Eliot, 1910. However, phylogenetic evidence (Fahey & Gosliner, 2004) shows that they are a subgroup within *Aegires*. Additionally, they are all more closely related to each other than to other species of *Aegires*.

Aegires serenae (Gosliner & Behrens, 1997)
Size: 90 mm   Western Pacific Ocean
ID: Grey with black markings and yellow rhinophores; large appendages surrounding the gill. Differs from other large species of *Aegires*, all of which are yellow in color. On the sponge *Leucetta primigenia* together with other species of *Aegires* at 10- 20 m.

Aegires citrinus (Bergh, 1875)
Size: 50 mm   Western Pacific Ocean
ID: Uniformly yellow without any black lines or spots; body rigid, elongate; gill protected by blunt appendages. Relatively shallow water, 10-20 m, where it feeds on the sponge *Leucetta* sp.

Aegires gardineri (Eliot, 1906)
Size: 80 mm   Indian and western Pacific oceans
ID: Bright yellow with black mottling rather than distinct lines as in *Aegires minor*. On the yellow sponges *Leucetta primigenia* and *Pericharax heterographis* on reef crests and slopes at 10-20 m.

Aegires sp. 10
Size: 60 mm   Maldives
ID: Yellow with large black spots. Rhinophores with black apices. Similar to *Aegires minor*, but with yellow body and black spots rather than lines.

Aegires minor (Eliot, 1904)
Size: 100 mm   Indian and western Pacific oceans
ID: Bright yellow with black lines and spots; body rigid and hard to the touch. Feeds on the yellow calcareous sponge

Leucetta primigenia and the brown sponge *Pericharax heterographis* on reef crests and slopes at 10-20 m. The egg mass is a bright yellow ribbon.

Gymnodorididae Odhner, 1941

There are 30 described and at least 60 undescribed species of *Gymnodoris* (Knutson & Gosliner, in preparation). Many species descriptions are very incomplete and it is often extremely difficult to establish what the names of the most common species actually represent. For example, species referred to as *Gymnodoris bicolor* and *G. alba* probably represent about 20 different species. *Gymnodoris* are very closely related to the Polyceridae and likely belong in this family. Most species are white with yellow or orange markings, and are small, less than 20 mm in length. A few species are quite large and brightly colored. All *Gymnodoris* are predatory and most feed on other species of opisthobranchs. Their systematics has only recently been reviewed (Knutson & Gosliner, 2014) but is in great need of further study and synthesis.

Species usually larger than 50 mm

Members of this group are characterized by their large size, their external coloration and gill morphology are variable.

Gymnodoris ceylonica (Kelaart, 1858)
Size: 120 mm   Indian and western Pacific oceans
ID: White with large orange spots; gill with orange lines; rhinophores tipped with orange. Shallow grass beds and sandy areas, feeds upon *Stylocheilus striatus*; active nocturnally. Shown here with its egg mass.

Gymnodoris aurita (Gould, 1852)
Size: 100 mm   Indian and western Pacific oceans
ID: Red-orange with yellow tubercles; rhinophores the same color as the tubercles; huge, highly-branched gill consisting of about 12 leaves. On shallow reefs, where it is active nocturnally and feeds on several species of *Marionia*.

Gymnodoris striata (Eliot, 1908)
Size: 55 mm   Indian and western Pacific oceans
ID: White with an elevated, light orange notal rim and longitudinal lines; orange also present on the gill and on the upper half of the rhinophores; gill branches flattened and leaf-like, forming an arc across the notum. Feeds upon *Plakobranchus ocellatus*.

Gymnodoris rubropapulosa (Bergh, 1905)
Size: 60 mm   Indian and western Pacific oceans
ID: White with numerous large orange spots; red orange pigment all over the gill and on the rhinophores. On shallow reefs in 10-25 m. It produces a bright orange spiral egg mass; often feeds on chromodorid nudibranchs.

Gymnodoris sp. 1
Size: 120 mm   Indonesia
ID: Uniformly red; gill large, with highly pinnate branches forming a complete circle; rhinophores relatively small, darker than rest of body; head wider than rest of the body. Shallow areas with sand covered coral rubble.

Gymnodoris sp. 2
Size: 110 mm   New Caledonia, Australia
ID: Body brown with translucent white tubercles.

Smaller species with a complete or nearly complete circle of gill branches

This informal group of species includes smaller animals in which the gill forms a complete circle of branchial leaves around the anus as shown in the photograph below.

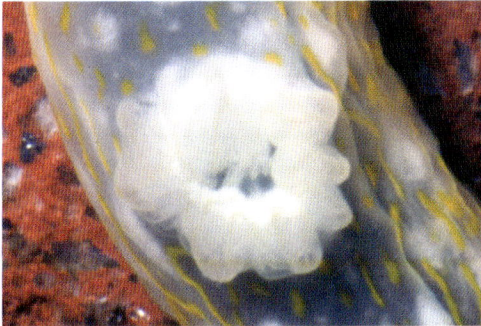

Gymnodoris okinawae Baba, 1936
Size: 25 mm   Widespread in the Indo-Pacific
ID: Translucent white with scattered opaque white pustules and orange squiggles on the notum; gill circle complete; rhinophoral club pale brown. On shallow water reefs from the intertidal zone to 15 m; feeds on sacoglossans including *Plakobranchus ocellatus*.

Gymnodoris sp. 3
Size: 20 mm   Widespread in the Indo-Pacific
ID: Translucent white with scattered opaque white pustules and minute orange spots. Similar to *Gymnodoris okinawae* but has larger pustules, and the gill circle is not complete posteriorly. From 2-12 m on patch reefs under rubble; food unknown.

Gymnodoris inornata Bergh, 1880
Size: 60 mm   Western Pacific
ID: Orange with darker pustules; gill circle complete. On shallow reef flats, it has been observed feeding on several species of nudibranchs including, *Dendrodoris fumata*, *Doriopsilla miniata* and *Goniobranchus lineolatus*. It has a bright orange egg mass.

Nudibranchia - "nudibranchs"

Gymnodoris sp. 4
Size: 34 mm   Marshall Is.
ID: Uniformly orange with a rugose, wrinkled body covered with small tubercles with white tips; rhinophores relatively narrow; gill well-developed, forming complete circle. On a patch of the green alga *Halimeda* in a lagoon, 8 m.

Gymnodoris sp. 5
Size: 30 mm   Western Indian Ocean
ID: Light orange with a rough body surface covered with low, rounded, dark orange tubercles; gill circle complete; rhinophores dark orange. On intertidal reef flats.

Gymnodoris sp. 6
Size: 18 mm   Indian and western Pacific oceans
ID: Yellow with yellow-orange spots over the entire body; gill large, yellow; gill branches pinnate, forming complete circle; rhinophores bulbous, yellow. Steep drop-offs in areas with small boulders.

Gymnodoris tuberculosa Knutson & Gosliner, 2014
Size: 55 mm   Western Pacific Ocean
ID: Uniformly white; rhinophores with a light yellow tinge; large rounded tubercles cover the body, the tubercles may be sparsely or densely distributed; gill forming a complete circle. On shallow reefs, feeding upon *Hypselodoris maculosa* and *Dendrodoris nigra*.

Gymnodoris sp. 7
Size: 55 mm   Indian and western Pacific oceans
ID: Uniformly white; rhinophores with opaque white markings; gill forming a complete circle with opaque white pigment; huge rounded tubercles cover the body. On shallow patch reefs and drop-offs to 25 m.

Gymnodoris sp. 8
Size: 55 mm   Tanzania, Red Sea
ID: Uniformly yellowish-white with large, rounded, white tubercles; gill large, highly pinnate, forming a complete circle; rhinophores white. Shallow sandy flats with isolated patches of coral, 1-10 m.

Gymnodoris citrina (Bergh, 1877)
Size: 30 mm   Widespread in the Indo-Pacific
ID: White to yellowish or orange with numerous scattered orange spots; anterior margin of the head with a row of conical tubercles; gill branches forming a complete circle; anterior end of the foot ends in a single lobe per side. On rocky reefs in 20 m. It has been observed cannibalizing members of its own species.

Gymnodoris sp. 9
Size: 25 mm   Indian and western Pacific oceans
ID: White to light yellowish or orange with numerous scattered orange spots situated evenly over the entire surface; anterior margin of the head with a distinctive row of low tubercles; gill branches form a complete circle; anterior end of the foot ends in two lobed sensory folds on each side. On shallow intertidal benches to 10 m.

Gymnodoris sp. 10
Size: 25 mm   Vanuatu
ID: White, with small orange spots evenly scattered over the body; gill with orange lines on the branches; rhinophores bulbous; head smooth, rounded; anterior end of the foot with a single lobe per side. Shallow rocky reefs.

Gymnodoris sp. 11
Size: 25 mm   Papua New Guinea, Indonesia
ID: White with orange spots and a large gill with fine orange lines on the pinnations. Similar to *Gymnodoris rubropapulosa* but the rounded head terminates just anterior to the rhinophores, also the lower anterior portion widens and is bordered by low orange tubercles. Feeds on *Nakamigawaia spiralis* and *Chelidonura sandrana*.

Gymnodoris sp. 12
Size: 25 mm   Western Pacific Ocean
ID: Dirty grey with yellowish orange rounded tubercles; anterior margin of the head bilobed, with well-developed tubercles; gill highly branched, forming a complete circle; foot broad, with broad tentacles anteriorly. Shallow reefs in silty areas.

Gymnodoris sp. 13
Size: 30 mm   Philippines
ID: Uniformly white with rows of large orange spots on the notum; anterior margin with large orange tubercles; gill white relatively small, consisting of pinnate branches forming an incomplete circle; rhinophores bulbous with orange tips. Shallow silty sandy, 10 m.

Gymnodoris sp. 14
Size: 8 mm   Papua New Guinea, Australia
ID: White with rows of small orange spots; gill white with simple branches forming a complete circle; rhinophores white to light orange; a series of sensory folds on the sides of the head and foot. Rocky reefs in 12 m.

Gymnodoris sp. 15
Size: 25 mm   Papua New Guinea
ID: White with lines of small orange spots; gill small, white with a few pinnate branches arranged in a nearly complete circle; rhinophores light brownish, bulbous, very close to each other and tipped with orange; foot broad with elongate tentacular extensions. Shallow reefs in 3-19 m.

Gymnodoris sp. 16
Size: 35 mm   Papua New Guinea
ID: White with lines of small orange spots; gill small, white with a few pinnate branches arranged in a nearly complete circle; rhinophores orange, conical, well separated; foot broad with elongate triangular extensions. Shallow reefs in 12 m; egg mass orange.

Gymnodoris sp. 17
Size: 20 mm   Philippines
ID: White with rows of small orange spots; gill white with simple branches forming a complete circle; rhinophores orange; foot with simply lobed elaborations around the mouth; head with a row of orange tubercles. Shallow clean sand in 7 m; active nocturnally.

Gymnodoris sp. 18
Size: 15 mm   Philippines
ID: White with rows of large orange spots; gill posterior, low in profile; gill branches simple, with orange lines, forming a complete circle; rhinophores bulbous, orange; body short, wide; head orange with simple lobes on the anterior margin. Shallow sandy areas, in 5 m; active nocturnally.

Gymnodoris sp. 19
Size: 15 mm   Philippines
ID: Pink with a complex pattern of opaque white frosting and large pink spots; gill small; gill branches simple, forming a complete circle; rhinophores bulbous, white basally and pink on the outer half. Shallow patch reefs in 10 m.

Gymnodoris sp. 20
Size: 15 mm   Widespread in the Indo-Pacific
ID: Translucent white with orange spots and a series of opaque white dorsal patches visible through the thin skin; conical rhinophores and gill branches tipped with orange. On shallow reefs under rubble in 1-20 m.

Gymnodoris sp. 21
Size: 15 mm   Papua New Guinea, Japan
ID: White with small orange spots; cylindrical rhinophores with orange apices; circular gill with numerous (20+) unbranched leaves with orange tips; an opaque white diamond behind rhinophores. In 10 m under coral rubble.

Gymnodoris alba species complex
Many species have been lumped under this name. Genetic studies have shown that these species are not only distinct, but they are not each other's closest relatives.

Gymnodoris alba (Bergh, 1877)
Size: 20 mm   Widespread in the Indo-Pacific
ID: White, with a series of large orange spots over the surface of the notum; pinnate gill branches white, forming a complete circle around the anus; tips of the rhinophores orange. Shallow water patch reefs under coral rubble; feeds on species of *Elysia* and small aeolids.

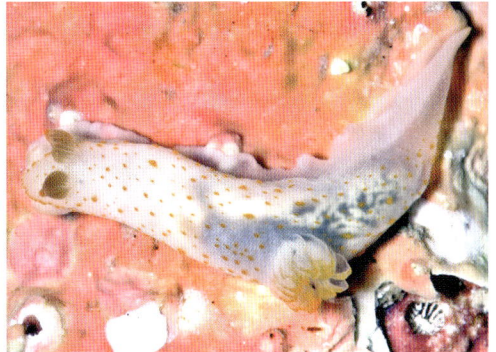

Gymnodoris sp. 22
Size: 30 mm   Vanuatu
ID: White with a series of large orange spots over the surface of the notum; gill branches simple, forming a complete circle around the anus; rhinophores and gill branches orange. Shallow water parch reefs under coral rubble; prey unknown.

Nudibranchia - "nudibranchs"

Gymnodoris sp. 23
Size: 7 mm   Malaysia
ID: White with isolated small orange spots; gill small, white; gill branches simple, forming a complete circle; rhinophores bulbous, white, with orange tips. Shallow reef slopes on algae, in 12 m.

Gymnodoris sp. 24
Size: 20 mm   Indian and western Pacific oceans
ID: White with scattered large orange spots; gill large, white; gill branches divided, forming a complete circle; rhinophores bulbous, orange. Along drop-offs of channel in lagoon, 12 m.

Gymnodoris sp. 25
Size: 12 mm   Papua New Guinea, Indonesia
ID: White with isolated small orange spots; gill small, white; gill branches simple, forming a semicircle; rhinophores bulbous, white. Along drop-offs on rocky reefs, 12 m.

Gymnodoris sp. 26
Size: 10 mm   Papua New Guinea
ID: White with isolated small orange spots; gill small, white; gill branches pinnate, forming a complete circle; rhinophores bulbous, white, with orange tips; body hourglass-shaped. Along drop-offs on rocky reefs in 12 m.

Gymnodoris bicolor (Alder & Hancock, 1864)
Size: 22 mm   Widespread in the Indo-Pacific
ID: White to pink or orange with small orange spots; gill with orange lines; rhinophores yellowish; gill forming a nearly complete circle, gill branches slightly ramified. Under coral slabs in relatively exposed areas in 1-10 m. Difficult to identify from the original description.

Gymnodoris sp. 27
Size: 21 mm   Marshall Is.
ID: White with a few large orange spots; gill small, gill branches simple with orange lines, forming a nearly complete circle; rhinophores orange. Shallow sandy lagoon in 10 m.

Gymnodoris sp. 28
Size: 20 mm   Papua New Guinea, Philippines
ID: White with rows of orange tubercles along the head and notal margin; other isolated orange spots on the dorsum; gill white with simple branches forming an incomplete circle; rhinophores bulbous, orange; body thin and elongate. On clean sand in 3 m; active nocturnally.

Gymnodoris sp. 29
Size: 10 mm   Philippines
ID: White, with rows of small orange spots; gill orange, situated at the posterior end of the body; gill branches simple, arranged in a complete circle; rhinophores bulbous, orange; body short with a rounded posterior end; foot short. On clean sand in 3 m; active nocturnally.

Gymnodoris sp. 30
Size: 12 mm   Philippines
ID: Head pointed anteriorly with a prominent orange line; rows of orange and opaque white spots on the notum and sides of the body; gill white, consisting of simple branches forming a complete circle; rhinophores bulbous, with orange tips. Mixed rocky reef and sand in 10 m.

Gymnodoris sp. 31
Size: 12 mm   Saudi Arabia
ID: White with small orange spots; gill white, small; gill branches slightly branched forming a nearly complete circle; rhinophores light yellow. On floating docks at a marina.

Gymnodoris sp. 32
Size: 18 mm   Seychelles
ID: Translucent white with a few small orange spots; opaque white defensive glands on either side of the body; gill large, highly pinnate, with opaque white glands at the base. Under rubble in 1 m on fringing reefs.

Gymnodoris sp. 33
Size: 10 mm   Gold coast Seaway (Australia)
ID: White with fine orange speckling on the dorsum; head pointed anteriorly with a prominent orange line; gill orange, consisting of simple branches forming a semicircle; rhinophores bulbous, orange. Shoreward seaways in 3 m.

Nudibranchia - "nudibranchs"

Species with uniform translucent coloration

Gymnodoris **sp. 34**
Size: 12 mm   Western and Central Pacific Ocean
ID: White with fine orange speckling on the back; gill white, consisting of simple branches forming a complete circle; rhinophores bulbous, orange; head pointed anteriorly with a prominent orange line. Drop-offs and patch reefs.

Gymnodoris nigricolor **Baba, 1960**
Size: 8 mm   Western Pacific
ID: Uniformly black including the rhinophores and gill, which forms a complete circle. It crawls on the fins of goby fishes (*Ctenogobiops* spp. and *Amblyeleotris* spp.) and slowly engulfs the soft tissue of the fin.

Gymnodoris **sp. 35**
Size: 10 mm   Papua New Guinea
ID: Light brown with a few small orange spots on the body; gill relatively large; head rounded anteriorly. Under coral rubble in 7 m on shallow reefs.

Gymnodoris **sp. 36**
Size: 15 mm   Papua New Guinea, Philippines
ID: Translucent light brownish-white with minute opaque white spotting; viscera clearly visible through the body; gill forming a complete circle. In 7-10 m on shallow reefs under coral rubble.

Gymnodoris **sp. 37**
Size: 25 mm   Philippines
ID: Uniformly translucent, almost transparent; gill low, forming a complete circle; gill branches only slightly ramified, with orange lines; rhinophores bulbous, white. Deep areas of fine coral rubble, in 30 m.

Gymnodoris **sp. 38**
Size: 15 mm   Philippines
ID: Uniformly translucent white with a few minute orange spots; gill white, small, with a few simple branches forming almost a complete circle; rhinophores white, conical. Shallow silty sandy, 10 m.

Gymnodoris sp. 39
Size: 10 mm   Papua New Guinea, Japan
ID: White with two lines of orange spots; rhinophores share a common stalk; gill reduced to a single, undivided triangular lobe. Burrows into sand on shallow slopes in 10-12 m.

Gymnodoris sp. 40
Size: 12 mm   Indonesia
ID: Translucent white with a few small dark brown spots; gill not visible; rhinophores black; viscera visible through the nearly transparent skin. Shallow sandy areas.

Gymnodoris pattani Swennen, 1996
Size: 23 mm   Thailand
ID: Uniformly translucent green; gill massive forming a complete or nearly complete circle, some larger gill branches with a few ramifications; a network of yellowish defensive glands visible through skin. Shallow algal mats in 0.3 m; food unknown.

Gymnodoris sp. 41
Size: 20 mm   Singapore, Indonesia, Australia
ID: Uniformly translucent green; gill large forming a nearly complete circle; foot broad, rhinophores conical. Shallow sandy areas.

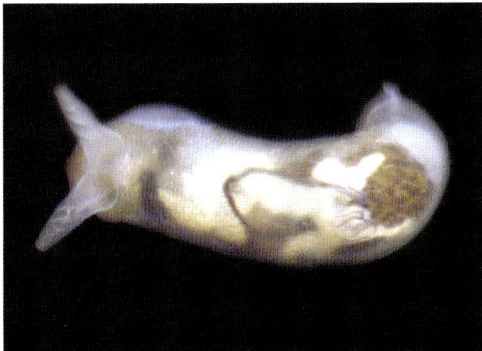

Gymnodoris sp. 42
Size: 7 mm   Sunshine Coast (Australia), Thailand
ID: Uniformly translucent green with internal organs readily visible; gill small consisting of a series of simple branches forming an almost complete circle; rhinophores conical with few lamellae. Shallow rocky reefs.

Gymnodoris sp. 43
Size: 30 mm   Madagascar
ID: Uniformly translucent green; gill small consisting of simple branches forming a complete or nearly complete circle; rhinophores conical; a network of dark green defensive glands visible through the skin.

Gymnodoris sp. 44
Size: 25 mm   Vanuatu
ID: Uniformly translucent green; gill small, consisting of simple branches forming a complete circle; rhinophores conical; head rounded anteriorly, wider than the rest of the body. Shallow rocky reefs.

Gymnodoris sp. 45
Size: 30 mm   Philippines, Indonesia
ID: Uniformly bright yellow; gill large, with slightly divided branches forming a nearly complete circle; rhinophores bulbous. Shallow sandy areas; active nocturnally.

Gymnodoris sp. 46
Size: 7 mm   Vanuatu
ID: Yellowish white with darker yellow spots; gill and rhinophores also yellow; anterior part of the head and mouth greatly expanded.

Species with an arc or line of gill branches

This informal group of species includes smaller animals in which the gill forms an arc or line of branchial leaves normally covering the anus as shown in the photograph below.

Gymnodoris pseudobrunnea Knudson & Gosliner, 2014
Size: 11 mm   Philippines
ID: White with a slight brownish tinge and orange spots arranged in linear rows; gill with orange lines; rhinophores tipped with orange; two white patches of the internal organs visible; both behind the gill. Active nocturnally in shallow silty areas in 5 m; prey unknown.

Gymnodoris brunnea Knudson & Gosliner, 2014
Size: 8 mm   Philippines
ID: White with a brownish tinge and orange spots arranged in linear rows; gill with orange lines; rhinophores tipped with orange; two white patches of the internal organs visible, one in front of gill and one behind. Active nocturnally in shallow silty areas in 5 m; prey unknown.

Gymnodoris sp. 47
Size: 30 mm   Philippines
ID: White, with a series of small orange spots over the surface of the notum; anterior margin with small orange tubercles; gill branches white, consisting of simple branches in a linear arrangement; rhinophores bulbous with orange tips; body elongate. Shallow sandy and rubble slopes in 15 m.

Gymnodoris sp. 48
Size: 45 mm   Philippines
ID: White with numerous red-orange spots; gill large with red lines on the numerous, simple branches, arranged in line; rhinophores bulbous, red-orange; body broad, foot wide with a red margin. Sandy and mixed rock slopes, in 15 m.

Gymnodoris subflava Baba, 1949
Size: 20 mm   Indian and western Pacific oceans
ID: Uniformly yellow or white with a few orange spots; widely separated, fan-shaped branchial leaves. In 1-5 m in areas of mixed sand and rubble.

Gymnodoris sp. 49
Size: 30 mm   Eastern Australia, Papua New Guinea
ID: White with orange conical tubercles; anterior end of the foot expanded into a lobate propodium; about 7 simple gill branches, each tipped with orange, arranged in a horizontal line or arc. Nocturnally active on shallow water sandy slopes in 10-15 m; it has been observed feeding upon *Stylocheilus striatus*.

Gymnodoris sp. 50
Size: 28 mm   Palau, Philippines
ID: White with red conical tubercles; anterior end of the foot red, expanded into a lobate propodium; 14-15 small and densely crowded gill branches. On shallow sandy slopes at night in 10-15 m.

Gymnodoris sp. 51
Size: 20 mm   Widespread in the Indo-Pacific
ID: White to reddish with a series of opaque white pustules and longitudinal red-orange lines; an opaque white diamond on the head between the rhinophores; gill with 8-10 simple branches. In 10-20 m crawling on the slopes of lagoon pinnacles; both diurnally and nocturnally active.

Gymnodoris sp. 52
Size: 12 mm   Papua New Guinea
ID: White with opaque white pustules and small orange spots; 5 gill branches; an opaque white triangle posterior to the rhinophores. During the day in shallow silty habitats in 2-4 m.

Gymnodoris sp. 53
Size: 15 mm   Indonesia
ID: White with orange tubercles forming lines, more densely arranged along the notal margin; rhinophores orange; gill leaves relatively highly branched. In shallow water, 3-5 m, under coral rubble.

Gymnodoris sp. 54
Size: 10 mm   Malaysia
ID: White with small lines of orange spots; body elongate with a rounded head; gill situated far back, near the posterior end of the animal with 9 branches. At night on shallow reefs.

Gymnodoris sp. 55
Size: 20 mm   Philippines
ID: Translucent white with conical orange tubercles; rhinophores conical and tapered; elongate, tentacular extensions on the anterior foot margin. Nocturnally active in shallow sandy areas in 1-5 m.

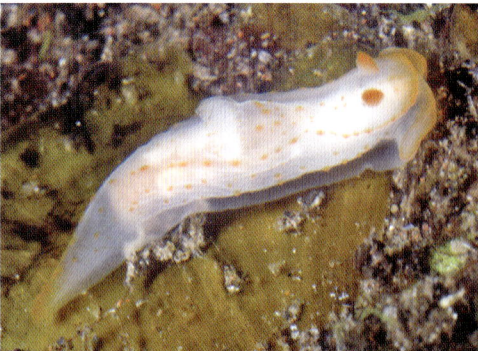

Gymnodoris sp. 56
Size: 15 mm   Indonesia, Philippines, Japan
ID: White with orange conical tubercles along the notal and anterior margins; head broad with two laterally extended portions of the foot. Burrows in sand in shallow water, 5-12 m.

Gymnodoris sp. 57
Size: 10 mm   Papua New Guinea, Philippines
ID: White with orange spots; gill situated on the posterior third of the body; head narrows near the rhinophores, foot wide, simply rounded. Under rubble in 5-10 m.

Gymnodoris sp. 58
Size: 8 mm   Tanzania
ID: White with a few orange spots; rhinophores immediately adjacent to each other; body short with a rounded head. In 2-3 m under coral rubble.

Gymnodoris sp. 59
Size: 10 mm   Papua New Guinea
ID: White and light orange with complex blotches; gill white with orange on the simple branches, arranged in a linear row; rhinophores bulbous, orange. Shallow sandy areas.

Gymnodoris sp. 60
Size: 9 mm   Philippines, Indonesia
ID: Brownish with a series of yellow longitudinal lines; rhinophores yellow with brownish lamellae and apex.

Gymnodoris sp. 61
Size: 20 mm   Philippines
ID: Reddish-orange with a series of lighter longitudinal lines; gill large with linear branches. Similar to *Gymnodoris* sp. 60, but with red-orange elevated linear ridges on the body.

Cryptobranchia - "cryptobranch dorids"

This is the largest group of dorids in terms of number of species. Members of Cryptobranchia are characterized by having a gill that is retractile into a distinct pocket. The body is normally oval with a pair of retractile rhinophores. All members of this group feed on sponges. The classification of this group has been reviewed by Valdés & Gosliner (2001) and Valdés (2002a). A substantial diversity of Indo-Pacific deep sea species known only from preserved specimens is not included in this book.

Dorididae Rafinesque, 1815

Species of this family have auriculate rather than tentacular oral tentacles. Notum typically with simple, spiculate tubercles.

Doris nucleola Pease, 1860
Size: 30 mm   Widespread in Indo-Pacific
ID: Deep cobalt blue with a whitish hour-glass making; rhinophores white; gill forming a complete circle, blue with white tips. Feeds on a deep blue sponge on which it is very cryptic; often found together with *Doris pecten*, which has a pectinate rather than circular gill; intertidal zone to 30 m.

Doris sp. 1
Size: 40 mm   Papua New Guinea, Philippines
ID: Orange; a prominent mid dorsal ridge situated between the gill and rhinophores. Under rubble on a shallow reefs at 10 m.

Nudibranchia - "nudibranchs"

Doris immonda (Risbec, 1928)
Size: 18 mm   Widespread in the Indo-Pacific
ID: Brownish with a median opaque white marking. Usually in
the rocky intertidal zone or in coral rubble on shallow reefs.

Doris sp. 2
Size: 30 mm   Philippines
ID: Orange with a y-shaped opaque white marking anterior to
the gill. Under dead coral rubble in 10 m.

Doris sp. 3
Size: 20 mm   Philippines
ID: Light salmon-pink with darker brown and opaque white;
tubercles of variable size, irregularly distributed; rhinophores
pink with brown; gill pink, forming a complete circle; body with
a high profile. On sand in 6 m.

Doris sp. 4
Size: 40 mm   Mauritius
ID: Greenish-brown with black spots on the notum in between
the large and spherical tubercles; gill black; rhinophores
greenish with black apices. On reefs in 10 m.

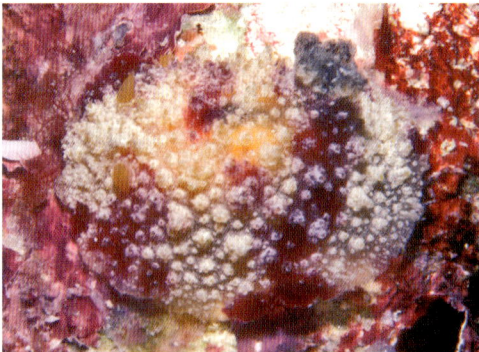

Doris sp. 5
Size: 40 mm   Marshall Is.
ID: Translucent grey with orange and purple areas; tubercles
irregularly distributed, of variable size, cream, each with a
darker spot at the apex; rhinophores pink; gill grey with white,
forming a complete circle.

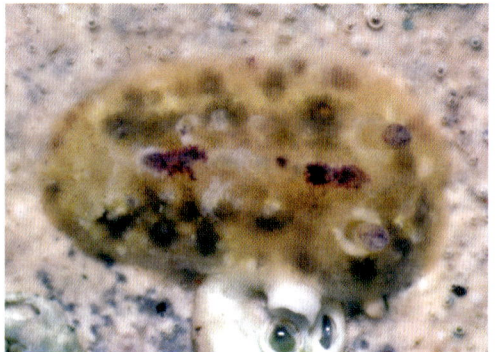

Doris sp. 6
Size: 12 mm   Port Elizabeth region (South Africa)
ID: Brown with darker and lighter markings on the large
rounded tubercles and some purple areas; rhinophores with
purple and white pigment; gill pale brown. Under a small
stone in about 10 m.

Doris sp. 7
Size: 15 mm   Kwazulu Natal (South Africa)
ID: Brown; tubercles smaller and more numerous than the preceding species; rhinophores and gill with the same color as the body. Shallow rock pools in the intertidal zone.

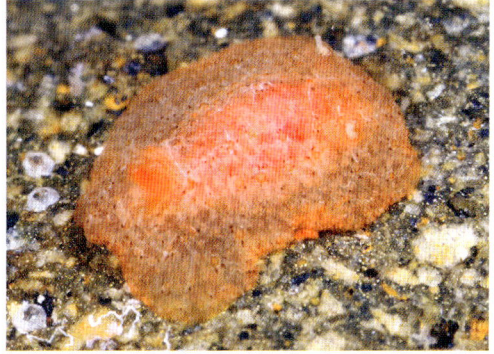

Doris sp. 8
Size: 12 mm   Philippines
ID: Orange with darker specks and fine opaque white lines; rhinophoral apices white. Under volcanic rocks, 4 m.

Doris ananas Lima, Tibriça & Simone, 2016
Size: 30 mm   Western Indian Ocean
ID: Yellow with rounded tubercles, some tipped with black pigment; rhinophores and gill also black. Under stones on shallow coral reefs to 20 m.

Doris sp. 9
Size: 30 mm   Marshall Is.
ID: Yellow with rounded tubercles, some tipped with black pigment; gill also with black pigment; rhinophores yellow. Under stones on shallow coral reefs to 20 m.

Doris pecten Collingwood, 1881
Size: 20 mm   Widespread in the Indo-Pacific
ID: Uniform dark blue including rhinophores and the pectinate gill. Under rocks in shallow water on sponges of the same color as the animal where it is well camouflaged.

Doris granulosa (Pease, 1860)
Size: 20 mm   Widespread in the Indo-Pacific
ID: Uniformly yellow; gill pectinate, posteriorly directed. Commonly under stones and rubble from the intertidal zone to about 3 m; feeds on yellow sponges where it can be extremely cryptic.

Nudibranchia - "nudibranchs"

Doris viridis (Pease, 1861)
Size: 20 mm   Indo-Pacific and eastern Pacific
ID: Green; gill pectinate. Under rocks from the intertidal zone to shallow reefs

Doris sp. 10
Size: 18 mm   Papua New Guinea
ID: Uniformly dark blue; rhinophores thin and white with a blue spot; gill blue, pectinate. Under rocks on submerged reefs in 15 m.

Doris sp. 11
Size: 25 mm   Western Pacific Ocean
ID: Orange; gill pectinate. On shallow submerged reefs and coral rubble.

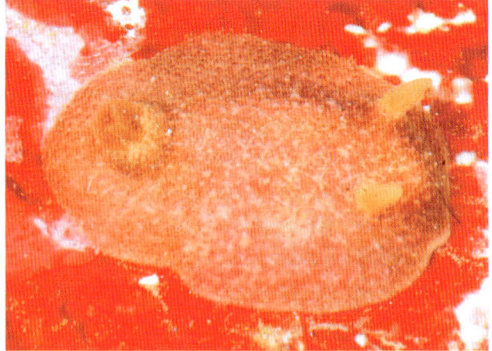

Pharodoris philippinensis Valdés, 2001
Size: 20 mm   Philippines, Indonesia
ID: Pinkish with distinctive yellow rhinophores and pale cream gill; branchial sheath very elevated, resembling a tower. On sand; nocturnally active, in 5-85 m.

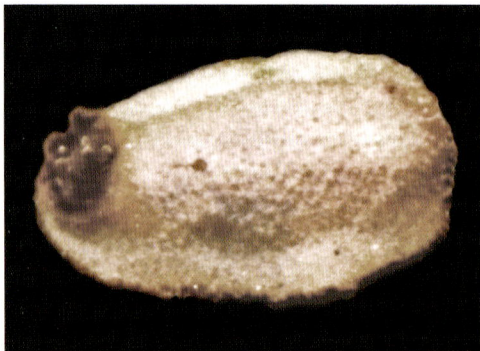

Goslineria callosa Valdés, 2001
Size: 21 mm   Philippines
ID: White with brown gill and mantle margin; ugly dorid with large and numerous copulatory spines. In deep water species down to 172 m.

Aphelodoris sp.
Size: 30 mm   Indonesia
ID: Opaque white with brown markings and black pigment around the edge of the notum, gill branches and rhinophores; cream pigment on the gill and on the tips of the rhinophores.

Aphelodoris gigas Wilson, 2003
Size: 70 mm   Western Australia
ID: Opaque white with a dense covering of dark brown markings; highly convoluted mantle margin, dark brown with a white marginal band; rhinophores with opaque white apices. On sponges in 12 m.

Aphelodoris karpa Wilson, 2003
Size: 100 mm   Australia
ID: Brown with orange pustules on the notum; an orange ring around each rhinophoral sheath and gill pocket; body margin with a white band and a broad orange submarginal band. Swims by dorsal ventral flexure. From the intertidal to 20 m.

Cadlinidae Bergh, 1891

Molecular evidence indicates that the mostly temperate and cold water genus *Cadlina* is not a chromodorid, but it is closely related to *Aldisa* (Johnson, 2011). These two groups are now included in the family Cadlinidae, which is characterized by having denticulate radular teeth. There are no tropical Indo-Pacific representatives of *Cadlina*, but there are several species of *Aldisa* described below.

Aldisa erwinkoehleri Perrone, 2001
Size: 20 mm   Thailand
ID: Light blue with opaque white tubercles; rhinophores dark; yellow pigment on tubercles immediately posterior to the rhinophores. Color pattern similar to *Phyllidiella pustulosa*.

Aldisa albatrossae Elwood, Valdés & Gosliner, 2000
Size: 21 mm   Japan, Philippines, Indonesia
ID: Translucent white with opaque white tubercles; anterior and posterior tubercles with yellow markings; head with a dark T-shaped marking. Appears to be a mimic of *Phyllidiella pustulosa*.

Aldisa williamsi Elwood, Valdés & Gosliner, 2000
Size: 18 mm   Papua New Guinea, Indonesia
ID: Bluish pigment with white tubercles and black markings; rhinophores cream colored. Shallow reefs, in close proximity to three other species with a similar color pattern: *Discodoris liturata*, *Goniobranchus geometricus* and *Phyllidiella pustulosa*.

Nudibranchia - "nudibranchs"

Aldisa andersoni Gosliner & Behrens, 2004
Size: 30 mm   Sri Lanka
ID: Bright blue with a yellow saddle behind the rhinophores and another in front of the gill; tubercles forming longitudinal ridges with black pigment in between and extending into the mantle margin; rhinophores blue. Inhabits shallow reefs, from about 8 m.

Aldisa sp. 1
Size: 25 mm   New Caledonia
ID: Blue with white gill and rhinophores; yellow lines and blotches present on the notum, with a single large black spot.

Aldisa sp. 2
Size: 9 mm   Enewetak Atoll (central Pacific Ocean)
ID: Translucent white with opaque white tubercles; center of the notum devoid of tubercles, with a series of brown spots; gill and rhinophores white. On a deep reef collected by a submersible in 131 m.

Aldisa sp. 3
Size: 30 mm   Madagascar
ID: Reddish orange with a network of well-elevated ridges tipped with lighter orange; blue spots in depressions between ridges near the center of the body; deep pits along the midline; rhinophores red, gill red brownish.

Aldisa sp. 4
Size: 40 mm   Mozambique
ID: Largely red with opaque white mottling; tubercles rounded with black tips; rhinophores and gill red. Found in tidepools in 1.5 m.

Aldisa pikokai Bertsch & S. Johnson, 1982
Size: 20 mm   Hawai'ian and Marshall Is.
ID: Red with transverse ridges and three depressions that mimic the oscula of sponges. Common on shallow subtidal reefs, often exposed or feeding on encrusting red sponges at night.

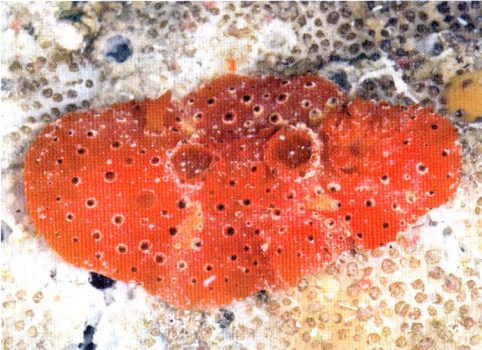

Aldisa fragaria Tibiraça, Pola, Cervera, 2017
Size: 40 mm   Philippines, Australia
ID: Red with two depressions surrounded by rings of tubercles; tubercles brown to black, each surrounded by a lighter ring. Intertidal zone, near the reef crest under dead coral slabs.

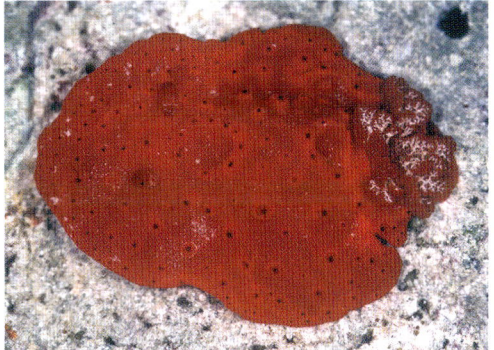

Aldisa sp. 5
Size: 55 mm   Japan
ID: Dark red with opaque white spots and dark markings on the rounded tubercles; rhinophores red; gill red with opaque white pigment. In 14 m on rocky reefs.

Aldisa zavorensis Tibiraça, Pola, Cervera, 2017
Size: 15 mm   Western Pacific Ocean
ID: Pale red with fine opaque white spots; two marked depressions; rhinophores red; gill mostly opaque white. On the top of barrier reefs under coral rubble.

Aldisa sp. 6
Size: 30 mm   Kwazulu Natal (South Africa)
ID: Orange; three depressions along the midline and a network of ridges on the notum; depressions pale cream to yellow with darker spots inside the holes. Subtidally on rocky reef habitats in 15-32 m.

Aldisa sp. 7
Size: 20 mm   New Caledonia
ID: Bright red with translucent white areas surrounded by bright blue rings; rhiniphores and gill red with opaque white markings.

Aldisa sp. 8
Size: 25 mm   Hawai'ian Is., Japan
ID: Red with yellow and bluish markings on the notum; two dorsal depressions; rhinophores red; gill branches red with white apices. Subtidally on rocky reef habitats.

89

Aldisa sp. 9
Size: 20 mm   Philippines
ID: Orange. Similar to *Aldisa pikokai* in having a series of interconnecting ridges on the notum; also lacks opaque white patches on the notum. On shallow reefs at night crawling on coral rubble.

Discodorididae Bergh, 1891

Species of this family have distinct, tentacular or conical oral tentacles. Most have a notum with simple, spiculate tubercles but some species have dorsal ridges or complex caryophyllidia tubercles with a ring of protruding spicules and cilia. The anterior, ventral side of the foot is transversely grooved and longitudinally notched as seen in the photo below. Dayrat (2010) reviewed the systematics of Discodorididae.

All members of the Discodorididae feed on sponges and are normally found on rocky substrates. Some species are able to autotomize sections of the mantle margin when disturbed.

Discodoris lilacina (Gould, 1852)
Size: 60 mm   Widespread in the Indo-Pacific
ID: Grey with brown and black patches; gill ochre. One of the most common dorids in shallow waters, from the intertidal zone to about 10 m. It feeds on grey sponges.

Discodoris sp. 1
Size: 50 mm   Philippines, Vanuatu
ID: Brown with dark patches. Similar to *Discodoris lilacina*, but has more brown pigment and a series of opaque white spots on the notum. Under rocks and coral rubble in shallow water to about 15 m.

Discodoris sp. 2
Size: 13 mm   Marshall Is.
ID: Orange with black spots on the dorsum forming irregular patches; gill orange; rhinophores pale brown; dorsum oval, covered with small conical tubercles; mantle margin, surrounded by densely arranged opaque white dots. Under a rock in an atoll lagoon; 6 m.

Discodoris coerulescens Bergh, 1888
Size: 30 mm   Indian and western Pacific oceans
ID: Translucent white with numerous black spots, some densely arranged in patches; opaque white spots on the notal margin. Under rubble in shallow waters to about 10 m.

Discodoris boholiensis Bergh, 1877
Size: 70 mm   Indian and western Pacific oceans
ID: Brown with black and white spots and white lines; body fairly flat with a central hump in the middle of the dorsum. Feeds on sponges, but is also seen crawling about in the open or underneath rocks in relatively shallow water.

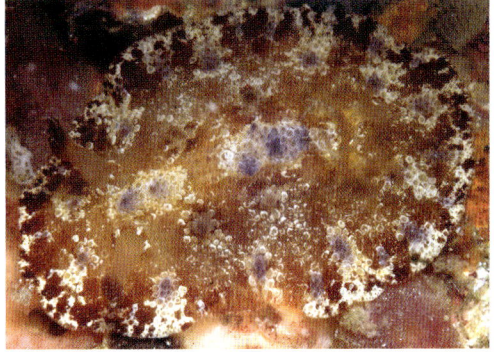

Discodoris cebuensis Bergh, 1877
Size: 40 mm   Widespread in the Indo-Pacific
ID: Mottled brown, white and cream, with purple markings; body relatively soft covered with conical tubercles; rhinophores and gill brown. Under rubble from the intertidal zone to 15 m.

Discodoris sp. 3
Size: 18 mm   Philippines
ID: Translucent white with numerous black spots, some densely arranged in patches; dark pigment surrounding the rhinophoral and gill openings. Under rubble in 12 m.

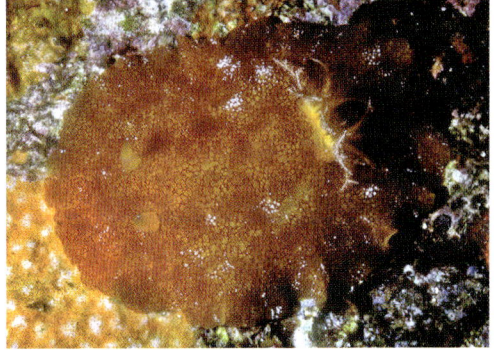

Discodoris sp. 4
Size: 30 mm   Indonesia
ID: Reddish with dark brown to black lines between the low, rounded tubercles and occasional opaque white spots. In relatively shallow water.

Discodoris sp. 5
Size: 30 mm   Indonesia
ID: Brownish with darker brown patches; body with a network of ridges connecting the round tubercles. On sandy substrate in shallow water.

Discodoris sp. 6
Size: 40 mm   Transkei coast (South Africa)
ID: Brownish with darker brown patches; body with rounded tubercles arranged in a stellate pattern. Under rocks in the mid-intertidal zone.

Nudibranchia - "nudibranchs"

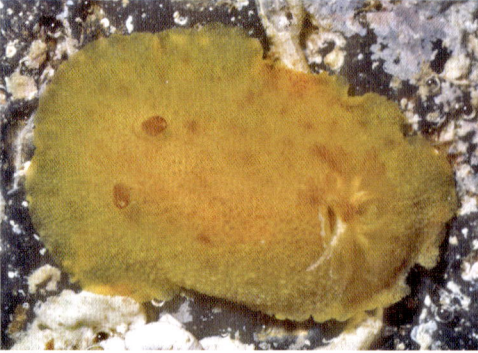

Geitodoris sp. 1
Size: 30 mm   Hawai'ian Is.
ID: Yellow with patches of opaque white near the gill and on the gill branches; rhinophores light brownish with white apices. Under rocks in the lower intertidal zone.

Geitodoris sp. 2
Size: 20 mm   Indonesia
ID: Yellowish-grey with a fine network of opaque cream-white pigment, scattered black dots and shades of brown on the center of the dorsum; tubercles cream-white, low and conical; rhinophores and gill brown with white pigment; body wide and short. Shallow silty areas and rocky slopes.

Sebadoris nubilosa (Pease, 1871)
Size: 200 mm   Indian and Pacific oceans
ID: Grey with brown patches on the notum; tubercles long and conical. Capable of swimming; can detach large portions of its mantle when disturbed.

Sebadoris fragilis (Alder & Hancock, 1864)
Size: 60 mm   Widespread in the Indo-Pacific
ID: Brownish with darker brown patches and occasional opaque white patches; gill large, well-developed, tripinnate. In 1-2 m under dead coral heads.

Paradoris erythraeensis (Vayssière, 1912)
Size: 30 mm   Indian and western Pacific oceans
ID: Yellowish to white with a few black spots scattered over the dorsal surface and opaque white markings on the elevated tubercles. From the intertidal to shallow subtidal reefs under coral rubble.

Paradoris sp. 1
Size: 20 mm   Southern Tanzania
ID: Drab colored with patches of darker brown and a few minute opaque white spots; large pores in the mantle surface. Intertidal zone under coral rubble.

Paradoris sp. 2
Size: 30 mm   Tanzania
ID: Greyish to yellow with pinkish patches; rhinophores and gill brown; surface with a sandy texture. Intertidal zone to a few meters under rocks.

Paradoris sp. 3
Size: 20 mm   Western Pacific Ocean
ID: White or yellow with longitudinal black dashes; gill white with brown apices; rhinophores black. On shallow reefs from 3-10 m.

Paradoris sp. 4
Size: 15 mm   Madagascar, Malaysia
ID: Yellowish with two longitudinal black lines and small white tubercles; rhinophores and gill leaves white with black apices. Under coral rubble on shallow patch reefs in 3-4 m.

Paradoris sp. 5
Size: 15 mm   Kenya
ID: Pale brown with numerous low and rounded white tubercles; a wide, black circular line separates the center of the dorsum from the mantle margin; mantle margin white, narrow; rhinophores and gill branches white with black apices. Under coral heads on shallow reefs.

Paradoris sp. 6
Size: 15 mm   Madagascar
ID: Translucent white with numerous, densely arranged, opaque white, small, rounded tubercles; dorsum with few curved black lines; rhinophores black. Shallow rocky reefs.

Paradoris sp. 7
Size: 30 mm   Tanzania, Madagascar
ID: Pink with a few, irregular, black longitudinal lines; tubercles few, large, conical and white; rhinophores black; gill pale grey. Shallow reefs under dead coral.

Paradoris sp. 8
Size: 30 mm   Madagascar, Seychelles Is., Indonesia
ID: Yellow with the dorsum covered with numerous opaque white tubercles; a few dark, short brown lines; rhinophores and gill yellow with black apices. On patch reefs in 5-15 m.

Paradoris sp. 9
Size: 20 mm   Vanuatu
ID: White with diffuse narrow, irregular lines of dark brown or black; rhinophores and gill white with black apices. On shallow reefs from 10-20 m.

Paradoris sp. 10
Size: 15 mm   Papua New Guinea, Philippines
ID: Yellow with numerous, small, rounder yellowish tubercles; mantle margin with a few radiating, dark brown lines; rhinophores and gill yellow with black apices. Under dead coral rubble, in 7 m.

Paradoris sp. 11
Size: 30 mm   Indonesia
ID: Uniformly cream; scattered conical tubercles, some of them very large, with cream bases, golden-yellow apical areas and opaque white tips; some tubercles surrounded by a network of golden-yellow pigment; rhinophores and gill golden yellow. Feeds on cream colored sponge on shallow reefs.

Paradoris liturata (Bergh, 1905)
Size: 30 mm   Eastern Indian and western Pacific oceans
ID: Pink with opaque white tubercles and a network of black lines. Part of a mimicry complex that includes *Phyllidiella pustulosa* and other species. Secretes an opaque white liquid when disturbed; also retracts its gill readily to increase its resemblance to *P. pustulosa*. On sponges on the outer sides of barrier reefs in 10-20 m.

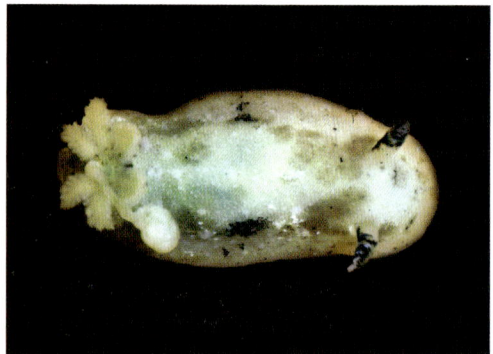

Paradoris imperfecta Valdés, 2001
Size: 13 mm   New Caledonia
ID: Cream with few irregular pale brown spots and numerous small dark brown dots; rhinophores with black apices; gill cream. In deep waters down to 274 m.

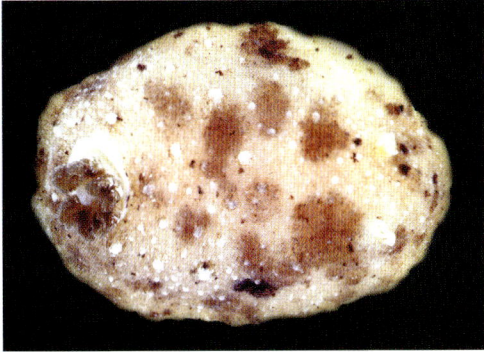

Paradoris araneosa Valdés, 2001
Size: 35 mm   New Caledonia
ID: Pale brown with scattered dark brown spots; larger tubercles opaque white; gill dark brown. In deep waters down to 464 m.

"Taringa" caudata (Farran, 1905)
Size: 25 mm   Indian Ocean
ID: White with a yellow marginal line and a few scattered yellow patches on the dorsum; rhinophores black; gill with grey rachises. "Taringa" luteola is a synonym. On relatively shallow reefs from the intertidal zone to 10 m.

"Taringa" halgerda Gosliner & Behrens, 1998
Size: 50 mm   Western Pacific Ocean
ID: White with yellow spots on the large dorsal tubercles. Similar to "Taringa" caudata but lacks a marginal yellow band and has yellow spots. On shallow reef faces from 10-25 m.

Carminodoris estrelyado (Gosliner & Behrens, 1998)
Size: 40 mm   Indian and western Pacific oceans
ID: Mottled with a pattern of tubercles that resemble fried eggs. Shallow water in the open or under coral rubble.

Carminodoris bifurcata Baba, 1993
Size: 30 mm   Western and central Pacific Oceans
ID: Mottled with a central notal patch of darker brownish pigment; dorsal tubercles small and rounded. From the intertidal zone to 15 m.

Carminodoris flammea (Fahey & Gosliner, 2003)
Size: 30 mm   Indonesia
ID: Mottled with a fiery red mid-dorsal pigment patch on the notum. On sponges on rocky patches between sand slopes in 10-20 m.

Nudibranchia - "nudibranchs"

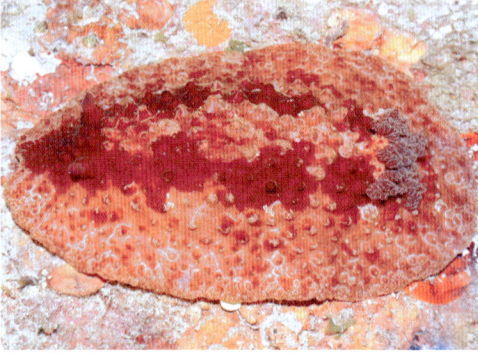

Carminodoris sp. 1
Size: 45 mm   Philippines
ID: Reddish with irregular opaque white pigment surrounding some tubercles and a dark brown band around the center of the dorsum; tubercles large, conical; rhinophores brown; gill brown with white lines. Under dead coral heads on shallow reefs, in 12 m.

Carminodoris sp. 2
Size: 20 mm   Hawai'ian Is.
ID: Reddish-brown with opaque white pigment on the gill and tips of the rhinophores; tubercles more numerous than other members of the genus. Under rocks in 10-15 m, on reef slopes.

Carminodoris armata Baba, 1993
Size: 25 mm   Indonesia, Japan
ID: Reddish brown with opaque white rings around some tubercles; tubercles large, spherical, yellow to brown with brown tips; rhinophores and gill brown with white spots. Silty and rocky slopes, in 10-20 m.

Carminodoris grandiflora (Pease, 1860)
Size: 50 mm   Widespread in the Indo-Pacific
ID: Mottled, lacking a central notal region of darker pigment; relatively large body; large rounded dorsal tubercles. In relatively shallow water under dead coral slabs and rubble.

Carminodoris sp. 3
Size: 15 mm   Philippines
ID: Brown with opaque white markings on the notum, gill branches, and rhinophoral tips. On shallow reef flats under coral rubble.

Carminodoris sp. 4
Size: 55 mm   Philippines
ID: Mottled, with large, rounded tubercles and distinct red circles widely separated from each other.

96

Peltodoris rubra (Bergh, 1905)
Size: 60 mm   Western and central Pacific Ocean
ID: Light reddish brown with darker patches; dorsum covered by low rounded tubercles many of which have a black spot at the apex. *Archidoris hawaiiensis* is a synonym. From the lower intertidal zone to approximately 10 m.

Peltodoris murrea (Abraham, 1877)
Size: 30 mm   Indian and western Pacific oceans
ID: White with pinkish patches; body rough, with a sandy texture. *Peltodoris mauritiana* is a synonym. Intertidal zone to a few meters, under rocks.

Peltodoris fellowsi Kay & Young, 1969
Size: 54 mm   Western and central Pacific Ocean
ID: White with black on the gill and rhinophores. From the intertidal zone to 20 m, under rocks or in the open.

Peltodoris sp.
Size: 15 mm   South Africa
ID: White with dark brown to black transverse bands and markings; gill and rhinophores translucent white. In 42 m.

Thordisa luteola Chan & Gosliner, 2007
Size: 30 mm   Tropical South Africa
ID: Yellow; elongate conical papillae, gill and rhinophores dark grey-brown. In rock pools at low tide.

Thordisa tahala Chan & Gosliner, 2007
Size: 15 mm   Madagascar, Indonesia, Marshall Is.
ID: Dark grey with light brown pigment on the gill and rhinophores; low conical papillae interconnected by low ridges. Shallow water, less than 5 m, under dead coral rubble.

Nudibranchia - "nudibranchs"

Thordisa villosa (Alder & Hancock, 1864)
Size: 70 mm   Indian and western Pacific oceans
ID: Yellowish brown with black pigment around the notal margin and in the center of the notum; transparent, long conical papillae. Relatively rare, found sporadically from a few isolated localities; usually on sandy substrate.

Thordisa sanguinea Baba, 1955
Size: 20 mm   Philippines, Japan
ID: Reddish orange with elongate papillae; mid-dorsal papillae with opaque white markings. In 64 m.

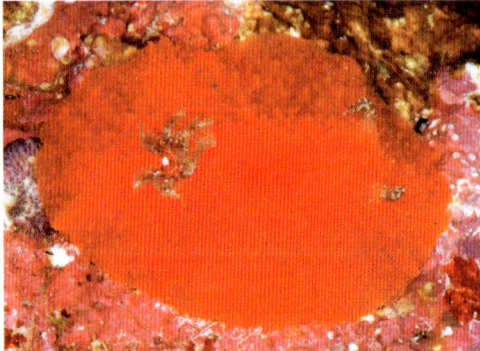

Thordisa sp. 1
Size: 55 mm   Philippines
ID: Uniformly bright orange-red; dorsum covered with brown elongate tubercles; rhinophores and gill brown with white pigment. On silty slopes in coral rubble, 20 m.

Thordisa sp. 2
Size: 18 mm   Indonesia
ID: Uniformly yellow; dorsum densely covered with elongate tubercles with spherical tips; rhinophores and gill yellow with opaque white pigment. Shallow rocky reefs.

Thordisa sp. 3
Size: 20 mm   Indonesia
ID: Brown with numerous opaque white pigment and a network of grey ridges surrounding dark brown pits; rhinophores and gill grey with abundant opaque white pigment. Under coral rubble, 1 m.

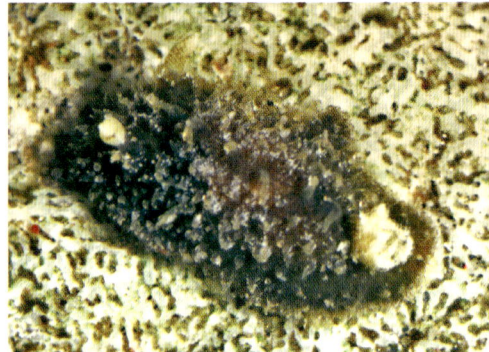

Thordisa oliva Chan & Gosliner, 2007
Size: 20 mm   Tropical South Africa, Kerama Is. (Japan)
ID: Green with opaque white pigment on the gill and rhinophores; body with elongate conical tubercles. In shallow water on patch reefs.

98

***Thordisa* sp. 4**
Size: 20 mm   Marshall Is.
ID: Pale orange with dark brown spots; tubercles rounded, small, pale brown; gill white; rhinophores pale brown with white lamellae. In a lagoon under rocks, 6 m.

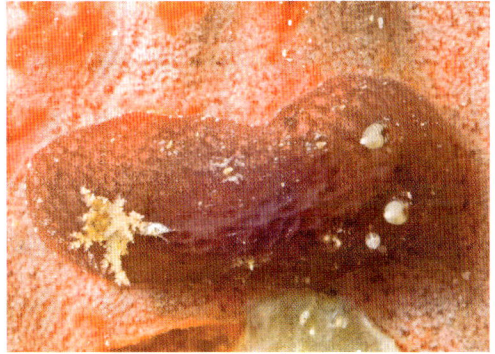

***Thordisa albomacula* Chan & Gosliner, 2007**
Size: 30 mm   Western and central Pacific Ocean
ID: Reddish brown with varying amounts of opaque white pigment; a linear patch of opaque white pigment immediately anterior to the gill. On reefs under coral rubble in 5-10 m.

***Thordisa* sp. 5**
Size: 20 mm   Tuamotu Archipelago
ID: Grey with dark brown patches; tubercles very small, mostly conical, some elongate with opaque white tips; gill white; rhinophores grey with white tips. Under coral rubble, 1 m.

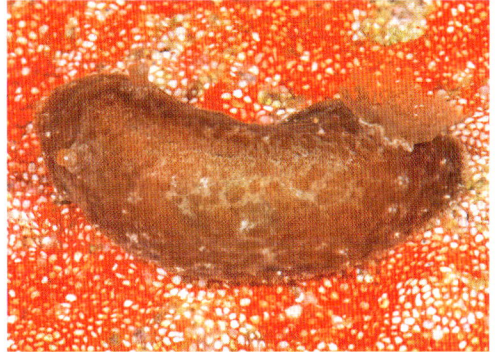

***Thordisa* sp. 6**
Size: 24 mm   Philippines
ID: Pale brown with dark reddish-brown patches; tubercles very small, mostly conical, some elongate with opaque white tips; gill and rhinophores brown with white pigment. Under dead coral slabs in 12 m.

***Thordisa* sp. 7**
Size: 18 mm   Philippines
ID: Dark grey with a pale brown area in the center of the dorsum; tubercles conical, some longer, opaque white; rhinophores dark grey with white apices; gill pale brown. Under small volcanic rocks, in 7 m.

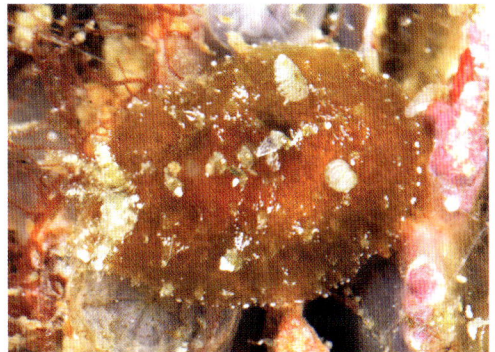

***Thordisa* sp. 8**
Size: 14 mm   Philippines
ID: Brown with scattered opaque white dots; dorsum with conical tubercles, some much larger than the rest, pale brown; rhinophores and gill white. Under dead coral heads, 15 m.

99

Nudibranchia - "nudibranchs"

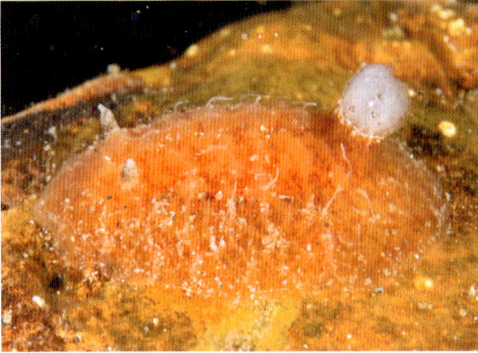

Thordisa sp. 9
Size: 30 mm   Philippines
ID: Orange-brown with some dark brown spots; dorsum covered with densely arranged conical tubercles, some opaque white, much longer than the rest; gill white; rhinophores white with brown pigment. Under dead coral on rocky reefs, in 14 m.

Thordisa sp. 10
Size: 40 mm   Widespread in the Indo-Pacific
ID: Yellow; delicate compound papillae with opaque white bases; rhinophores dark yellow; gill pale brown with white pigment. On shallow patch reefs in 5-10 m.

Thordisa sp. 11
Size: 20 mm   Indonesia, Philippines, Japan
ID: Uniform dark brownish-grey; dorsum with clusters of black compound papillae; rhinophores black with white dots; gill pale cream. On shallow reefs under coral slabs.

Thordisa sp. 12
Size: 22 mm   Philippines
ID: Light brown with a row of darker brown spots on either side of notum; tubercles stellate. Under coral rubble, 15 m.

Thordisa sp. 13
Size: 100 mm   Indonesia
ID: Uniformly brown with numerous tubercles bearing thin unbranched processes; rhinophores and gill lighter yellowish brown.

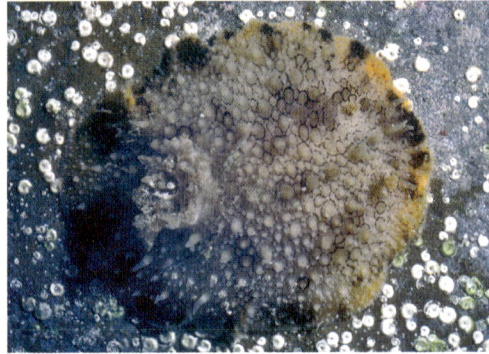

Thordisa sp. 14
Size: 50 mm   Tropical South Africa
ID: Brownish with black rings around the large conical tubercles; tubercles surrounded by a ring of smaller rounded tubercles. At the rock sand interface of the lower intertidal zone, where it feeds on sponges.

100

Thordisa sp. 15
Size: 12 mm   Western Australia
ID: Translucent grey with dense black spots; large tubercles with white frosting around their bases and orange-brown apices; gill and rhinophores orange-brown.

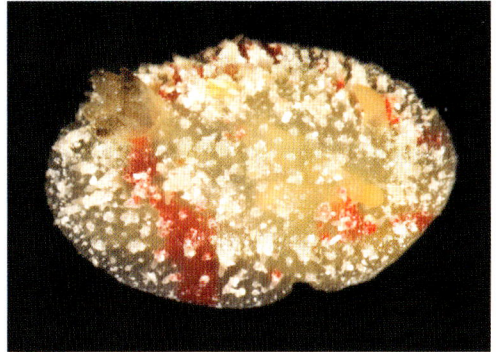

Thordisa sp. 16
Size: 25 mm   Papua New Guinea
ID: Pale orange with irregular red patches; tubercles cream, compound, with elongate conical, opaque white apices; rhinophores orange; gill pale orange with brown pigment. On outer edges of reef faces, 20 m.

Thordisa sp. 17
Size: 26 mm   Philippines
ID: Yellow with brown patches; tubercles elongate with compound tips formed of conical papillae; rhinophores white; gill not visible. At the base of a steep slope under coral rubble, in 15 m.

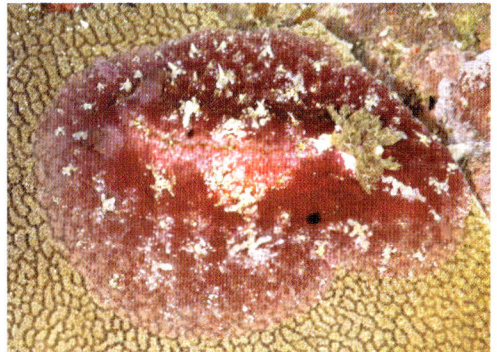

Thordisa sp. 18
Size: 55 mm   Saudi Arabian Red Sea
ID: Pink with reddish pigment covering large portions of the dorsum; tubercles conical, opaque white, some with very elongate tips; gill brown; rhinophores reddish. Under coral rubble on a steep sandy slope, 17 m.

Asteronotus hepaticus (Abraham, 1877)
Size: 350 mm   Western Pacific Ocean
ID: Reddish purple with occasional opaque white spots; more numerous tubercles than in *Asteronotus cespitosus*. Nocturnally active, crawling over the surface of large coral heads.

Asteronotus spongicolus Gosliner & Valdés, 2002
Size: 30 mm   Indian and western Pacific oceans
ID: Light to dark brown; similar in appearance to *Asteronotus mimeticus* but has a more elongate body and a mid-dorsal line of lighter pigment between the rhinophores and gill. On the underside of the lobate sponge, *Carteriospongia* sp. in shallow water on patch reefs.

Nudibranchia - "nudibranchs"

Asteronotus cespitosus (van Hasselt, 1824)
Size: 400 mm   Widespread in the Indo-Pacific
ID: Brownish of different shades, some specimens with opaque white spots; large tubercles arranged in concentric rings. Under large rocks or coral heads during the day, crawls on sand or reef flats during the night. Feeds upon sponges including *Dysidea* sp.

Asteronotus mimeticus Gosliner & Valdés, 2002
Size: 40 mm   Western Pacific Ocean
ID: Grey to brown; texture highly variable, it may have tubercles (left photo) or entirely smooth (right photo). On the underside of sponges such as *Phyllospongia lamellosa* and *Carteriospongia* sp. The egg mass is a flat, tightly coiled spiral of 2-3 whorls.

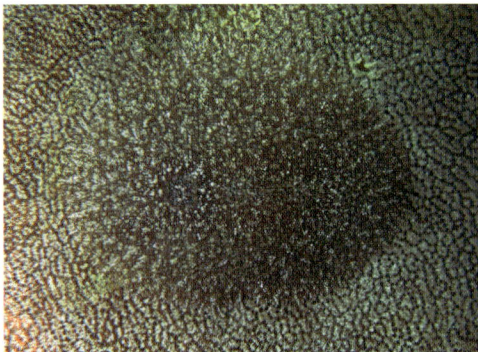

Asteronotus sp.
Size: 35 mm   Saudi Arabian Red Sea
ID: Dark grey with scattered light grey pigment. Under foliose sponges on reef flats, in 9 m.

Otinodoris raripilosa (Abraham, 1877)
Size: 70 mm   Palau
ID: Mottled with isolated patches of red-orange; compound elongate papillae. On shallow fringing reefs where it is nocturnally active.

Otinodoris sp. 1
Size: 100 mm   Philippines
ID: Cream with brown compound papillae, reddish and purple concavities, and opaque white pigment; large tubercles and concavities lined with black rings. Active at night, on a reef slope in approximately 12 m.

Otinodoris sp. 2
Size: 50 mm   Northern Philippines
ID: Brown with a few opaque white patches scattered over the notum; granular texture with thin papillae and rounded tubercles over the surface. Nocturnally active, crawling in the open on shallow reefs and sandy areas.

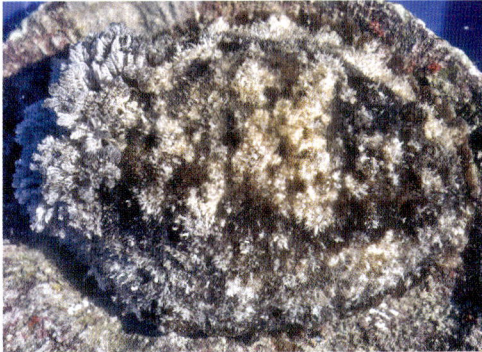

Otinodoris sp. 3
Size: 120 mm   East coast of Madagascar
ID: Grey, densely covered by compound opaque white papillae. On the underside of large, dead coral heads in 2-3 m.

Otinodoris sp. 4
Size: 40 mm   Indonesia
ID: Grey with golden brownish tubercles and papillae extending from them; gill and rhinophores with opaque white pigment. On silty sand in relatively shallow water.

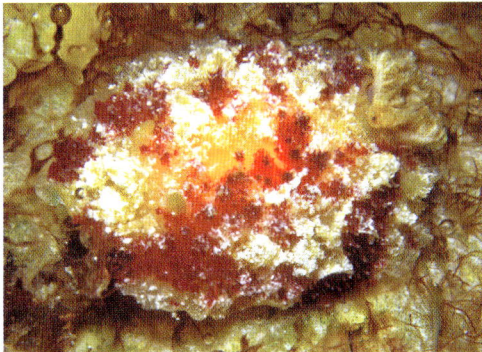

Otinodoris sp. 5
Size: 60 mm   Marshall Is.
ID: Pale orange with irregular red patches; tubercles compound, with elongate conical, opaque white apices; rhinophores orange; gill pale orange with brown pigment.

Otinodoris sp. 6
Size: 55 mm   Philippines
ID: Reddish-brown with opaque white patches; dorsum covered with irregular tubercles and elongate papillae; rhinophores and gill brown. Under coral rubble on steep sandy slopes, in 17 m.

Nudibranchia - "nudibranchs"

Otinodoris sp. 7
Size: 80 mm   Papua New Guinea
ID: Yellowish white with darker mottling; notum with elongate branched appendages; rhinophores dark grey.

Discodorid sp. 1
Size: 30 mm   Western Pacific Ocean
ID: Translucent with numerous reticulations and opaque white and black spots; a longitudinal brown ridge present mid-dorsally. Under coral rubble in 3-10 m.

Discodorid sp. 2
Size: 70 mm   Philippines
ID: Opaque white with brown and opaque white pigment on the central part of the dorsum; brown pigment also present on the notal reticulations and a single black spot on the notum behind the rhinophores.

Discodorid sp. 3
Size: 70 mm   Papua New Guinea
ID: Translucent brownish with two lines of large brown spots on the notum; tubercles yellowish with brown centers; mantle margin undulating.

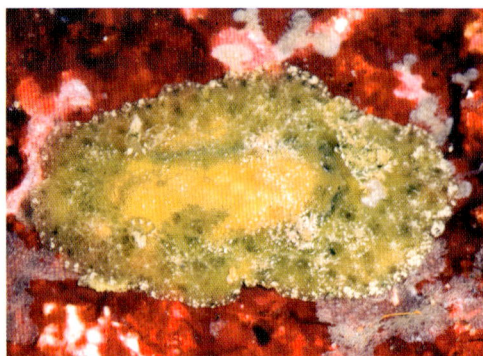

Discodorid sp. 4
Size: 24 mm   Philippines
ID: Pale orange with scattered black and white pigment; dorsum with small conical tubercles, some with white tips; rhinophores and gill pale orange with dark brown and cream pigment. Under coral rubble on shallow reef flats, in 10 m.

Discodorid sp. 5
Size: 35 mm   Indonesia
ID: Uniformly reddish-purple with minute dark purple dots; tubercles small, conical; rhinophores brownish with white tips; gill purple-red.

Discodorid sp. 6
Size: 30 mm   Indonesia
ID: White with few brown spots; tubercles small, conical; rhinophores white; gill white with brown lines.

Discodorid sp. 7
Size: 48 mm   Indonesia
ID: White with a few brown spots; tubercles rounded; body wide and flat; rhinophores white; gill not visible.

Discodorid sp. 8
Size: 25 mm   Indonesia
ID: Translucent, almost transparent; yellow viscera visible; dorsum with a network of opaque white pigment and a transverse band in the middle; rhinophores and gill translucent cream with white apices. Under coral rubble on rock reefs.

Halgerda dalanghita Fahey & Gosliner, 1999
Size: 30 mm   Widespread in the Indo-Pacific
ID: Orange with lighter lines on top of the interconnecting ridges; small black spots may also be present along the surface of the ridges; rhinophores with a black basal patch and a black apical portion. On orange sponges in shallow water from 10-15 m.

Halgerda sp. 1
Size: 30 mm   Philippines
ID: Orange with lighter lines on top of the interconnecting ridges. Similar to *Halgerda dalanghita* but with more diffuse dark pigment on the rhinophores and more numerous yellow spots situated on the notal surface between ridges.

Halgerda sp. 2
Size: 55 mm   Philippines
ID: Uniformly yellow with ridges of the same color. Similar to *Halgerda paliensis* but with more highly elevated tips to ridges with a more acute apex; the apices in *H. paliensis* are rounded rather than angular.

Nudibranchia - "nudibranchs"

Halgerda paliensis (Bertsch & S. Johnson, 1982)
Size: 70 mm   Hawai'ian Is.
ID: Uniformly yellow with ridges of the same color; one of the largest species of *Halgerda*. Commonly on shallow water patch reefs in 10-15 m.

Halgerda sp. 3
Size: 30 mm   Philippines
ID: Orange with black spots situated in polygons between the ridges; apices of ridges tipped with white apex; gill leaves white with black lines; rhinophores with black apices, each with a basal mark. In rubble, 20 m.

Halgerda sp. 4
Size: 25 mm   Philippines
ID: Orange with black spots situated in polygons between ridges. Similar to *Halgerda* sp. 3 but with black spots on between ridges and at the apices of ridges; lacks white spots on the apices. In coral rubble, 20 m.

Halgerda sp. 5
Size: 70 mm   French Polynesia
ID: Greyish-white with an orange marginal band; tubercles large with opaque white rounded tips; rhinophores and gill white with black spots. Often in groups on vertical walls of the outer reef slope, in 10-55 m.

Halgerda punctata Farran, 1905
Size: 50 mm   Indian Ocean
ID: White with a series of yellowish tubercles along the ridges and black spots between the ridges; a black line along the posterior side of the rhinophoral base. Outer reef habitats to about 25 m.

Halgerda onna Fahey & Gosliner, 2001
Size: 19 mm   Japan, Guam
ID: White with a marginal yellow band and scattered black spots; additional yellow markings on the middle of the dorsum. Shallow water reefs in 3 m.

106

***Halgerda brunneomaculata* Carlson & Hoff, 1993**
Size: 25 mm   Indian and western Pacific oceans
ID: Yellowish with orange ridges and a single large spot between the ridges; mantle with a white rim; rhinophores and gill white with black pigment. On shallow reefs from 10-20 m.

***Halgerda dichromis* Fahey & Gosliner, 1999**
Size: 60 mm   Mozambique, Kwazulu Natal (South Africa)
ID: White with elongate orange lines and black patches along the dorsal ridges; rhinophores, each with a black basal patch and a black rhinophoral club. On patch reefs from 3-36 m.

***Halgerda formosa* Bergh, 1880**
Size: 30 mm   Widespread in the Indian Ocean
ID: Translucent white with orange pigment on the dorsal ridges; scattered spots absent or present in variable density; rhinophores, each with a basal black patch and a black club. On relatively shallow reefs in the open during the day.

***Halgerda elegans* Bergh, 1905**
Size: 25 mm   Western Pacific Ocean
ID: White with orange lines and a series of perpendicular black lines along the margin; rhinophores and gill translucent white with black apices. On patch reefs from 5-13 m.

***Halgerda guahan* Carlson & Hoff, 1993**
Size: 48 mm   Guam
ID: White with orange lines along the ridges and additional orange lines between the ridges; rhinophores and gill white with black spots. On shallow reefs.

***Halgerda toliara* Fahey & Gosliner, 1999**
Size: 40 mm   Western Indian Ocean
ID: Off-white to yellowish white; rhinophoral clubs black but lacking the basal patch of black present in *Halgerda formosa*. In 3-30 m on fringing reefs.

107

Nudibranchia - "nudibranchs"

Halgerda bacalusia Fahey & Gosliner, 1999
Size: 52 mm   Myanmar, Thailand
ID: Opaque white with a series of broad orange lines on the dorsal ridges and orange spots on the tips of the tubercles; smaller orange spots on the surface between the ridges. On outer reef slopes in 10-28 m.

Halgerda diaphana Fahey & Gosliner, 1999
Size: 40 mm   Ryūkyū and Kerama Is. (Japan)
ID: White with orange lines on the ridges and occasional additional orange lines on the notum. On relatively shallow reefs from 7-20 m.

Halgerda tessellata (Bergh, 1880)
Size: 40 mm   Western Pacific
ID: Color pattern composed of a series of triangular orange ridges with brown pigment, orange markings and white spots; large white spots around the mantle margin. On shallow patch reefs among coral rubble.

Halgerda sp. 6
Size: 40 mm   Western Indian Ocean
ID: Color complex, with a series of triangular orange ridges with brown pigment, orange markings and white spots. Similar to *Halgerda tessellata*, but without white markings around the margin of the mantle. Molecular studies support the distinction between these two species.

108

***Halgerda willeyi* Eliot, 1904**
Size: 80 mm   Western and central Pacific
ID: Translucent white with several yellow ridges and a series of yellow and black lines between them. On living reefs crawling in the open or under rocks.

***Halgerda malesso* Carlson & Hoff, 1993**
Size: 60 mm   Guam, Marshall Is.
ID: Translucent white with numerous orange lines. Similar to *Halgerda batangas*, but the orange lines coalesce to form spots and are present as a series of submarginal bands. On shallow reefs in 8-30 m.

***Halgerda* sp. 7**
Size: 55 mm   Red Sea
ID: White with yellow ridges and thick black lines between them; yellow tubercles at the intersection of ridges; rhinophores and gill white with black spots. Often mistaken for *Halgerda willeyi* but has a larger gill with more numerous branches having small black spots rather than distinct lines. On shallow reefs and on steep slopes of fringing reef face, down to 25 m. Introduced into the Adriatic via the Suez Canal.

Nudibranchia - "nudibranchs"

Halgerda sp. 8
Size: 50 mm   Mozambique, Reunion
ID: White with numerous brown lines and spots. Similar to *Halgerda* sp. 7, but with more numerous black lines and numerous scattered spots present around mantle margin. Reefs, 20 m.

Halgerda johnsonorum **Carlson & Hoff, 2000**
Size: 26 mm   Marshall Is., New Caledonia
ID: White with orange lines on the ridges and a series of narrow black lines; ridges less prominent than in *Halgerda willeyi*. In caves and on reef ledges.

Halgerda sp. 9
Size: 70 mm   Indonesia
ID: White with large, yellow-orange tubercles and black circles between them; ridge apices tall, orange.

Halgerda okinawa **Carlson & Hoff, 2000**
Size: 114 mm   Indonesia, Japan
ID: White with large, yellow-orange tubercles and ridges; black pigment present between the ridges. In 20-58 m.

Halgerda albocristata **Gosliner & Fahey, 1998**
Size: 20 mm   Western and central Pacific Ocean
ID: Translucent white with the central portion of the notum covered with yellow pigment; a network of opaque white lines covering the ridges. On shallow reefs, 5-15 m.

Halgerda wasiniensis **Eliot, 1904**
Size: 50 mm   Indian Ocean
ID: White with most of the dorsum covered by black pigment; orange lines on the surface of the ridges, these are broader in South African specimens. On reefs from 3-30 m.

Halgerda stricklandi Fahey & Gosliner, 1999
Size: 35 mm   India, Thailand, Myanmar
ID: Translucent white with a series of orange tubercles arranged randomly, not interconnected by ridges. On reef faces from 7-21 m.

Halgerda carlsoni Rudman, 1978
Size: 40 mm   Western Pacific Ocean
ID: Translucent white with a series of orange-tipped tubercles forming interrupted ridges; minute, scattered orange spots between the tubercles; gill large. Never common, occasionally under coral heads and rubble, feeding on sponges.

Halgerda terramtuentis Bertsch & S. Johnson, 1982
Size: 35 mm   Hawai'ian Is.
ID: Translucent cream with white tipped tubercles and a network of orange lines; the only member of this group of *Halgerda* species with white rather than orange on the tips of the tubercles. In the open on reefs from 15-25 m.

Halgerda batangas Carlson & Hoff, 2000
Size: 40 mm   Western and central Pacific Ocean
ID: Translucent white with a network of orange lines between the tubercles rather than orange spots. On shallow reefs, 10-20 m.

Halgerda aurantiomaculata (Allan, 1932)
Size: 50 mm   Western and central Pacific Ocean
ID: Opaque white with orange spots over the surface of the notum and smaller spots on the tips of the tubercles. On shallow reefs, 10-20 m.

Halgerda sp. 10
Size: 45 mm   Mozambique, Mayotte
ID: Translucent white with a series of orange-tipped tubercles forming ridges; pits between ridges grey, with orange spots; gill large, black; rhinophores white with black pigment. On rocky reefs, in 14 m.

Nudibranchia - "nudibranchs"

Halgerda abyssicola Fahey & Gosliner, 2000
Size: 26 mm   Coral Sea
ID: White with pale yellow-white ridges and tubercles; dark lines outline both sides of each ridge; thick, dark lines perpendicular to the mantle edge, and dark spots along the mantle margin; rhinophores and gill white with black pigment. In 207-420 m.

Halgerda sp. 11
Size: 55 mm   Philippines
ID: Translucent white with an opaque white line around the notum; tubercles extremely large, conical, each with a series of radiating black lines; rhinophores and gill white with black pigment. On deep reefs in the mesophotic zone, 55 m.

Halgerda sp. 12
Size: 60 mm   Philippines
ID: Translucent white with black spots on the mantle margin; dorsum with large, conical tubercles and black ridges between them; rhinophores and gill white with black pigment; gill very large. On deep reefs in the mesophotic zone, 60 m.

Halgerda sp. 13
Size: 35 mm   Philippines
ID: White with yellow tubercles connected by ridges, some of which are yellow; black spots and lines in the areas between ridges; rhinophores and gill white with black lines. On deep reefs in the mesophotic zone, 60 m.

Halgerda sp. 14
Size: 50 mm   Philippines
ID: Bluish-white with black spots on the mantle margin and a white line on the edge of the mantle; dorsum with conical tubercles, each with a radiating pattern of black lines; rhinophores and gill white with black lines. On deep reefs in mesophotic zone, 85 m.

Halgerda fibra Fahey & Gosliner, 2000
Size: 45 mm   New Caledonia, Philippines
ID: White with thin, dark lines radiating from the gill pocket and from each tubercle; additional lines in the depressions between ridges; mantle margin with small dark spots or lines; rhinophores and gill white with brown pigment. Trawled from deep water, in 90-550 m.

112

Halgerda sp. 15
Size: 25 mm   New Caledonia
ID: Uniformly white with black lines along the ridges; gill base yellow; a few black spots and lines on the gill branches and a single black line on the rhinophores.

Halgerda sp. 16
Size: 25 mm   Madagascar, Mayotte
ID: Uniformly white with a yellow medial line; black rhinophore clubs and black tips on the gill branches. On reef faces from 6-19 m.

Halgerda sp. 17
Size: 25 mm   Indonesia
ID: Uniformly white with black lines along the ridges and dark spots around the mantle margin; rhinophores white each with a single dark brown line; gill branches white with dark rachises. On reefs.

Halgerda sp. 18
Size: 60 mm   Vanuatu
ID: Translucent white with yellow tubercles and black ridges; black lines on the gill and the posterior side of the rhinophores. Relatively deep water.

Halgerda sp. 19
Size: 25 mm   Mozambique, South Africa
ID: White with network of yellow-orange lines on low ridges; rhinophoral club and outer portion of gill branches black. Shallow to medium depth reefs 12-33 m.

Halgerda sp. 20
Size: 42 mm   Mozambique
ID: White with orange lines outlining ridges; black spots found in depressions between ridges; rhinophoral club and gill branches black. Deep reefs from 32-42 m.

Nudibranchia - "nudibranchs"

Halgerda sp. 21
Size: 31 mm   Mozambique
ID: White with well elevated, thin orange ridges; black spots on the notum, mostly between the ridges; a dark brown spot on each rhinophoral base, with a black club; gill branches numerous with black rachises. Shallow reefs, 16 m.

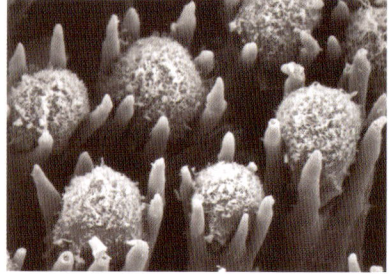

Atagema echinata (Pease, 1860)
Size: 12 mm   Western and central Pacific Ocean
ID: White with yellowish pigment and brown spots; compound tubercles comprised of numerous caryophyllidia; rhinophores white with brownish pigment. On patch reefs in relatively calm water in 3-8 m.

Atagema cf. scabriuscula (Pease, 1860)
Size: 20 mm   Indonesia, Hawai'ian Is
ID: Dark grey with dark grey spots on the holes between ridges. On sponges in sandy areas in shallow water.

Caryophyllidia-bearing discodorids

Members of this subgroup of Discodorididae have the dorsum covered by microscopic organs called caryophyllidia, composed of spicules surrounding a central knob, covered with cilia. The function of these organs is unknown, but evidence indicates that they evolved only once in cryptobranch dorids, therefore all the species bearing caryophyllidia are derived from a single common ancestor (Valdés & Gosliner, 2001).

Atagema intecta (Kelaart, 1858)
Size: 80 mm   Widespread in the Indo-Pacific
ID: Brown with a medial white line; dorsum with large tubercles covered by caryophyllidia. Under coral rubble on shallow reefs from the intertidal zone to about 10 m.

Atagema spongiosa (Kelaart, 1858)
Size: 200 mm   Indian and western Pacific oceans
ID: Grey with brown pigment; bumpy dorsal surface with deep black pits resembling the oscula of sponges. On shallow reefs, in rubble areas usually mixed with sand.

114

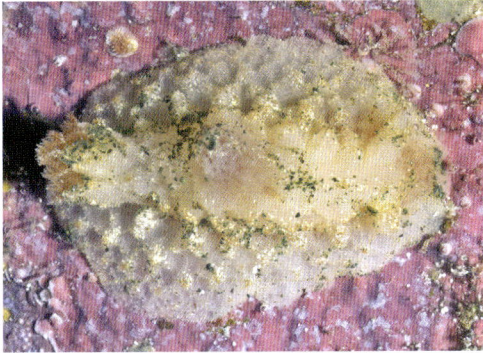

Atagema sp. 1
Size: 35 mm   Papua New Guinea
ID: Yellowish white with opaque white spots; central area of the notum devoid of stellate clusters of caryophyllidia. On white encrusting sponges embedded in silty sand, on slopes in 10 m.

Atagema cf. osseosa (Kelaart, 1859)
Size: 25 mm   Widespread in the Indo-Pacific
ID: Uniformly greyish white; opaque white pigment on the tips of the rhinophores; caryophyllidia arranged in compound stellate clusters. Under coral rubble in 20 m; feeds on sponges.

Atagema sp. 2
Size: 35 mm   Philippines
ID: Brownish with darker brown patches evenly distributed over the body; caryophyllidia not forming elevated compound clusters. In 10 m under coral rubble.

Atagema sp. 3
Size: 18 mm   Philippines
ID: Orange; dorsum covered with large and short compound stellate clusters of purple caryophyllidia; rhinophores orange with purple and white tips; gill brown with white tips. On sandy and rubble slopes in 15 m.

Atagema sp. 4
Size: 35 mm   Philippines
ID: Greenish with the dorsum covered with ridges and spherical tubercles with caryophyllidia; pits between ridges dark grey; rhinophores and gill brownish. Under rubble on shallow reefs in 12 m.

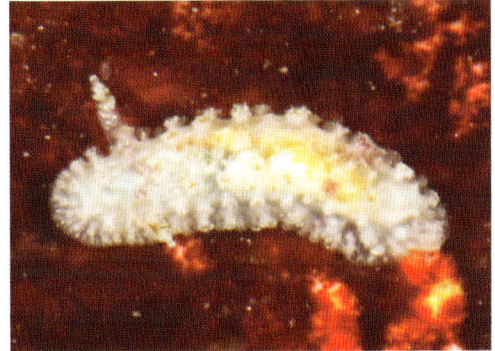

Atagema sp. 5
Size: 12 mm   Papua New Guinea
ID: White with yellow and purple pigment; dorsum covered with stalked tubercles with apical caryophyllidia forming stellate clusters; rhinophores translucent with purple and opaque white pigment; gill not visible. Under dead coral slabs, in 13 m.

Nudibranchia - "nudibranchs"

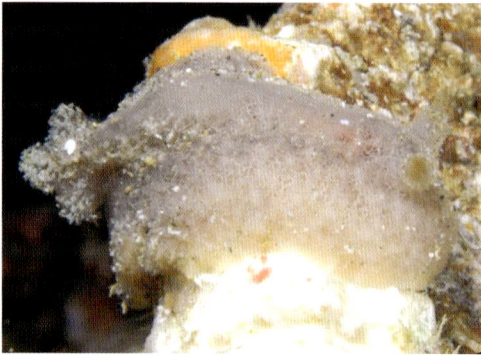

Atagema sp. 6
Size: 45 mm   Philippines
ID: Uniformly grey; dorsum with a complex network of ridges and compound stellate clusters of caryophyllidia; gill sheath with three lobes; rhinophores brown. Under coral rubble in 14 m.

Atagema sp. 7
Size: 40 mm   Philippines
ID: Uniformly translucent grey including rhinophores and gill; dorsum with a complex network of ridges and compound stellate clusters of caryophyllidia. Shallow rocky reefs under coral rubble.

Atagema sp. 8
Size: 20 mm   Philippines
ID: Uniformly white with ridges around grey circular depressions; rhinophores and gill white. In shallow water on patch reefs.

Atagema sp. 9
Size: 20 mm   Philippines
ID: Light grey with opaque white spots and a lighter mid-dorsal hump; gill and rhinophores grey; gill pocket elongate extending posteriorly; rhinophoral sheaths highly elevated. On shallow reefs at night crawling on coral rubble.

Atagema sp. 10
Size: 20 mm   Madagascar
ID: Grey with opaque white spots on the tips of the relatively small clusters of compound caryophyllidia; rhinophores and gill pale brown. Under coral rubble in 1-2 m.

Atagema sp. 11
Size: 15 mm   Aldabra Atoll, Philippines
ID: Light grey with darker grey reticulations in the lowest parts of the notum; brown pigment on the yellowish rhinophores. Under coral rubble in 1-8 m. Only two specimens have been found from widely separate localities.

116

Atagema sp. 12
Size: 35 mm   Philippines
ID: Uniformly white with a network of small caryophyllidia; gill posteriorly directed with three protective lobes; rhinophores yellowish. Shallow patch reefs, 15 m.

Atagema sp. 13
Size: 30 mm   Philippines
ID: Grey with darker spots between ridges; some caryophyllidia with opaque white apices; three elongate gill branches. Shallow reefs, 15 m.

Atagema sp. 14
Size: 30 mm   Philippines
ID: Light brownish with a row of black spots on either side of body; tips of compound tubercles and gill branches opaque white. Shallow reefs, 15 m.

Sclerodoris coriacea Eliot, 1904
Size: 25 mm   Indian Ocean
ID: Brownish with opaque white pigment on the notum, especially on the elevated, rounded tubercles; body texture granular, composed of a dense covering of caryophyllidia. In tide pools at night and on shallow reef flats.

Sclerodoris apiculata (Alder & Hancock, 1864)
Size: 50 mm   Indian and western Pacific oceans
ID: Tan with a network of interconnected caryophyllidia; some elevated tubercles terminate in a fleshy papilla. On sponges from the intertidal zone to 20 m.

Sclerodoris sp. 1
Size: 40 mm   Philippines
ID: Orange with encrusting greyish-white pigment on the dorsum; tubercles low, irregular; rhinophores and gill reddish-brown. Under coral rubble on a steep sandy slope, 17 m.

Nudibranchia - "nudibranchs"

Sclerodoris rubicunda (Baba, 1949)
Size: 20 mm   Western and central Pacific Ocean
ID: Red with a series of depressions and two large bands of opaque white. Originally described as a species of *Halgerda*, but has a solid body with caryophyllidia. In relatively shallow water feeding on red sponges.

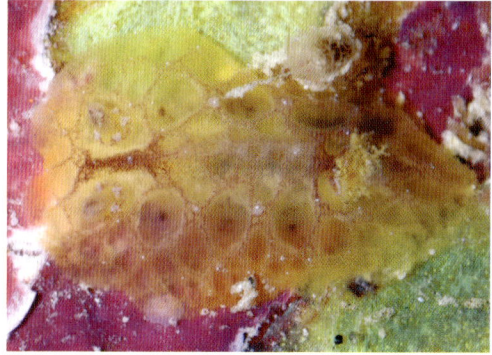

Sclerodoris sp. 2
Size: 40 mm   Vanuatu, Papua New Guinea
ID: Translucent brown. Similar to *Sclerodoris apiculata* but with more regular depressions that resemble sponge oscula; dark spots in the center of each depression. On shallow sandy bottoms.

Sclerodoris tuberculata Eliot, 1904
Size: 50 mm   Indian and western Pacific oceans
ID: Color highly variable, ranging from yellow and red to black, often with opaque white patches; a series of round depressions on the notum resemble sponge oscula. In shallow water on variously colored sponges; it adopts the pigments of the prey sponges on which it is highly cryptic.

Sclerodoris sp. 3
Size: 40 mm   Hawai'ian Is.
ID: Reddish-brown with a series of dark depressions that resemble sponge oscula and opaque white pigment; rhinophores dark brown with white dots; gill pale grey. On a red sponge under a basaltic boulder in 1-2 m.

Sclerodoris sp. 4
Size: 25 mm   Philippines, Indonesia
ID: Pinkish grey with numerous deep black pits of different sizes; tubercles translucent, nipple-shaped; rhinophores with various shades of brown; gill cream. On shallow reef slopes under coral rubble, in 12 m.

Jorunna funebris (Kelaart, 1859)
Size: 150 mm   Indian and western Pacific oceans
ID: White with black rings; fuzzy appearance owing to the presence of dense caryophyllidia. In relatively shallow water, usually associated with the bright blue sponge, *Haliclona* sp.

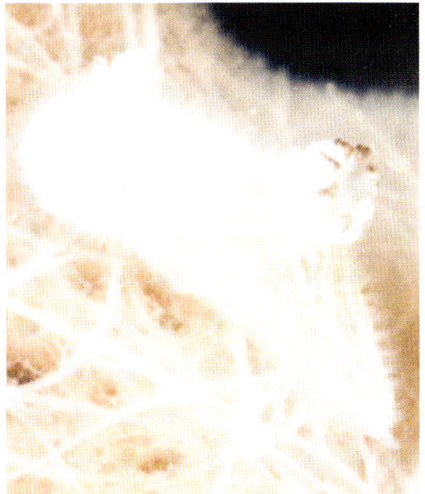

Jorunna labialis (Eliot, 1908)
Size: 20 mm   Red Sea, Madagascar, Tanzania
ID: Brown, sometimes grey, with darker brown spots on the notum; gill branches tipped with opaque white. *Jorunna malcomi* is a synonym. Under volcanic rocks in the intertidal zone to 2 m, in relatively sandy areas.

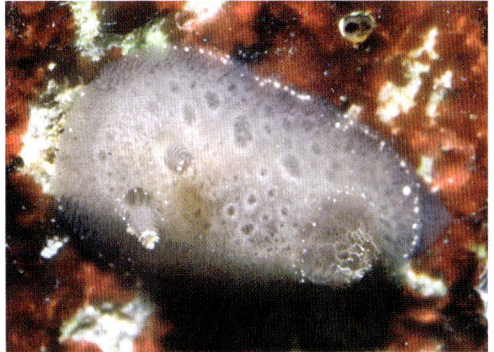

Jorunna ramicola Miller, 1996
Size: 20 mm   Indian and western Pacific oceans
ID: Light grey with darker grey spots surrounded by white rings; caryophyllidia with opaque white tips around the edge of the rhinophoral sheaths, gill cavity and edge of the mantle. Under coral rubble on shallow reefs where it feeds on grey sponges.

Jorunna rubescens (Bergh, 1876)
Size: 200 mm   Indian and western Pacific oceans
ID: White with brown lines and yellow spots; juveniles (right photo) white with opaque white lines; body large, oddly shaped, with a high profile. It was once placed in a distinct genus, *Kentrodoris*. On shallow water reefs; feeds on sponges.

Jorunna parva (Baba, 1938)
Size: 25 mm   Indian and Western Pacific oceans
ID: Brown or orange with a series of black-tipped caryophyllidia; mantle glands opaque white along the edges of the mantle; rhinophores and gill black. In shallow water; feeds on unidentified sponges.

Jorunna alisonae Ev. Marcus, 1976
Size: 35 mm   Indonesia, Marshall Is., Hawai'ian Is.
ID: Grey with circles of darker grey and opaque white apices in some of the caryophyllidia; rhinophores brownish; tips of the gill branches with opaque white. Intertidal zone to 10 m on the underside of coral rubble where it feeds on grey sponges.

***Jorunna* sp. 1**
Size: 18 mm   Philippines
ID: Reddish-grey with darker patches; rhinophores grey with white pigment; gill translucent white with the branches curved inward. Under coral rubble on a reef flat, 2 m.

***Jorunna* sp. 2**
Size: 27 mm   Marshall Is.
ID: Dark brown with scattered opaque white pigment; rhinophores and gill brown with white pigment; gill branches curved inward. In a lagoon on a patch of *Halimeda* algae, in 10-12 m.

***Jorunna* sp. 3**
Size: 18 mm   Philippines
ID: Pinkish grey to grey with faint opaque white circles; rhinophores white; gill branches grey, held erect. Under rubble, shallow reefs to 20 m.

Jorunna sp. 4
Size: 25 mm   Philippines
ID: Dark brown with opaque white on notum gills and rhinophore apices; gill branches erect; body elongate. Sand areas, on sponges, 20 m.

Jorunna sp. 5
Size: 20 mm   Philippines
ID: Yellowish with opaque white on some caryophyllidia, rhinophoral apices and gill branches; body wide. Together with *Jorunna* sp. 3 and *J.* sp. 4.

Jorunna sp. 6
Size: 18 mm   Philippines
ID: Pinkish with small caryophyllidia and darker depressions on the notum; rhinophores with horizontal lamellae as in *Rostanga*.

Jorunna sp. 7
Size: 15 mm   Philippines
ID: Brownish with opaque white on most caryophyllidia; rhinophores uniformly brown, darker than body.

Jorunna sp. 8
Size: 28 mm   Philippines
ID: White to pink with several grey depressions. Similar to *Jorunna* sp. 9 but differs by having more circular opaque white markings and the radular morphology. Predator of *Kallypilidion* sponges, 25 m.

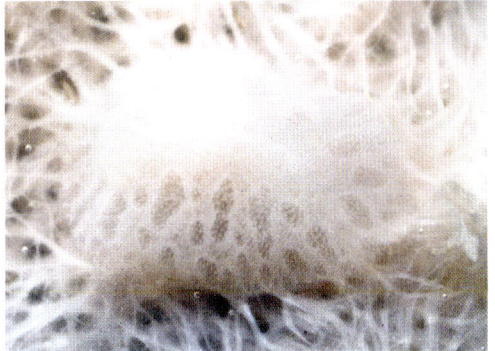

Jorunna sp. 9
Size: 20 mm   Papua New Guinea, Philippines
ID: White to pink with several grey depressions. Lives inside the tubes of the pink sponge *Kallypilidion* sp. where is very cryptic. On shallow reefs in 5-20 m.

121

***Jorunna* sp. 10**
Size: 20 mm   Papua New Guinea
ID: Pinkish grey with a complex network of grey lines;
rhinophores white; gill grey with the branches curved inward.
Found on sponges of similar color pattern in which the
nudibranch is well camouflaged, as seen in the photo on the
right. Previously thought to be a *Rostanga*.

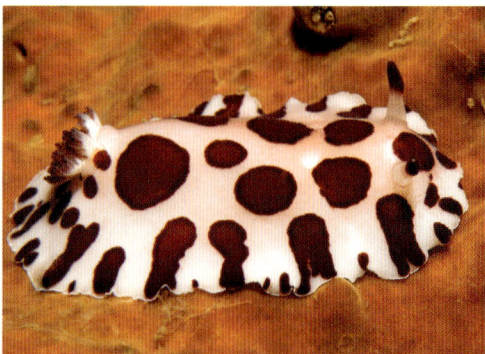

***Diaulula* sp. 1**
Size: 15 mm   Papua New Guinea
ID: Dark brown with darker spots on the notum; gill opaque
white; rhinophores brown with opaque white apices;
caryophyllidia surrounding the rhinophoral sheaths and gill
pocket with opaque white tips. On patch reefs in 8 m.

***Diaulula* sp. 2**
Size: 20 mm   Philippines, Indonesia
ID: Greyish white with dark brown to black symmetrical
patches; rhinophoral club dark brown with a white tip; gill
white with black apices. On shallow reef flats.

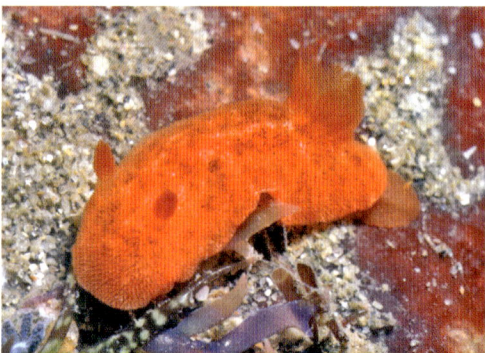

***Diaulula* sp. 3**
Size: 22 mm   Indonesia
ID: Translucent white with light brown spots; gill large,
emerging from an elongate sheath; rhinophores white. Fine
volcanic sand, 20 m.

***Rostanga bifurcata* Rudman & Avern, 1989**
Size: 25 mm   Widespread in the Indo-Pacific
ID: Red or orange, usually with darker patches and opaque
white spots on the notum; radular morphology distinctive. On
red sponges under coral rubble in shallow water.

Rostanga sp. 1
Size: 18 mm   Philippines
ID: Orange-red with opaque white pigment; rhinophores pale orange; gill orange-red with the branches curved inward. Sandy slopes under rubble, in 20 m.

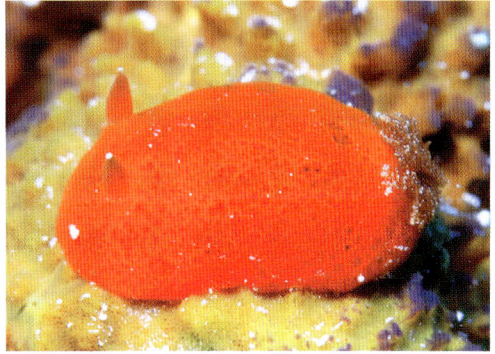

Rostanga sp. 2
Size: 15 mm   Marshall Is.
ID: Red with dark red spots; gill with brown branches laying flat against the body; rhinophores red with white apices. On *Halimeda* algal patches in lagoons, in 9-10 m.

Rostanga sp. 3
Size: 30 mm   Vanuatu
ID: Reddish orange with opaque white spots on the edge of the mantle; gill the same color as the body, gill branches oriented inward; conical rhinophores brownish with a lighter apex. Under rocks in deep reefs.

Rostanga sp. 4
Size: 13 mm   Indonesia
ID: Uniform orange-red; gill red with branches having elongate tips; rhinophores with pronounced lamellae, orange with white apices. Sandy slopes on coral rubble.

Rostanga sp. 5
Size: 35 mm   Philippines
ID: Bright reddish with a dense covering of opaque white spots; gill branches oriented inward, overlapping. In 20 m, crawling over the surface of coral rubble.

Rostanga lutescens (Bergh, 1905)
Size: 25 mm   Widespread in the Indo-Pacific
ID: Cream to yellowish or orange with scattered darker spots and patches of opaque white; rhinophores and gill darker yellowish. Under coral rubble in 10-20 m; feeds on yellow sponges.

123

Nudibranchia - "nudibranchs"

Rostanga aureamala Garovoy, Valdés & Gosliner, 2001
Size: 50 mm   South Africa
ID: Pale orange with pale patches and abundant reddish spots; gill and rhinophores red, rhinophores tipped with opaque white. On sponges on rocky ledges in 20 m.

Rostanga sp. 6
Size: 20 mm   Papua New Guinea, Indonesia
ID: Reddish orange with darker patches; some caryophyllidia with yellowish-white apices; gill and rhinophores the same color as the body, but the conical rhinophores may have and opaque white apex. On encrusting red sponges on the undersides of coral rubble.

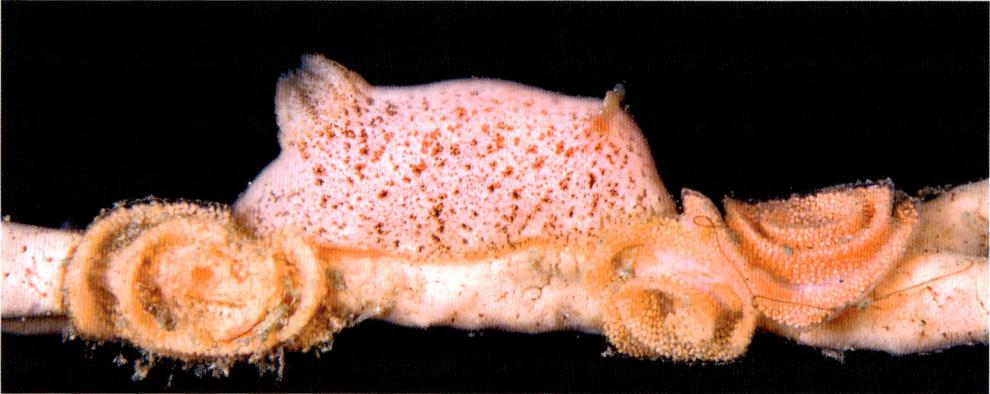

Rostanga sp. 7
Size: 24 mm   Indonesia
ID: Pink with small dark brown depressions; rhinophores and gill pink; gill branches curved inward. On sponges together with its small circular egg masses.

Platydoris inframaculata (Abraham, 1877)
Size: 120 mm   Indian and western Pacific oceans
ID: Dark brown with grey, opaque white and yellow markings; ventral surface with large brown spots and a yellow or orange ring outside the spots. On patch reefs and reef flats in 10-15 m; active at night; produces a bright red egg mass.

Platydoris scabra (Cuvier, 1804)
Size: 100 mm   Indian and western Pacific oceans
ID: Blotched grey with an orange marginal ring and orange rhinophores; dark lines on the gill branches. Shallow water under coral heads, often crawling in the open during the night.

Platydoris cruenta (Quoy & Gaimard, 1832)
Size: 100 mm   Widespread in the Indo-Pacific
ID: White with a dense covering of brown lines; red patches frequently present on the notum; gill branches outlined with dark grey or black pigment. *Platydoris striata* is a synonym. On shallow reef flats where it is nocturnally active.

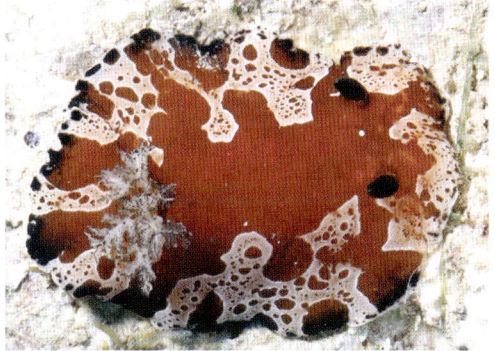

Platydoris dierythros Fahey & Valdés, 2003
Size: 40 mm   Western Australia
ID: Cream with a patchwork of red pigment; rhinophores black with white tips; gill white, covered with brownish spots. On shallow reefs in 15 m.

Platydoris ellioti (Alder & Hancock, 1864)
Size: 150 mm   Indian and western Pacific oceans
ID: Yellow with darker spots; opaque white pigment may also be present on the notum; underside yellow with large black spots. Sandy habitats among coral rubble.

Platydoris sabulosa Dorgan, Valdés & Gosliner, 2002
Size: 125 mm   Philippines
ID: Sandy brown with light and dark brown markings; under surface with large brown spots as in *Platydoris inframaculata* and *Platydoris ellioti*. On shallow reef flats.

Platydoris cinereobranchiata Dorgan, Valdés & Gosliner, 2002   Western Pacific, possibly Seychelles Is.
Size: 200 mm
ID: Tan with numerous small black dots and fewer, larger red blotches; gill branches uniformly dark bluish-grey. Under coral rubble in shallow reefs to 15 m.

Platydoris inornata Dorgan, Valdés & Gosliner, 2002
Size: 40 mm   Indian and western Pacific oceans
ID: Light tan with darker tan blotches; gill white with brown speckles. Under coral rubble in 10-20 m.

Nudibranchia - "nudibranchs"

Platydoris formosa (Alder & Hancock, 1864)
Size: 120 mm   Widespread in the Indo-Pacific
ID: Tan with red and opaque white pigment; yellow and black pigment around the gill pocket and rhinophoral sheaths; distinct black lines outlining the gill. On shallow reef flats, active at night.

Platydoris ocellata Dorgan, Valdés & Gosliner, 2002
Size: 250 mm   Western Pacific Ocean
ID: Brown with white circles surrounded by a narrow black rings; mantle with a cream or yellow marginal band. On sandy slopes in 10-20 m, nocturnally active.

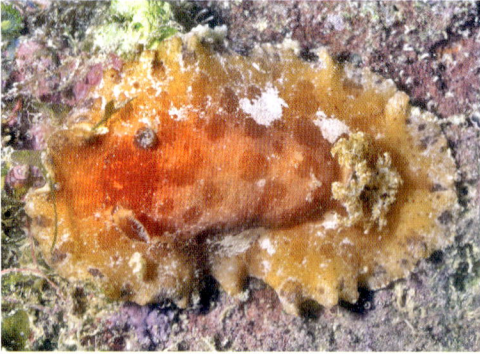

Platydoris pulchra Eliot, 1904
Size: 50 mm   Western and central Indian Ocean
ID: White, covered with orange and large darker orange

spots; a purple-brown marginal band along the edge of the notum. Under coral rubble in shallow water 1-5 m.

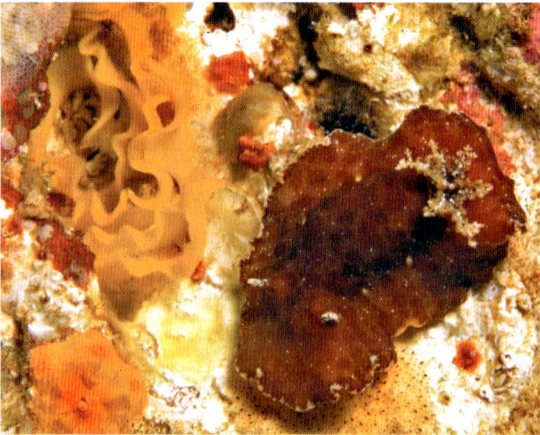

Platydoris sanguinea Bergh, 1905
Size: 40 mm   Western Pacific Ocean
ID: Uniformly dark red or red-orange with white spots; light and dark individuals observed mating with each other; gill white with small black spots. At night in sandy areas in 5-10 m.

126

***Platydoris* sp. 1**
Size: 55 mm   Philippines
ID: Orange with darker reddish-orange patches; rhinophores dark brown; gill white with brown pigment. Nocturnally active on sandy and rocky slopes, in 20 m.

***Platydoris* sp. 2**
Size: 20 mm   Marshall Is.
ID: Greyish-brown, mottled with dark brown pigment forming a pattern of ocelli; rhinophores and gill dark brown.

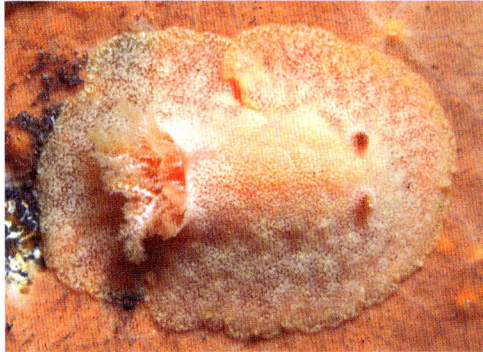

***Platydoris* sp. 3**
Size: 30 mm   Indonesia
ID: Light reddish orange with abundant white pigment on the notum; gill branches the same color as the dorsum with white rachises. On red sponges on sandy slopes mixed with small coral heads.

***Platydoris* sp. 4**
Size: 60 mm   Philippines
ID: Reddish pink with a series of large darker patches and light spots scattered within the patches; a lighter mid-dorsal hump; gill yellowish with brown spots; rhinophores brown with lighter apices. On shallow reefs at night where it is crawling on coral rubble.

The following species have caryophyllidia but their generic placement is uncertain

Caryophyllidia dorid sp. 1
Size: 25 mm   Philippines
ID: Reddish to orange with a series of darker patches punctuated by clusters or darkly tipped caryophyllidia; gill

whitish with darker spots; rhinophores with the same color as the rest of the body. Under basaltic rocks in shallow reefs.

Nudibranchia - "nudibranchs"

Caryophyllidia dorid sp. 2
Size: 20 mm   Papua New Guinea, Philippines
ID: Off-white with a series of darker patches punctuated by clusters or darkly tipped caryophyllidia. Under coral rubble on shallow patch reefs.

Caryophyllidia dorid sp. 3
Size: 25 mm   Papua New Guinea
ID: Yellow with clusters of darkly tipped caryophyllidia; gill branches edged with brown pigment, tipped with opaque white. A sheltered lagoon fringing reef in 10 m.

Caryophyllidia dorid sp. 4
Size: 25 mm   Papua New Guinea, Philippines
ID: Brown with white speckling and a lighter brown mid-dorsal stripe; opaque white pigment on the inner portions of the gill. Under coral rubble in shallow reef flats.

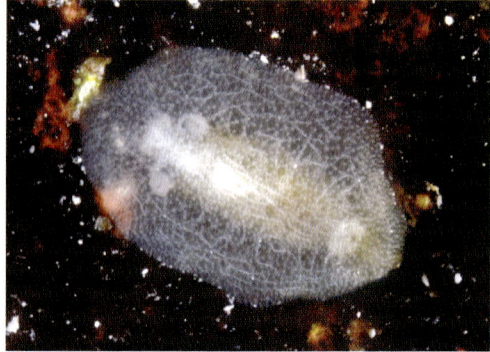

Caryophyllidia dorid sp. 5
Size: 12 mm   Papua New Guinea
ID: Uniformly yellowish white, including gill and rhinophores; dorsum with interconnecting ridges and relatively large caryophyllidia. Under coral rubble in shallow reef flats.

Caryophyllidia dorid sp. 6
Size: 10 mm   Papua New Guinea, Japan
ID: White with numerous minute black spots on the notum and opaque white spots along the notal margin; gill and rhinophores white. Under coral rubble on shallow reef flats.

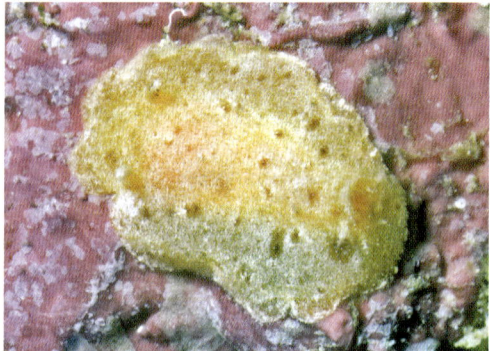

Caryophyllidia dorid sp. 7
Size: 20 mm   Papua New Guinea
ID: Yellowish orange with darker spots and opaque white patches; dark pigment areas appear as depressions, but are at the same level as the rest of the notum. On shallow fringing reefs in areas of strong water current.

Caryophyllidia dorid sp. 8
Size: 70 mm   Reunion
ID: Orange with darker mottling between caryophyllidia; rhinophores elongate, conical, brownish with white apices.

Caryophyllidia dorid sp. 9
Size: 28 mm   Kerama Is., Japan
ID: Similar to Caryophyllidia dorid sp. 2, but with a dark grey series of patches of caryophyllidia situated over the surface of the mantle.

Actinocyclidae O'Donoghue, 1929

Members of this group are closely related to chromodorids because of the presence of denticulate radular teeth, jaws covered with rodlets, and a soft body, lacking spicules. Most species are very cryptic on their food source or natural substrate. Two genera are recognized as valid, *Actinocyclus* and *Hallaxa*, mainly differentiated on the basis of anatomical characteristics. The taxonomy of this group was reviewed by Gosliner & S. Johnson (1994) and Valdés (2002b).

Actinocyclus verrucosus Ehrenberg, 1831
Size: 60 mm   Widespread in the Indo-Pacific
ID: Cream to brown or black, often with darker tubercles covering the relatively soft, rubbery body; gill branches numerous and unipinnate. On shallow reefs where it feeds on sponges that lack spicules.

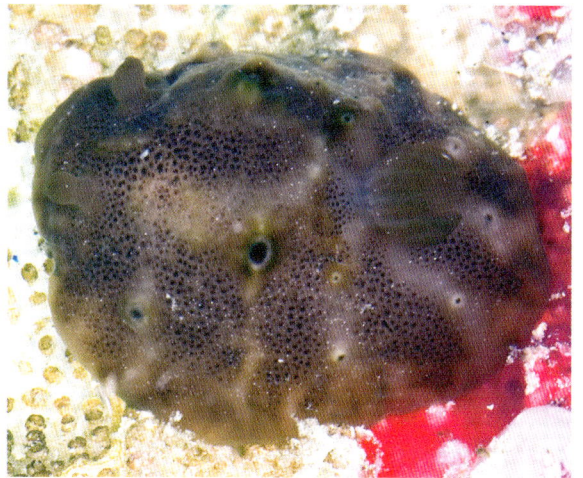

Actinocyclus papillatus (Bergh, 1878)
Size: 50 mm   Western Pacific Ocean
ID: Whitish with a series of dark grey lines on the notum; tubercles simple, rounded, tipped with orange-brown. Under coral slabs on shallow water reefs, in 8 m.

Hallaxa transluscens Gosliner & S. Johnson, 1994
Size: 20 mm   Philippines
ID: Translucent grey with a dense network of opaque white;
rhinophores uniformly brownish. Under rocks in shallow near-
shore reefs where it feeds on identically colored sponges.
Shown here with its egg mass.

Hallaxa fuscescens (Pease, 1871)
Size: 20 mm   Indian and western Pacific oceans
ID: Translucent dark grey with black spots; gill and
rhinophores also black. *Hallaxa atrotuberculata* and *H.
decorata* are synonyms. Under rocks in shallow water.

Hallaxa albopunctata Gosliner & S. Johnson, 1994
Size: 6 mm   South Africa
ID: Translucent pale green with small opaque white
punctuations; gill and rhinophores paler greenish white;
internal organs visible. Under small rocks in 2-3 m.

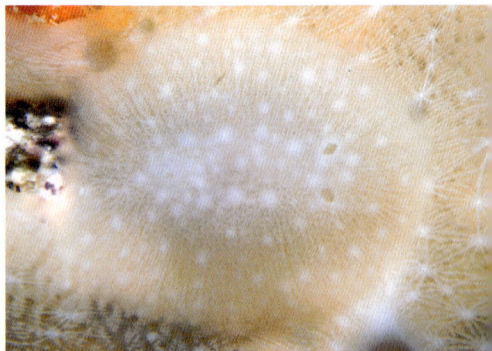

Hallaxa cryptica Gosliner & S. Johnson, 1994
Size: 25 mm   Indian and western Pacific oceans
ID: Brown or pale whitish with a series of opaque pustules
on the notum; gill and rhinophores with the same color as
the notum; rhinophores with opaque white apices. On the
underside of coral rubble where it feeds on non-spiculate
sponges.

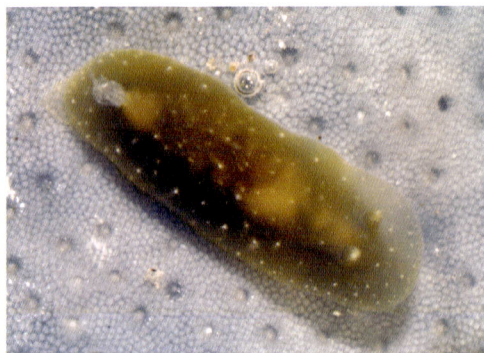

Hallaxa elongata Gosliner & S. Johnson, 1994
Size: 12 mm   Aldabra Atoll
ID: Greenish with opaque white spots; gill branches and
rhinophores tipped with opaque white. Fine coral rubble in
shallow portions of atoll lagoons, 1-2 m.

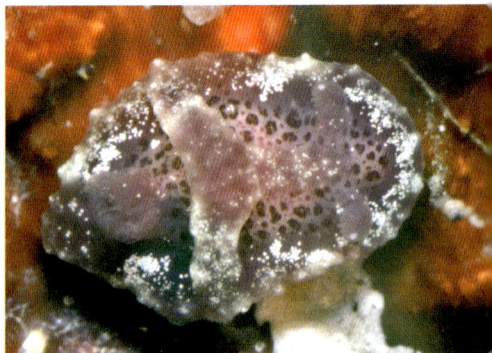

Hallaxa hileenae Gosliner & S. Johnson, 1994
Size: 13 mm   Western Pacific Ocean
ID: Purplish with dark grey patches and opaque white on the
notum; dorsum with a Y-shaped ridge. Under coral rubble in
1-8 m.

Hallaxa iju Gosliner & S. Johnson, 1994
Size: 10 mm   Western and central Pacific ocean
ID: Reddish brown to dark grey or black with small opaque white flecks; opaque white pigment on the upper two-thirds of the rhinophoral club. Under coral rubble on shallow reefs in 1-8 m.

Hallaxa indecora (Bergh, 1905)
Size: 12 mm   Indian and western Pacific oceans
ID: Light to dark purplish plum; white pigment spots may be present on the notum and on the tips of the rhinophores. Under coral rubble on shallow reefs.

Hallaxa paulinae Gosliner & S. Johnson, 1994
Size: 18 mm   Indonesia, Palau, Japan
ID: Translucent white with a dense covering of opaque white that leaves horizontal translucent "windows" visible on the notum; rhinophores tipped with a black or brown stripe. On the edge of patch reefs under coral rubble; feeds on a soft sponge with an identical color pattern.

Hallaxa sp. 1
Size: 15 mm   Philippines
ID: Purple with diagonal patches, punctuated with lighter pigment and darker spots; gill purple; rhinophores brown with opaque white lamellae. In 20 m crawling over the surface of coral rubble. Resembles a sponge.

Hallaxa sp. 2
Size: 18 mm   Philippines
ID: Translucent with abundant opaque white spots. Similar to Hallaxa cryptica but with more spots, which are not as elevated as in H. cryptica. Under coral rubble in 10 m.

Hallaxa sp. 3
Size: 22 mm   Okinawa (Japan)
ID: Translucent grey with a network of opaque white. Similar to Hallaxa paulinae and H. translucens but lacks black pigment on the rhinophoral club and differs in its internal anatomy. In 12 m.

Hallaxa sp. 4
Size: 17 mm   Malaysia
ID: Translucent white; large pustules on the body, which are outlined with a opaque white reticulation; rhinophores and gill white. Underneath coral rubble; feeds on aspiculate sponges.

Hallaxa sp. 5
Size: 22 mm   Philippine
ID: Uniformly black. Similar to *Hallaxa fuscescens* but lack the distinct rounded tubercles; numerous unipinnate g branches. In rock pools in the intertidal zone.

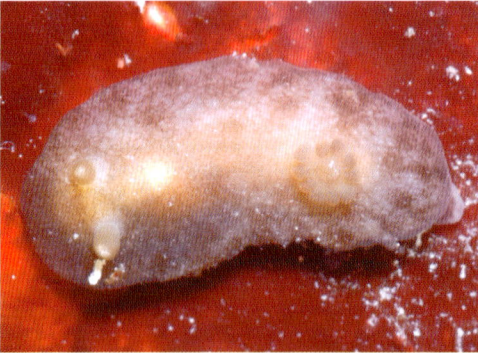

Hallaxa sp. 6
Size: 20 mm   Vanuatu
ID: Light pink with darker pink patches; gill and rhinophores with the same color. On relatively deep reefs.

Chromodorididae Bergh, 1891

This is the largest family of Indo-Pacific sea slugs with mor than 360 species, many of which are still undescribed. Th name means colorful sea nymph, and most species ar brightly colored and elaborately patterned. The differen taxa can be distinguished by some external features, but ar primarily separated by their radular teeth. The systematic of this group has undergone a major revision with rearrangement of many taxa (R. Johnson 2010; R. Johnso & Gosliner 2012). Most significantly, Indo-Pacific specie previously included in *Chromodoris* (see Rudman 1984) ar now split into to two genera, *Chromodoris* and *Goniobranchus* Species of *Glossodoris* are now split between *Glossodoris Doriprismatica* and *Ardeadoris*. Species of *Risbecia* are no included in *Hypselodoris*. Other smaller changers are als reflected here.

Cadlinella Thiele, 1931

Cadlinella is the most basal group of chromodorids. It i characterized by having large, elongate tubercles on th dorsum as well as other distinct anatomical characters.

Cadlinella subornatissima Baba, 1996
Size: 9 mm   Japan, Indonesia
ID: White with orange pigment only in the center of the dorsum, not covering the margins of the notum; papillae elongate and pointed with red pigment on the apices. In 40 m.

Cadlinella ornatissima (Risbec, 1928)
Size: 35 mm   Indian and western Pacific ocean
ID: Yellow with tall pink tipped tubercles; rhinophores and gi white; a series of flask shaped mantle glands along the edg of the mantle. Common on reef flats and reef faces, ofte under coral heads.

Cadlinella hirsuta Rudman, 1995
Size: 15 mm   New Caledonia, Chesterfield Reefs
ID: Yellow-orange; dorsum covered with white, thin, elongate
papillae; rhinophores and gill white. In 25 m, on brown
sponges.

Chromodoris Alder & Hancock, 1855

Chromodoris is now restricted to the species that have a flat
egg mass (R. Johnson & Gosliner 2012), as shown in the
photo below. Most species in this group display a pattern
of longitudinal black lines, with a few exceptions such as
Chromodoris aspersa. Despite the fact it has dots instead
of lines it is included in *Chromodoris* due the shape of its
egg mass and genetic data that also support its placement
in this group.

Chromodoris magnifica (Quoy & Gaimard, 1832)
Size: 90 mm   Western Pacific Ocean
ID: White with an orange submarginal band; dorsum
with black pigment in the center and white lines; gill and
rhinophores orange. Deep-water animals (right photo) are

paler. Most similar to *Chromodoris africana*, but the orange
band is inside a white band. On outer reef walls and slopes;
feeds on non-spiculate sponges.

Chromodoris africana Eliot, 1904
Size: 73 mm   Indian Ocean
ID: White with a wide orange marginal band and three wide
black longitudinal stripes; gill and rhinophores reddish-
orange. On outer reef walls and slopes in 15-30 m.

Chromodoris quadricolor (Rüppell & Leuckart, 1830)
Size: 45 mm   Red Sea, Tanzania
ID: White with three black longitudinal stripes; a thin white
marginal band, followed by a wide orange band; center of the
mantle with a bluish tinge between the black stripes. Feeds
on the tall fire sponge, *Latrunculia magnifica* as well as black
sponges of the genus *Semitaspongia*.

Nudibranchia - "nudibranchs"

Chromodoris elisabethina Bergh, 1877
Size: 25 mm   Western Pacific Ocean
ID: Blue dorsum, encircled in black and white; a mid-dorsal longitudinal black line, which may be broken into a series of short lines; a thick, yellow marginal line. Feeds on foliose sponges in 5-30 m.

Chromodoris sp. 1
Size: 40 mm   Eastern Malaysi
ID: Blue dorsum, encircled in black and white, with severa black longitudinal lines. Genetically distinct from *Chromodc ris elisabethina*.

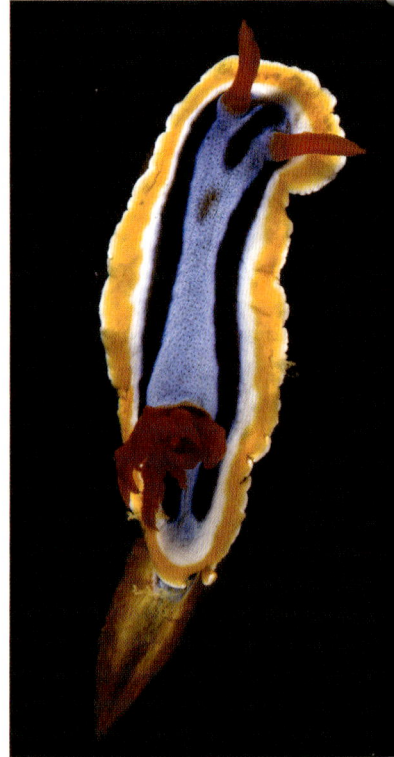

Chromodoris colemani Rudman, 1982
Size: 25 mm   Western and central Pacific Ocea
ID: White with a series of thin longitudinal blac lines and orange to orange-brown lines betwee the black lines. On reef slopes; generally les common than the other reef members of this grou Layton, Gosliner & Wilson (2018) have show the extreme geographical mimics of this specie depicted here – top left: Philippines, middle lef Western Australia, bottom left: Queensland, righ Timor-Leste.

134

Chromodoris westraliensis (O'Donoghue, 1924)
Size: 26 mm   Western Australia
ID: Black with a wide orange marginal band; large granular blue patches around the gill and between the rhinophores; a thin blue patch just inside the anterior edge of the marginal band; rhinophores and gill deep orange. On offshore reefs and slopes in 10-30 m.

Chromodoris kuiteri Rudman, 1982
Size: 60 mm   Eastern Australia, Lord Howe Is.
ID: Black with longitudinal white lines; mantle margin orange with a white band separated from the orange by black pigment; gill and rhinophores orange. On shallow reefs where it feeds on sponges of the genus *Dysidea*.

Chromodoris joshi Gosliner & Behrens, 1998
Size: 60 mm   Eastern Indian and western Pacific oceans
ID: Buttery yellow with a darker golden margin; white flecks scattered over the yellow areas; a wide black submarginal band encircles the notum; a black stripe of the same width begins anteriorly at the submarginal bands and follows the

center line to the gill; gill and rhinophores yellow-orange to orange. On outer rock walls to 30 m deep. The color morph shown on the right is genetically identical to the typical *Chromodoris joshi* (left).

Chromodoris michaeli Gosliner & Behrens, 1998
Size: 46 mm   Indonesia, Philippines
ID: Powdery blue with a white line on the edge of the notum; an orange band inside the white, followed by a blue area and a black band, which encircles the animal; this band is broken on the head and behind the gill; randomly distributed black spots within the black band; gill and rhinophores orange. On reef slopes and walls.

Chromodoris annae Bergh, 1877
Size: 40 mm   Widespread in the Indo-Pacific
ID: Blue with darker markings and lacking a mid-dorsal longitudinal line; small black specks within the blue areas. On open rock walls and reef faces where it feeds on aplysillid sponges in 15-30 m.

Nudibranchia - "nudibranchs"

Chromodoris hamiltoni Rudman, 1977
Size: 65 mm   Western Indian Ocean
ID: Blue, with several dark blue-black longitudinal lines, often with a central patch of orange pigment; margin with a wide orange-brown band; rhinophores and gill orange. On patch reefs and slopes to 20 m.

Chromodoris sp. 2
Size: 65 mm   Western Indian Ocean
ID: Blue with various degrees of black pigment; black central line expanded anteriorly; orange markings, if present, to the sides of the center black line rather than being centrally situated; margin with a wide orange-brown band; rhinophores and gill orange. Often confused with *Chromodoris hamiltoni* but genetically and morphologically distinct.

Chromodoris sp. 3
Size: 50 mm   Philippines
ID: Light blue with longitudinal black lines. Differs from *Chromodoris lochi* in having an orange marginal band and by the wide space between the marginal band and the black lines. On deep mesophotic reefs, 100 m.

Chromodoris sp. 4
Size: 40 mm   Red Sea
ID: Light blue with several black lines and orange patches. Similar to *Chromodoris quadricolor* but with lighter blue pigment and additional longitudinal black lines on the notum.

Chromodoris sp. 5
Size: 29 mm   Mozambique, South Africa
ID: Light blue with an outer orange marginal band and an inner black band. On meosphotic reefs from 40-60 m.

Chromodoris sp. 6
Size: 30 mm   Tahiti
ID: Light blue with narrow black longitudinal lines on the dorsum and foot, which may be interrupted; rhinophores and gill honey-yellow with opaque white lines. Deep reefs on flat massive sponges, may be abundant, in 40-50 m.

Chromodoris dianae Gosliner & Behrens, 1998
Size: 60 mm   Western Pacific Ocean
ID: Powder blue due to white punctuations over a blue background; mantle margin white; a discontinuous black submarginal band encircles the medial area; all specimens with a spot between the orange rhinophores; gill branches white with orange apices. Common on reef faces where it feeds on foliose sponges such as *Carteriospongia*.

Chromodoris sp. 7
Size: 60 mm   Western Pacific Ocean
ID: Powder blue due to white punctuations over a blue background; mantle margin white with orange marginal spots. Similar and confused with *Chromodoris dianae*, differs by its orange marginal spots and gill with orange over entire surface of gill branches. On shallow reefs, feeds on sponges such as *Carteriospongia*.

Chromodoris willani Rudman, 1982
Size: 35 mm   Western Pacific Ocean
ID: Blue with longitudinal black lines; mangle edge white; opaque white spots on the gill and rhinophores. On exposed reef walls and slopes, where it feeds on foliose sponges such as *Carteriospongia*.

137

Nudibranchia - "nudibranchs"

Chromodoris sp. 8
Size: 40 mm   Kenya
ID: Light blue with black longitudinal lines on the dorsum and foot; orange pigment on the margin of the notum; rhinophores and gill orange with opaque white spots, which distinguish this species from *Chromodoris willani* whose gill and rhinophores are grey. Shallow reef flats.

Chromodoris lochi Rudman, 1982
Size: 35 mm   Widespread in the Indo-Pacific
ID: Pale blue with a dark blue submarginal band and middorsal line; rhinophores and gill range from yellow to pink. On the walls on the outside of fringing and barrier reefs where it feeds on sponges. Indian Ocean specimens have been considered to be a separate species, *Chromodoris boucheti*, but molecular evidence suggests they are the same species.

Chromodoris strigata Rudman, 1982
Size: 20 mm   Widespread in the Indo-Pacific
ID: White with dark longitudinal patches on the dorsum arranged in a pattern; marginal band wide, yellow-orange; rhinophores and gill dark yellow-orange. Common on reef faces and flats where it feeds on foliose sponges such as *Carteriospongia*.

138

Chromodoris buchananae Gosliner & Behrens, 2000
Size: 48 mm   New South Wales (Australia)
ID: Translucent cream with small brown specks over the notum; wide orange marginal band within which is a think white band; two opaque white lines running the length of the body; gill and rhinophores orange.

Chromodoris sp. 9
Size: 19 mm   Marshall Islands
ID: Translucent orange with fine black longitudinal lines; submarginal band opaque white; marginal band orange; rhinophores and gill orange; gill with red lines. Under dead coral or debris on lilac colored sponges; 5-8 m.

Chromodoris sp. 10
Size: 25 mm   French Polynesia
ID: Light blue with black longitudinal lines on the back and foot; marginal band orange, followed by a light blue area, and a black line; rhinophores and gill orange.

Chromodoris sp. 11
Size: 35 mm   Philippines
ID: Light brown with numerous black lines; gill rachis orange. Similar to *Chromodoris burni* but with black spots present between margin and black lines. Coral rubble, 20 m.

Chromodoris burni Rudman, 1982
Size: 20 mm   Eastern Australia
ID: Light brown with numerous black lines and white, light blue patches; marginal band orange; gill and rhinophores orange; gill rachis with parallel black lines. On shallow reefs in the open.

Chromodoris lineolata van Hasselt, 1824
Size: 30 mm   Western Pacific Ocean
ID: Dark brown to black, densely covered with fine opaque white longitudinal lines; a wide yellow-orange marginal band. Feeds on *Dysidea* sponges on shallow reefs.

139

Nudibranchia - "nudibranchs"

Chromodoris mandapamensis Valdés, Mollo & Ortea, 1999
Size: 30 mm — Indian Ocean
ID: Cream-white; numerous dark brown to black spots concentrating in some areas forming large patches; mantle margin with orange spots; gill and rhinophores cream with opaque white dots. Under coral rubble in 3-10 m.

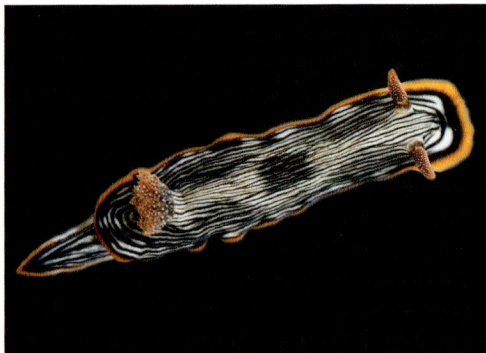

Chromodoris striatella Bergh, 1877
Size: 30 mm — Western Pacific Ocean
ID: Cream-white with numerous dark brown lines; mantle margin with orange marginal band; gill and rhinophores dark reddish-brown with white dots. Feeds on brownish sponges and inhabits shallow waters.

Chromodoris sp. 12
Size: 45 mm — Philippines, Indonesia
ID: Cream-white with numerous dark brown lines and dark brown patches on the notum; broken orange spots along the mantle margin. On coral rubble in silty habitats, 20 m.

Chromodoris sp. 13
Size: 18 mm — Papua New Guinea, Vanuatu
ID: Cream-white with numerous dark brown lines aggregating in some areas to form patches; marginal band orange; gill and rhinophores reddish-brown with opaque white spots. On shallow water reefs.

Chromodoris sp. 14
Size: 18 mm — Indonesia
ID: Opaque white with areas of grey and black, and orange spots; marginal orange band; rhinophores and gill orange with opaque white spots. Shallow reefs, under dead coral heads, in 15 m.

Chromodoris sp. 15
Size: 18 mm — Philippines, New Caledonia
ID: Opaque white with numerous black spots surrounded by grey pigment; discontinuous mantle orange margin; rhinophores and gill orange with opaque white spots.

Chromodoris sp. 16
Size: 25 mm   Western Australia
ID: Cream-white with numerous dark brown lines; two opaque white patches on the center of the notum. Genetically distinct from all other species of *Chromodoris*.

Chromodoris sp. 17
Size: 15 mm   Eastern and western Australia
ID: Purplish brown with irregular white patches; mantle margin surrounded by spots rather than a continuous orange line. Previously mistaken as *Chromodoris striatella*.

Chromodoris aspersa (Gould, 1852)
Size: 26 mm   Widespread in the Indo-Pacific
ID: White with a yellow or orange marginal band and numerous purple spots; spots vary in size between individuals and become more diffuse near the edges creating the impression that are not in focus. From intertidal and shallow subtidal patch reefs to 10 m; produces a flat egg mass.

Chromodoris sp. 18
Size: 25 mm   Red Sea
ID: Uniformly cream-white with large black spots that cover the dorsum and foot; a submarginal orange band present on the notum and foot; rhinophores orange; gill yellowish-cream; body oval rather than elongate. Genetically distinct from *Chromodoris aspersa*.

Goniobranchus Pease, 1866
This group of chromodorids is distinct from *Chromodoris* by having a more ovoid body shape and different kinds of glands around the edge of the mantle. Species in this group produce egg masses that are attached by the narrow edge and are elevated from the surface.

The *Goniobranchus tinctorius* group
While this complex of species (having a network of red markings) has been considered as a single variable species, there are consistent differences between specimens from different geographical localities. The entire group is in need of major revision. We prefer to consider the different forms as distinct species and they are treated here in that manner.

Goniobranchus tinctorius (Rüppell & Leuckart, 1830)
Size: 95 mm   Oman, Red Sea
ID: White with a yellow marginal band, followed by a white clearing, with several rows of darker red spots; red reticulate pigment broken, giving the appearance of white specks and spots; mantle undulated. Common on shallow reefs, crawling in the open.

Nudibranchia - "nudibranchs"

Goniobranchus cf. alderi (Collingwood, 1881)
Size: 45 mm   Indian Ocean
ID: White with a fine red-orange reticulated pattern on the center of the dorsum; an orange marginal band and a maroon submarginal band that is differentiated from the rest of the reticulate pattern, which may be interrupted as a series of red patches; gill branches lined with red. Under dead coral rubble from the intertidal to about 10 m.

Goniobranchus sp. 1
Size: 55 mm   Widespread in the Indo-Pacific
ID: White overlain by a purple-red reticulated pattern that forms blotches of color toward the golden-yellow marginal edge; distinct red spots on the tips of tubercles, surrounded by a red ring; a pale orange marginal band; rhinophores pale orange without opaque white markings. On relatively shallow water from 5-15 m.

Goniobranchus sp. 2
Size: 50 mm   Northwest Hawai'ian Is.
ID: White with a red reticulate dorsal pattern and an orange marginal band; a few large dark red spots inside the orange band; rhinophores pale orange without any opaque white markings. On lagoon patch reefs in 10-15 m, crawling in the open.

Goniobranchus reticulatus (Quoy & Gaimard, 1832)
Size: 60 mm   Western Pacific Ocean
ID: A reticulated network of red lines over the surface of the mantle; lacks submarginal spots; distinct tubercles over the surface of the body; marginal band absent, or less commonly with a faint orange band; gill with inner opaque white rachises. Frequently under coral rubble in moderately shallow reefs.

Goniobranchus sp. 3
Size: 40 mm   Indonesia
ID: White with red spots, in some specimens forming rings, mainly on the center of the dorsum; mantle margin with a orange band.

Goniobranchus sp. 4
Size: 75 mm   Hong Kong (China)
ID: White with white tubercles with red apices and red rings around the them; mantle margin with a yellow band; gill and rhinophores red.

Goniobranchus sp. 5
Size: 40 mm   Western Pacific Ocean
ID: Dorsum covered by a diffused reticulated region of red lines, a branched mid-dorsal papilla anterior to the gill; distinct red lines along the rachis of each gill branch. In the same habitat as *Goniobranchus reticulatus*.

Goniobranchus sp. 6
Size: 50 mm   Tahiti
ID: White with a diffuse red reticulated network surrounding conical tubercles; submarginal band opaque white and an orange marginal band; rhinophores light brown with white lines on the lamellae; gill white with red on the rachis and branches. On reefs inside lagoons, 8-12 m.

Goniobranchus sp. 7
Size: 95 mm   New Caledonia, Marshall Is.
ID: White with a complex reticulation of faint red lines; reticulations more concentrated submarginally forming a distinct ring around the notum; dorsum densely covered with tubercles, with two dark brown bands running between the rhinophores and the gill.

Goniobranchus sp. 8
Size: 45 mm   Okinawa (Japan)
ID: Reticulated region of red lines in the center of the dorsum; a broad area of white between the yellow marginal band and the reticulate region; darker red spots at the margin of the reticulated area; rhinophores with a series of opaque white spots rather than continuous lines. In 4-50 m.

Goniobranchus sp. 9
Size: 70 mm   Myanmar, Malaysia
ID: White with irregularly shaped dark red markings on the center of the dorsum, sparse to absent near the margin; marginal band pale orange; juveniles with less red on the

dorsum (right photo). On shallow water reefs, crawling in the open. The specimen shown here is host to the commensal shrimp, *Periclimenes imperator*.

Nudibranchia - "nudibranchs"

Species that raise and lower the anterior portion of the head

The next twelve species appear to be closely related and exhibit the characteristic behavior of raising and lowering the frontal portion of the head and mantle as seen in the photograph below.

Goniobranchus conchyliatus **(Yonow, 1984)**
Size: 35 mm   Indian Ocean
ID: Purplish with opaque white or yellow tubercles and a network of thin black lines; gill and rhinophores dark red or reddish-orange.

***Goniobranchus* sp. 10**
Size: 18 mm   Fiji
ID: Light brown with opaque white rounded tubercles on the dorsum; front of the head opaque white; rhinophores and gill honey colored with opaque white spots.

***Goniobranchus* sp. 11**
Size: 17 mm   Marshall Is.
ID: Purple with cream pustules and black lines on the dorsal surface; rhinophores and gill white with purple lines. Under coral heads and on reef faces, 2-8 m.

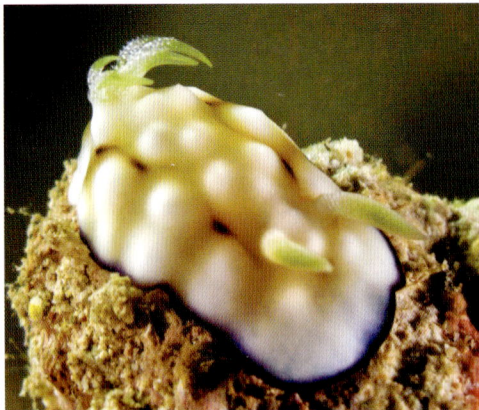

***Goniobranchus* sp. 12**
Size: 30 mm   French Polynesia
ID: White with white rounded tubercles; light brown pigment and black spots between the tubercles; a marginal purple band surrounding the notum; rhinophores and gill pale green with opaque white spots. On rocky reefs in 7-22 m.

Goniobranchus hintuanensis **(Gosliner & Behrens, 1998)**
Size: 16 mm   Western Pacific Ocean
ID: White with a deep violet mantle edge; small circles of deep magenta encircle opaque white areas, rounded nodules on the medial area and at the base of the rhinophores; plum color forms an irregular network on the dorsum; rhinophores and gill plum colored. Shallow, silty habitats, usually in less than 5 m.

Goniobranchus geometricus (Risbec, 1928)
Size: 35 mm   Indian and western Pacific oceans
ID: Purplish with opaque white tubercles and a network of thick black lines; gill and rhinophores with bright green tips. On shallow patch reefs, usually under stones or coral rubble, but also in the open.

Goniobranchus vibratus (Pease, 1860)
Size: 30 mm   Marshall Is., Hawai'ian Is., Japan
ID: Yellow with large, low white tubercles; a series purple "indentation-like" patches along the mantle margin; rhinophores and edges of the gill also purple. Feeds on a purple-black sponge.

Goniobranchus sp. 13
Size: 40 mm   Moorea, Tuamotu Archipelago
ID: White with a network of yellow pigment; dark brown spots along the yellow network; a marginal dark blue band surrounding the notum; rhinophores and gill white basally with dark blue tips. In shallow bays on sandy and rocky areas, less than 5 m.

Goniobranchus roboi (Gosliner & Behrens, 1998)
Size: 50 mm   Indian and western Pacific oceans
ID: Yellow-orange with varying size patches of blue and lavender, and brown; bright blue blocks of color form a series separated by black along the edge of the mantle; rhinophores and gill blue-black.

Goniobranchus sp. 14
Size: 60 mm   Reunion Is.
ID: Light blue with a large area of yellow with white circles; each circle outlined in darker yellow; dark blue to black lines radiate from the yellow to the margin of the body; a submarginal black band around on the notum; rhinophores and gill light blue with darker blue. Rocky reefs, in 17 m.

Nudibranchia - "nudibranchs"

Goniobranchus sp. 15
Size: 28 mm   Queensland (Australia), Philippines
ID: Yellow-orange with varying size light blue patches; mantle margin with a thick black line followed by a wide light blue area broken with transverse black lines; gill and rhinophores with red pigment. On shallow water reefs on the side of steep slopes, in the open.

Goniobranchus sp. 16
Size: 20 mm   Indonesia, Philippines
ID: Pale blue with a series of transverse yellow bars that end in darker patches; rhinophores and gill blue; mantle glands clearly visible along edge of mantle.

Goniobranchus sp. 17
Size: 23 mm   Philippines
ID: Pale blue with a series of transverse yellow bars that end in darker patches; rhinophores and gill yellow-orange. Deep reefs in 30 m.

Goniobranchus sp. 18
Size: 20 mm   Indonesia
ID: Bluish-white, with several broad, solid bands of yellow on the center of the mantle, and short, bifurcated black pigment on the sides of the yellow bands; rhinophores and gill yellow-orange.

Mantle raising and lowering
The next species of *Goniobranchus* raise and lower the entire mantle edge while they crawl, as seen in the photograph below.

Goniobranchus geminus (Rudman, 1987)
Size: 35 mm   Indian Ocean
ID: Yellow with four bands around the mantle edge, outermost white, followed by greyish-purple, then bluish-white, then yellow; middle of the dorsum with numerous purple-brown spots ringed with bluish-white.

Goniobranchus gleniei (Kelaart, 1858)
Size: 50 mm   Indian Ocean
ID: White with a characteristic orange pattern on the dorsum surrounded by a black line and containing irregular black spots; marginal band white followed by a dull purple submarginal band; rhinophores and gill white to yellow to brown.

Goniobranchus tritos (Yonow, 1994)
Size: 40 mm   Maldives
ID: Cream with a wide dull purple marginal band; dorsum with large black spots surrounded by white diffuse areas; rhinophores and gill light greyish-brown.

Goniobranchus charlottae (Schrödl, 1999)
Size: 60 mm   Red Sea
ID: Adults (left photo) reddish-brown with scattered red spots; marginal band yellow, followed by dark blue, then light blue spots; juveniles (right photo) reddish-brown with large cream-white areas and a submarginal light blue band rather than spots; rhinophores and gill pale brown with numerous opaque white spots; rhinophoral apices purple. In relatively shallow water in silty habitats.

147

Nudibranchia - "nudibranchs"

Goniobranchus coi (Risbec, 1956)
Size: 50 mm   Western and central Pacific
ID: Yellow with a tan rose to pink central area surrounded by white and black undulating lines, often with a few black spots; mantle margin purple, followed by a white band and a tan wider band. Sheltered habitats on the inside of barrier reefs.

Goniobranchus kuniei (Pruvot-Fol, 1930)
Size: 75 mm   Indian, western and central Pacific oceans
ID: Yellowish with a purple and blue marginal band; center of the dorsum brown with black spots or rarely rings, surrounded by purple and yellowish areas. Generally in moderate depths in fairly sheltered habitats.

Goniobranchus sp. 19
Size: 20 mm   Moorea
ID: Bright yellow with opaque white rounded tubercles; marginal band wide, purple; rhinophores and gill white to light yellow with opaque white spots. In shallow bays in sandy and rocky areas, 5-10 m.

Species of *Goniobranchus* with rings or spots, not flapping

This group includes animals that have rings or spots on the dorsum but do not flap the mantle. Species such as *Goniobranchus annulatus* (below) display considerable external color variation but can be recognized by the presence of rings.

Goniobranchus annulatus (Eliot, 1904)
Size: 100 mm   Indian and western Pacific oceans
ID: White with a purple marginal band and two large purple circles surrounding the gill and the rhinophores; dorsum covered with large orange spots. Specimens from Thailand exhibit considerable variation in color. From the intertidal zone to about 15 m on reef flats.

Goniobranchus sp. 20
Size: 30 mm   Marquesas Is.
ID: White with two interrupted black circles and a yellow marginal band on the notum; rhinophores and gill white basally and orange apically. Inside bays, 1 m.

Goniobranchus sp. 21
Size: 50 mm   South Africa, Mozambique, Reunion
ID: White with a brown pattern broken by large white spots with red circles inside; rhinophores and gill white with purple apices. On shallow water reefs.

Nudibranchia - "nudibranchs"

Goniobranchus sp. 22
Size: 40 mm   United Arab Emirates
ID: White with large purple spots over surface of the notum; marginal band yellow; rhinophores with orange tips; gill white with longitudinal orange lines on gill branches. On blue sponges.

Goniobranchus sp. 23
Size: 40 mm   United Arab Emirates
ID: White with blood red spots over the surface; mantle margin yellow and purple; rhinophores and gill white with opaque white markings.

Goniobranchus sp. 24
Size: 25 mm   Oman
ID: Uniformly white with large isolated yellow spots encircled with red rings; rhinophores and gill white with opaque white lines. Shallow water rocky reefs.

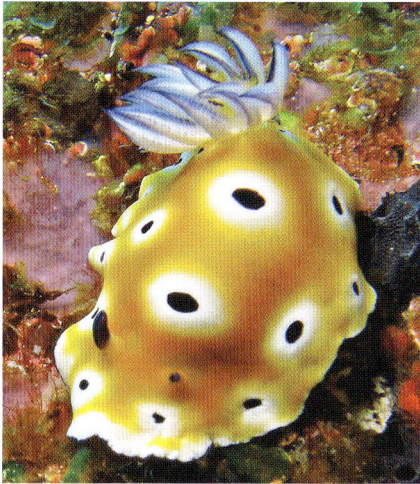

Goniobranchus leopardus (Rudman, 1987)
Size: 60 mm   Widespread in the Indo-Pacific
ID: White with a brown pattern broken by large white areas containing purple or purple-brown spots and rings; marginal band purple followed by white. On relatively shallow reefs out in the open.

Goniobranchus sp. 25
Size: 75 mm   Western Pacific Ocean
ID: Complex color pattern with brownish pigment on the white notum and opaque white spots as well as blue and yellow markings near the notal margin; rhinophores and gill dark grey with opaque white dots or lines; triangular tubercles on the notum. On shallow water reefs.

Goniobranchus collingwoodi (Rudman, 1987)
Size: 44 mm   Western Pacific Ocean
ID: Central portion of the dorsum reddish brown with black and white spots; an irregular purple marginal band; a white region separates the purple and brown and has a series of yellow spots; some larger purple spots may be found here also. Feeds on a dark green sponge.

Nudibranchia - "nudibranchs"

Goniobranchus fidelis (Kelaart, 1858)
Size: 30 mm   Widespread in the Indo-Pacific
ID: Creamy white with a wide, wavy, orange marginal band; a wine red line divides the marginal band from the creamy dorsum; gill and rhinophores black. Common inhabitant of patch reefs in 2-15 m.

Species of *Goniobranchus* with a white mantle and various marginal bands

Several species of *Goniobranchus* are characterized by having a white mantle with one or more marginal and submarginal bands. These species also have varied colored rhinophores and gill.

Goniobranchus preciosus (Kelaart, 1858)
Size: 30 mm   Western and central Pacific Ocean
ID: White with three colored marginal bands: thin opaque white, then deep red, followed by yellow; central region of the notum solid or mottled white; rhinophores dark brown with opaque white lamellae; gill lighter brown with white edges. Common in shallow subtidal lagoons and calm waters.

Goniobranchus galactos (Rudman & S. Johnson in Rudman, 1985)
Size: 25 mm   Marshall Is.
ID: White with either an orange, yellow, red or purple marginal band, or some combination of these; a submarginal reddish-maroon or purplish band with scattered bright white spots, which are probably glandular in nature.

Goniobranchus verrieri (Crosse, 1875)
Size: 17 mm   Widespread in the Indo-Pacific
ID: White with areas of transparency; outer red marginal band and inner yellow or orange submarginal band; rhinophoral clubs red to brown with white edging on the lamellae. Common from the intertidal zone to several meters, under coral rubble.

Goniobranchus sinensis (Rudman, 1985)
Size: 20 mm   Western Pacific Ocean
ID: White with dark red to black pigment on the gill and rhinophores; successive blue, black and orange-yellow marginal bands; orange spotting may be present on the notum. On shallow water reefs crawling in the open during the day.

Goniobranchus sp. 26
Size: 25 mm   Marshall Is.
ID: Yellow to orange with with opaque white and red submarginal bands and a reddish-brown marginal band; rhinophores and gill brown with opaque white lining on the gill branches and rhinophoral lamellae. Common on shallow reefs under coral rubble and debris; feeds on the sponge, *Chelonaplysilla violacea*.

Goniobranchus albonares (Rudman, 1990)
Size: 15 mm   Western Pacific Ocean
ID: White with translucent and opaque white pigment on the gill and rhinophores; an orange-yellow marginal band; orange spotting can be present on the notum. On shallow water reefs.

Goniobranchus sp. 27
Size: 22 mm   Papua New Guinea
ID: White with bright red spots on the notum; marginal line blue, thin, followed by a brown and a yellow band with a dense concentration opaque white mantle glands inside; gill and rhinophores reddish-brown with white dots. In shallow areas of mixed sand and rubble where it crawls in the open.

Nudibranchia - "nudibranchs"

Goniobranchus trimarginatus (Winckworth, 1946)
Size: 30 mm   India
ID: Pale grey with reddish spots irregularly scattered over the central part of the dorsum; mantle edge with a white, thin band, then a band of deep red and on the inside a slightly wider band of yellow; rhinophores and gill white.

Goniobranchus sp. 28
Size: 15 mm   Western Malaysia
ID: White with brown and opaque tubercles; gill and rhinophores white; successive translucent whitish red and orange-yellow marginal bands; scattered dark brown spots inside the marginal bands. On shallow water reefs.

Goniobranchus sp. 29
Size: 15 mm   Western Thailand
ID: White to yellow with a red mantle margin followed by black and opaque white submarginal bands. Similar to *Goniobranchus rubrocornutus* but with translucent white rhinophores and gill. On shallow reefs.

Goniobranchus rubrocornutus (Rudman, 1985)
Size: 13 mm   Western and central Pacific Ocean
ID: White to yellow with a either red, yellow or orange mantle edge followed by black and opaque white submarginal bands; gill and rhinophores white to red; some specimens with white rhinophoral lamellae. In shallow reefs under coral rubble.

Other varied species of *Goniobranchus*
The following species display variable color patterns and do not fit any of the categories above, therefore they are all listed together in this informal group.

Goniobranchus albopunctatus Garrett, 1879
Size: 30 mm   Widespread in the Indo-Pacific
ID: Yellow to red reticulated color, giving rise to white rings and specks; mantle margin blue, followed by dark blue, then yellow; foot yellow. On subtidal reefs in 5-20 m, often under coral rubble or out in the open.

154

Goniobranchus alius (Rudman, 1987)
Size: 40 mm   Indian Ocean
ID: Creamy white with six irregular greyish patches along the inner notum; mantle covered with small translucent pits, each with a yellow spot, giving the dorsum an uneven appearance; mantle margin with elongate purple marks and a diffuse creamy-yellow submarginal band. From the intertidal and shallow-patch reefs to 3 m.

Goniobranchus aureopurpureus (Collingwood, 1881)
Size: 40 mm   Western Pacific Ocean
ID: White with yellow and dull brown irregular spots over the mid-region; mantle margin with a diffuse purple band, with a series of large blue spots; rhinophores red-brown with white edges; gill brownish. On shallow patch reefs and in silty areas.

Goniobranchus rufomaculatus (Pease, 1871)
Size: 30 mm   Western and central Pacific Ocean
ID: White with small yellow spots and three translucent regions near the margin; marginal band made up of a series of broken, short blue lines; gill white; rhinophores dark brown to purple with white edges. On shallow patch reefs and nearshore areas.

Goniobranchus albopustulosus (Pease, 1860)
Size: 30 mm   Hawai'ian Is.
ID: Light yellow with large white tubercles; marginal band continuous or made up of a series of purple spots; gill white; rhinophores brown with white edges. Commonly under dead coral heads from the lower intertidal zone to a few meters.

Goniobranchus obsoletus (Rüppell & Leuckart, 1831)
Size: 40 mm   Persian Gulf, Red Sea
ID: White with tubercles and orange-brown reticulations; gill and rhinophores white; successive orange and black marginal bands. On shallow water reefs.

Goniobranchus sp. 30
Size: 25 mm   Indonesia
ID: Light blue with a white margin; two pinkish longitudinal lines meet in front of the rhinophores; rhinophores and gill pinkish. Could be a *Chromodoris* but the egg mass is unknown. On shallow rocky reefs.

Nudibranchia - "nudibranchs"

Goniobranchus decorus (Pease, 1860)
Size: 20 mm   New Caledonia, Japan, Hawai'ian Is.
ID: Translucent white with broad white longitudinal lines; line along the midline often forking in a "Y" just in front of the gill; mantle edge white, followed by orange-brown; large purple and small white spots scattered over the dorsum. From the intertidal zone to a few meters, often under coral rubble.

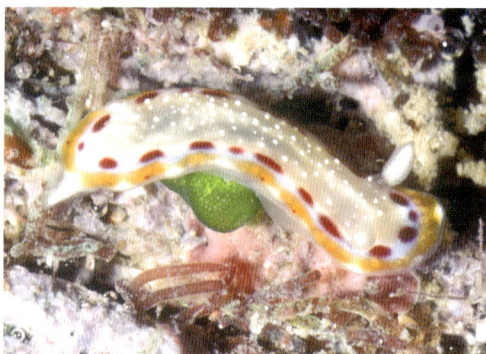

Goniobranchus lekker (Gosliner, 1994)
Size: 22 mm   Western Indian Ocean
ID: Translucent white; an interrupted marginal white line followed by a submarginal band of burnt orange; a band of light purple, central to the orange, with a series of large, dark purple to black spots; center of the dorsum with scattered opaque white tubercles; gill and rhinophores opaque white. From the intertidal zone to shallow subtidal reefs.

Goniobranchus sp. 31
Size: 30 mm   Marquesas Is.
ID: Translucent white with irregular frosting of opaque white; submarginal orange band; marginal band light blue with purple spots; rhinophores light brown with opaque white markings; gill white. Rocky reefs, 8 m.

Goniobranchus sp. 32
Size: 22 mm   Philippines
ID: Cream to brown with opaque white spots over most of the notum; undulating orange submarginal band with a few black spots at its widest areas; marginal blue band with large purple-black spots; rhinophores orange; gill brown with white spots.

Goniobranchus sp. 33
Size: 20 mm   Tahiti
ID: Cream to brown with opaque white tubercles over most of the notum; marginal band orange with a few black spots; submarginal purple-black spots; rhinophores and gill white.

Goniobranchus setoensis (Baba, 1938)
Size: 20 mm   Widespread in the Indo-Pacific
ID: Color pattern virtually identical to that of *Goniobranchus decorus* with the exception that the white lines are very fine and lack associated purple spots. Additional work is necessary to determine whether these are color variants or distinct species. Often under coral heads in 3-15 m.

Goniobranchus sp. 34
Size: 29 mm   Saudi Arabia
ID: Translucent grey with opaque white on the front and hind ends and near the outer edges; longitudinal opaque white lines and purple spots on the dorsum; a marginal orange band with opaque white spots; rhinophores translucent white with opaque white bands; gill white with orange tips. Shallow fringing reefs on sponges, in 5-10 m.

Goniobranchus pruna (Gosliner, 1994)
Size: 6 mm   South Africa, Madagascar
ID: Opaque white with a translucent white band and irregular orange patches along the margin; irregular dark plum spots on the notum; rhinophores and gill white with opaque white spots, tipped with orange. From the intertidal zone to a few meters.

Goniobranchus naiki (Valdés, Mollo & Ortea, 1999)
Size: 13 mm   India, Myanmar, Thailand
ID: Translucent white with numerous opaque white dots on the dorsum; scattered maroon patches with orange spots inside around the margin; gill and rhinophores light brown.

Goniobranchus tennentanus (Kelaart, 1859)
Size: 25 mm   Indian Ocean
ID: Cream-white with a marginal irregular blue band and large yellow spots; central portion of the body brown with large purple spots; rhinophores pale brown; gill off-white with dark grey lines. Intertidal zone and shallow reefs to 10 m.

Goniobranchus kitae (Gosliner, 1994)
Size: 18 mm   Madagascar, South Africa
ID: Translucent white with dark purple spots scattered over the mantle and along the mantle margin; marginal spots with concentrations of reflective yellow or orange-yellow granules; gill and rhinophores with white dots. Under small stones and coral rubble in 1-3 m.

Goniobranchus sp. 35
Size: 25 mm   Indonesia
ID: White with prominent dark purple conical tubercles; gill and rhinophores brownish grey with opaque white lines or spots; successive blue and orange-yellow marginal bands. On shallow rubble slopes.

157

Nudibranchia - "nudibranchs"

Goniobranchus cavae (Eliot, 1904)
Size: 50 mm   Western Indian Ocean
ID: Variable from cream to dirty brown with numerous black spots surrounded by white pigment; edge of the mantle purple; rhinophores and gill white with purple tips. Shallow rock reefs, intertidal zone to 24 m.

Goniobranchus tumuliferus (Collingwood, 1881)
Size: 18 mm   Western Pacific Ocean
ID: White with large crimson spots; clear margin followed by a yellow submarginal band; mantle glands along the edge of the mantle; rhinophores and gill pale translucent grey with opaque white apices.

Goniobranchus sp. 36
Size: 30 mm   United Arab Emirates
ID: Translucent white with a few large red or reddish purple spots; gill and rhinophores white; purple pigment on the notal and foot margins. On shallow water reefs.

Goniobranchus petechialis (Gould, 1852)
Size: 70 mm   Hawai'ian Is.
ID: Straw colored body with an orange mantle margin; dorsum with irregularly shaped red spots; gill white with red edging; rhinophores bright orange. It has not been seen in 50 years and there has been some speculation that it might be extinct. On shallow water reefs.

Goniobranchus orientalis (Rudman, 1983)
Size: 70 mm   Japan, Hong Kong (China), and Korea
ID: Translucent white with an orange marginal band; scattered dark brown spots or more dense spots, as in the present specimen, on the dorsum; gill may be lined with orange or black; rhinophores are orange. On shallow water reefs.

Goniobranchus sp. 37
Size: 35 mm   Okinawa (Japan)
ID: Translucent white with an opaque white marginal band; dorsum covered with red spots; rhinophores red; gill white. Under deal coral slabs in 10-20 m.

Goniobranchus sp. 38
Size: 15 mm   India
ID: Translucent white with large opaque white and brown patches and black spots; blue spots submarginally; grey submarginal band with orange spots; rhinophores and gill white with orange; notum with small conical tubercles. Intertidal on brown sponges.

Goniobranchus cazae (Gosliner & Behrens, 2004)
Size: 70 mm   Gulf of Oman
ID: Translucent white with scattered maroon patches on the notum and around the margin, having orange spots inside; gill and rhinophores white; successive orange and maroon marginal bands. On shallow water reefs.

Goniobranchus sp. 39
Size: 25 mm   Philippines, Indonesia
ID: White with numerous yellow spots; rhinophores and gill branches red-orange; mantle margin purple posteriorly and laterally and burnt orange anteriorly. Shallow rubble, 15 m.

Goniobranchus sp. 40
Size: 7 mm   Tropical Japan
ID: White with a series of longitudinal orange lines; rhinophores and gill with dark blue pigment. Under dead coral in 16 m.

Goniobranchus sp. 41
Size: 20 mm   Western and central Pacific Ocean
ID: Translucent white or yellowish orange with scattered opaque white spots over the surface of the body. In 1-15 m, under coral rubble.

Goniobranchus sp. 42
Size: 10 mm   Western and central Pacific Ocean
ID: Pink with successive red, yellow, and opaque white marginal bands; rhinophores orange with opaque white spots; off white gill also with opaque white spots. Under coral heads in 10-15 m.

Nudibranchia - "nudibranchs"

Goniobranchus sp. 43
Size: 20 mm   Western Pacific Ocean
ID: Greyish white with numerous opaque white pustules; a thin orange marginal band at the edge of the notum; gill and rhinophores with opaque white spots; rhinophores tipped with orange. Under coral heads in 25 m.

Goniobranchus sp. 44
Size: 10 mm   Indonesia
ID: Wine red covered with opaque white spots; additional purple, orange and opaque white pigment as well as scattered black spots near the notal margin; rhinophores and gill uniformly reddish.

Goniobranchus sp. 45
Size: 15 mm   Guam, Palau, Marshall Is.
ID: Opaque white with dirty brown mottling over the dorsal surface; marginal band orange; rhinophores white; gill covered with opaque white. Usually under rocks or in small caves in 5-20 m.

Goniobranchus sp. 46
Size: 15 mm   Indonesia
ID: Greyish with lighter radiating lines coming to elevated points; a series of purplish blue spots along the midline of the body; gill white; rhinophores tipped with red.

Goniobranchus sp. 47
Size: 20 mm   Marshall Is.
ID: Uniformly grey with a granular texture; rhinophores grey each with a yellow-orange band; gill also grey. Very cryptic on the sponges in which it feeds.

Goniobranchus sp. 48
Size: 30 mm   Indonesia, Marshall Is., Vanuatu
ID: White, densely mottled with brown; gill and rhinophores reddish; dorsum with high tubercles; it appears to be highly spiculate. On quiet lagoons; its appearance resembles the sponge on which it feed, *Dysidea arenaria*.

Mexichromis Bertsch, 1977

Species in this genus are distinguished by having a unique radular morphology. Most Indo-Pacific species have simple or complex tubercles on the notum. Species formerly included in *Pectenodoris* and *Durvilledoris* are now also included in *Mexichromis* (R. Johnson & Gosliner 2012).

Mexichromis multituberculata (Baba, 1953)
Size: 30 mm   Western Pacific Ocean
D: Yellowish cream with a series of purple spots along the edge of the mantle; notal surface covered with tall conical compound tubercles, tipped in purple; orange spots may be present along the edge of the notum. Protected waters on silty substrate in 5-20 m.

Mexichromis mariei (Crosse, 1872)
Size: 30 mm   Indian and western Pacific oceans
D: Pink to lavender with an orange submarginal band; tall tubercles on the dorsal surface with reddish-purple pigment. Generally on shallow silty substrate where it feeds on the sponge, *Dysidea* sp.

Mexichromis lemniscata (Quoy & Gaimard, 1832)
Size: 23 mm   Widespread in the Indo-Pacific
ID: Purple with a wide creamy yellow marginal band; a wide cream-white band along the mid-line, flanked by a thin wine red line, then a yellowish band and another thin red line. In the intertidal zone and on shallow patch reefs; feeds on sponges; egg ribbon white.

Mexichromis pusilla (Bergh, 1874)
Size: 20 mm   Widespread in the Indo-Pacific
ID: Pale pink to peach with a wide cream-white to yellowish marginal band, notched several times, purple fills the notches; an elongate white patch between the rhinophores and in front of the gill. From the intertidal zone to 20 m under coral rubble.

Mexichromis similaris (Rudman, 1986)
Size: 5 mm   Widespread in the Indo-Pacific
ID: Pink to purple; a white marginal band and a single white longitudinal line down the midline and encircling the gill; diffuse purple patches on the inside of the marginal line. Shallow water under coral rubble.

Mexichromis aurora (R. Johnson & Gosliner, 1998)
Size: 20 mm   Western Pacific Ocean
ID: Pink, darkening to maroon at the edges; three wide whitish-yellow longitudinal bands, each with a thin white outline; numerous dark pink to purple spots, and occasional white spots. On *Dysidea* sponges in 5-20 m.

Mexichromis sp. 1
Size: 30 mm   Tanzania
ID: Translucent white with numerous purple spots covering the dorsum; marginal band opaque white, with orange mantle glands.

Mexichromis sp. 2
Size: 12 mm   Vanuatu
ID: White with a red marginal band; dorsum with small purple spots; purple pigment only on the apices of the gill branches. On shallow reefs.

Mexichromis sp. 3
Size: 25 mm   Papua New Guinea
ID: Creamy white with scattered rounded tubercles, each with a purple spot at the apex; orange patches along the margin; a purple line along the edge of foot; rhinophores and gill white with purple tips. Sandy and silty habitats, 15 m.

Mexichromis sp. 4
Size: 45 mm   Philippines
ID: Pinkish purple fading to white towards the margin; orange patches forming an interrupted line around the margin; a purple line along edge of foot; rhinophores purple; gill white with purple lines on outer side of branches. Sandy and silty slopes, 20 m.

Mexichromis trilineata (A. Adams & Reeve, 1850)
Size: 12 mm   Western Pacific Ocean
ID: Purple with a thin marginal white line; three longitudinal lines on the dorsum, which can be yellow with a white edge on each side; in some specimens the lines are broken or

only the medial line is present. Feeds on the sponge, *Dysidea* sp. in which the animals may entirely embed themselves; on shallow reefs to 30 m.

Glossodoris Ehrenberg, 1831
Members of *Glossodoris* have flexible undulations of their mantle. The vibrating gill is composed of branches arranged in a double spiral.

Glossodoris acosti Matsuda & Gosliner, 2018
Size: 50 mm   Papua New Guinea, Philippines
ID: Mottled reddish brown and white; marginal light blue, followed by dark green, and lighter yellow-green; gill large. Mistakenly identified as *Glossodoris cincta*, but differs in having three marginal bands. Shallow reefs, under rubble.

163

Glossodoris sp. 1
Size: 50 mm   Philippines
ID: Mottled reddish brown and white; margin with three successive marginal bands of light blue, dark blue and bright yellow. Shallow reefs under coral rubble.

Glossodoris cincta **(Bergh, 1888)**
Size: 50 mm   Reunion, Mauritius
ID: Mottled reddish brown and white; margin with two lines outermost blue, followed by black. Animals with differently colored marginal lines constitute distinct species. Relatively shallow water on patch reefs, in the open or beneath coral rubble.

Glossodoris aeruginosa **Rudman, 1995**
Size: 70 mm   Australia, New Caledonia, Vanuatu
ID: Color complex, dominated by a regular pattern of raised white patches edged with a narrow brown line; patches aggregated into clusters, leaving some quite large blue-green regions; a broken brown submarginal band; mantle edge with a diffuse bluish band that darkens right at the mantle edge.

Glossodoris andersoni **Matsuda & Gosliner, 2018**
Size: 45 mm   Saudi Arabia
ID: Irregularly mottled with white and brown; brown more prominent centrally; submarginal band of yellow spots followed by black and light blue bands; rhinophores and gill with the same color as the body; gill laying flat on the body; mantle edge undulating. Under coral rubble on shallow reef flats, 7 m.

Glossodoris hikuerensis **(Pruvot-Fol, 1954)**
Size: 140 mm   Widespread in the Indo-Pacific
ID: Brown mottled with white; mantle margin with wide bands: pale brown, white, and almost black. In shallow water on patch reefs, generally under rubble; secretes a dense white liquid when disturbed.

Glossodoris gregorius **Rudman, 1986**
Size: 7 mm   Tanzania
ID: Brownish with scattered white spots; a marginal black band followed by a yellow submarginal band and a diffuse bluish inner region; gill white with black edges; rhinophores black with white specks. Known only from a single specimen.

Glossodoris rufomarginata (Bergh, 1890)
Size: 32 mm　　　　Widespread in the Indo-Pacific
ID: Pale grey speckled with orange-brown; a brown marginal band with a white submarginal band. On open rocky surfaces from 1-30 m.

Glossodoris sp. 2
Size: 42 mm　　　　Tropical southern Africa
ID: Translucent white with an opaque white marginal band; gill and rhinophores opaque white. On shallow to deep rocky reefs, in 15-42 m.

Glossodoris vespa Rudman, 1990
Size: 70 mm　　　　Queensland (Australia)
ID: Dark charcoal grey with black marginal and yellow submarginal bands; gill and rhinophores the same color as the notum. Crawling on rocky surfaces in 20 m on reefs.

Glossodoris bonwanga Matsuda & Gosliner, 2018
Size: 45 mm　　　South Africa, Mozambique, Tanzania
ID: Pinkish with opaque white spots; a wide black marginal band followed by a yellow submarginal band; gill lined with black lines; notum lacks tubercles. Feeds on a pink encrusting sponge.

Glossodoris sp. 3
Size: 60 mm　　　　Red Sea
ID: Snow-white with a narrow dark blue marginal band and a wider lighter blue submarginal band; gill light tan; rhinophores white.

Glossodoris sp. 4
Size: 40 mm　　　　Indonesia
ID: Milky white with an opaque white marginal band and a yellow submarginal band; Rhinophores and gill reddish brown.

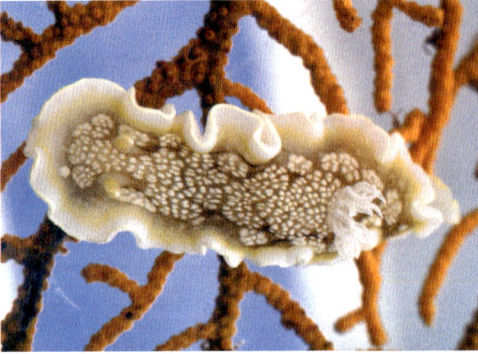

Glossodoris sp. 5
Size: 70 mm   Natal (South Africa)
ID: Light brown with small opaque white pustules; gill and rhinophores with opaque white pigment. Relatively deep water, 34 m, on rocky reefs.

Glossodoris sp. 6
Size: 39 mm   Philippines, Okinawa (Japan)
ID: Translucent white with numerous opaque white pustules over the entire surface; rhinophores and gill with opaque white and yellowish pigment. On shallow to deep reefs, 10-67 m.

Glossodoris sp. 7
Size: 55 mm   Papua New Guinea
ID: Uniformly yellow with a thin orange marginal band and a broad white submarginal band. The single specimen was collected from a sloping wall on a stretch of rugged limestone coastline, in 10 m.

Glossodoris buko Matsuda & Gosliner, 2018
Size: 18 mm   Philippines, New Guinea, Australia
ID: Translucent white with central opaque markings and a yellowish marginal band; rhinophores and gill cream-white. Virtually identical to *Glossodoris pallida*, but with larger white patch around gill and geographically isolated to the western Pacific. Feeds on yellowish-brown sponges.

Glossodoris pallida (Rüppell & Leuckart, 1831)
Size: 40 mm   Red Sea and western Indian Ocean
ID: Translucent white with central opaque markings and a yellow marginal band; rhinophores and gill cream-white. Walls and patch reefs in 3-30 m, on the tan sponge shown here.

Glossodoris sp. 8
Size: 30 mm   Madagascar
ID: Milky white with opaque white makings on the center of the notum forming a submarginal band; marginal line thin, orange; rhinophores and gill white with red markings; mantle edge undulating. Rocky reefs in shallow water.

Glossodoris sp. 9
Size: 25 mm   Sri Lanka
ID: White with numerous tiny black dots; isolated rounded tubercles, each tipped with light yellow; marginal band yellow; rhinophores dark brown apically; gill white with yellow pigment; margin slightly undulate.

Glossodoris pullata Rudman, 1995
Size: 50 mm   New Caledonia
ID: White with reticulate pattern of brown and white over most of the mantle; each rhinophore with white stalk and black club with white apex; gill whitish with black lines; mantle margin black.

Glossodoris sp. 10
Size: 30 mm   Philippines, Australia
ID: White with reticulate pattern of brown and white extending to the grey and white mantle margin; rhinophores and gill brown with white markings.

Glossodoris aureola Rudman, 1995
Size: 48 mm   New Caledonia
ID: Translucent white with bright orange spots; marginal band pale yellow; gill extremely large with an orange line on each branch; rhinophores whitish with orange markings.

167

Nudibranchia - "nudibranchs"

Doriprismatica d'Orbigny, 1839

Members of this group have more rigid undulations of the mantle edge and a narrower body shape than *Glossodoris*.

Doriprismatica misakinosibogae (Baba, 1988)
Size: 30 mm   Japan, Korea
ID: Translucent white body with an opaque white, slightly undulating margin; gill and rhinophores black. On shallow water reefs in 10-20 m, in the open during the day.

Doriprismatica paladentata (Rudman, 1986)
Size: 20 mm   Western Pacific Ocean
ID: White with scattered brown blotches; a submarginal bluish band around the edge of the mantle; gill whitish lined with black and brown; rhinophores black. Under rocks on shallow reef flats under rubble.

Doriprismatica sibogae (Bergh, 1905)
Size: 100 mm   Western Pacific
ID: Deep yellow with a black marginal line and a thick submarginal white band; gill and rhinophores black; mantle edge undulating. Under coral heads and on sponges inhabiting exposed vertical surfaces on outer reefs.

Doriprismatica plumbea (Pagenstecher, 1877)
Size: 55 mm   Western Indian Ocean, Red Sea
ID: Brown or reddish-brown with white speckling; notal edge with an inner broad diffuse yellow inner band, a narrow irregular greenish blue band, and marginal black band; rhinophores with opaque white lines; gill lined with black.

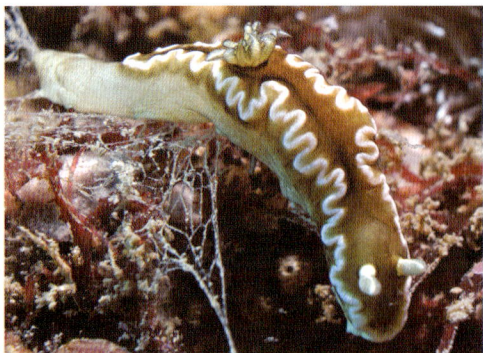

Doriprismatica dendrobranchia (Rudman, 1990)
Size: 100 mm   Queensland (Australia)
ID: Uniformly brown with an opaque white notal margin; rhinophores and gill whitish, gill branches subdivided near their tips. Known only from a handful of specimens.

Doriprismatica atromarginata (Cuvier, 1804)
Size: 100 mm   Widespread in the Indo-Pacific
ID: Light yellow with a black marginal line; gill and rhinophores black; mantle edge undulating. Under coral heads and on sponges inhabiting exposed vertical surfaces on outer reefs.

Doriprismatica stellata (Rudman, 1986)
Size: 130 mm   Western Pacific
ID: Black with white specks; mantle merges smoothly with the posterior end of the foot. The name refers to the Milky Way owing to the numerous white dots that appear like a galaxy. On rocky outcrops in the open in 15-20 m; feeds on foliose sponges.

Doriprismatica tibboeli (Valdés & M. J. Adams, 2005)
Size: 50 mm   Guam, Indonesia
ID: Black with a wide white marginal band; black rhinophores and gill. On submerged pinnacles, in areas of strong current where it feeds on a black sponge.

Doriprismatica balut Matsuda & Gosliner, 2018
Size: 35 mm   Philippines, Indonesia
ID: White with grey pigment and black and white spots; successive white, black, white, and brown marginal bands; rhinophores with the same color as the body and a thin black line on their posterior face; gill charcoal grey. Under

coral rubble in 3 m; feeds on the sponges, _Candidaspongia flabellata_ and _Phyllospongia lamellosa_.

Doriprismatica sp. 1
Size: 22 mm   Okinawa (Japan)
ID: White with a submarginal yellow band; gill and rhinophores black. On a mixed live and dead stony coral reef, approximately 5 m from the reef front.

Doriprismatica sp. 2
Size: 30 mm   Indonesia
ID: White with chocolate brown pigment in its center; marginal band yellow; rhinophores and gill dark brown.

Doriprismatica rossi Matsuda & Gosliner, 2018
Size: 40 mm   Saudi Arabia
ID: Whitish with fine dusting of brown and black speckles, giving the whole animal a brownish cast; submarginal band broad, golden-brown, followed by a narrow turquoise band and a black marginal band; rhinophores black with white lines on the rachises and lamellae; gill white and brown. Shallow areas of sand and mixed coral; nocturnally active, in 3 m.

Doriprismatica marinae Matsuda & Gosliner, 2018
Size: 30 mm   Madagascar
ID: Tan with opaque white speckles on the notum; marginal band black; rhinophores black with white lines; gill brownish with black lines; body edge highly undulate. On shallow reefs under dead coral slabs.

Doriprismatica sp. 3
Size: 30 mm   Indonesia
ID: White with brown and opaque white speckling over its surface; rhinophores and gill with opaque white pigment over their surface.

Doriprismatica sp. 4
Size: 45 mm   Indonesia
ID: Cream with brown speckling over the entire notum; marginal lines on the rhinophores and gill charcoal grey; a black line along the margin of the gill pocket and around the openings of the rhinophoral sheaths. Under coral rubble in 3 m.

Ardeadoris Rudman, 1984
Members of this group have bodies with numerous undulations of the mantle edge. Most species are whitish in color. Some species previously included in *Glossodoris* and *Noumea* (see Rudman, 1984) are now considered members of *Ardeadoris*, based on molecular evidence.

Ardeadoris egretta Rudman, 1984
Size: 100 mm   Western Pacific
ID: White body; gill and rhinophores with an orange marginal band. On relatively shallow reef flats, often seen crawling in the open over the surface of living reefs.

Ardeadoris scottjohnsoni Bertsch & Gosliner, 1989
Size: 30 mm   Okinawa (Japan), Hawai'ian Is.
ID: White with an orange marginal band; gill and rhinophores black. Under ledges on limestone reefs in 10-20 m.

***Ardeadoris* sp. 1**
Size: 45 mm   Solomon Is.
ID: Cream-white with an opaque white submarginal band and a red-orange marginal band; rhinophores translucent white with an opaque white line on the posterior side and a red line at the base; gill branches opaque white with red bases. On fringing reefs, in 8-12 m.

Ardeadoris averni (Rudman, 1985)
Size: 55 mm   Western Pacific Ocean
ID: Pure white with an orange to bold red band along the highly ruffled margin; rhinophores the same red color as

mantle margin; gill brownish to white. Relatively deep water, 20-30 m.

***Ardeadoris* sp. 2**
Size: 20 mm   Tuamotu Archipelago
ID: Uniformly bluish-white; rhinophores and gill bright red; mantle margin undulated, edged in pale yellow. Shallow lagoons, 2 m.

Ardeadoris angustolutea (Rudman, 1990)
Size: 25 mm   Western and central Pacific Ocean
ID: Translucent cream with a diffuse white medial region; submarginal band creamy-yellow; marginal border white, with a very narrow yellow line along the edge; gill and rhinophores edged with reddish-brown. On shallow patch reefs under coral rubble in 3-15 m.

Nudibranchia - "nudibranchs"

Ardeadoris sp. 3
Size: 60 mm   Philippines
ID: Yellowish brown over most of the notum, white towards the mantle margin, surrounded by narrow red line; rhinophore solid red, lacking white lines; gill uniformly red. Shallow reefs under rocks, 5 m.

Ardeadoris sp. 4
Size: 50 mm   Philippines
ID: Cream notum with red marginal band; posterior side of each rhinophore with basal orange line; gill white with orange markings at base. Shallow reefs, 15 m.

Ardeadoris electra (Rudman, 1990)
Size: 40 mm   Indian and western Pacific oceans
ID: Milky white with a bright yellow marginal band followed by an opaque white submarginal band; an opaque white line on the center of the anterior face of the rhinophores and dashes of brownish pigment on the gill. In deep water at 70 m.

Ardeadoris cruenta (Rudman, 1986)
Size: 55 mm   Western Pacific Ocean
ID: Cream with blood red spots and broad white and yellow marginal bands. On reef fronts and drop-offs in water from 1-30 m.

Ardeadoris symmetrica (Rudman, 1990)
Size: 45 mm   Widespread in the Indo-Pacific
ID: Light brown with symmetrical opaque white markings on the notum; marginal band red; rhinophores and gill apices also red. Under rocks and coral heads in 10-25 m.

Ardeadoris rubroannulata (Rudman, 1986)
Size: 80 mm   New Caledonia, Australia
ID: Pinkish to yellow with a yellow marginal band followed by a narrow red band and an inner opaque white band; gill and rhinophores reddish.

Ardeadoris sp. 5
Size: 20 mm   Tahiti
ID: Light tan with opaque white spots; marginal band white; rhinophores orange; gill slate blue with white; mantle margin slightly undulated. In lagoons in relatively deep water, 30 m.

Ardeadoris undaurum (Rudman, 1985)
Size: 66 mm   Indian Ocean
ID: Translucent white with large opaque white blotches over the dorsal surface; yellow marginal band; gill white, tipped in red; rhinophores also white with yellow apices. Crawling on rock surfaces in 3 m.

Ardeadoris tomsmithi (Bertsch & Gosliner, 1989)
Size: 35 mm   Japan, Marshall Is., Hawai'ian Is.
ID: Brownish with a marginal band that varies from white to yellow; dorsal surface crowded with large white or yellow spots; rhinophores vary from brown in the Marshall Is. to blue-black in the Hawai'ian Is.; highly undulating margin. On shear faces and sponge covered overhangs.

Ardeadoris carlsoni (Rudman, 1986)
Size: 55 mm   Fiji
ID: Pale orange-yellow, with paler patches especially between the gill and rhinophores; a thick bright orange-red marginal band and a broad whitish submarginal band. Known only from a single specimen collected by Bruce Carlson.

Ardeadoris poliahu (Bertsch & Gosliner, 1989)
Size: 35 mm   Hawai'ian Is., possibly Thailand
ID: Dorsum greyish-white to pale reddish-brown, with patches of darker pigment and scattered white flecks; marginal band

white, followed by a red submarginal line, and a wide white band; rhinophores and gill white to pale brown with red lines. On relatively shallow rocky outcrops in 20-30 m.

173

Nudibranchia - "nudibranchs"

Verconia Pruvot-Fol, 1931

Members of this group are relatively small and have a distinctive radula with an inner lateral tooth that is much wider than the other teeth.

Verconia decussata (Risbec, 1928)
Size: 12 mm   Indian and western Pacific oceans
ID: Pink or white with reddish markings on the gill and rhinophores. Very similar to *Noumea simplex*, but with an undulating mantle margin that gives the body a cruciform appearance. Feeds on pink sponges on relatively shallow reefs.

Verconia romeri (Risbec, 1928)
Size: 20 mm   Western Pacific Ocean
ID: Pink with a white marginal band; gill and rhinophores orange. On a pink, aplysillid sponge; gill vibrates while crawling.

Verconia sudanica (Rudman, 1985)
Size: 20 mm   Red Sea
ID: Translucent white with small scattered orange spots on the notum; mantle margin yellowish-orange; gill and rhinophores translucent white with opaque white lines.

Verconia simplex (Pease, 1871)
Size: 12 mm   Widespread in the Indo-Pacific
ID: Color variable from white to pink; border of the mantle sometimes with a broken orange band; gill and rhinophores tipped with deep orange. Feeds on pink sponges, including *Darwinella*.

Verconia hongkongiensis (Rudman, 1990)
Size: 6 mm   Japan, Hong Kong (China)
ID: Uniformly translucent white; gill and rhinophores translucent white with bright red lines.

Verconia sp. 1
Size: 15 mm   South Africa, Madagascar
ID: White with scatted orange spots on the notum and an orange marginal line; rhinophores and gill white; rhinophores with orange tips. Under coral rubble on shallow reefs, 3-10 m.

Verconia sp. 2
Size: 12 mm   Papua New Guinea
ID: White with orange spots around the margin and smaller orange spots scattered over the surface of the notum; gill and rhinophores translucent grey, rhinophores with opaque white apices. Under coral rubble on patch reefs and barrier reefs.

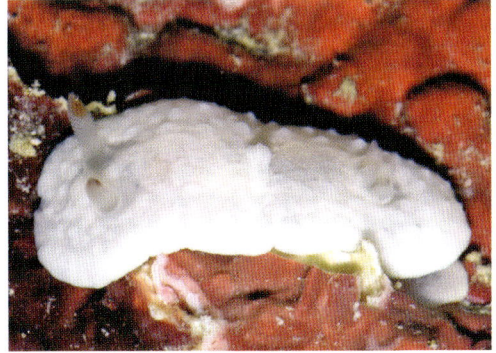

Verconia sp. 3
Size: 15 mm   Vanuatu
ID: Uniformly opaque white; gill white with opaque orange lines; rhinophores with an orange apex; dorsum with rounded tubercles.

Verconia subnivalis (Baba, 1987)
Size: 30 mm   Japan
ID: White with an orange-yellow marginal band and an inner yellow band; rhinophores reddish purple with opaque white lines; gill translucent white with opaque white lines.

Verconia nivalis (Baba, 1937)
Size: 20 mm   Japan, Korea, Hong Kong (China)
ID: Uniformly translucent white with a few scattered orange spots and a yellow margin; gill and rhinophores translucent white with light orange apices. On shallow reefs from 3-10 m.

Verconia sp. 4
Size: 15 mm   Papua New Guinea, Marshall Is.
ID: Pinkish-red with a faint opaque white network on the dorsum; marginal band white; bright red rhinophores and red lines on the gill branches, both with white bases.

Verconia cf. *laboutei* (Rudman, 1986)
Size: 15 mm   Western Pacific Ocean
ID: Yellow with red gill and rhinophores. Similar to *Noumea laboutei* described from New Caledonia but is not certain whether that species has the reticulations on the mantle present in specimen in this photo. Feeds on sponges with striations closely matching the white reticulations.

Verconia sp. 5
Size: 20 mm   Papua New Guinea
ID: Yellow with white reticulations; gill and rhinophores red. Similar to *Noumea verconiforma* but is unclear whether the yellow mantle represents variation or is characteristic of a distinct species. Under coral rubble on the crest of barrier reefs near passes; vibrates its gill.

Verconia sp. 6
Size: 15 mm   Vanuatu
ID: Yellowish green with dark reddish brown rhinophores; reddish brown lines on the gill.

Verconia verconiforma (Rudman, 1995)
Size: 12 mm   Western and central Pacific Ocean
ID: White with red rhinophores and gill. Its reticulated pattern of lines resembles the structure of a sponge on which it feeds. Under coral rubble in relatively shallow water; vibrates its gill.

Verconia alboannulata (Rudman, 1986)
Size: 25 mm   Indian and western Pacific oceans
ID: Translucent pink with a wide cream colored marginal band; a series of reddish purple spots along the inside of this band; a distinctive white midline branches between the rhinophores, then forms an oval that encircles the gill; gill and rhinophores orange.

Verconia norba (Er. Marcus & Ev. Marcus, 1970)
Size: 25 mm   Widespread in the Indo-Pacific
ID: Pink to purplish-orange or purple; broad cream marginal band, with reddish-purple submarginal markings; mid-dorsal band of similar white or cream color, it may break halfway to the gill, then forms a patch that circles the gill; gill and rhinophores tinged with orange-red.

Verconia sp. 7
Size: 12 mm   Hawai'ian Is.
ID: Purple with a broad white marginal band, and a purple submarginal line; a straight, uninterrupted mid-dorsal white band. Under small stones in 3 m.

Verconia sp. 8
Size: 15 mm   Papua New Guinea, Philippines
ID: Purple with red, dark purple and white markings; a distinct white, wide, irregular mid-dorsal band. Under rocks on shallow patch reefs from 3-15 m.

Verconia varians (Pease, 1871)
Size: 15 mm   Widespread in the Indo-Pacific
ID: Translucent with the internal viscera giving it a pink to orange appearance; marginal band wide, cream, with a thin red line along its inner edge; a broken white line down the center of the dorsum; gill and rhinophores red-orange. Under coral rubble on shallow reefs.

Verconia purpurea (Baba, 1949)
Size: 15 mm   Japan
ID: Bright pinkish purple, with a wide medial white band, which extends from the rhinophores to the gill; marginal band opaque white to creamy-yellow, with a thin series of red submarginal specks; gill and rhinophores orange-red.

Verconia sp. 9
Size: 14 mm   Marshall Is.
ID: Pinkish-red with a thin white margin; rhinophores and gill pinkish-red with red lines; mantle edge undulating. Shallow water under coral heads on pink sponges, in 4-12 m.

Verconia sp. 10
Size: 8 mm   Madagascar
ID: Pink with opaque white pustules on the notum; a solid orange marginal band on the edge of the notum; rhinophores and gill pale grey. Under coral rubble in 1-2 m.

Nudibranchia - "nudibranchs"

Verconia catalai (Rudman, 1990)
Size: 12 mm   New Caledonia
ID: Opaque white with bright red radiating markings on the notum; rhinophores bright orange; gill pale purple. Feeds on a yellow sponge in about 6 m.

Verconia sp. 11
Size: 25 mm   Australia
ID: Yellowish body with a yellow marginal band and an opaque white inner band; gill and rhinophores dark purple.

Verconia sp. 12
Size: 25 mm   Kwazulu Natal (South Africa)
ID: Uniformly translucent white with an opaque white marginal band; opaque white and oblong to round mantle glands visible away from the notal margin; gill and rhinophores translucent white with bright red lines.

Verconia sp. 13
Size: 20 mm   Papua New Guinea
ID: Pale red; a light area in the center with fine opaque white spots; mantle glands large, orange; rhinophores and gill white with orange tips; mantle edge slightly undulating.

Diversidoris Rudman, 1987

This group includes a few species that are distinguishable from other chromodorids by having small tubercles on the dorsum and a wide, undulating mantle similar to that of species of *Glossodoris*, but the branchial leaves do not move rhythmically.

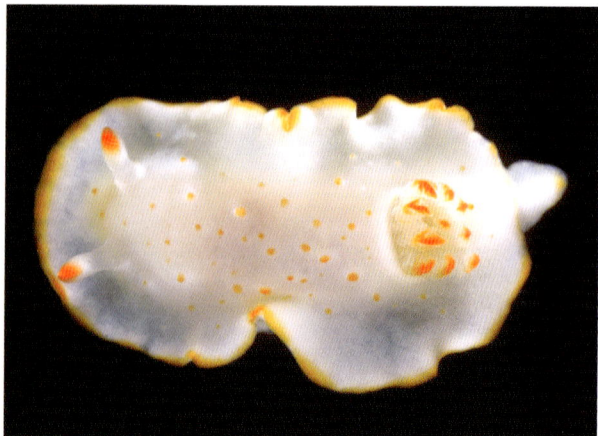

Diversidoris aurantionodulosa Rudman, 1987
Size: 20 mm   Indian and western Pacific
ID: White with orange spots on elevated tubercles; marginal band orange; gill leaves with an orange line on the primary axis of each branch; rhinophores with an orange apex. Feeds on the pink sponge *Darwinella* sp. on shallow reefs.

178

Diversidoris sp. 1
Size: 15 mm　　　　　　　　　Papua New Guinea
ID: Translucent white with opaque white close to the mantle margins; red lines on the anterior and posterior ends; rhinophores and gill white basally with red tips; body smooth. Under coral rubble on shallow reefs, in 7 m.

Diversidoris sp. 2
Size: 25 mm　　　　　　　　　　　　　Indonesia
ID: Bluish white with opaque white pustules on the notum; submarginal band white, marginal band orange; rhinophores and gill bluish basally with brown tips.

Diversidoris flava (Eliot, 1904)
Size: 15 mm　　　　Widespread in the Indo-Pacific
ID: Bright yellow; a series of red-orange spots form an irregular line along the border of the mantle; gill and rhinophores bright yellow. Feeds on yellow sponges on shallow reefs.

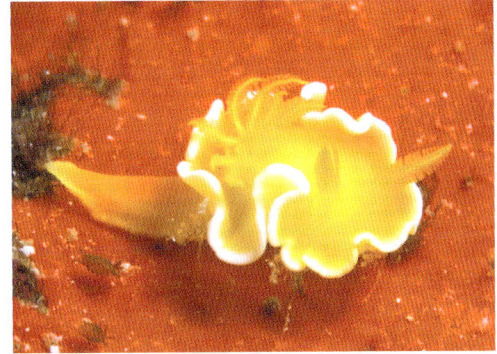

Diversidoris crocea (Rudman, 1986)
Size: 25 mm　　　　Western and central Pacific Ocean
ID: Bright yellow with a thick opaque white marginal band; gill and rhinophores yellow; mantle margin undulating. Feeds on yellow sponges in relatively shallow water.

Thorunna Bergh, 1878
Species of *Thorunna* have either mantle glands restricted to the anterior and posterior ends of the animal or more typically, entirely absent. The body is elongate with a relatively high profile and the gill vibrates.

Thorunna australis (Risbec, 1928)
Size: 15 mm　　　　　　　　Indo-Pacific
ID: Rose pink with white lines and blue spots; opaque white mantle glands at both ends; rhinophores white, each with a red band. Similar to some species of *Hypselodoris* and *Noumea*, but lacks contrasting pigment in the center. Frequently beneath coral rubble in shallow patch reefs.

Nudibranchia - "nudibranchs"

Thorunna kahuna R. Johnson & Gosliner, 2001
Size: 30 mm   Hawai'ian Is.
ID: Purple with a darker purple submarginal line; gill and rhinophores red; mantle glands visible as opaque white spots at both ends of the animal. On shallow water reefs and in harbors where they feed on the sponge, *Dysidea* sp.

Thorunna purpureopedis Rudman & S. Johnson *in* Rudman, 1985
Size: 10 mm   Marshall Is., Japan
ID: Purple with an undulating broad orange to red band that extends around the entire margin of the notum; gill and rhinophores dark orange-red.

Thorunna sp. 1
Size: 20 mm   Philipiines
ID: Deep purple with an orange marginal band; gill and rhinophores orange. Similar to *Thorunna purpureopedis* but lacks inner red submarginal band. In coral rubble, 20 m.

Thorunna montrouzieri Rudman, 1995
Size: 14 mm   New Caledonia, possibly Japan
ID: White with broad red markings on the sides and anterior margin of the body; purple markings behind the anterior red patch and also at the posterior end of the mantle; gill and rhinophores red.

Thorunna sp. 2
Size: 10 mm   Western Pacific Ocean
ID: Deep purple with an orange-yellow marginal band; gill and rhinophores reddish orange. On shallow reef slopes.

Thorunna furtiva Bergh, 1878
Size: 20 mm   Western Pacific Ocean
ID: Opaque white with an orange to brown marginal band; an orange line up the anterior and posterior midline of the rhinophores and along the outer edge of the gill. Feeds on the sponge *Dysidea herbacea* on intertidal and shallow subtidal limestone platforms.

***Thorunna africana* Rudman, 1984**
Size: 20 mm   Tanzania and the Red Sea
ID: White with a yellow-gold marginal band; tips of the rhinophores and lines on the gill brown. The gill wiggles rhythmically as the animal crawls; feeds on *Dysidea* sp.

***Thorunna daniellae* (Kay & Young, 1969)**
Size: 15 mm   Widespread in the Indo-Pacific
ID: White with a "smudged" purple submarginal band on the mantle and posterior part of the foot; gill and rhinophores orange-red; mantle glands absent. On shallow reefs, 3-30 m.

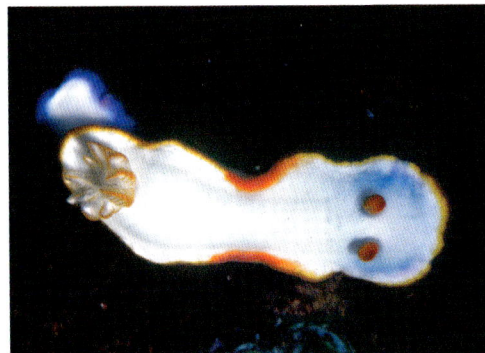

***Thorunna horologia* Rudman, 1984**
Size: 12 mm   Western Indian Ocean
ID: White with a red outer and yellow-orange inner marginal line, which thickens midway down the body; a purple marginal line present on the foot. In shallow waters.

***Thorunna* sp. 3**
Size: 20 mm   Marquesas Is.
ID: Pink with a white longitudinal line on the anterior part of the notum; submarginal opaque white band and marginal purple band; foot with a purple band; rhinophores and gill white basally and orange apically. On shallow rocky reefs, 8 m.

***Thorunna* sp. 4**
Size: 20 mm   Thailand
ID: Translucent white with opaque white spots centrally; reddish orange and opaque white patches with black spots on the mantle edge; rhinophores red-orange basally, white apically; gill translucent white with opaque white.

***Thorunna* sp. 5**
Size: 10 mm   Marshall Is.
ID: Pinkish with a translucent margin surrounded by purple spots; opaque white spots on the anterior and posterior ends; four broad longitudinal white bands on the notum; a red-orange band on the anterior margin. On shallow reef pinnacles.

Thorunna sp. 6
Size: 15 mm   Philippines
ID: Rose pink with white lines and blue spots; mantle margin with purple spots; rhinophores uniformly red; white mantle glands visible anteriorly. Similar to *Thorunna australis* but with shorter, wider body and more opaque lines on the dorsum.

Thorunna sp. 7
Size: 10 mm   Madagascar
ID: Pinkish with a translucent margin surrounded by purple spots; four broad longitudinal white bands on the notum; a red-orange band and an opaque white patch on the anterior margin; white rhinophores with purple apices. On sea mounts in 20 m.

Thorunna florens (Baba, 1949)
Size: 10 mm   Western Pacific Ocean
ID: Translucent whitish-purple with a darker purple submarginal band or a series of spots; dorsum with a double ring of outer yellow and inner white circles; rhinophores and gill with red pigment; red yellow and white pigment on the anterior margin. On shallow slopes in volcanic sand.

Thorunna punicea (Rudman, 1995)
Size: 12 mm   Indian and western Pacific oceans
ID: Deep purple with a narrow opaque white marginal line; base of the gill and rhinophores dark purple with the outer two-thirds bright orange. On reefs from 10 to 87 m.

Thorunna halourga R. Johnson & Gosliner, 2001
Size: 20 mm   Western Pacific Ocean
ID: Pinkish purple, darker purple at the anterior and posterior ends; submarginal band opaque white; gill and rhinophores red-orange. On shallow water reefs under coral rubble.

Thorunna sp. 8
Size: 25 mm   Australia
ID: Purple with a few orange spots with red centers; additional red spots submarginally; gill and rhinophores dark purple; anterior end of the body with a yellow-orange line.

Thorunna sp. 9
Size: 10 mm   Marquesas Is.
ID: Deep pinkish purple with an orange marginal band and an opaque white central band that surrounds the gill pocket; gill and rhinophores reddish; deep purple mantle glands surrounded by opaque white located at the anterior and posterior ends of the body.

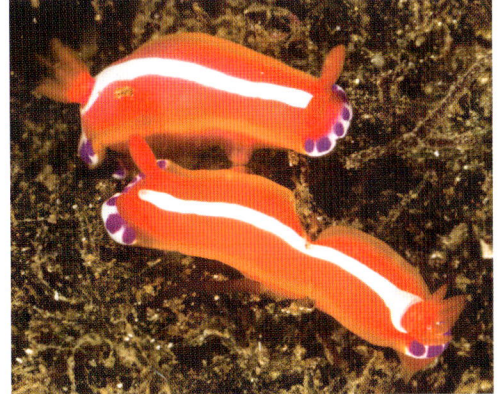

Hypselodoris Simpson, 1855
Species of *Hypselodoris* usually have a high body profiles relative to other chromodorids. Their radular teeth have a bifid cusp. *Hypselodoris* was most recently reviewed by Gosliner and R. Johnson (1999) but there are still several undescribed species in the Indo-Pacific tropics.

Species with dense alternating mantle glands
The four species below have mantle glands that extend the entire perimeter of the mantle and are densely packed with alternating large and small glands.

Hypselodoris purpureomaculosa Hamatani, 1995
Size: 35 mm   Western Pacific Ocean
ID: White with a thick orange marginal band; dorsum with a series of burgundy to purple markings; rhinophores and gill dark orange. On shallow ledges where it feeds on non-spiculate sponges.

Nudibranchia - "nudibranchs"

Hypselodoris iacula Gosliner & R. Johnson, 1999
Size: 50 mm   Indian and western Pacific oceans
ID: Pinkish-white with a thick scalloped orange mantle margin, interrupted by opaque white spots; a purple spot on the apex of each scallop; a white network of opaque white lines covers the dorsum; Rhinophores and gill orange. On steep walls among sponges in 20-25 m.

Hypselodoris maridadilus Rudman, 1977
Size: 35 mm   Widespread in the Indo-Pacific
ID: Yellow with a purple margin on the mantle and foot; dorsum with 5 longitudinal purple lines, between these lines are a series of diffuse violet transverse bands; gill and rhinophores bright orange-red. From the intertidal zone to 20 m.

Hypselodoris alburtuqali Gosliner & Johnson in Epstein et al., 2018
Size: 30 mm   Red Sea
ID: Reddish-cream with opaque white areas at the anterior and posterior ends; longitudinal opaque white lines and dark red spots on the notum; marginal band red; rhinophores white with two red bands; gill white with orange and red pigment. Closely resembles *Goniobranchus* sp. 29. Shallow reef flats under coral rubble in 7 m.

Species with purple or white longitudinal lines
The following species are characterized by having a series of longitudinal purple or white lines, in some cases with other lines or spots of different colors.

Hypselodoris emma Rudman, 1977
Size: 40 mm   Indian and western Pacific oceans
ID: Pale cream, with a purple margin on the mantle and foot; 3 purple longitudinal lines on the dorsum, between which there are brown lines; the latter vary greatly depending upon location; gill and rhinophores red. On shallow reefs from the intertidal to 20 m.

Hypselodoris whitei (A. Adams & Reeve, 1850)
Size: 35 mm   Indian and western Pacific oceans
ID: Whitish with a purple marginal band and 5 longitudinal purple lines; dorsal surface with pustules; rhinophores red-orange; gill red. Often confused with *Hypselodoris maridadilus*. Crawling in the open on shallow reefs flats in 10-20 m.

Hypselodoris sp. 1
Size: 15 mm   Tuamotu Archipelago
ID: Translucent pinkish with longitudinal opaque white lines and purple patches on the head, posterior end of mantle and margin of the foot; marginal band red with whitish areas at several points; mantle glands white, prominent at both ends of the body; rhinophores white with three red bands; gill red. Shallow reef flats under coral rubble near passes, in 1 m.

Hypselodoris maculosa (Pease, 1871)
Size: 40 mm   Widespread in the Indo-Pacific
ID: White centrally, brown or purple marginally, with a series of thin white lines, some of which may be broken into specks; purple and opaque white spots distributed between the white lines; rhinophores white with two red bands. Abundant in shallow water reefs.

Hypselodoris decorata (Risbec, 1928)
Size: 30 mm   Western Pacific Ocean
ID: Cream centrally, orange marginally, with a series of thin white lines; purple and opaque white spots between the white lines. Similar to _Hypselodoris maculosa_ but with three rather than two rhinophoral red rings. Shallow reefs, 10-15 m.

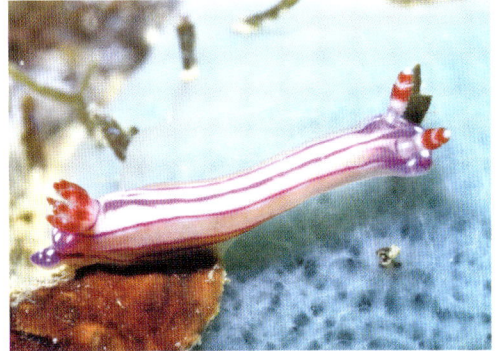

Hypselodoris juniperae Gosliner & R. Johnson _in_ Epstein _et al.,_ 2018
Size: 15 mm   Western Indian Ocean
ID: Light purple with a pale orange marginal band, dorsum with distinct opaque spots and larger dark purple spots; rhinophores with two red rings.

Hypselodoris alboterminata Gosliner & R. Johnson, 1999
Size: 15 mm   Hawai'ian Is.
ID: Yellow-white with longitudinal purple lines; front and rear portions of the mantle purple, with raised opaque white spots; rhinophores white with 2-3 red bands. On reefs in 3-20 m.

Hypselodoris yarae Gosliner & R. Johnson *in* Epstein *et al.,* 2018
Size: 20 mm   Madagascar, Philippines, Marshall Is.
ID: White centrally, with a broad and undulating brown to purple marginal band; dorsum with a series of white lines

and brown spots; rhinophores white with 2-3 red bands. On shallow reef flats.

Hypselodoris insulana Gosliner & R. Johnson, 1999
Size: 50 mm   Midway, Kure (Leeward Hawai'ian Is.)
ID: Salmon-pink with about 20 opaque white longitudinal lines and a purple submarginal band; margin transparent with opaque white mantle glands visible; gill white basally with red rachises; rhinophores with 1-2 red rings each. Feeds on blue sponges.

Hypselodoris violabranchia Gosliner & R. Johnson, 1999
Size: 20 mm   Hawai'ian Is.
ID: Salmon with fine white lines; anterior and posterior ends of the body and foot purple; gill translucent with a purple outer edge; rhinophores with a violet line on their posterior face. On shallow reefs and breakwaters in 10-20 m.

Hypselodoris peasei (Bergh, 1880)
Size: 20 mm   Northern Hawai'ian Is.
ID: White with a series of purple spots and numerous opaque white longitudinal lines; a violet-purple band on the margin of the mantle and foot; rhinophores with 1-2 red-orange bands; gill with opaque white pigment and red-orange apices. In shallow water along rock faces where it aggregates to feed upon the yellow sponge, *Luffariella* sp.

Hypselodoris bertschi Gosliner & R. Johnson, 1999
Size: 25 mm   Northern Hawai'ian Is., perhaps Japan
ID: Pink-white with longitudinal opaque white lines; marginal band orange and purple spots on the notum; rhinophores white with orange tips. Although superficially similar to other "white-lined" species of *Hypselodoris* it is more closely related to species without white lines. Under rocks in the lower intertidal zone to 5 m.

Hypselodoris sp. 2
Size: 25 mm   Oman
ID: Dense brown pigment with white spots arranged in longitudinal lines on the center of the dorsum; submarginal band white, with black spots; marginal band opaque white with blue spots; rhinophores red with white tips; gill translucent white with red on the branches. May be a color variant of *H. carnea*. On shallow rocky reefs.

Hypselodoris carnea (Bergh, 1889)
Size: 45 mm   Western Indian Ocean
ID: White with brownish pigment on the notum as well as opaque white lines and black spots; marginal band purple; gill and rhinophores red. From the lower intertidal zone to 20 m on rocky reefs.

Hypselodoris reidi Gosliner & R. Johnson, 1999
Size: 50 mm   Indonesia, Philippines
ID: White, covered with a yellow reticulated pattern; a distinctive pink band along the margin of the head and the posterior end of the body; notum with a brown saddle with evenly distributed pinkish white spots; gill and rhinophores tan. In 3-25 m, feeding on the sponge *Dysidea* sp.

Hypselodoris rudmani Gosliner & R. Johnson, 1999
Size: 45 mm   Western Indian Ocean
ID: Translucent white with scattered opaque white, black, and yellow spots; marginal band purple-blue; rhinophores dark-red; gill white with a thin orange-red line on each side of the rachis of each branch. From the intertidal zone in rock pools to 30 m.

Species with an elevated gill peduncle
The following species have an elevated gill that is reminiscent of a volcano. Both molecular and morphological evidence suggest these species are more closely related to each other than to other species of *Hypselodoris*.

Hypselodoris krakatoa Gosliner & R. Johnson, 1999
Size: 55 mm   Western Pacific Ocean
ID: Mottled red with tan patches; a purple band along the edge of the foot and on the anterior end of the notum; a series of black longitudinal lines bordered by an opaque white, almost silvery, stippling. On shallow to deep reefs, under coral heads or out in the open.

Hypselodoris cerisae Gosliner & R. Johnson _in_ Epstein _et al.,_ 2018
Size: 45 mm   Taiwan, Japan, Malaysia
ID: White a series of black longitudinal lines and pink pigment centered on the notum. Similar but genetically distinct from *Hypselodoris krakatoa*.

Hypselodoris regina Er. Marcus & Ev. Marcus, 1970
Size: 45 mm   Western Indian Ocean
ID: Orange with bluish white patches and black lines on the notum, foot and sides of the body; gill and rhinophores red-orange. On shallow reefs where it feeds on the sponge, *Dysidea* sp.

Hypselodoris jacksoni Wilson & Willan, 2007
Size: 60 mm   Australia
ID: Translucent white with a network of thick dark brown lines, yellow spots, and an orange notal margin; gill and rhinophores red. In the open on shallow rocky reefs, in 10-30 m.

Hypselodoris iba Gosliner & R. Johnson *in* Epstein *et al.,* 2018
Size: 40 mm   Indonesia, Philippines
ID: White with a yellow or white marginal band and a purplish, diffuse submarginal band; a prominent reddish saddle may be present on the center of the notum in some specimens; gill and rhinophores orange to red. Purple specimens and white specimens with a brownish saddle have been observed mating with each other and are genetically identical. On shallow water reefs.

Species with a yellow marginal line and red or purple lines or spots

This group includes the next three, closely related species that are respectively from the Hawai'ian Is., the western Pacific and the western Indian Ocean.

Hypselodoris paulinae Gosliner & R. Johnson, 1999

Size: 65 mm   Hawai'ian Is.
ID: Opaque white with a wide yellow marginal band, and large red spots; foot with a purple marginal band; rhinophores red-orange; gill white with red-orange rachises. On volcanic rock faces in 20-30 m.

Hypselodoris kaname Baba, 1994

Size: 45 mm   Western Pacific Ocean
ID: Opaque white with a yellow marginal band and a purple submarginal band; notum with well-developed mid-dorsal lines and few reddish purple spots. Shallow to deep water on reefs in 7-48 m; feeds on non-spiculate sponges.

Hypselodoris fucata Gosliner & R. Johnson, 1999

Size: 50 mm   Western Indian Ocean
ID: Pinkish white with three thin opaque white longitudinal lines; an orange-red line flanks each of these; other broken red and white lines along the edge of the mantle; submarginal band broad, broken, pinkish-purple; marginal band yellow; rhinophores orange red. From the intertidal zone to about 25 m.

Species with yellow spots

The next several species have yellow spots on the notum, but are not necessary closely related evolutionarily.

Hypselodoris bollandi Gosliner & R. Johnson, 1999

Size: 43 mm   Philippines, Japan
ID: White with the dorsum covered with yellow spots; dark blue lobed markings on each side of the body and frontal mantle; rhinophores white basally with dark orange-red on the club; gill white with dark orange-red markings. On the steep slopes of fringing reefs in 10-20 m.

Nudibranchia - "nudibranchs"

Hypselodoris sp. 3
Size: 19 mm   Marshall Is.
ID: Translucent greyish-white with an opaque white patch posterior to the rhinophores and in front of the gill connected by a longitudinal band; black spots present on areas away from opaque white band; marginal band opaque white with yellow and purple marginal spots; rhinophores and gill bright red. Under dead coral or debris, in 5-8 m.

Hypselodoris roo Gosliner & R. Johnson in Epstein et al., 2018
Size: 42 mm   Western Pacific
ID: White to pale purple with numerous yellow and black spots on the notum. Genetic studies indicate it is distinct from *Hypselodoris kanga* and has black spots instead of lines. Relatively shallow water in 10-20 m.

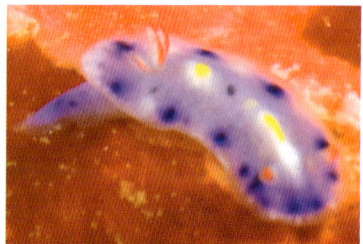

Hypselodoris infucata (Rüppell & Leuckart, 1831)
Size: 50 mm   Widespread in the Indo-Pacific
ID: White or blue with dusky grey to dark blue-black regions, laterally; body covered with yellow and blue spots; gill and rhinophores red. Feeds on the sponge, *Dysidea* sp. Introduced into the Mediterranean via the Suez Canal.

Hypselodoris confetti Gosliner & R. Johnson *in* Epstein *et al.,* 2018
Size: 50 mm   Western Pacific
ID: White to bluish towards the margins; numerous yellow and black spots; rhinophores with black bases and red tips; gills with yellow, black and red pigment. Similar to *Hypselodoris kanga* and *H. roo* but with yellow, purple and black spots rather than purple lines on the notum; like *H kanga* has blue rather than red on the gill.

Species with red-brown or black lines

Hypselodoris sagamiensis (Baba, 1949)
Size: 20 mm   Indonesia, Vanuatu, Japan
ID: White with a few yellow spots just inside the mantle margin; numerous black or dark blue spots on the notum; rhinophores and gill with red pigment. This specimen from Indonesia is similar to the original description from Japan, but further study is necessary to verify this.

Hypselodoris skyleri Gosliner & R. Johnson *in* Epstein *et al.,* 2018
Size: 12 mm   Philippines, Indonesia, Marshall Is.
ID: White with a series of longitudinal brown lines on the notum and opaque white spots; purple spots along the notal margin; gill with red and opaque white markings; rhinophores white with two red-orange rings. On shallow reefs under coral rubble in 15 m.

Hypselodoris katherinae Gosliner & R. Johnson *in* Epstein *et al.,* 2018
Size: 20 mm   Indonesia, Malaysia, Philippines
ID: White with a series of longitudinal red-brown lines on the notum; blue spots along the notal margin; brown pigment may be present on the notum together with opaque white pigment on the elevated tubercles. On sandy and rubble slopes in 10-25 m.

Hypslodoris paradisa Gosliner & R. Johnson *in* Epstein *et al.,* 2018
Size: 10 mm   Papua New Guinea
ID: Pinkish centrally, cream marginally, with thin white lines, some of which may be broken into specks; red and brown spots between the white lines, opaque white dots on the head and posterior end; red v-shaped marking on the anterior portion of the notum; rhinophores white with two red bands. On deep reefs, 39 m.

Nudibranchia - "nudibranchs"

Hypselodoris maritima (Baba, 1949)
Size: 20 mm   Western Pacific Ocean
ID: White, with a blue marginal and a yellow sub-marginal band; central portion of the dorsum with variable numbers of brown-black lines. Relatively uncommon, on reefs in relatively shallow water.

Hypselodoris nigrolineata (Eliot, 1904)
Size: 40 mm   Indian Ocean
ID: White with a greenish area in the center of the body with numerous black longitudinal lines; purple mantle margin with diffuse bluish patches submarginally. Shallow rock pools in the intertidal zone.

Hypselodoris zebrina (Alder & Hancock, 1864)
Size: 20 mm   India, Thailand, Malaysia
ID: Translucent bluish-white with orange to yellow spots and transverse purple lines; rhinophores and gill white with crimson outlines.

Hypselodoris kanga Rudman, 1977
Size: 45 mm   Indian Ocean
ID: White with yellow spots and interconnecting black lines; gill branches lined with blue and with yellow spots on their outer margins. In 1-20 m.

Hypselodoris zephyra Gosliner & R. Johnson, 1999
Size: 20 mm   Indian and western Pacific oceans
ID: White with parallel black lines except on a large area behind the gill; foot with a thick purple marginal band; rhinophores dark orange-red with white tips; gill dark orange-red with white spots on the outer side. Feeds on non-spiculate sponges on shallow reef flats and slopes.

Hypselodoris nigrostriata (Eliot, 1904)
Size: 40 mm   Indian Ocean
ID: Bluish with zigzagging black lines and large yellow patches. Similar to Hypselodoris zephyra but has a larger body size, the gill branches lack white spots and the rhinophores lack an opaque white tip.

Hypselodoris sp. 4
Size: 35 mm   Philippines
D: Opaque white with black spots on the back and foot; submarginal band orange to yellow; marginal band blue; rhinophores and gill red-orange.

Species with red purple rings or spots

Hypselodoris dollfusi (Pruvot-Fol, 1933)
Size: 50 mm   Indian Ocean
ID: Translucent pinkish-white, with a bright yellow-orange marginal band and a series of deep pink-purple rings, which surround a circle of lavender. In 10-20 m; feeds on *Dysidea* sponges.

Hypselodoris sp. 5
Size: 25 mm   Oman
ID: Translucent white with red spots; red spots near margin with purple rings; marginal band narrow, opaque white; rhinophores light tan with white apices; gill translucent white with opaque white lines.

Hypselodoris peri Gosliner & R. Johnson *in* Epstein *et al.*, 2018
Size: 35 mm   Philippines, Indonesia
ID: Translucent white with a red longitudinal line on the center of the dorsum; additional red spots near the margin with purple at their outer edges; a red ring surrounds the base of the gill pocket; submarginal bands opaque white and yellow; marginal band orange; rhinophores and gill reddish-orange. On deep reefs, in 40 m.

Species with an elevated gill with a pink or purple body color

The following species are members of the *Hypselodoris bullockii* complex. Most lack mantle glands or have only a few glands posteriorly. At present most of these species are considered to be *H. bullockii*, but consistent differences in color pattern and molecular data suggest that several distinct species exist. All species have a pinkish or purple body color with a gill peduncle that is well elevated from the notum.

Hypselodoris apolegma (Yonow, 2001)
Size: 100 mm   Western Pacific Ocean
ID: Brilliant purple; gill and rhinophores orange; marginal band diffuse, reticulate, white. Recently described as a distinct species. Conspicuous when crawling on reefs and slopes in 5-30 m.

Hypselodoris bullockii **(Collingwood, 1881)**
Size: 45 mm   Western and central Pacific
ID: Light pink-orange with a thin opaque white marginal line; gill and rhinophores white basally with reddish tips. On shallow water reefs crawling in the open; feeds on the sponge *Euryspongia* sp. Records from the Indian Ocean are *Thorunna punicea*.

Hypselodoris variobranchia Gosliner & R. Johnson *in* Epstein *et al.*, 2018
Size: 50 mm   Malaysia, Philippines
ID: Brilliant deep purple; gill purple or orange; rhinophores bright orange. Differs from other species in the *Hypselodoris bullockii* complex in that the marginal band is wide and solid, not diffuse. Commonly on shallow water reefs in 10-20 m.

Hypselodoris sp. 6
Size: 35 mm   Marshall Is.
ID: Translucent pink with yellowish irregular markings; purple pigment on the head and on the posterior end of the foot; rhinophores and gill white with purple pigment at the base and orange at tips. Nocturnally active on outer edges of leeward reefs.

Hypselodoris violacea Gosliner & R. Johnson *in* Epstein *et al.*, 2018
Size: 50 mm   Philippines, Malaysia
ID: Violet with a broad white marginal band; rhinophores and gill violet. Shallow reefs, 7-10 m.

Hypselodoris rositoi Gosliner & R. Johnson *in* Epstein *et al.*, 2018
Size: 40 mm   Philippines
ID: Salmon pink with an opaque white marginal band; rhinophores and gill orange; foot white. On deep reefs, 30-40 m.

Hypselodoris melanesica Gosliner & R. Johnson *in* Epstein *et al.*, 2018
Size: 25 mm   Papua New Guinea, Solomon Is.
ID: Deep purple with a darker purple ring at the base of the gill and rhinophores; gill and rhinophores orange above the purple base. On patch shallow reef habitats in 10-20 m. A similar colored form found in Reunion (Indian Ocean).

Hypselodoris sp. 7
Size: 50 mm   Indonesia, Palau
ID: Light purple with a thick white marginal band; rhinophores and gill orange.

195

Nudibranchia - "nudibranchs"

Hypselodoris brycei Gosliner & R. Johnson *in Epstein et al.,* 2018
Size: 40 mm   Western Australia
ID: White with a narrow, deep purple marginal band; rhinophores and gill bright crimson. This form appears quite distinct from other members of the *Hypselodoris bullockii* complex. On shallow reefs in 1-20 m; feeds on the sponge, *Euryspongia* sp.

Hypselodoris flavomarginata Rudman, 1995
Size: 40 mm   Vanuatu, New Caledoni
ID: Bright purple with a broad cream-yellow marginal band gill and rhinophores deep purplish red. On deep reefs, in 18 30 m; feeds on sponges.

Hypselodoris babai Gosliner & Behrens, 2000
Size: 25 mm   Western Pacific Ocean
ID: White with a rich red-brown central region; long irregular oval white spots distributed over the mantle; a wide white band edges the mantle and foot; gill and rhinophores red. In relatively deep waters, 40-60 m.

Hypselodoris lacteola Rudman, 1995
Size: 30 mm   New Caledonia
ID: White with purple pigment on the posterior end of the foot rhinophores and gill wine-red. In 36 m.

Other varied species of *Hypselodoris*

***Hypselodoris* sp. 8**
Size: 20 mm   Indonesia
ID: Translucent greyish-white, with a network of cream-white pigment; purple spots near the mantle edge; rhinophores and gill white basally with opaque white and red-orange on the tips.

Hypselodoris lacuna Gosliner & R. Johnson *in Epstein et al.,* 2018
Size: 12 mm   Indian and western Pacific oceans
ID: Opaque white with purple spots; many of the spots located in translucent circles on the notum; gill and rhinophores tipped with red orange. Under coral rubble on shallow water reefs.

Hypselodoris sp. 9
Size: 30 mm   Western Australia
ID: Pale grey with numerous yellow and black dots; broad red markings near the margin of the notum; gill with opaque white markings at the base of gill leaves.

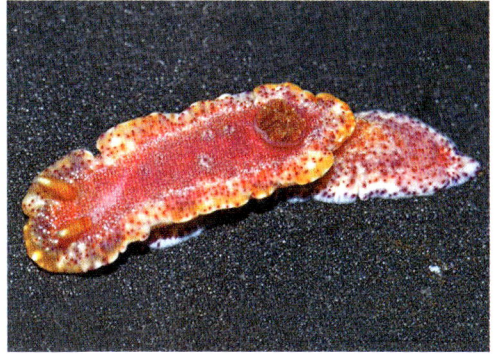

Hypselodoris sp. 10
Size: 25 mm   Walters Shoals (Indian Ocean)
ID: Reddish with purple spotting; orange pigment near the mantle margin; rhinophores and gill red-orange.

Species of *Hypselodoris* whose gill vibrates and exhibit "trailing behavior"

These species of *Hypselodoris* used to be included in *Risbecia* (see Rudman, 1984) and can be recognized by a high body profile with a mantle edge that is well extended from the sides of the body. The gill vibrates as the animals move. Specimens of the various species often exhibit "trailing behavior" where one or more individuals follow each other.

Hypselodoris tryoni (Garrett, 1873)
Size: 70 mm   Western and central Pacific
ID: Mottled light and dark tan with black spots and a blue marginal band. Similar in color to *Goniobranchus leopardus*, *G. geminus*, and *G. kuniei* but these species have a low rounded body typical of *Goniobranchus*. Raises and lowers the head as it crawls.

Hypselodoris sp. 11
Size: 50 mm   Western Pacific
ID: White with pink mottling; an undulating dark blue margin and a series of inwardly directed undulations; scattered yellow spots over the entire body. Similar to *Hypselodoris imperialis* but has a more dense yellow spotting and red pigment rather than blue on the gill branches. Feeds on the grey sponge, *Euryspongia* sp.

Nudibranchia - "nudibranchs"

Hypselodoris pulchella (Rüppell & Leuckart, 1830)
Size: 110 mm   Indian Ocean
ID: White with a reticulated pattern of violet patches on the dorsum and numerous yellow spots; border on the mantle purple; rhinophores purple with white dots; gill branches white with red rachises. On shallow reefs in protected areas.

Hypselodoris ghardaqana (Gohar & Aboul-Ela, 1957)
Size: 50 mm   Red Sea, Oman, Myanmar, Thailand
ID: White with few, large yellow-orange spots; border of the mantle purple. Similar to *Hypseldoris pulchella* but has fewer much larger orange spots and lacks the reticulate pattern on the notum.

Hypselodoris imperialis (Pease, 1860)
Size: 50 mm   Society Is., Hawai'ian Is.
ID: White with an undulating dark blue margin and a series of inwardly directed undulations; large, scattered yellow spots over the entire body; gill white lined with blue; rhinophores blue with white spots on the lamellae. Feeds on the blue grey sponge, *Dysidea fragilis.*

Hypselodoris sp. 12
Size: 45 mm   Indonesia, Philippines
ID: White with a pattern of violet pigment on the dorsum and irregular patches of bright yellow; border on the mantle purple; rhinophores purple with white dots; gill branches white with purple rachises. In 15-30 m on sandy slopes among coral rubble.

Ceratosoma J. E. Gray, 1850 *in* M. E. Gray, 1850
Members of this group have an irregularly shaped undulating mantle with mantle glands reduced to the posterior end or to elaborate appendages situated behind the gill.

Ceratosoma gracillimum Semper *in* Bergh, 1876
Size: 120 mm   Western Pacific Ocean
ID: Color varies from yellow to orange or brick red-brown, with various degrees of opaque white to cream mottling; mantle lacks a distinct edge between the head and the well-developed lateral lobes. Often crawling on shallow reefs among rubble at night.

198

Ceratosoma trilobatum (J. E. Gray, 1827)
Size: 120 mm   Indian and western Pacific oceans
ID: Red with white circles or yellow spots; mantle margin with a continuous, not broken purple line, thicker on the head; distinct notal margin edged with purple; two lobes opposite to the gill much larger than the rest. Feeds on a siliceous sponge; egg mass orange.

Ceratosoma sp. 1
Size: 12 mm   Widespread in the Indo-Pacific
ID: Translucent rose pink to red with a wide cream marginal band or opaque white flecks; center of the dorsum with irregular, opaque white mottling. From the intertidal zone to about 10 m on the undersurface of rocks.

Ceratosoma sp. 2
Size: 30 mm   Outer Hawai'ian Is.
ID: Yellow with scattered opaque white spots; submarginal band purple, followed by orange and white; purple on the posterior end of foot; rhinophores and gill orange with purple; mantle edge slightly undulating.

Ceratosoma sp. 3
Size: 20 mm   Indonesia
ID: Red with longitudinal white lines; marginal band opaque white; rhinophores and gill white with red lines; mantle edge undulating. On coral reefs in shallow water.

Nudibranchia - "nudibranchs"

Ceratosoma palliolatum Rudman, 1988
Size: 75 mm   Australia, Japan, Marshall Is
ID: Mottled orange with scattered purple spots around the mantle edge; rhinophores tipped with purple; gill translucent reddish lacks a prominent lobe behind the gill. In 5-20 m.

Ceratosoma tenue Abraham, 1876
Size: 120 mm   Widespread in the Indo-Pacific
ID: Color variable, grey, orange or red, with spots of different colors; posterior two lobes joined by a ridge, outlined with a broken purple line. Similar to *Ceratosoma trilobatum* and *C. gracillimum*, but the lobes are subequal and narrower than in the other two species. On shallow sand and rubble flats and slopes in 5-20 m.

Miamira Bergh, 1874
Body shape variable from ovoid to highly lobed, often with a mid-dorsal elevation behind gill, which contains concentrations of defensive mantle glands. Similar to *Ceratosoma*, but genetically distinct.

Miamira alleni (Gosliner, 1996)
Size: 50 mm   Philippines and Indonesia
ID: Creamy-tan with a series of elongate nodular appendages that resemble soft coral branches. On shallow reefs dominated by a xeniid octocoral, which it closely mimics, in about 10 m; it is unlikely that it feeds on octocorals, but rather on sponges.

200

***Miamira magnifica* Eliot, 1910**
Size: 70 mm   Indian and western Pacific oceans
ID: Bright purple with red patches; red also on the edge of the ridges; marginal band white followed by purple; gill red with opaque white lines; rhinophores red; body highly ridged with three prominent high points. On shallow reefs to 25 m.

***Miamira moloch* (Rudman, 1988)**
Size: 112 mm   Western Pacific Ocean
ID: Reddish-orange with a series of pink elongate nodular appendages that resemble sponges. Feeds on sponges, which it closely resembles.

***Miamira* sp. 1**
Size: 20 mm   Philippines
ID: Pink with lighter mottling reminiscent of sponge tissue; tips of the appendages orange and conical in shape. Shallow water, among rubble in 10 m.

Nudibranchia - "nudibranchs"

Miamira miamirana (Bergh, 1875)
Size: 75 mm Indo-Pacific
ID: Color varies from green to green-brown and red-brown, with low cream-colored pustules and blue spots ringed with red; body wider than in other *Miamira*; mantle with rounded lobes around the edge and round depressions near the middle; dorsal tubercles compound. In shallow water, 5-15 m, on reef slopes and flats.

Miamira sinuata (van Hasselt, 1824)
Size: 45 mm Widespread in the Indo-Pacific
ID: Greyish or greenish with yellow, white and blue spots; gill and rhinophores green with white specks; body covered with low tubercles. In 5-30 m, in association with sponges of the genus *Dysidea*, sometimes together with the cephalaspideans, *Sagaminopteron ornatum* and *S. nigropunctatum*.

Nudibranchia - "nudibranchs"

Miamira sp. 2
Size: 150 mm   Mozambique, Reunion
ID: White with brown concentric rings and smaller red rings; gill large, highly pinnate. This remarkable new species has superficial similarities to species of *Dendrodoris*. Crawling on sand in shallow water.

Porostomata - "Radula-less dorids"

Members of this group of dorid nudibranchs lack radular teeth and feed by secreting digestive enzymes into sponges and sucking the partially digested tissue. Dendrodorids have a prominent gill on the back. Phyllidiids have no dorsal gill but a secondary set of gills along the underside of the body margins. Porostomata are cryptobranch dorids since they have a cavity into which the gill can be retracted (Valdés & Gosliner, 1999). This is also true for the Phyllidiidae, which retain a gill cavity even though the original gill has been lost. The Phyllidiidae were reviewed most recently by Brunckhorst (1993).

Dendrodorididae O'Donoghue, 1924

Members of this family are externally indistinguishable from other cryptobranch dorids, except for that the oral tentacles are reduced and fused together, giving the appearance that there are no oral tentacles. Many species have a characteristic spicy taste derived from drimane sesquiterpenoids that the nudibranchs synthesize independently from their food source and store in their mantle for defense. Dendrodorids are found in tropical, subtropical, and temperate regions of the Atlantic, Pacific and Indian Oceans.

Doriopsilla Bergh, 1880

Members of this group have a relatively rigid body with spicules providing skeletal support. *Doriopsilla* is more diverse in temperate regions than in the tropics.

Doriopsilla sp. 1
Size: 25 mm   South Africa
ID: Light brownish with darker brown spots on the notum; dorsal surface covered with rounded tubercles that may have radiating opaque white lines at the base. Under rocks in the lower intertidal zone.

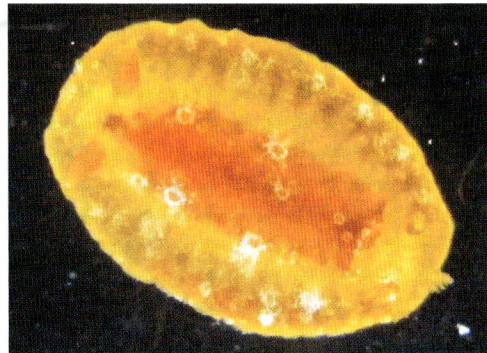

Doriopsilla miniata (Alder & Hancock, 1864)
Size: 30 mm   India, Australia, Japan
ID: Color variable from pale orange to deep orange; usually with a distinctive pattern of intersecting opaque white lines, in some cases the white pigment forms circles with radiating white lines. From the intertidal zone to 15 m. Records from temperate South Africa are *Doriopsilla areolata*.

203

Nudibranchia - "nudibranchs"

***Doriopsilla* sp. 2**
Size: 20 mm Hawai'ian Is.
ID: Yellowish orange or brownish; notum covered with rounded tubercles some of which have a dark spot at the apex. On shallow patch reefs in 3-5 m.

***Doriopsilla* sp. 3**
Size: 12 mm Papua New Guinea
ID: Light orange with a series of opaque white markings on the notum; rhinophores with dark brown bases and an opaque white tips. Under coral rubble on the crest of barrier reefs.

***Doriopsilla* sp. 4**
Size: 15 mm Philippines
ID: Whitish to grey with low rounded tubercles often with orange spots on the apices; an orange ring at around each rhinophoral sheath. Looks similar to *Dermatobranchus fortunatus* in its color pattern, but differs in having an obvious gill at the posterior end of the mantle.

Dendrodoris Ehrenberg, 1831
Species of *Dendrodoris* have a soft body and have spicules only as juveniles. Internally, they have a distinct type of digestive gland to aid in dissolving sponge tissue.

Species with an elongate body
One group of *Dendrodoris* species is unusual in having highly elongate bodies with the gill situated near the posterior end of the animal. Additionally, these animals have the ability to greatly extend their bodies making them extremely long.

***Dendrodoris elongata* Baba, 1936**
Size: 60 mm Indo-Pacific and eastern Pacific
ID: Translucent white with irregular brown and whitish stellate markings of varying sizes; small tubercles on the surface of the body. Under rocks on shallow reefs in 1-5 m.

Dendrodoris albopurpura Burn, 1957
Size: 150 m   Widespread in the Indo-Pacific
ID: Grey with a distinctive pattern of white pustules, each tipped with a brown or purple spot; body elongate and covered with small tubercles; gill set far back on the body. Under coral rubble in shallow water.

Dendrodoris sp. 1
Size: 100 mm   Philippines
ID: Whitish with dark grey blotches over the surface; gill large with dark lines in the center of each branch. Mesophotic, 100 m.

Dendrodoris sp. 2
Size: 30 mm   South Africa
ID: White with black spots of varying sizes; rhinophores and gill white. Similar to *Dendrodoris* sp. 4, but with larger spots.

Dendrodoris albobrunnea Allan, 1933
Size: 70 mm   Indian and western Pacific oceans
ID: Grey with numerous irregular brown spots; lacks opaque white markings or purple tubercles on the notum. Under rocks in relatively shallow water, 1-10 m.

Dendrodoris sp. 3
Size: 30 mm   Papua New Guinea
ID: Light grey with white tubercles, black spots and a fine network of grey pigment; rhinophores with subapical black pigment. Under rocks in rubble areas on shallow reef flats in 10 m.

205

Dendrodoris sp. 4
Size: 30 mm   Saudi Arabian Red Sea
ID: Translucent white with the internal organs visible; body elongate; dorsum smooth with numerous black spots, mainly on the center of the body, and opaque white dots, mainly on the mantle margin; rhinophores white, each with a large black spot; gill with brown pigment. Under dead coral rubble, 13 m.

Dendrodoris sp. 5
Size: 200 mm   Marshall Is.
ID: Greenish-grey with irregular dark grey pigment; body elongate, covered with numerous small rounded tubercles, white with black apices; mantle margin narrow, ruffled, with radial dark lines; rhinophores and gill greenish grey. In caves at night, 14 m.

Species with large complex tubercles
The following five species have large complex tubercles on the notum. Four of the five species are widespread in the Indo-Pacific and often occur together.

Dendrodoris tuberculosa (Quoy & Gaimard, 1832)
Size: 200 mm   Widespread in the Indo-Pacific
ID: Color very variable, from pale green to yellowish brown; dorsum covered with large, fleshy compound tubercles; underside of the mantle with large round white spots. Under stones during the day and actively crawling over shallow reefs at night; mantle secretions may cause a painful sting; egg ribbon bright yellow.

Nudibranchia - "nudibranchs"

Dendrodoris denisoni (Angas, 1864)
Size: 60 mm   Widespread in the Indo-Pacific
ID: Creamy-white with large brown and white fleshy tubercles
and bright blue spots in depressions between tubercles. On
shallow reefs in the open or under rocks, occasionally in
deep water trawls down to 120 m.

Dendrodoris coronata Kay & Young, 1969
Size: 45 mm   Western and central Pacific Ocean
ID: Black with numerous white tubercles; a band of large
tubercles just in front of the gill gives it the appearance of a
small living cowry; mantle margin orange-brown.

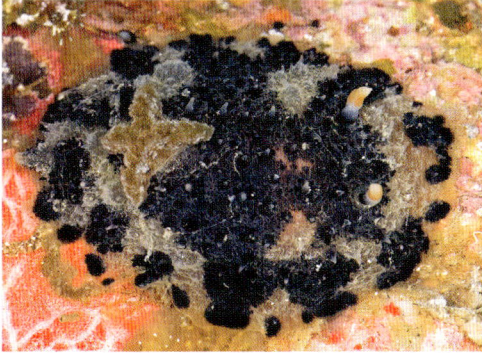

Dendrodoris atromaculata (Alder & Hancock, 1864)
Size: 85 mm   India, Fiji, Australia, Philippines
ID: Pale yellow to brownish-orange with irregular dark brown
patches; dorsum covered with complex tubercles, each with
a narrow stalk and a swollen midsection bearing many finger-
like papillae, which radiate out in a stellate pattern. Intertidal
zone.

Dendrodoris carbunculosa (Kelaart, 1858)
Size: 750 mm   Indo-Pacific and eastern Pacific
ID: Brown with darker areas at the bases of the tubercles;
larger tubercles ringed with smaller tubercles; underside
brown lacking white spots. Under stones during the day,
actively crawling over shallow reefs at night; mantle
secretions may cause a painful sting; egg ribbon bright
yellow.

Species with a smooth notum
The following species have oval to elongate,
smooth bodies, lacking tubercles and spicules. The systematics of some of these species has been most recently clarified by Brodie
et al. (1997) and Brodie & Calado (2006).

Dendrodoris rainfordi Allan, 1932
Size: 170 mm   Thailand, Malaysia, Australia
ID: Whitish with irregular brown to black patches
and characteristic brown spots resembling
atolls; mantle margin with purple spots. On
mixed sand and mud in a sheltered bays.

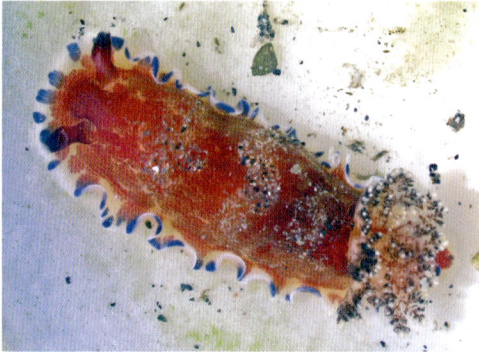

Dendrodoris elizabethina (Kelaart, 1859)
Size: 20 mm   Sri Lanka and Gulf of Oman
ID: Translucent grey, almost completely covered with reddish brown pigmentation; mantle margin with large blue patches; rhinophores reddish brown and black with white tips. Intertidal zone.

Dendrodoris sp. 6
Size: 30 mm   Widespread in the Indo-Pacific
ID: Reddish-orange with several opaque white, conical tubercles surrounded by mottled opaque white pigment; mantle margin lighter, narrow; rhinophores dark brown with white apices; gill uniformly dark brown. Under rocks, tide pools to 15 m.

Dendrodoris guttata (Odhner, 1917)
Size: 60 mm   Western Pacific Ocean
ID: Yellow to orange brown with scattered black spots, each ringed with a diffuse white band; mantle margin highly ruffled. Shallow water habitats in silty areas usually at night in 3-15 m.

Dendrodoris sp. 7
Size: 50 mm   Marshall Is.
ID: Uniformly red with a cream-white line around the mantle margin; rhinophores red with white apices; gill cream with reddish-brown pigment. Under rocks, 15 m.

Dendrodoris arborescens (Collingwood, 1881)
Size: 80 mm   Western Pacific Ocean
ID: Black with no white spots and a red marginal band instead of submarginal. Very similar to *Dendrodoris nigra* these two species are often mistaken, differences include color pattern, eggs and larvae. Under coral rubble in shallow water.

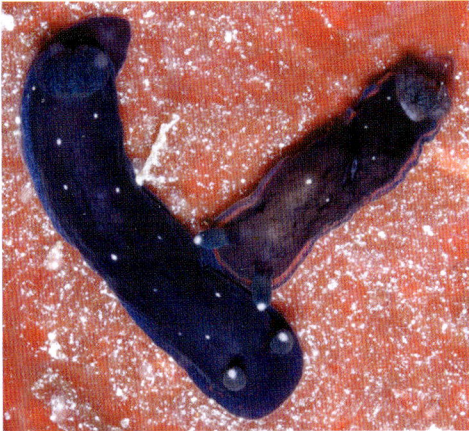

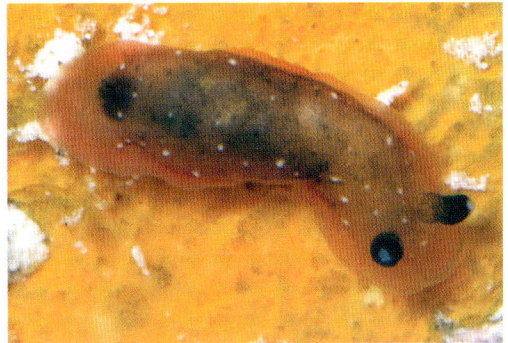

Dendrodoris nigra (Stimpson, 1855)
Size: 80 mm   Widespread in the Indo-Pacific
ID: Adults black, often with white spots; if red is present forms a submarginal band; juveniles (bottom right photo) vary from pink to orange; more than 6 gill branches, compact, curved inward, never reaching the edge of the mantle. Feeds on the sponge, *Halichondria dura;* glands produce a noxious white milky secretion. In 1-5 m, well hidden during the day.

Dendrodoris fumata (Rüppell & Leuckart, 1831)
Size: 100 mm   Widespread in the Indo-Pacific
ID: Color variable from pink to red or reddish-orange in juveniles, turning to black in adults, occasionally with irregular dark patches; differs from *Dendrodoris nigra* in having fewer (5) large gill branches, which spread and extend to the edge of the mantle, lacking white spots. Under coral rubble in shallow water, 1-5 m.

Nudibranchia - "nudibranchs"

Phyllidiidae Rafinesque, 1814

This group includes relatively tough bodied porostomes in which the primary gill is absent and secondary respiratory structures are situated underneath the mantle, in the hyponotum. Species are distinguished by variations in color and the shape and spacing of the notal tubercles. Distinguishing anatomical characteristics between the genera are largely internal. The systematics of this group was reviewed by Brunckhorst (1993).

Many species have a characteristic odor derived from sesquiterpene isocyanides that the nudibranchs obtain from their prey and store in their mantle for defense. Phyllidiid chemicals are extremely toxic and can kill other organisms kept in aquaria together with the nudibranchs. Phyllidiids are exclusively found in tropical and subtropical regions of the Atlantic, Pacific and Indian Oceans, reaching depths below 700 m.

Phyllidia Cuvier, 1797

These are medium to large phyllidiids, often with large tubercles, sometimes forming longitudinal ridges. The oral

tentacles are not fused together. Internally, the pharyngeal bulb has large glandular bodies partly protruding from it.

Phyllidia elegans Bergh, 1869
Size: 63 mm   Widespread in the Indo-Pacific
ID: Pink with black lines and spots; tubercles opaque white, a few tipped with yellow; rhinophores yellow; foot sole with a black line. In the same habitat as *Phyllidia coelestis*, commonly on reef faces at moderate depths, 1-40 m.

Phyllidia cf. *elegans* Bergh, 1869
Size: 50 mm   Papua New Guinea
ID: White with black lines and spots; rhinophores yellow. Similar to *Phyllidia elegans* but lacks yellow pigment on the tubercles and has black spots rather than lines submarginally. Distinctness of this species needs further study.

Phyllidia varicosa Lamarck, 1801
Size: 115 mm   Widespread in the Indo-Pacific
ID: Blue with black pigment between the ridges; tubercles and rhinophores yellow; a black line on the foot sole. Probably the most common and widespread species of *Phyllidia*; in the open on patch reefs or reef faces; egg mass flat.

Phyllidia coelestis Bergh, 1905
Size: 60 mm   Indian and western Pacific oceans
ID: Blue with black lines between the ridges; tubercles and rhinophores yellow; differs from *Phyllidia varicosa* by having a Y-shaped black marking in front of the rhinophores and lacking a black line on the foot sole. Common on open reef slopes to 20 m, frequently observed on walls in the open; feeds on sponges.

Phyllidia alyta Yonow, 1996
Size: 50 mm   Indian Ocean
ID: Greyish-pink with opaque white tubercles and four parallel black lines that rarely intersect. Crawling in the open on shallow patch reefs in 5-20 m.

Phyllidia madangensis Brunckhorst, 1993
Size: 60 mm   Western Pacific Ocean
ID: Black with granular opaque white tubercles capped in bright yellow; tubercles sparsely scattered, widely spaced, without smaller tubercles between the larger ones; rhinophores yellow; foot lacks a black median stripe. Shallow water patch reefs to 15 m.

Species with a black mantle with yellow tubercles
Species in this informal group have a black mantle with a series of yellow tubercles.

Phyllidia tula Er. Marcus & Ev. Marcus, 1970
Size: 86 mm   Micronesia
ID: Black with numerous rounded yellow tubercles; bases of the tubercles often with white rings; tubercles gradually decrease in size towards the margin of the notum; rhinophores gold; foot, ventral gills, and hyponotum grey; foot sole with a black longitudinal stripe. On reef faces and in coral rubble.

Phyllidia carlsonhoffi Brunckhorst, 1993
Size: 70 mm   Western and central Pacific Ocean
ID: Black with yellow tubercles; tubercles broad, largest at the center, not forming ridges; large conical tubercles alternate with small rounded ones; rhinophores yellow; hyponotum grey with a hatched pattern; foot and ventral gills grey; foot sole with a medial black line. Bays and lagoons.

Species with black circles or swirls

The following species of *Phyllidia* are characterized by having a pale color with black circles or swirls contrasting with the lighter background.

Phyllidia babai Brunckhorst, 1993
Size: 65 mm   Eastern Indian and western Pacific Ocean
ID: Bluish-grey with minute, scattered opaque white spots on the notum; black rings at the base of some tubercles; marginal border pale yellow. On shallow patch reefs, usually in the open.

Phyllidia sp. 1
Size: 25 mm   Philippines
ID: Bluish appearance due to the presence of numerous opaque white dots covering the dark grey notum; dorsum covered with irregular yellow tubercles, larger in the center of the body, and an irregular network of thick black lines between the tubercles; rhinophores yellow. Mixed rocky and sandy slopes, 15 m.

Phyllidia sp. 2
Size: 40 mm   Philippines
ID: Bluish-grey with numerous opaque white dots; dorsum with irregular opaque white tubercles, larger in the center of the body; some tubercles with faint yellow pigment; a series of thick black lines or patches between the tubercles; rhinophores orange. Sheltered rocky slopes, 30 m.

Phyllidia willani Brunckhorst, 1993
Size: 50 mm   Western Pacific Ocean
ID: Bluish-white with minute white dots giving the dorsum a granular appearance; tubercles large with yellow tips and white lateral granules, some surrounded by black pigment; undulating swirls of black laterally; margin of the notum lacks a yellow line. On shallow reefs in 10-20 m.

Phyllidia exquisita Brunckhorst, 1993
Size: 23 mm   Widespread in the Indo-Pacific
ID: Bluish appearance due to the widely spaced arrangement of opaque white dots; undulating swirls of black laterally; yellow marginal line, at least anteriorly; rhinophores yellow. Occurs on reef faces and flats in 5-15 m.

***Phyllidia ocellata* Cuvier, 1804**
Size: 70 mm   Widespread in the Indo-Pacific
ID: Yellow to golden-yellow or orange, often with black circles or lines surrounded by white or yellow; tubercles large, irregular, yellow or white; extremely variable in its color pattern, even from a single locality. On relatively shallow reefs (1-20 m), almost always conspicuously in the open.

Nudibranchia - "nudibranchs"

Phyllidia multifaria Yonow, 1986
Size: 40 mm   Red Sea
ID: Greyish-white with yellow pigment on some of the elevated tubercles; a network of black lines at the base of the tubercles; rhinophores yellow. In the open on shallow reefs.

Phyllidia schupporum Fahrner & Schrödl, 2000
Size: 30 mm   Northern Red Sea
ID: White with burnt-orange tubercles and a network of thick, black lines projecting towards the mantle margin; rhinophores orange-yellow. On shallow reefs in 5-12 m.

Phyllidia sp. 3
Size: 35 mm   Philippines
ID: Center of the dorsum bluish; mantle margin bright orange; dorsum with rounded white tubercles, some with orange apices; two longitudinal thick black lines and black spots on the dorsum; rhinophores deep red. Deep reefs on drop-offs, 35 m.

Phyllidia sp. 4
Size: 20 mm   Philippines
ID: Bright red center of the dorsum; opaque white mantle margin; dorsum with three longitudinal ridges formed by small tubercles; additional small tubercles scattered over the mantle margin; large black spots forming three longitudinal lines; rhinophores bright red. Coral rubble on deeper reefs, 20 m.

Phyllidia polkadotsa Brunckhorst, 1993
Size: 15 mm   Widespread in the Indo-Pacific
ID: Bright yellow with three rows of black spots; rhinophores yellow. On patch reefs and shallow slopes in 5-10 m.

Phyllidia scottjohnsoni Brunckhorst, 1993
Size: 26 mm   Western and central Pacific Ocean
ID: White with black spots; small tubercles; cream to white rhinophores.

Phyllidia koehleri Perrone, 2000
Size: 15 mm   Maldives
ID: Dark yellow with a large, thick, black circle surrounding the visceral hump and a central longitudinal black line; three longitudinal crests; rhinophores uniformly orange. On shallow reefs in 16-26 m.

Phyllidia sp. 5
Size: 12 mm   Madagascar
ID: Pinkish-white with black lines and a bright yellow marginal line on the anterior end. In the open on a shallow patch reef in a sheltered lagoon.

Species with pale coloration

The following species of *Phyllidia* has a pale coloration with small spots, very different from other species of Phyllidiidae from the tropical Indo-Pacific, which generally have a combination of bright colors. This phyllidiid is more similar to other species found in Indo-Pacific deep waters, or in the Atlantic and eastern Pacific.

Phyllidia goslineri Brunckhorst, 1993
Size: 14 mm   Papua New Guinea
ID: Semi-transparent notum covered with evenly spaced, minute dark brown spots, giving the animal a brown appearance; rhinophores cream. Known from a single specimen collected from an emerging pinnacle in 20 m.

Species with a ventral anus

Species of *Phyllidia* with a ventral anus were formerly placed in a separate genus, *Frye-ria*. But more recent studies have shown this is simply a sub-group of *Phyllidia* (Valdés & Gosliner, 1999).

Phyllidia rueppelii (Bergh, 1869)
Size: 42 mm   Red Sea
ID: Dark blue to black; mantle margin edged with yellow-orange; large, isolated central tubercles with whitish-blue bases and yellow-orange tips, oval and rounded in profile; rhinophores yellow-orange. In coral rubble.

Nudibranchia - "nudibranchs"

Phyllidia marindica (Yonow & Hayward, 1991)
Size: 40 mm   Indian Ocean
ID: Pale blue with black bars and markings; two black longitudinal black bands running on either side of a single medial longitudinal ridge; medial ridge blue-grey, joining with coalesced tubercles; larger tubercles capped with yellow; rhinophores gold. On reef faces.

Phyllidia picta Pruvot-Fol, 1957
Size: 45 mm   Western Pacific Ocean
ID: Blue with a network of black pigment on the notum; tubercles gold, single, isolated; medial tubercles alternate: 1, 2, 1, 2; large crescent shaped blue areas along the margin, with small gold capped tubercles; rhinophores gold. Shallow water reefs in the open, in 5-10 m.

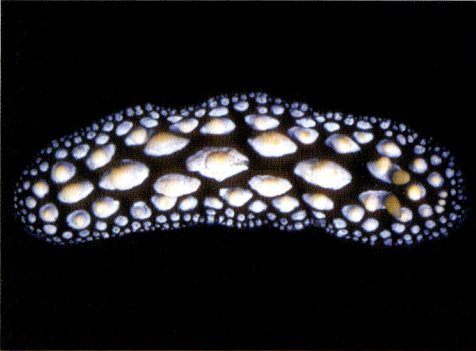

Phyllidia guamensis (Brunckhorst, 1993)
Size: 35 mm   Mariana Is., possibly Marquesas Is.
ID: Largely black with light blue pigment at the base of the tubercles, each with a yellow apex; rhinophores yellow. Similar to *Phyllidia tula* but with a ventral anus. In the open on shallow reefs.

Phyllidia sp. 6
Size: 25 mm   Hawai'ian Is.
ID: Blue with a network of black pigment on the notum; tubercles gold; black pigment surrounds the tubercles and extends laterally. On shallow reefs out in the open in 10-20 m.

Phyllidia sp. 7
Size: 50 mm   Marquesas Is.
ID: Black with a bluish mantle margin; center of the dorsum covered with large, spherical, yellow tubercles, surrounded by white circles; mantle margin with small black spots; rhinophores orange, emerging within the white circles of other tubercles. Found on walls or reef faces, in 25 m.

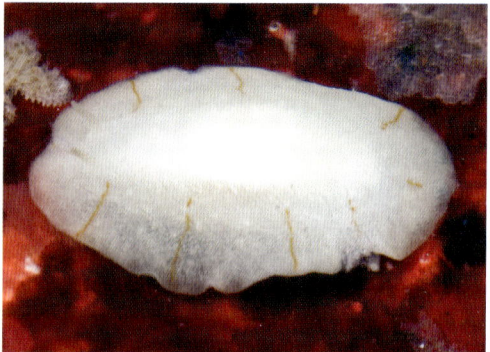

Phyllidia larryi (Brunckhorst, 1993)
Size: 6 mm   Guam, Philippines
ID: White with red transverse lines on the mantle margin; rhinophores yellow.

Deep-water species
The following two species of *Phyllidia* occur deeper than 50 m. Many more deep water phyllidiids, known from preserved animals only, are not included here.

***Phyllidia* sp. 8**
Size: 60 mm   Philippines, Indonesia, possibly Japan
ID: Light blue, largely the result of the presence of a small opaque white spots; ridges greatly reduced with only a few tubercles; a Y-shaped black patch between the rhinophores, followed by a black transverse band and other varied black markings. At the base of relatively steep slopes in 25-30 m.

***Phyllidia* sp. 9**
Size: 60 mm   Philippines
ID: Light blue, largely the result of the presence of a small opaque white spots; with only a few orange tubercles. Similar to *Phyllidia* sp. 8 but with elongate black markings rather than transverse bands. Mesophotic, 100 m.

***Phyllidia* sp. 10**
Size: 35 mm   Philippines
ID: Opaque white with a black patch covering the center of the body; dorsum with numerous large, irregular, white tubercles; tubercles in the center of the body larger, with orange apices; rhinophores orange. Deep reefs, 80 m.

***Phyllidia orstomi* Valdés, 2011**
Size: 20 mm   New Caledonia
ID: Pale grey with bright yellow tubercles; mantle margin with black spots; broken longitudinal black lines. In deep water, 270-300 m.

Phyllidiella Bergh, 1869
Species in this group are typically medium sized phyllidiids, with the dorsum covered with simple or compound tubercles, coalesced into groups, or fused into ridges. The oral tentacles are not fused together. Internally, the pharyngeal bulb is covered with a large mass of oral glands.

***Phyllidiella hageni* Fahrner & Beck, 2000**
Size: 50 mm   Papua New Guinea
ID: Pinkish-red with black lines between ridges. Similar to *Phyllidia zeylanica* but has lower ridges and the tubercles have white apices. On shallow reef flats and slopes, where they crawl in the open.

Phyllidiella nigra (van Hasselt, 1824)
Size: 63 mm   Indian and western Pacific oceans
ID: Black with pink tubercles; tubercles evenly scattered, not arranged in rows, often compound with 2-3 coalescing tubercles; rhinophores black. In coral rubble in shallow water.

Phyllidiella zeylanica (Kelaart, 1859)
Size: 80 mm   Indian and western Pacific oceans
ID: Pinkish with black lines between ridges; up to nine irregular tuberculate ridges; ridges vary greatly, some may be broken or interrupted; medial ridges may be separated into two longitudinal groups; individual tubercles pink; mantle edge smooth; rhinophores black, ventral gills grey, foot sole white. A common inhabitant of reef flats in 10-20 m.

Phyllidiella rosans (Bergh, 1873)
Size: 35 mm   Widespread in the Indo-Pacific
ID: Black with longitudinal pink rounded ridges; the ridges may be interrupted, especially in Pacific specimens; anus opens at the apex of one of the posterior tubercles; rhinophoral stalk pink and clavus black; foot and ventral gills grey. In coral rubble on shallow reef flats.

Phyllidiella sp. 1
Size: 30 mm   Western Indian Ocean
ID: Pinkish grey with several of longitudinal ridges formed by series of small tubercles; some ridges merge at the posterior end of the body; black lines between ridges; rhinophores black. Shallow areas on reef faces and rubble, 10-20 m.

Phyllidiella annulata (J. E. Gray, 1853)
Size: 31 mm   Indian and western Pacific oceans
ID: Pinkish-white with a series of black lines forming rings; small tubercles occur within the rings but there are no tubercles in the center of each ring, only black pigment; rhinophores black. In coral rubble.

Phyllidiella rudmani Brunckhorst, 1993
Size: 60 mm   Indian and western Pacific oceans
ID: Pale pink with two longitudinal black stripes; pink and rounded notal tubercles, tipped with white, more or less arranged in longitudinal rows, but never forming a ridge; rhinophores black apically and pink basally. On shallow reefs where it feeds on the sponge, *Phakellia* sp.

Phyllidiella pustulosa (Cuvier, 1804)
Size: 70 mm   Widespread in the Indo-Pacific
ID: Highly variable in color pattern, predominantly black with pink or white tubercles; tubercles arranged in small clusters, becoming more separated as the animal grows. In shallow water reefs to deep reef slopes, 5-40 m; one of the most common phyllidiid on Indo-Pacific reefs; the flatworm *Pseudoceros imitatus* mimics this species.

Phyllidiella sp. 2
Size: 45 mm   Saudi Arabian Red Sea
ID: White with a network on dorsal black lines; dorsum covered with large conical tubercles arranged in groups of 2-5; rhinophores black. Rocky patch reefs in protected lagoons, 20 m.

Phyllidiella cooraburrama Brunckhorst, 1993
Size: 40 mm   Fiji, Bali, Australia
ID: Pinkish with a network on dorsal black lines; very large, isolated dorsal tubercles with broad pink bases and elongate multicompound apices; rhinophores black. On shallow reefs where it feeds on orange sponges.

219

Nudibranchia - "nudibranchs"

Phyllidiella meandrina (Pruvot-Fol, 1957)
Size: 55 mm   Indian Ocean
ID: Pinkish with black markings that encircle the tubercles; rhinophores black. On shallow water reefs in the open in 10-20 m.

Phyllidiella sp. 3
Size: 30 mm   Heron Island (Australia)
ID: Pink with black lines that run both longitudinally and horizontally; tubercles rounded, with opaque white tips; rhinophores pink. In shallow water, 2-5 m.

Phyllidiella granulata Brunckhorst, 1993
Size: 40 mm   Western Pacific Ocean
ID: Granular grey with up to ten circling black bands, dividing the mantle into 2-3 large patches, and extending to the rhinophores and behind the anus; tubercles tall, acute, sometimes compound; rhinophores black; foot sole grey. On reef flats at 5-20 m.

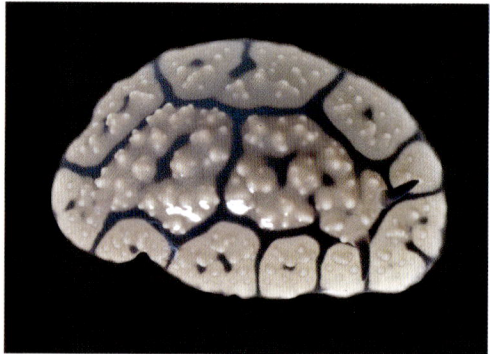

Phyllidiella backeljaui Domínguez, Quintas & Troncoso, 2007
Size: 25 mm   Papua New Guinea
ID: Pinkish-grey with a network of black lines and irregular black spots; tubercles complex with paler apices; rhinophores black.

Phyllidiella lizae Brunckhorst, 1993
Size: 36 mm   Australia, Indonesia
ID: Pale pink with simple, rounded, pale pink tubercles; narrow black lines crossing the dorsum; rhinophores black, white and pink. On shallow reefs in 10 m.

Phyllidiella sp. 4
Size: 45 mm   Papua New Guinea
ID: Uniformly pinkish; dorsum covered with numerous small, rounded white spots; rhinophores pale brown. Exposed reefs on reef faces, 25 m.

Phyllidiopsis Bergh, 1876

Species in this group are typically small to medium in size; most have flattened bodies, relatively smooth, with small, simple tubercles and/or low ridges, but a few species have a high profiles with large compound and/or coalesced tubercles. The main characteristics of this group are the oral tentacles completely fused together forming a squarish shape, and the presence of a very elongate and narrow pharyngeal bulb, completely covered with tightly packed, minute, oral glands.

Phyllidiopsis shireenae Brunckhorst, 1990
Size: 110 mm   Widespread in the Indo-Pacific
ID: White with opaque white spots and a prominent longitudinal mid-dorsal ridge covered with large tubercles; ridge encircled by a black ring with radiating black lines; mantle margin with smaller tubercles; rhinophores pale salmon pink. In 20-30 m on steep reef slopes and walls.

Phyllidiopsis krempfi Pruvot-Fol, 1957
Size: 65 mm   Indian and western Pacific oceans
ID: Pink with irregular, black, longitudinal lines that meander between the tubercles; long spicules visible though the translucent pink notum; medial tubercles compound with tips lighter than the body; rhinophores pink, black posteriorly. Crawling on reef flats in 10-15 m.

Phyllidiopsis gemmata (Pruvot-Fol, 1957)
Size: 40 mm   Indian and western Pacific oceans
ID: Pink with a series of longitudinal ridges with black lines; radiating black lines often at the mantle margin; rhinophores pink with black posteriorly. On shallow reefs in 10-15 m.

Phyllidiopsis fissurata Brunckhorst, 1993
Size: 80 mm   Western Pacific Ocean
ID: Grey with tall, multicompound pink tubercles; dark grey to black pigment forming lines and deep fissures between the tubercles; rhinophores pink with black posteriorly. On sharp drop-offs and walls.

Phyllidiopsis sinaiensis (Yonow, 1988)
Size: 80 mm   Northern Red Sea
ID: Pink with a network of black lines; a tuberculate central ridge and numerous, large and multicompound tubercles; rhinophores black apically and pink basally. On shallow reefs in the open in 10-20 m.

Phyllidiopsis pipeki Brunckhorst, 1993
Size: 85 mm   Western Pacific Ocean
ID: Grey with a pinkish hue and two longitudinal black lines; some specimens with a few black spots or several black rays extending to the edge of the mantle; tubercles large, single or compound; rhinophores black and pink, with a black line posteriorly. On reef flats in 10-20 m.

Phyllidiopsis sp. 1
Size: 5 mm   French Polynesia
ID: Yellowish white with a central longitudinal ridge formed by small tubercles and some small ridges on the sides; black dorsal pigment forming a network around the ridges in the center of the dorsum; rhinophores yellowish. Shallow rocky reefs.

Phyllidiopsis striata Bergh, 1889
Size: 20 mm   Western and central Pacific Ocean
ID: Bluish-white with three low, white longitudinal ridges bordered by black lines and an outer black ring; central ridge always shorter, terminating just behind the rhinophores; rhinophores lemon yellow. On shallow reef flats from 1-20 m.

Phyllidiopsis dautzenbergi (Vayssière, 1912)
Size: 19 mm   Red Sea
ID: White with a thick black circle on the center of the dorsum and black radiating projections that reach the mantle margin; dorsum with low longitudinal ridges. On hard bottoms in 15 m.

Phyllidiopsis annae Brunckhorst, 1993
Size: 20 mm   Indian and western Pacific oceans
ID: Bluish-white with three low, blue, tipped in white, median longitudinal ridges, bordered by black lines and an outer black ring; mantle perimeter granulose with a few tiny black spots; rhinophores black. On shallow reef flats and slopes in 5-15 m.

Phyllidiopsis phiphiensis Brunckhorst, 1993
Size: 29 mm   Madagascar, Thailand
ID: Translucent white with three longitudinal black lines, and black spots on the margin; two low white ridges between the lines unite at the anus; anteriorly the ridges pass through the rhinophoral sheaths to the anterior margin of the mantle; rhinophores white. In 1-10 m; feeds on a red sponge.

222

Phyllidiopsis sphingis Brunckhorst, 1993
Size: 23 mm   Western and central Pacific Ocean
ID: Cream with blue pigment around the margins; numerous longitudinal and radiating black lines and spots; rhinophores cream to yellow. On moderately steep reef slopes in the open.

Phyllidiopsis sp. 2
Size: 20 mm   Madagascar
ID: Bluish white with a central black stripe; two longitudinal ridges bordered by black lines with radiating branches to the mantle edge; shorter black lines extend from the mantle edge inward a short distance; rhinophores black. On barrier reef flats and slopes in 10-25 m.

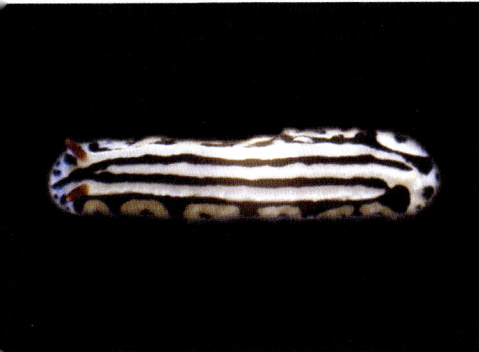

Phyllidiopsis sp. 3
Size: 25 mm   Hawai'ian Is.
ID: Whitish with four black longitudinal lines; outer lines with radiations to the mantle margin; blue pigment at the anterior and posterior ends; rhinophores red. Relatively deep water, in 30 m.

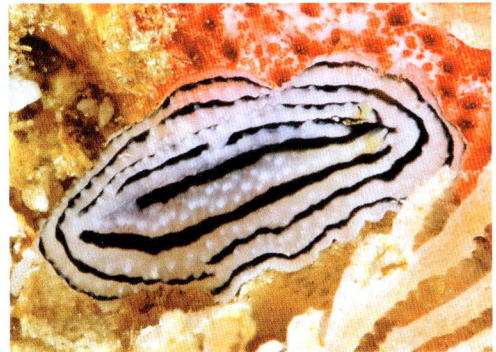

Phyllidiopsis sp. 4
Size: 22 mm   Kenya
ID: White with several longitudinal rows of small tubercles; a series of concentric black rings and longitudinal lines occupy the areas between tubercles; rhinophores yellowish. Under coral rubble, 15 m.

Phyllidiopsis loricata (Bergh, 1873)
Size: 26 mm   Widespread in the Indo-Pacific
ID: White with a series of 10-12 large marginal black to brown spots; mantle texture appears rough due to the numerous conical, rounded tubercles; rhinophores white to cream. In coral rubble.

Phyllidiopsis sp. 5
Size: 15 mm   Thailand
ID: Yellow with a bluish mantle margin; large black patches surround the yellow center; small black dots on the mantle edge.

223

Nudibranchia - "nudibranchs"

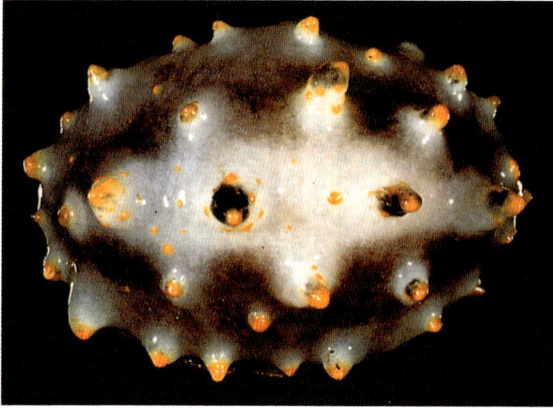

Phyllidiopsis holothuriana Valdés, 2001
Size: 58 mm   New Caledonia, Vanuatu
ID: Dark grey to black with gold-yellow large conical tubercles, some with black at the base. In deep water, 100-550 m.

Phyllidiopsis brunckhorsti Valdés, 2001
Size: 50 mm   New Caledonia
ID: Opaque white with the digestive gland visible as a pale cream area; mantle margin with several radiating black lines and spots. In deep water, 280-350 m.

Phyllidiopsis cardinalis Bergh, 1876
Size: 65 mm   Widespread in the Indo-Pacific
ID: Yellow, red-orange or red-brown, often with shades of dark olive and purple; tubercles isolated, large and compound; two medial rows of large tubercles with reddish veins; mantle margin yellow to olive-yellow with dark grey-black spots; rhinophores with olive apices. Coral rubble, in 0-10 m.

Phyllidiopsis sp. 6
Size: 15 mm   Maldives Is.
ID: Yellow with longitudinal black lines having lateral extensions into the mantle margin and isolated black spots; tubercles rounded; rhinophores yellow.

Phyllidiopsis monacha (Yonow, 1986)
Size: 20 mm   Red Sea and Indonesia
ID: Translucent white with a pattern of connected black patches, a yellow median line and several yellow patches on the mantle margin; rhinophores uniformly yellow. On soft bottoms at 42 m.

Reticulidia Brunckhorst, 1990
Species of this group have smooth reticulate ridges on the dorsum, unfused oral tentacles, and a pharyngeal bulb, composed of radially arranged glandular discs.

Reticulidia suzanneae Valdés & Behrens, 2002
Size: 70 mm   Indian Ocean
ID: Bright yellow-orange with notal ridges; white lines along the crests of the ridges and a large dense black spot at the center of each of the depression between the ridges. In 10-25 m.

Reticulidia halgerda Brunckhorst & Burn *in* Brunckhorst, 1990
Size: 65 mm   Western and central Pacific Ocean
ID: Black with orange ridges and white apical crests; rhinophores red. On exposed walls in moderately deep water, 14-65 m.

Reticulidia fungia Brunckhorst & Gosliner *in* Brunckhorst, 1993
Size: 42 mm   Widespread in the Indo-Pacific
ID: Bluish-white with a few broad, smooth, orange ridges with white crests; black areas between the ridges; mantle margin with a grey-blue line. On reef slopes and walls in 20-40 m.

Reticulidia sp. 1
Size: 45 mm   Philippines
ID: White with black markings between the ridges; lacks any orange pigment; rhinophores yellow. Mesophotic, 100 m.

225

Nudibranchia - "nudibranchs"

Reticulidia sp. 2
Size: 15 mm   Vanuatu, Papua New Guinea
ID: Orange with a series large black markings surrounded by opaque white bands; rhinophores orange. On shallow water reefs in 10 m.

Ceratophyllidia Eliot, 1903
Species of this group have unusually bodies with spherical, stalked and autotomizable tubercles on the dorsum and lack oral glands on the pharyngeal bulb.

Ceratophyllidia africana Eliot, 1903
Size: 40 mm   Indian and western Pacific oceans
ID: Whitish-cream with soft, detachable papillae scattered with black markings. Beneath stones or coral heads on relatively shallow reefs.

Ceratophyllidia sp. 1
Size: 35 mm   Papua New Guinea, Guam
ID: White, with a series of large, inflated, solidly dark grey to black tubercles around the margin; rhinophores white. Further study is required to determine whether this represents a species distinct from Ceratophyllidia africana. Under coral rubble in relatively shallow water.

Ceratophyllidia sp. 2
Size: 15 mm   Papua New Guinea, Philippines, Guam
ID: White with 10-16 tan brown to red spots, arranged approximately in two lines medially; a series of large inflated tubercles with reddish brown apices around the margin of the mantle; rhinophores cream-brown. In shallow water.

Ceratophyllidia sp. 3
Size: 35 mm   Tropical Japan
ID: Pale yellowish, with numerous white papillae; dark pigment concentrated on the central papilla with sparse or no pigment on the marginal ones; rhinophores white.

Ceratophyllidia sp. 4
Size: 30 mm   Philippines
ID: Bright yellow with large, spherical papillae covering the body; papillae with different degrees of black pigment, some almost completely black, others almost completely white; rhinophores opaque white. Steep reef face among coral rubble, 30 m.

Clade 2: Cladobranchia - "cladobranchs"

so known as Cladohepatica, this is the second major group of nudibranchs. Cladobranchs are characterized by having branched digestive gland. The phylogeny of this group has been recently investigated by Pola & Gosliner (2010) and oodheart *et al.* (2015, 2017). Some of the subgroups described below are likely paraphyletic (unnatural groups).

Arminina - "arminids"

its traditional sense, Arminina is an unnatural group of nudibranchs (Goodheart *et al.* 2015, 2017), as members are only ited by having an oral veil, which has originated independently in different groups. The Arminidae feed on soft corals and natulaceans, while the group to which *Janolus* belongs, feeds on bryozoans. Several other taxa have been lumped into this oup, which is in need of a new classification.

Arminidae Iredale & O'Donoghue, 1923

here are many species of arminids found in the Indo-Pacific opics. Most are in the genera *Armina* and *Dermatobranchus* d have a series of longitudinal ridges on the body. Species Arminidae are commonly found on soft sandy bottoms, om shallow waters down to great depths. They feed on soft orals and sea pens using their jaws and radula to bite off eces of flesh.

rmina Rafinesque, 1814

embers of *Armina* are characterized by having a series of econdary respiratory leaves between the mantle and the ot (as seen on the photograph on the right), on the sides the body. Also, the anterior edge of the mantle, behind e rhinophores, is normally complete. Many species have a eries of longitudinal lines on the dorsum.

Armina magna Baba, 1955
Size: 150 mm   Japan, Philippines
ID: Black with white longitudinal lines and yellow to orange margins of the mantle and foot; margin of the oral veil also orange but interrupted; rhinophores mainly black with orange dots on the tips. On sandy and muddy bottoms, collected in fishing nets and from trawls in 100-138 m.

Armina sp. 1
ize: 200 mm   Indonesia
O: Black with white longitudinal lines; yellow to orange nargins of the mantle, foot and oral veil; rhinophores black with orange apices. Feeds on the sea pen, *Pteroides* sp. in m.

Armina paucifoliata Baba, 1955
Size: 100 mm   Philippines, Japan
ID: Black with yellowish white longitudinal lines; white margins of the mantle, foot and oral veil; rhinophores black with a white apex. Together with *Armina magna* in 100 m.

227

Armina variolosa (Bergh, 1904)
Size: 50 mm   Japan, Hong Kong (China), Philippines
ID: Reddish with longitudinal, irregular rows of rounded tubercles each with a white apex; rhinophores narrow, reddish with white tips; foot wide, with a white edge. On sandy and mud bottoms, on sandy slopes in 7-20 m.

Armina occulta Mehrotra, Caballer & Chavanich, 201
Size: 80 mm   Western Pacific Ocea
ID: Black with white longitudinal stripes; foot with a blu marginal band; oral veil and mantle with an orange margin band; bright blue curved lines extending from the rhinophore to the extremities of the oral veil. On sandy areas in 3-20 n appears to feed on the sea pen, *Pteroides* sp.

Armina sp. 2
Size: 105 mm   Philippines
ID: Black with white longitudinal stripes; mantle and foot with an orange margin followed by a blue band in the foot; blue pigment also present at the base of the rhinophores and on the anterior portion of the oral veil. Nocturnally active in 10-55 m; feeds on the sea pen, *Virgularia* sp.

Armina scotti Mehrotra, Caballer & Chavanich, 201
Size: 60 mm   Western Pacific Ocea
ID: Black with white longitudinal stripes; foot and oral veil wit an orange marginal band and a submarginal blue band; ora veil white; foot with distinct triangular foot corners. On sand and gravelly bottoms, often together with *Armina* sp. 3. in 1C 15 m; feeds on the sea pen, *Virgularia* sp.

Armina sp. 3
Size: 60 mm   United Arab Emirates
ID: Black with yellow longitudinal stripes; foot and oral veil with a pale yellow marginal band and a submarginal pale blue band; oral veil white with two black stripes. On sandy substrate from 8-14 m; feeds on the sea pen, *Virgularia* sp.

Armina sp. 4
Size: 40 mm   Vanuat
ID: Grey with dark brown to black longitudinal lines; ora veil with a series of concentric fine dark lines and a yellov margin. Trawled from deep water on soft substrate.

228

rmina sp. 5

ize: 60 mm   United Arab Emirates

): Dark grey with longitudinal yellowish lines and irregular
ack mottling on the notum; oral veil with a series of
regularly radiating white lines; rhinophores golden yellow.
andy bottoms.

Armina sp. 6

Size: 80 mm   Philippines

ID: Black with longitudinal white lines and irregular black
mottling on the notum; mantle and foot with an orange
margin; oral veil black, edged in orange; rhinophores orange.
Nocturnally active on sandy rubble in 20 m; feeds on the sea
pen, *Pteroides* sp.

rmina sp. 7

ize: 35 mm   Philippines

): Dark grey with longitudinal brownish-yellow lines; mantle
ith a yellowish margin, rhinophores blue with bright red
pices. On sandy rubble, in 20 m; feeds on the sea pen,
teroides sp.

Armina sp. 8

Size: 50 mm   Philippines

ID: Black with longitudinal white ridges, each with a thin
orange central line; dorsum with large unpigmented areas
and an orange marginal line; foot and head bluish; velum
white with an orange marginal line and a central blue area,
densely mottled with black; rhinophores red. Active during
the day on sandy rubble in 35 m; feeds on sea pens.

rmina sp. 9

ize: 40 mm   Philippines

): Black with numerous white longitudinal ridges interrupted
y transversal regions of black pigment; notal margin white
ith a thin marginal orange line; foot white; velum pale orange
ith an orange edge; rhinophores orange apically. Nocturnally
ctive on sand, 15 m; feeds on the sea pen, *Virgularia* sp.

Armina sp. 10

Size: 60 mm   Philippines

ID: White with pale orange longitudinal lines, some areas
between ridges with black pigment; foot bluish; velum white
with a black central area and an orange marginal line; two
vertical lines on the head below the orange rhinophores. On
sandy rubble where it feeds on sea pens.

229

Nudibranchia - "nudibranchs"

Armina cygnea (Bergh, 1876)
Size: 100 mm   Australia
ID: Black with numerous white longitudinal lines extending into the oral veil; foot with a marginal yellow line and submarginal pale blue pigment. Shallow water on sandy substrate; feeds on the soft coral, *Dendronephthya* sp.

Armina sp. 11
Size: 125 mm   South Afric
ID: Black with a few white longitudinal lines; white band along the margins of the notum, foot and oral veil; oral ve extremely wide; rhinophores black with white apices. O coarse sand in 36 m.

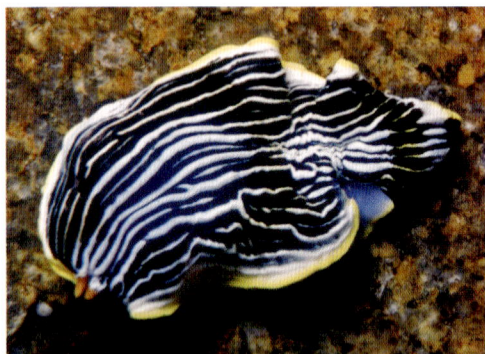

Armina sp. 12
Size: 80 mm   Kwazulu Natal (South Africa)
ID: Black with numerous white longitudinal lines; margin of the notum yellow; rhinophores with an orange apex; foot with blue pigment.

Armina papillata Baba, 1933
Size: 100 mm   Philippines, Japa
ID: Black with longitudinal white ridges and a white margina line; velum black, edged in white, with several white papillae rhinophores black with white apices. Nocturnally active o sand rubble in 10 m; feeds on the sea pen, *Pteroides* sp.

Armina cf. **comta** (Bergh, 1880)
Size: 40 mm   Western Pacific Ocean
ID: Black with yellow longitudinal lines and yellow margins of the notum and oral veil; rhinophores black with a yellow apex; yellow papillae on the oral veil. On shallow sandy substrates; feeds on the sea pen, *Veretillum* sp.

Armina sp. 13
Size: 35 mm   Vanuat
ID: Pinkish red with a series of longitudinal faint white line on the notum; foot broad with wide, angular extension anteriorly; mantle narrowing near the middle where lines c dark brown and opaque white form a girdle. Trawled fron relatively deep water.

Armina babai (Tchang, 1934)
Size: 80 mm   Pakistan, Singapore, China
ID: Grey with an irregular pinkish tinge; one of the few species *Armina* lacking longitudinal ridges and undoubtedly one of the least attractive Indo-Pacific nudibranchs, we can only be thankful that it spends most of its time buried under intertidal sand flats to relatively deep water; presumably feeds on sea pens.

Armina sp. 14
Size: 100 mm   Western Australia
ID: Grey with numerous irregular, opaque white longitudinal ridges on the dorsum; velum and foot grey with opaque white marginal lines; rhinophores grey with white apices. Fine silty sand.

Armina sp. 15
Size: 30 mm   Vanuatu
ID: White with fine black longitudinal lines; notum with a yellow marginal line; oral veil white with black spots and a yellow band. Trawled from deep water on soft substrate.

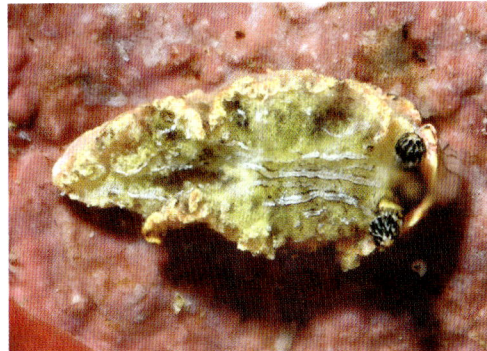

Armina sp. 16
Size: 25 mm   Vanuatu
ID: Yellow with a few white longitudinal lines and isolated black pigment; oral veil grey with a yellow margin; rhinophores black with yellow pigment on the lamellae and apex. On gravelly bottoms.

Armina sp. 17
Size: 40 mm   United Arab Emirates
ID: Light grey with longitudinal white lines and irregular black mottling on the notum; oral veil with irregular tubercles; rhinophores dark grey to black. On gravelly bottoms.

Armina sp. 18
Size: 40 mm   Philippines
ID: Chocolate brown with longitudinal white lines; oral veil with a few elongate tubercles; rhinophores brown basally with orange clubs. On gravelly bottoms in 15 m.

Nudibranchia - "nudibranchs"

Dermatobranchus van Hasselt, 1824

Members of *Dermatobranchus* are characterized by lacking secondary respiratory leaves on the sides of the body. Also, the anterior edge of the mantle, behind the rhinophores, is normally incomplete, fused with the head. Many species have irregular ridges or tubercles on the dorsum.

Dermatobranchus gonatophorus van Hasselt, 1824

Size: 40 mm   Indian and western Pacific oceans
ID: Grey with black and yellow lines and an orange marginal band; rhinophores with black clubs. Feeds on the soft coral, *Eleutherobia greyi* on sandy habitats in 15-53 m.

Dermatobranchus ornatus (Bergh, 1874)

Size: 80 mm   Indian and western Pacific oceans
ID: Green with white flat-topped scattered tubercles having orange apices; marginal band around the notum and oral veil orange, followed by a submarginal white area with black spots; black spots also on the foot. In 12-56 m, active during the day; it appears to feed on gorgonians and soft corals.

Dermatobranchus pustulosus van Hasselt, 1824

Size: 70 mm   Western Pacific, possibly South Africa
ID: Brownish mottled mantle with a series of irregular pustules covering the notum; in mature specimens pustules tipped with black spots; rhinophores very bulbous, brownish, each with a dark ring. On shallow water reefs in the open and under coral rubble; feeds on xeniid soft corals.

Dermatobranchus kalyptos Gosliner & Fahey, 2011

Size: 50 mm   Indonesia
ID: Purplish pink with white and brown pigment; notum with irregular pustules, but fewer than in *Dermatobranchus pustulosus*; veil white with scattered brown pigment; rhinophores dark brown with white dots.

Dermatobranchus phyllodes Gosliner & Fahey, 2011

Size: 40 mm   Western Pacific Ocean
ID: White with scattered brownish spots; notum with a series of diagonal ridges on the outer halves, leaving most of the central notum free of ridges; rhinophores dark brown with white lamellae. On reefs in 10-20 m where soft corals are abundant.

Dermatobranchus diagonalis Gosliner & Fahey, 2011
Size: 35 mm   Papua New Guinea
ID: Greyish-green with a white head and oral veil, and scattered brown pigment; notum with diagonal ridges extending all the way from the center to the edge; ridges with opaque white lines; a thin orange marginal line on the notum and oral veil. Shallow protected lagoons in 15 m.

Dermatobranchus caesitius Gosliner & Fahey, 2011
Size: 20 mm   South Africa
ID: Bluish with a series of interrupted partial, well elevated ridges; notum with scattered black spots; oral veil white with blue pigment; rhinophores dark grey with white lamellae. Intertidal zone; feeds on xeniid soft coral, *Sansibia flava*.

Dermatobranchus tuberculatus Gosliner & Fahey, 2011
Size: 18 mm   Malaysia, Philippines
ID: Whitish with brown pustules and pinkish purple spots on the notum; a brown triangular area may be present in the mid dorsal region. In areas densely covered with the soft coral, *Cespitularia* sp., in 3-5 m.

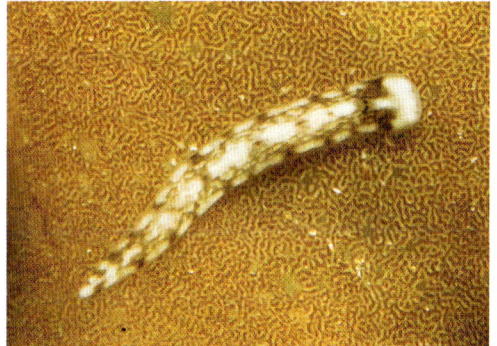

***Dermatobranchus* sp. 1**
Size: 10 mm   Tahiti
ID: White mottled with brown pigment leaving a series of white areas in the center of the dorsum; rhinophores dark brown; body very elongate. In 15 m.

Dermatobranchus fortunatus (Bergh, 1888)
Size: 12 mm   Widespread in the Indo-Pacific
ID: White, devoid of obvious longitudinal ridges, with a series of brown patches along the mantle edge; orange pigment on the rhinophores as well as on the margins of the oral veil and

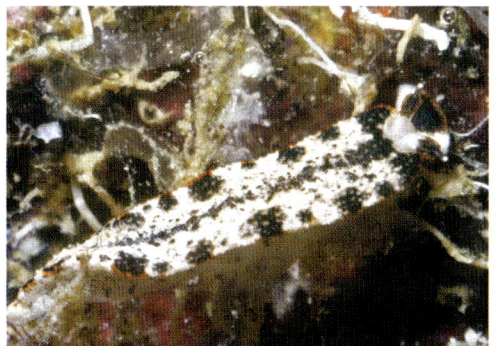

mantle; a single brown patch on the anterior end of the oral veil. Commonly under coral rubble on reefs from the intertidal zone to 5 m.

Dermatobranchus sp. 2
Size: 60 mm   Philippines
ID: White, mottled with irregular black pigment and with a series of longitudinal white ridges; mantle margin highly convoluted; rhinophores very large, wide and low, brown with white lamellae. Trawled from deep water on sandy substrate, 223-369 m.

Dermatobranchus sp. 3
Size: 40 mm   Philippines
ID: Mottled brownish, orange and grey with a series of irregular, rounded pustules; mantle and velum margins cream; dorsum and velum covered with numerous small dark dots, more densely arranged on the margin; rhinophores bulbous, orange-brown and black, with white apices.

Dermatobranchus sp. 4
Size: 15 mm   Kenya, Indonesia
ID: Varied shades of greyish-white and brown with thick, irregular dorsal longitudinal ridges; velum broad, white, with an orange edge; rhinophores dark grey with opaque white spots and apices.

Dermatobranchus fasciatus Gosliner & Fahey, 2011
Size: 15 mm   Philippines, Papua New Guinea
ID: White with two distinct transverse bands of brown pigment; brown rhinophores with opaque white spots. On shallow reefs in areas with abundant soft corals.

Dermatobranchus sp. 5
Size: 30 mm   Papua New Guinea
ID: Greyish-white with numerous opaque white longitudinal ridges; dorsum with scattered brown spots surrounded by areas of light brown pigment; rhinophores brown with white apices. On outer reef slopes in 20 m.

Dermatobranchus sp. 6
Size: 15 mm   Philippines, Indonesia
ID: White with longitudinal opaque white ridges and several areas of black pigment between the ridges; rhinophores black with orange apices; velum bluish edged in orange-cream.

***Dermatobranchus albus* (Eliot, 1904)**
Size: 10 mm · · · · · · · · · · Indian and western Pacific oceans
ID: Color variable from white to black with prominent dorsal longitudinal ridges, which may have orange pigment on them; margins of the mantle and oral veil orange; rhinophores black with orange apices. On reefs in 1-40 m, crawling in the open.

***Dermatobranchus semilunus* Gosliner & Fahey, 2011**
Size: 12 mm · · · · · · · · · · · · · · · Western Pacific Ocean
ID: Opaque white with longitudinal dark ridges; a distinct U-shaped band of dark brown on the anterior third of the notum; other brown spots on the notum and oral veil; rhinophores dark grey with white lamellae. On barrier reef crests, in 5-11 m.

***Dermatobranchus* sp. 7**
Size: 15 mm · · · · · · · · · · · · · · · · Tuamotu Archipelago
ID: Opaque white with faint brown longitudinal lines and black spots surrounded by yellow areas; black spots near the mantle margin, and forming a line in the center of the dorsum; rhinophores translucent with opaque white and black pigment. Protected bays and lagoons, in 1 m.

Nudibranchia - "nudibranchs"

Dermatobranchus funiculus Gosliner & Fahey, 2011
Size: 13 mm   Southern Japan, Philippines
ID: White to reddish-brown with numerous longitudinal ridges on the notum; yellowish glands on the margins of the notum; oral veil opaque white with an orange margin; rhinophores brown with opaque white lamellae and apices. Areas of dense rubble and strong currents in 12-20 m.

Dermatobranchus kokonas Gosliner & Fahey, 2011
Size: 7 mm   Papua New Guinea
ID: Opaque white without longitudinal ridges; rhinophoral clubs brown; anterior margin of the oral veil orange-brown. Under coral rubble on fringing reefs in 15 m.

Dermatobranchus caeruleomaculatus Gosliner & Fahey, 2011
Size: 20 mm   Indonesia, Malaysia, Philippines
ID: Whitish with reddish brown pigment covering most of the notum; longitudinal black lines and opaque white spots also present; an orange margin and blue markings on the edge of the notum, foot and oral veil. In 10-20 m; feeds on the soft coral, *Dendronephthya* sp.; it displays trailing behavior.

Dermatobranchus oculus Gosliner & Fahey, 2011
Size: 15 mm   Southern Japan
ID: Opaque white with longitudinal brown ridges; a few
arge translucent ocelli with black spots along the notum;
rhinophores with black clubs. In 12 m.

Dermatobranchus piperoides Gosliner & Fahey,
2011
Size: 8 mm   Reunion Island
ID: Opaque white with scattered black spots but lacking
longitudinal ridges on the notum; velum with an orange
anterior patch. In 1-2 m under volcanic rocks.

Dermatobranchus rodmani Gosliner & Fahey, 2011
Size: 12 mm   Madagascar, eastern Malaysia
ID: Pale pinkish; smooth notum with brown patches,
occasionally with a few low longitudinal ridges; oral veil
and notum with a yellow margin having scattered brown
spots; rhinophores brown with opaque white markings. On
reefs, crawling in the open in areas with dense covering of
octocorals, in 5-10 m.

***Dermatobranchus* sp. 8**
Size: 18 mm   Philippines
ID: White with tan patches; small brownish ocelli between
the longitudinal ridges; oral veil with a faint orange margin;
rhinophores dark brown with orange on the lamellae; apex
yellow. Shallow patch reefs on soft corals, 10 m.

***Dermatobranchus* sp. 9**
Size: 25 mm   Philippines
ID: Brown with longitudinal black ridges and opaque white
areas; velum reddish, with a brown inner region and several
large opaque white spots; rhinophores with white stalks,
clubs black with white lamellae.

***Dermatobranchus* sp. 10**
Size: 30 mm   Indonesia
ID: Opaque white with longitudinal blue ridges; mantle and
velum with marginal yellow bands; rhinophores black with
light blue lamellae.

Nudibranchia - "nudibranchs"

Dermatobranchus sp. 11
Size: 25 mm   Philippines
ID: White; dorsum black covered with longitudinal white ridges; mantle and velum with orange marginal lines; rhinophoral stalks white with orange lines, club black with white vertical lamellae. Shallow patch reefs in silty areas, 10 m.

Dermatobranchus dendronephthyphagus Gosliner & Fahey, 2011
Size: 40 mm   Okinawa (Japan), Philippines
ID: White with black pigment and black longitudinal lines; margin of the notum light yellow; rhinophores with black and white pigment. In 45 m; feeds on the octocoral, *Dendronephthya* sp.

Dermatobranchus sp. 12
Size: 20 mm   Indonesia
ID: Bluish notum with thin dark blue longitudinal lines; mantle, foot and oral veil margins orange; rhinophores black with white lamellae.

Dermatobranchus leoni Gosliner & Fahey, 2011
Size: 40 mm   Philippines
ID: Reddish with numerous black longitudinal lines on the notum and opaque white spots; margins of the foot and oral veil orange with large black spots; rhinophores black with white apices.

Dermatobranchus striatus van Hasselt, 1824
Size: 35 mm   Western Pacific Ocean
ID: Black with longitudinal white markings on the notum; an alternating series of black and white rings on the oral veil, anterior to the rhinophores; margins of the notum, foot and oral veil light orange. In 30 m on sand; active at night.

Dermatobranchus cymatilis Gosliner & Fahey, 2011
Size: 23 mm   Southern Japan, Philippines
ID: Opaque white with black longitudinal lines on the orange-brown dorsum; foot margin with a white band and black spots; yellow pigment and black spots on the margins of the oral veil and notum. In 10-60 m.

Dermatobranchus sp. 13
Size: 20 mm   Vanuatu
ID: White with numerous black longitudinal lines on the notum; oral veil with yellowish orange pigment; rhinophores dark brown to black, with opaque white spots.

Dermatobranchus sp. 14
Size: 40 mm   Malaysia
ID: Opaque white with broken black ridges on the dorsum; notum and velum with orange marginal lines; velum white with blue pigment and large black spots; rhinophores with white stalks, clubs black with white lamellae.

Dermatobranchus rubidus (Gould, 1852)
Size: 50 mm   Western and central Pacific
ID: Pink to red with a series of longitudinal opaque white lines on the ridges; foot broad with wide, angular extensions anteriorly; oral veil with a scalloped margin. On sandy areas from the intertidal zone to 15 m; active at night.

Dermatobranchus sp. 15
Size: 40 mm   Indonesia
ID: Pale orange with numerous red tubercles on the notum; notum and foot margins white; rhinophores red.

Dermatobranchus sp. 16
Size: 20 mm   Indonesia
ID: Yellow brown; rhinophores white with black lines; notum with a series of longitudinal and diagonal ridges.

Dermatobranchus sp. 17
Size: 25 mm   Philippines
ID: White with interrupted longitudinal lines and black spots surrounded by lighter rings; rhinophores black with orange. Medium deep reefs, 22 m.

Dermatobranchus sp. 18
Size: 18 mm   Philippines
ID: Body greyish white; ridges parallel and diagonal with brownish pigment; rhinophores brown with orange pigment, Shallow reefs, under coral rubble.

Madrellidae Preston, 1911

This small family is closely related to the Proctonotidae but its members have an oral veil. Species of this group feed on bryozoans.

Madrella ferruginosa Alder & Hancock, 1864
Size: 45 mm   Indian and western Pacific oceans
ID: Reddish brown with opaque white pigment between the rhinophores, on the rhinophoral stalk, and on the cerata; rhinophores brownish with a swollen area containing numerous papillae and a narrow, long extension. From the intertidal zone to 15 m on reefs; feeds on calcareous, crustose bryozoans.

Madrella gloriosa Baba, 1949
Size: 40 mm   Tanzania, Japan
ID: Brown with white spots; cerata relatively thick, red with cream bases covered with opaque white spots and blue pigment; a nodular opaque white area between the rhinophores.

Madrella sp. 1
Size: 25 mm   Papua New Guinea
ID: Transparent brownish; cerata shaped like bottles or bowling pins, with a network of opaque white pigment. Under coral rubble in 7 m, on barrier reefs.

Madrella sp. 2
Size: 10 mm   Philippines
ID: Orange mottled with opaque white pigment; cerata short, curved, orange and white; rhinophores translucent white with a few papillae. Under coral rubble on a steep reef slope, 15 m.

240

Doridomorphidae Er. Marcus & Ev. Marcus, 1960

This small family contains a single tropical Indo-Pacific species. It is characterized by lacking oral tentacles, a gill, or secondary respiratory structures. These animals move away from the light relatively fast, which in addition to the flat body, and color camouflage on their coral prey, makes them very difficult to spot in the field.

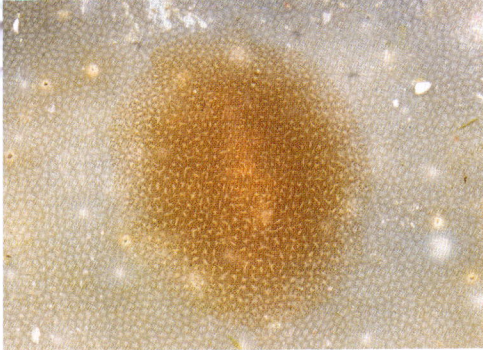

***Doridomorpha gardineri* Eliot, 1903**
Size: 20 mm   Indian and western Pacific oceans
ID: Brown; body flat with simple rhinophores. On shallow reefs; feeds exclusively on the blue coral, *Heliopora caerulea.*

Proctonotidae J. E. Gray, 1853

Most members of this family have a branched sensory structure between the rhinophores called the caruncle. The dorsum is covered with cerata, with or without branches of the digestive gland. Proctonotids feed on bryozoans. Species of *Janolus*, the most diverse genus, eat arborescent species. When disturbed many species autotomize the cerata, which are sticky and adhere to anything that they come in contact with.

***Janolus* sp. 1**
Size: 30 mm   Indonesia, southern Japan
ID: Cream with orange spots; cerata transparent, swollen, with orange, opaque white and purple spots; rhinophores red; caruncle white with orange spots. In 10-43 m.

Pinufiidae Er. Marcus & Ev. Marcus, 1960

This family includes a single species characterized by having a differentiated mantle with a series of cerata that disappear when the animal is starved for a few days. It has rhinophores but lacks oral tentacles.

***Pinufius rebus* Er. Marcus & Ev. Marcus, 1960**
Size: 10 mm   Western and central Pacific Ocean
ID: Brownish with opaque white spots; numerous elongate cerata extend from the body. On shallow reefs; feeds on *Porites* corals, on which it is remarkably well camouflaged.

***Janolus* sp. 2**
Size: 50 mm   Mauritius
ID: Translucent grey with transparent cerata in which the digestive gland branches are visible; each ceras with subapical yellow pigment and black pointed tips; rhinophores elongate with black tips. Soft bottoms in 24 m.

***Janolus* sp. 3**
Size: 30 mm   Western Pacific ocean
ID: Bright red orange with pointed yellow tips on the cerata; caruncle contrasting opaque white. In 10 m on outer barrier reefs.

Nudibranchia - "nudibranchs"

Janolus toyamensis Baba & Abe, 1970
Size: 50 mm   Western and central Pacific
ID: Light honey brown with translucent cerata, through which the digestive gland is visible; cerata with yellow pigment subapically and dark brown tips; many cerata bear opaque white lines. Feeds on arborescent bryozoans on rocky drop-offs in 5-10 m.

Janolus savinkini Martynov & Korshunova, 2012
Size: 70 mm   Western Pacific Ocean
ID: Opaque creamy-white; cerata and rhinophores cream with blue subapical rings and purple to brown apices; caruncle white. In 20-30 m on rubble fields; feeds on arborescent bryozoans.

Janolus sp. 4
Size: 50 mm   Indonesia
ID: Orange with dark purple rhinophores and a yellow caruncle; cerata orange, most with lighter orange subapical rings and purple apices, some with dense opaque white pigment covering the apices. Coral rubble in shallow water.

Janolus sp. 5
Size: 15 mm   New Caledonia
ID: Translucent white; cerata and rhinophores white with deep violet tips; brown branches of the digestive gland visible through the body wall; caruncle white, small.

242

Janolus sp. 6

Size: 30 mm   Indonesia
ID: Yellow-brown with brown and opaque white spots on the notum and on the bulbous cerata; rhinophores with opaque white papillae on their surface.

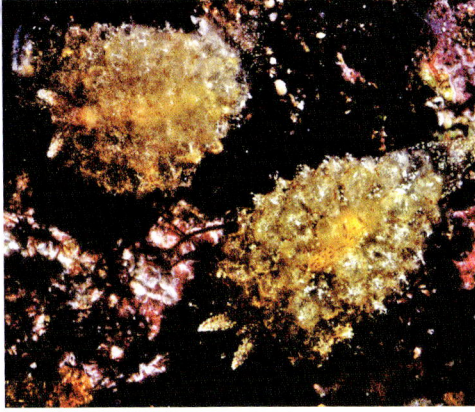

Janolus sp. 7

Size: 50 mm   Indian and western Pacific oceans
ID: Color variable from translucent white to pale brown; cerata with the same color as the body with blue purple apices, each with a yellow subapical ring and mottled cream spots below. In 20-30 m, on rubble fields and slopes where it feeds on arborescent bryozoans.

Janolus sp. 8

Size: 25 mm   Western Pacific Ocean
ID: Orange with opaque white pigment, and black and purple ceratal tips. Feeds on an arborescent bryozoans of the genus *Tricellaria* with curved apical branches; on steep reef walls and pinnacles in areas where strong currents are present in 20-40 m.

Nudibranchia - "nudibranchs"

Janolus sp. 9
Size: 5 mm   Great Barrier Reef (Australia)
ID: Pale brown with dark brown and opaque white pigment; cerata opaque white with dark purple rings. On bryozoans in 13 m.

Janolus mirabilis Baba & Abe, 1970
Size: 15 mm   Widespread in the Indo-Pacific
ID: Opaque white body and cerata, both with a dense covering of papillae; a distinct gap between anterior and posterior clusters of cerata. Together with *Janolus toyamensis* on arborescent bryozoans in 5-10 m.

Janolus sp. 10
Size: 18 mm   Marshall Is.
ID: Opaque white body and cerata, both with a dense covering of papillae; cerata with characteristic narrowings near the apices; each ceras with a large brown spot; rhinophores large and papillate. Under dead coral in lagoon reefs and pinnacles, in 4-15 m.

Janolus sp. 11
Size: 8 mm   Palau
ID: Translucent white body with opaque white spots, orange and blue markings on the cerata and rhinophores; cerata with subapical blue ring. Steep walls, on the bryozoan, *Tricellaria* sp.

Janolus sp. 12
Size: 18 mm   Indonesia, Marshall Is.
ID: Translucent white with abundant opaque white pigment covering the body, the cerata and the rhinophores; cerata

papillate with reddish-brown tips and dark brown digestive gland branches visible at the base; rhinophores very long, papillate. Under coral rubble, 1-5 m.

Dendronotina - "dendronotinids"

Members of this group are characterized by the presence of distinct rhinophoral sheaths that are elevated from the notum. Dendronotinids also have a series of lateral appendages on the sides of the body; some of these are highly branched and function as secondary gills. Recent phylogenetic studies have shown that dendronotinids do not constitute a single natural group, but represent a combination of two smaller groups (Goodheart *et al.* 2015, 2017).

Bornellidae Bergh, 1874

Species in this group have elongate bodies with highly branched dorsal appendages that function as secondary gills. They appear to be closely related to the mainly temperate Dendronotidae, but have distinguishing features of their reproductive anatomy. Most species of *Bornella* are rather drably colored.

Bornella anguilla S. Johnson, 1984
Size: 80 mm   Widespread in the Indo-Pacific
ID: Bright and complex color pattern with orange and black paddle-shaped appendages adjacent to the lateral appendages and rhinophores. On the undersides of rocks and on sertularid hydroid colonies in 5-20 m; when disturbed, it is capable of swimming rapidly by moving its body like an eel.

Bornella stellifer (A. Adams & Reeve *in* A. Adams, 1848)
Size: 30 mm   Widespread in the Indo-Pacific
ID: Translucent pale brown with orange and opaque white markings; orange subapical rings on the lateral appendages and on the branches of the rhinophoral sheaths. From the intertidal zone to 20 m in association with thecate hydroids, on which it feeds.

Bornella dotoides Pola, Rudman & Gosliner, 2008
Size: 25 mm   Papua New Guinea
ID: Brown with small opaque white spots; lateral appendages and rhinophoral sheaths with numerous small tubercles. Under coral rubble on relatively shallow reef flats in 7-15 m.

Bornella pele Pola, Rudman & Gosliner, 2008
Size: 30 mm   Western and central Pacific Ocean
ID: Translucent white covered with minute opaque white spots; red pigment on the anterior and posterior ends of the body and on the stalks of the rhinophoral sheaths; lateral appendages simple and fusiform with several elongate lateral branches and two bright red lines at their junction. On exposed volcanic slopes in 20-30 m.

Bornella hermanni Angas, 1864
Size: 50 mm   Indian and western Pacific oceans
ID: White with irregular brown pigment; similar to *Bornella stellifer*, but with the papillae on the rhinophoral sheaths subdivided and only three pairs of lateral appendages on either side of the body. On shallow reefs and walls where it feeds on thecate hydroids.

245

Bornella cf. adamsii J. E. Gray in M. E. Gray, 1850
Size: 50 mm   Borneo, Thailand, Malaysia
ID: Opaque white with orange mottling; similar to *Bornella stellifer*, but the rhinophoral sheaths are greatly enlarged. On sandy substrate in 15-25 m.

Bornella irvingi Edmunds & Preece, 1996
Size: 16 mm   Pitcairn Is., French Polynesia
ID: Opaque white with a dark brown patch on the head; rhinophores and velar tentacles orange; only two pairs of lateral appendages.

Bornella johnsonorum Pola, Rudman & Gosliner, 2008
Size: 25 mm   Marshall Is.
ID: White with a network of red lines; similar to *Bornella stellifer*, but lacks the orange subapical rings on the oral tentacles, rhinophoral sheaths and lateral processes; rhinophoral sheaths similar to those of *B. stellifer*, but the stalk is narrower and the posterior papilla more slender. On ledges at night in 12-15 m.

Bornella valdae Pola, Rudman & Gosliner, 2008
Size: 70 mm   Kwazlulu Natal (South Africa)
ID: Opaque white with a network of red pigment on the sides of the body; rhinophores and lateral appendages with white, red and yellow pigment. Feeds on thecate hydroids on moderately deep reefs in 25-45 m.

Bornella sp. 1
Size: 10 mm   Marshall Is.
ID: Pale translucent brown, covered with minute opaque white spots forming an irregular pattern; viscera visible as a yellow and black area.

Bornella sp. 2
Size: 9 mm   Philippines, Indonesia
ID: Translucent white with abundant opaque white spots all over the body; oral tentacles, rhinophores, rhinophoral sheath appendages and lateral processes orange.

246

Bornella sp. 3
Size: 15 mm   Indonesia
ID: Variable pattern of lighter and more intense orange reticulations on the notum; lateral processes tipped with opaque white.

Dendronotidae Allman, 1845

Members of this group have elongated bodies with numerous branching cerata on the dorsal sides. Dendronotids are most diverse in temperate and cold oceans but there are a few tropical Indo-Pacific species described below.

Dendronotus noahi Pola & Stout, 2008
Size: 15 mm   Papua New Guinea
ID: Translucent white; dark black digestive gland ducts entering the slightly branched lateral processes and rhinophoral sheaths; opaque white at the apex of the rhinophoral sheath branches; rhinophores bright yellow. Under coral in 20 m on exposed reef slopes.

Dendronotus orientalis (Baba, 1932)
Size: 25 mm   Widespread in the Indo-Pacific
ID: Translucent with opaque white spots; viscera visible as a brown mass; body wide with well-elevated rhinophores and an elongate, filamentous extension from the rhinophoral sheaths. On sandy areas in 1-2 m; feeds on the athecate hydroid, *Tubularia mesembryanthemum.*

Dendronotus sp. 1
Size: 17 mm   Okinawa (Japan)
ID: Uniformly greyish white; opaque white tips of the branches of the lateral appendages and rhinophoral sheath lobes; rhinophores light brown. Rubble-strewn areas in 69 m.

Dendronotus regius Pola & Stout, 2008
Size: 30 mm   Indonesia, Philippines
ID: Translucent white with alternating patches of olive green and brown; entire surface marked by small opaque white

spots; lateral appendages and rhinophoral sheaths with many small elongate papillae along the surface. On shallow reefs crawling out in the open.

Nudibranchia - "nudibranchs"

Dendronotus sp. 2
Size: 15 mm   Indonesia
ID: Translucent, with pale brown lateral processes, oral tentacles and rhinophoral sheath appendages with purple and white tips; rhinophores opaque white.

Dendronotus sp. 3
Size: 15 mm   Indonesia
ID: Pale with dark multifid tubercles over the surface of the body; lateral appendages darker than the body, highly branched.

Dendronotus cf. gracilis Baba, 1949
Size: 30 mm   Japan
ID: Translucent whitish with a series of large yellow spots on the notum; lateral appendages covered with black, highly branched with most apical appendages opaque white. Rubble-strewn areas of deep reefs in 69 m.

Dendronotus sp. 4
Size: 10 mm   Indonesia
ID: Translucent white with numerous brown spots; lateral appendages and rhinophoral sheaths ramified with white apices; lateral appendages translucent with the digestive gland branches visible.

Hancockiidae MacFarland, 1923

This is a small group of dendronotinids that are characterized by having "pulpit-like" rhinophores with a lobate sheath and a tapering club that ends in a rounded knob. Species of Hancockiidae feed on hydroids and are found in both tropical and temperate waters.

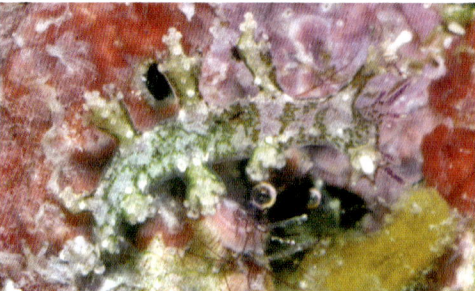

Hancockia sp. 1
Size: 12 mm   Papua New Guinea
ID: Pinkish with brown speckling; lateral appendages unbranched, with rounded tubercles on their surface. Under coral rubble on shallow reefs in 8 m.

Hancockia sp. 2
Size: 25 mm   Papua New Guinea
ID: Brown or greenish with a network of fine opaque white lines on the notum and on the four to five pairs of lateral appendages. On sertularid hydroids growing epibiotically on *Halimeda* plants on the edges of barrier reefs in 10-15 m. Occurs together with *Eubranchus* sp. 9 and 10.

Hancockia sp. 3
Size: 10 mm   Hawai'ian Is.
ID: Light brown with a few scattered opaque white spots on the notum and at the base of the branched lateral appendages; rhinophoral clubs larger than in either of the previous two species.

Hancockia sp. 4
Size: 10 mm   Indonesia
ID: Reddish-cream with numerous small purple dots; lateral appendages and rhinophoral sheaths highly branched with purple and white tips; velar appendages white.

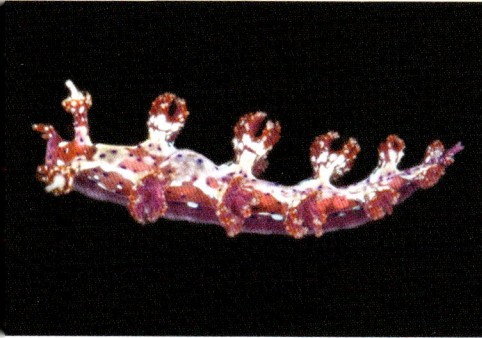

Hancockia sp. 5
Size: 20 mm   Marquesas Is., Papua New Guinea
ID: Reddish-purple with an greyish-white area on the dorsum that penetrates into the bases of the five pairs of lateral appendages and the rhinophoral sheaths; dorsum with numerous black spots; rhinophores white. Feeds on hydroids growing on the green alga *Halimeda* sp. in 1-6 m.

Hancockia sp. 6
Size: 20 mm   Madagascar
ID: Reddish-brown with an irregular network of white pigment on the dorsum penetrating into the base of the four pairs of lateral appendages and the rhinophoral sheaths; rhinophores white. Feeds on hydroids on shallow reefs, 10 m.

Hancockia sp. 7
Size: 8 mm   Indonesia
ID: White, with a network of pinkish pigment on the notum; four pairs of lateral appendages and rhinophoral sheaths with irregular pink and white pigment.

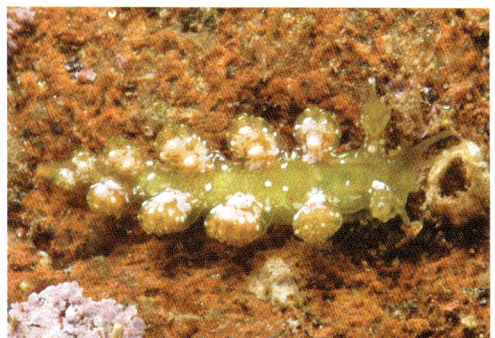

Hancockia sp. 8
Size: 8 mm   Indonesia
ID: Uniformly ochre with scattered opaque white spots of the notum; five pairs of lateral appendages with light brown and opaque white pigment; rhinophores with white apices.

249

Nudibranchia - "nudibranchs"

Phylliroidae Menke, 1830

A bizarre looking, heavily modified group of nudibranchs including pelagic species that feed on siphonophores and sea jellies.

***Phylliroe bucephalum* Lamarck, 1816**
Size: 25 mm   Circumtropical
ID: Transparent with the viscera visible; body tall, flattened laterally with a distinct tail; head with two smooth rhinophores. Swims by fast lateral undulations; feeds on sea jellies and other plankton, juveniles are parasitic on *Zanclea* medusae.

***Cephalopyge trematoides* (Chun, 1889)**
Size: 25 mm   Circumtropical
ID: Transparent with the viscera visible and rows of white or yellow photophores; body elongate with a distinct tail; head with two smooth, contractile rhinophores. Swims by fast lateral undulations; feeds on siphonophores.

Lomanotidae Bergh, 1890

Members of this small group have elongate bodies and a series of lobed lateral appendages. The appendages may be arranged in a continuous fashion or in one or two lobes of the notal margin. Species of Lomanotidae feed on a variety of hydroids. Most species are cryptic on their food source.

***Lomanotus vermiformis* Eliot, 1908**
Size: 30 mm   Possibly circumtropical
ID: White with brown pigment and a series of opaque white longitudinal curved lines; lateral appendages numerous and simple, each tipped with an opaque white spot; body long, worm-like. Extremely well camouflaged along the primary axis of its prey, the stinging hydroid, *Macrophynchia philippina*; on reefs in 1-20 m.

***Lomanotus* sp. 1**
Size: 20 mm   Marshall Is.
ID: Opaque white and brown with a network of opaque white lines; body wider near the rhinophores and again more posteriorly in two lobes. On the stinging hydroid, *Gymnangium gracilicaule* in 10-15 m.

***Lomanotus* sp. 2**
Size: 10 mm   Indonesia
ID: Pink with a concentration of brown pigment and opaque white spots; two lobes posterior to the head but not as well developed as in the preceding species. On the stinging hydroid, *Gymnangium gracilicaule* in shallow water.

Lomanotus sp. 3
Size: 20 mm   Philippines
ID: Light brownish with numerous simple lobed lateral appendages, covered with black pigment; black pigment also on the rhinophoral sheaths, the rhinophores, the oral tentacles, and the anterior margin. On shallow reefs in 10 m.

Lomanotus sp. 4
Size: 20 mm   Philippines
ID: Brown with opaque white lines on the notum; rhinophoral sheaths lacking opaque white apices, widely flared. On reefs in 15 m; feeds on finely branched thecate hydroids.

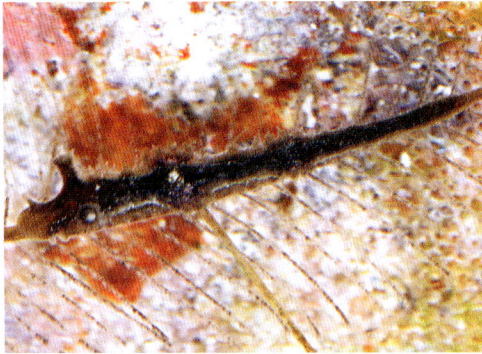

Lomanotus sp. 5
Size: 18 mm   Philippines
ID: Uniformly black with translucent lateral appendages and some opaque white dots; body very elongate, with short rhinophores and lateral appendages. Extremely well camouflaged along the primary axis of its hydroid prey; on rubble slopes, in 18 m.

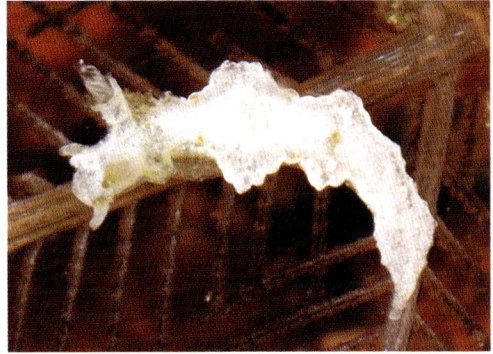

Lomanotus sp. 6
Size: 20 mm   Philippines
ID: Uniformly white with some brown pigment; body wider near the rhinophores and again more posteriorly forming two lobes. On the primary axis of its hydroid prey, *Gymnangium gracilicaule* on reef faces in 25 m.

Lomanotus sp. 7
Size: 8 mm   Indonesia
ID: Translucent white with brown pigment on the notal margins; rhinophores bright red. On the primary axis of its hydroid prey, *Gymnangium gracilicaule* on reef faces.

Lomanotus sp. 8
Size: 15 mm   Thailand
ID: Translucent white with a network of opaque white lines on the dorsum and brown pigment on the rhinophoral sheaths, head and notum; rhinophores black; lateral papillae short with the exception of four very large ones. Feeds on the hydroid, *Gymnangium gracilicaule* on reef faces.

Lomanotus sp. 9
Size: 12 mm · Indonesia
ID: Orange with red pigment on the notal margins, rhinophores and head. Lateral papillae short with the exception of a few longer ones. Feeds on the hydroid prey, *Gymnangium gracilicaule.*

Lomanotus sp. 10
Size: 10 mm · Philippines
ID: Orange with opaque white spots on the notum. Feeds on the hydroid, *Gymnangium grailicaule.*

Scyllaeidae Alder & Hancock, 1855

Members of this group are unusual in having one or two pairs of lobes extending from the body, which bear branched respiratory structures. Scyllaeids feed on epiphytic hydroids growing on brown algae or sea grasses. All species can swim by flexing the body, assisted by the erection and flattening of the rhinophoral sheaths and lateral appendages, which are used as "oars" and to increase the area of the body. Some groups are strictly benthic whereas others are associated with drifting, oceanic brown algae.

Crosslandia viridis Eliot, 1902
Size: 30 mm · Tanzania, Papua New Guinea
ID: Uniformly green, two very large lobes each with a short secondary lobe along the margin, such that the animal resembles a species of *Elysia*. Intertidally on thecate hydroids growing on the sea grass, *Thalassodendron ciliatum.*

Crosslandia sp. 1
Size: 25 mm · Papua New Guinea, Hawai'ian Is.
ID: Brownish with numerous, fine, transverse opaque white lines; differs from *Crosslandia viridis* in having two pairs of subequal lobes along the body. Under coral rubble in 3-10 m.

Crosslandia sp. 2
Size: 20 mm · French Polynesia
ID: Green with numerous small emerald dots forming transversal lines and a few larger bright blue spots; edges of the notum and rhinophoral sheaths yellow; two pairs of subequal lobes along the body. In 20 m.

Crosslandia sp. 3
Size: 18 mm   Red Sea
ID: Light brown with opaque white spots associated with minute papillae; parapodial lobes bilobed, each with a conical apical papilla. On algae on shallow reefs, 5 m.

Scyllaea fulva Quoy & Gaimard, 1824
Size: 40 mm   Western Pacific Ocean
ID: Brown with opaque white pigment and a few bright blue spots; body with two pairs of elongate branches; rhinophoral sheaths broad and flattened. On floating algae, especially *Sargassum*; feeds on epibiotic hydroids; capable of swimming using lateral undulations of its body.

Tethydidae Rafinesque, 1815

Members of this group have a well developed oral hood edged with numerous elongate papillae that are used for filter feeding and the capture of prey. *Melibe* are specialized predators upon crustaceans. Most species are capable of swimming by moving their body from side to side. All of the Indo-Pacific species have symbiotic zooxanthellae which accounts for their golden brown color. This group was most recently reviewed by Gosliner & Pola (2012).

Notobryon wardi Odhner, 1936
Size: 40 mm   Western and central Pacific Ocean
ID: Translucent white with the viscera visible through the body wall; anterior pair of lateral lobes much larger than the posterior pair; notum covered with small conical, opaque white papillae; posterior side of the rhinophoral sheaths with a short sail-like margin. On reefs in 10-20 m.

Melibe viridis (Kelaart, 1858)
Size: 200 mm   Widespread in the Indo-Pacific
ID: Translucent brownish-green; cerata large, with rounded tubercles on the surface; oral hood rounded; resembles a mass of algae. On sandy areas in 2-15 m; active diurnally and nocturnally; the egg mass is an elongate spiral string, attached to the sandy substrate; the largest and most widespread Indo-Pacific species of *Melibe*. Introduced into the Mediterranean, where it has migrated through the Suez Canal.

Melibe megaceras Gosliner, 1987
Size: 40 mm   Widespread in the Indo-Pacific
ID: Translucent with scattered brown pigment; large inflated cerata with 2-4 elongate branches at the apices; rhinophoral sheath with a single elongate papilla on the posterior surface. On clean sandy habitats.

Nudibranchia - "nudibranchs"

Melibe minuta Gosliner & V. Smith, 2003
Size: 15 mm   Okinawa (Japan)
ID: Dark brown; cerata flattened with an inrolled margin. On dead coral with growth of *Acanthophora* algae on shallow reefs in 3 m.

Melibe pilosa Pease, 1860
Size: 100 mm   Hawai'ian Is., Easter Is.
ID: Relatively translucent with grey brown pigment; cerata wedge-shaped and triangular with a laterally flattened surface. On algae such as *Acanthophora*, *Padina* and *Sargassum* on shallow reef flats with mixed sand and rubble.

Melibe engeli Risbec, 1937
Size: 45 mm   Widespread in the Indo-Pacific
ID: Virtually transparent with the viscera visible through the body wall; rhinophoral sheath with a sail like appendage on the posterior side; cerata with numerous elongate papillae and fimbriate appendages on the apices. On the algae, *Padina* and *Acanthophora* on reef flats of 1-5 m.

Melibe digitata Gosliner & V. Smith, 2003
Size: 35 mm   Philippines, Indonesia
ID: Dark brown; small oral veil; cerata with digitate to conical papillae over the surface. Under coral heads and on algae such as *Padina* on shallow reef flats.

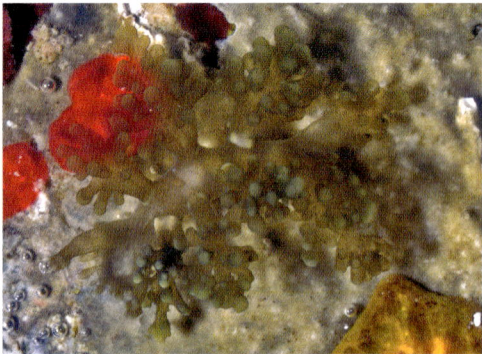

Melibe tuberculata Gosliner & V. Smith, 2003
Size: 20 mm   Philippines
ID: Dark brown; cerata with distinctly rounded tubercles. Often together with *Melibe digitata* under coral rubble on shallow reef flats.

Melibe sp. 1
Size: 70 mm   Indonesia
ID: Relatively translucent with a golden brown surface; cerata more or less cylindrical; numerous papillae extending from the cerata and body. Shallow water sandy substrate.

254

***Melibe colemani* Gosliner & Pola, 2012**
Size: 50 mm   Indonesia, Malaysia, Philippines
ID: Almost entirely transparent with opaque white threads that are visible through the body wall. Forages on sandy bottoms.

***Melibe coralophilia* Gosliner & Pola, 2012**
Size: 120 mm   Eastern Indian and Western Pacific oceans
ID: Uniformly dark brown; thick cerata covered with minute light spots; rhinophoral sheaths short and broad; oral hood small relative to the size of the animal. On reefs in 1-3 m, in areas where it is well protected among the branches of living coral colonies of *Porites* sp. and *Heliopora caerulea*.

***Melibe* sp. 2**
Size: 25 mm   Indonesia
ID: Uniformly green with inflated cerata. Superficially resembling *Stiliger smaragdinus*, but with a distinct oral hood and rhinophores emerging from hood. Found on *Caulerpa racemosa*, which it mimics.

Nudibranchia - "nudibranchs"

Melibe papillosa (de Filippi, 1867)
Size: 100 mm   Western Pacific Ocean
ID: Translucent golden brown with brown spots; few elongate papillae on the body and cerata; cerata wedge-shaped and triangular with laterally flattened surfaces. On algae and in sea grass beds on shallow reef flats with mixed sand and rubble.

Melibe bucephala Bergh, 1902
Size: 100 mm   Red Sea, Thailand
ID: Greenish; cerata covered with papillae and with several digitate extensions on the apex of each ceras; rhinophore sheaths with expanded wing-like posterior ends. On shallow reefs and sandy areas among sea grass and algae.

Tritoniidae Lamarck, 1809

The species in this group have paired secondary gill branches and rhinophores with a crown of papillae surrounding finger-like apices. Tritonids are specialized predators on octocorals, including soft corals, gorgonians and sea pens. The two largest groups are *Tritonia* and *Marionia*, differentiated by internal characters.

Tritonia Cuvier, 1798
Members of *Tritonia* are characterized by lacking stomach plates in the digestive system, and they usually have a smooth notum lacking tubercles.

Tritonia bollandi V. Smith & Gosliner, 2003
Size: 88 mm   Japan, Indonesia
ID: Bright olive green with opaque white secondary gills along the sides of the body; rhinophores elongate with a white base and a brownish club. Feeds on the red gorgonian, *Verrucella aurantia* in 59-75 m.

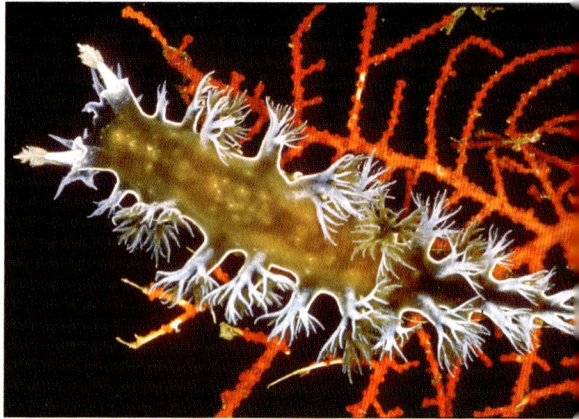

Tritonia sp. 1
Size: 25 mm   Philippines
ID: Opaque white with translucent brown secondary gills, rhinophores and velar appendages. Deep reefs on rubble bottom, 40 m.

Tritonia sp. 2
Size: 20 mm   Indonesia
ID: Greenish with opaque white pigment on the secondary gills and on a series of tubercles located in the center of the notum; four pairs of elongate velar tentacles. On a red gorgonian.

Tritonia sp. 3
Size: 15 mm   Philippines
ID: Mottled brown; secondary gills moderately branched, with dark brown tips; velar tentacles simple or bifid. Feeds on the brownish soft coral, *Paralemnalia* sp., which it closely resembles.

Tritonia sp. 4
Size: 15 mm   Papua New Guinea
ID: Opaque white with some green pigment; gill branches short and curled, resembling contracted xeniid soft corals; velar tentacles simple, short and rounded. On shallow reefs in 15 m, in areas with scattered colonies of *Anthelia* spp. octocorals.

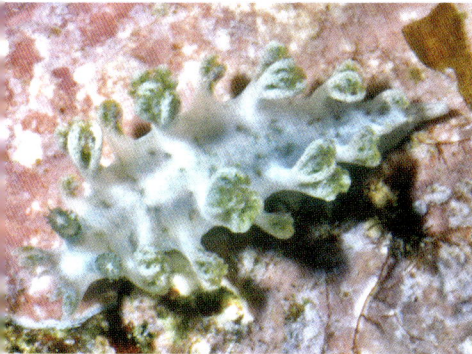

Tritonia sp. 5
Size: 15 mm   Indonesia
ID: Light grey with darker spots; secondary gills moderately branched, with brown tips; rhinophoral sheaths with a ring of dark grey spots along the margin.

Tritonia sp. 6
Size: 15 mm   Tanzania
ID: Uniformly grey with 5-6 pairs of secondary gills; four pairs of simple or bifid velar tentacles. Virtually identical to its octocoral prey, *Coelogorgia palmosa*; in less than 1 m on patch reefs.

Tritonia sp. 7
Size: 20 mm   Great Barrier Reef (Australia)
ID: Grey-brown; secondary gill branches mimic soft coral polyps making this species remarkably cryptic; rhinophoral sheath, stalks, and velar tentacles long and digitiform, also resembling the pinnate tentacles of an octocoral.

Tritonia sp. 8
Size: 18 mm   Papua New Guinea
ID: Orange with opaque white encrusting pigment on the lateral appendages and rhinophores; 4-5 simple or divided velar tentacles on each side of the bilobed velum. On shallow patch reefs in 10-15 m under coral rubble.

257

Nudibranchia - "nudibranchs"

Tritonia sp. 9
Size: 40 mm   Indian and western Pacific oceans
ID: Translucent whitish with orange or brown reticulating patches on the notum; notal and velar margins, as well as the secondary gills, outlined in opaque white; velar appendages elongate, with numerous secondary branches. On reefs under coral rubble in 15-20 m; capable of swimming by dorso-ventrally flexing its body.

Tritonia sp. 10
Size: 20 mm   Philippines, Japa
ID: Grey to brown with various shades that create a pattern alternating diamond-like color elements; dorsal surface wi minute opaque white punctuations; eight pairs of seconda gills finely branched; three or four pairs of simple or slight branched velar tentacles. On reefs in 10-15 m where xeni octocorals are abundant.

Tritonia sp. 11
Size: 15 mm   Philippines
ID: Orange with numerous opaque white tubercles and triangular darker areas on the dorsum; lateral appendages and rhinophores translucent white; five pairs of branched lateral processes. On pink gorgonians, possibly *Euplexaura* sp., in 25 m.

Tritonia sp. 12
Size: 18 mm   Keny
ID: Opaque white with several oval darker areas on th dorsum; lateral processes ramified with short branche velum with a few short, unbranched papillae.

Tritonia sp. 13
Size: 45 mm   South Africa
ID: Greyish-pink with opaque white encrustations; rhinophores orange-red; no distinct secondary gills, only an undulating notal margin. On relatively deep reefs in 44 m.

Tritoniopsis Eliot, 1905

Members of *Tritoniopsis* differ from species of *Tritonia* and *Marionia* by the radular teeth morphology. They also have highly branched secondary gills. Most species are very variable in color.

Tritoniopsis alba Baba, 1949
Size: 27 mm   Indian and western Pacific oceans
ID: Normally white, sometimes orange or reddish, with minute brown dots; entire body surface with small conical tubercles;

secondary gills highly branched, always held parallel to the substrate. On reefs in 10-20 m, under coral rubble.

Tritoniopsis elegans (Audouin *in* Savigny, 1826)
Size: 60 mm   Indian and western Pacific oceans
ID: Translucent white, orange, or yellow, with opaque white markings on the smooth notum and on the highly branched, congested secondary gills. A predator of the soft corals, *Lobophyton* sp., *Sinularia* sp., *Briareum* sp., *Scleronephthya* sp., *Dendronephthya* sp., and *Pachyclavularia* sp.; on shallow water reefs, 5-20 m; a pest from live rock in aquarium trade.

Tritoniopsis sp.
Size: 25 mm   Papua New Guinea
ID: Pale orange with minute brown dots; a radiating pattern of branches from the notum to the secondary gills; tubercles rounded and more sparsely distributed than in *Tritoniopsis alba*. Under coral rubble on reef flats in 1-2 m.

Nudibranchia - "nudibranchs"

Marianina Pruvot-Fol, 1931

Traditionally this group has been placed in a separate family, but recent phylogenetic studies show it is clearly a tritoniid. It contains a single species.

Marianina rosea (Pruvot-Fol, 1930)
Size: 15 mm   Indian and western Pacific
ID: Pinkish purple with yellowish white bifid secondary gills and a pair of elongate, simple velar tentacles; rhinophores bright red. Unlike other tritoniids, it feeds on arborescent hydroids in 1-10 m on flats and reef slopes.

Marionia Vayssière, 1877

Members of *Marionia* are characterized by having stomach plates in the digestive system. Externally, species of *Marionia* usually have dorsal tubercles but are otherwise similar to species of *Tritonia* and *Tritoniopsis*.

Species with rounded tubercles on the notum
All the species in this section have the dorsum covered with rounded tubercles as shown in the photo below.

Marionia cyanobranchiata (Rüppell & Leuckart, 1831)
Size: 125 mm   Red Se
ID: Tan to light brown with dark blue-green, highly ramified secondary gill dark markings near the midline of the notum posterior to the rhinophore three pairs of velar tentacles, simple and unbranched. On reefs in 10-15 r

Marionia arborescens Bergh, 1890
Size: 65 mm   Indian and western Pacific oceans
ID: Greenish brown with dense, prominent tubercles on the notum; tubercles outlined basally with dark brown pigment, some covered with opaque white; velar tentacles simple; secondary gills highly ramified. Under coral rubble in 1-10 m.

Marionia rubra (Rüppell & Leuckart, 1831)
Size: 120 mm   Indian and western Pacific ocean
ID: Color variable from deep red to light green or brown notum with large, crowded tubercles, often with opaqu white pigment; 8-12 short velar appendages with multifid tips margins of the rhinophoral sheaths broad and undulating. O reefs in 2-15 m; feeds on soft corals.

Marionia hawaiiensis (Pease, 1860)
Size: 50 mm   Hawai'ian Is.
ID: Uniformly brownish with opaque white spots; notum covered by low rounded tubercles; secondary gills highly ramified; velar appendages subdivided into 2-4 branches. On shallow water reefs; feeds upon the soft coral, *Anthelia edmondsoni*.

Marionia sp. 1
Size: 35 mm   Indonesia
ID: Reddish-brown with a complex network of thin blue lines and spots; some dorsal areas lacking reddish-brown pigment; velar appendages green, subdivided into 2-3 branches; secondary gills small, highly branched, green with opaque white spots; rhinophores black with white apices.

Marionia sp. 2
Size: 70 mm   Indian and western Pacific oceans
ID: Greenish brown; similar to *Marionia arborescens* but with shorter secondary gills and taller, more dense notal tubercles with more opaque white; 3-4 pairs of simple, undivided velar tentacles. On reefs in 5-10 m, under coral rubble.

Marionia sp. 3
Size: 50 mm   Philippines
ID: Opaque white with brown and black spots; secondary gills highly branched and curved; notum with dorsal tubercles. On reefs, in areas of mixed sand and rubble, 15 m.

Marionia sp. 4
Size: 70 mm   Papua New Guinea, Philippines
ID: Grey; darker brown areas on either side of the bases of the secondary gills; this produces a symmetrical and striking color pattern; opaque white spots near the central portion of the notum; velar tentacles with bifid or trifid apices; notum with a complex reticulate pattern of low tubercles. Under large slabs of coral in 10-15 m.

Marionia sp. 5
Size: 55 mm   Philippines
ID: Brown with a dense covering of small low tubercles outlined with opaque white; secondary gills darker than the body, also with reticulations on their stalks and opaque white outlines; velar tentacles long with bifid and trifid tips. Under large coral slabs in 7 m.

Nudibranchia - "nudibranchs"

Species with transverse lines or grooves
All the species in this section have transverse lines or grooves on the dorsum as shown in the photo below.

Marionia distincta Bergh, 1905
Size: 60 mm   Western Pacific Ocean
ID: White with a series of brown transverse lines on the smooth notum; black spots at the base of the finely branched secondary gills; four pairs of simple or slightly branched velar tentacles. In 10 m, in areas dominated by xeniid soft corals.

Marionia levis Eliot, 1904
Size: 40 mm   Indian and western Pacific oceans
ID: White or yellowish, with a series of brown, opaque white or purple transverse lines; black spots at the base of the stalks of the secondary gills and rhinophoral sheaths; 3-4 pairs of velar tentacles, mostly simple or with bifid apices. Under coral rubble during the day and active nocturnally, when it is seen crawling in the open; feeds on the soft coral, *Rhytisma fulva*.

Marionia elongoreticula V. Smith & Gosliner, 200
Size: 70 mm   Indonesia, Philippine
ID: Pale yellow with a pattern of reddish brown lines formir reticulations across the surface; four pairs of velar tentacle simple or divided at their tips; narrow rhinophoral sheatl with a series of longitudinal lines at their apex. Under cor heads in shallow water patch reefs and rubble communitie feeds on gorgonians of the family Elisellidae.

Marionia elongoviridis V. Smith & Gosliner, 2007
Size: 70 mm   Philippines
ID: Greenish-yellow with transverse reddish-brown lines that do not meet in the middle; about 10 pairs of green secondary gills; velum with four pairs of digitiform tentacles, most simple, a few with bifid tips. Swims by opening the rhinophoral sheaths and undulating the body; under coral heads in shallow water patch reefs and rubble communities in 15 m; probably feeds on soft corals.

Marionia sp. 6
Size: 100 mm   Western Pacific Ocea
ID: Bright green with opaque white transverse lines and network on the secondary gill bases; light green seconda gills, short but highly pinnate; 3-4 pairs of divided or simp velar tentacles. In 3-15 m on shallow reef flats under rubbl active at night; feeds on the soft coral, *Lemnalia* sp.; it preyed upon by *Gymnodoris aurita*.

Marionia sp. 7
Size: 40 mm   Tanzania
D: Uniformly brownish with translucent white areas on the junctions of the transverse bands on the notum; a few opaque white spots on the notum; 3-4 pairs of unbranched velar tentacles. In 10 m among coral rubble.

Species with varied patterns
The following species do not match any of the patterns described above and show remarkable variability in their external morphology and coloration, therefore they cannot be included in a specific section and they are maintained in a different category.

Marionia sp. 8
Size: 40 mm   Indian and western Pacific oceans
ID: Brown with a pattern of reticulated polygons on the notum having patches of light and dark brown; junctions of the polygons with dark blue lines and at some of the junctions lighter, bright blue spots; velar tentacles with branched tips. Under rocks and coral rubble in 10-20 m.

Marionia sp. 9
Size: 22 mm   Philippines
ID: Brown a pattern of reticulated polygons on the notum, and numerous large bright blue spots; junctions of the polygons with black lines; secondary gills large, brown; velar tentacles with branched tips. On shallow shoreward reefs, 1-2 m.

Marionia sp. 10
Size: 20 mm   Indonesia, Philippines
ID: Translucent white with a dense covering of small brown and opaque white spots; relatively short secondary gills, covered in opaque white; velar tentacles short and simple.

Marionia sp. 11
Size: 70 mm   Philippines
ID: Uniformly drab brown with white speckling all over the body; rhinophoral sheaths stout, with a series of papillae forming a crown-shape; secondary gills short and sparse. Trawled from about 100 m.

Marionia sp. 12
Size: 45 mm   Kwazulu Natal (South Africa)
ID: Bright red-orange pigment on the body and gills and bright bluish purple spots over the notum and sides of the body.

Nudibranchia - "nudibranchs"

Marionia sp. 13
Size: 40 mm   Indonesia, Philippines
ID: Light brownish with a network of white pigment on the dorsum; secondary gills, velar tentacles and apices of the rhinophoral sheaths purple; rhinophores brownish-purple. On reefs, in areas of mixed sand and rubble, 15 m.

Marionia sp. 14
Size: 110 mm   Gulf of Oman
ID: Light brown with scattered dark brown patches and fine reticulating white lines; velar tentacles relatively short and united into a broad velum. On sandy substrate in relatively shallow water.

Marionia sp. 15
Size: 40 mm   Philippines
ID: Light brown with a uniform pattern of undulating darker brown longitudinal bands; large secondary gills with transverse branches across the notum; velar processes slightly branched. On reefs in areas with abundant soft corals, 15 m.

Marionia sp. 16
Size: 20 mm   Philippines
ID: Uniformly light brownish with darker brown reticulations; numerous rounded tubercles giving the entire animal a nodular appearance. In rubble fields in 20 m where soft corals are abundant.

Marionia sp. 17
Size: 25 mm   Philippines
ID: Reticulate pattern of brown and white with conical tubercles between reticulations; head white with black velar tentacles. On plexaurid or ellisellid gorgonians, in deep reefs, 35 m.

Marionia sp. 18
Size: 35 mm   Philippines
ID: Dark brown with a reticulate pattern of blue; two rows of blue spots on the notum and another on either side of body; body with conical tubercles.

Marionia sp. 19
Size: 25 mm   Philippines
ID: Grey with opaque white lines and charcoal grey secondary gills; charcoal grey on the tips of the rhinophores and rhinophoral sheaths.

Marionia sp. 20
Size: 25 mm   Philippines
ID: Brown with a reticulate pattern of blue. Similar to *Marionia* sp. 18 but with narrower body and less prominent mantle folds. On shallow reefs under coral rubble.

Marionia sp. 21
Size: 20 mm   Philippines
ID: Light brown with darker brown patches; middle two pairs of secondary gills bright orange; rhinophore sheaths tall, cylindrical

Marionia sp. 22
Size: 15 mm   Philippines
ID: Beige with darker brown patches on the notum, the tips of gills and the rhinophoral sheaths; body with small conical papillae. On soft corals in shallow reefs.

Nudibranchia - "nudibranchs"

Marionia sp. 23
Size: 45 mm   Philippines
ID: Elongate, narrow with a reticulate network of opaque white and plum polygons; gills, rhinophoral sheaths and rhinophores dark plum.

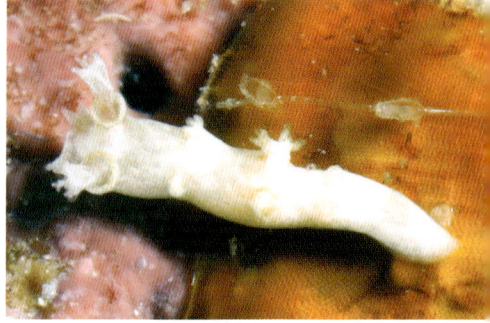

Marionia sp. 24
Size: 8 mm   Philippines
ID: Pale off white with slightly branched secondary gills; rhinophoral sheeths wide at opening. On soft corals in shallow reefs, 10-15 m.

Dotidae J. E. Gray, 1853

The species belonging to this group all have nodular cerata, often with spherical lobes such that each ceras resembles a cluster of grapes. The rhinophoral sheaths are cylindrical cups, each with a long simple cylindrical rhinophoral clavus in the center. The systematics of this group has been recently reviewed by Shipman & Gosliner (2015), who recognized two genera, *Doto* and *Kabeiro*.

Doto Oken, 1815
Species of *Doto* have relatively short bodies compared to members of *Kabeiro*.

Doto ussi Ortea, 1982
Size: 30 mm   Indian and western Pacific oceans
ID: Brownish grey with opaque white pigment; cerata grey, outlined in white or yellow; cerata large with numerous low rounded tubercles covering their surface. On the stinging hydroid, *Aglaophenia cupressina* on which is highly cryptic in 1-15 m; yellow egg masses at the base of the hydroids.

Doto sp. 1
Size: 14 mm   Philippines
ID: Uniformly dark grey to black; cerata large, dark grey with white apices; each ceras with numerous large, rounded, dark grey tubercles with black centers. On arborescent hydroids on rubble and silty slopes, 20 m.

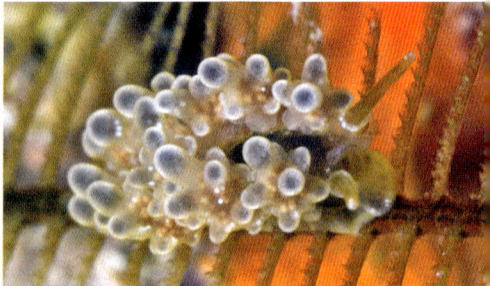

Doto racemosa Risbec, 1928
Size: 10 mm   Western Pacific Ocean
ID: Brown; cerata brown with grey rounded lobes and a few opaque white spots; rhinophoral sheath rims opaque white. On reefs in 10 m; feeds on the plumularid hydroid shown in the photo.

266

Doto sp. 2
Size: 20 mm   Philippines
ID: Brown; cerata yellow, densely crowded, covered with long tubercles. At 20 m on a sandy and rubble bottom; shown here on its hydroid prey together with its egg mass.

Doto sp. 3
Size: 20 mm   Philippines
ID: White with bright yellow pigment; head with a dark longitudinal patch; cerata white or yellow with brown tipped rounded tubercles; rhinophores and sheaths black. Rubble fields in 20 m, on erect thecate hydroids.

Doto sp. 4
Size: 8 mm   Indonesia
ID: Brownish-grey with black and white dots; rhinophoral sheaths with opaque white dots, forming a ring around the margin; rhinophores elongate with some opaque white spots, more densely arranged on the apex; cerata with small tubercles, transparent, with the cream branches of the digestive gland visible, and a few black and white dots.

Doto sp. 5
Size: 10 mm   Philippines
ID: Brown; cerata orange covered with large brown tubercles; apical tubercles with opaque white; rhinophoral sheaths broad at their opening, each with an orange line around the margin. On the hydroid, *Aglaophenia* sp. on shallow water reefs in 3-10 m.

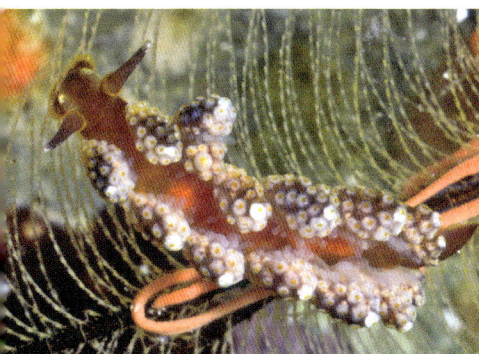

Doto sp. 6
Size: 20 mm   Philippines
ID: Brown; seven pairs of large cerata with the secondary gills visible on the inner side; cerata covered with rounded tubercles with orange apices; apical tubercles with opaque white. In 20 m in areas of strong current; feeds on the delicate plumularid hydroid shown in the photo; egg mass also present on the hydroid colony.

Doto sp. 7
Size: 5 mm   Seychelles
ID: Brownish grey with a few minute opaque white spots; cerata pinkish with rounded tubercles; rhinophoral sheaths and rhinophores with opaque white pigment. Under coral rubble in 1-2 m in passes of coral atolls.

Nudibranchia - "nudibranchs"

Doto sp. 8
Size: 7 mm　　　　　　　　　　　　　Papua New Guinea
ID: Brown; cerata with somewhat pointed tubercles, each with a dark grey to black tip; rhinophores and their sheaths with opaque white spots. On low growing hydroids in 2-3 m, on fringing reefs.

Doto sp. 9
Size: 15 mm　　　　　　　　　　　　　　　Indonesia
ID: White with a mid-dorsal brown line that extends to the anterior end of the head; cerata white with brown tipped rounded tubercles; rhinophores brown; red lines on the head and sides of the body. On plumularid hydroids; egg mass visible in the photo.

Doto sp. 10
Size: 7 mm　　　　　　　　　　　　　　Marshall Is.
ID: Brown with mottled black pigment and opaque white dots; rhinophores translucent with dense opaque white dots; cerata reddish with large, round black tubercles. On floating docks in harbors.

Doto sp. 11
Size: 20 mm　　　　　　　　　　　　　　　Indonesia
ID: Bright red-orange; remarkably long cerata, each with a few scattered elongate tubercles; rhinophoral sheaths red-orange; rhinophores orange. Orange egg masses shown in the photo.

Doto greenamyeri Shipman & Gosliner, 2015
Size: 15 mm　　　　　　　　　　　　　Papua New Guinea
ID: White; cerata with a series on concentric rings of grey and gold; foot with gold lines and a grey border; rhinophores black. On an unidentified species of plumularid hydroid.

Doto sp. 12
Size: 11 mm　　　　　　　　　　　　　　　Indonesia
ID: White; cerata white with large black spots on the apices of the tubercles; apical tubercles yellowish-orange with a black center; rhinophoral sheaths with a black ring around the apex.

Doto sp. 13
Size: 9 mm — Japan
D: Opaque white; cerata elongate, with bright red conical tubercles; rhinophores and oral margin also red; margin of the rhinophoral sheaths narrow and even. On feathery thecate hydroids in 20 m.

Doto sp. 14
Size: 7 mm — Indonesia, Hong Kong, Japan
ID: Bright orange with opaque white areas on either side of the notum; cerata short with pinnate tubercles on their anterior and posterior sides; rhinophoral sheaths with up to three papillae extending from the margin. Shown here on a plumularid hydroid.

Doto sp. 15
Size: 15 mm — New Caledonia, Indonesia
D: Translucent white with orange on the head; cerata orange with opaque white tubercles; rhinophores black, elongate.

Doto sp. 16
Size: 4 mm — Philippines
ID: Translucent white with brownish cerata and brown or opaque white on tubercles. On thecate hydroids where it produces a yellowish egg mass with direct-developing larvae, 20 m.

Doto sp. 17
Size: 15 mm — Indonesia
ID: Translucent white body; elongate, irregular cerata with opaque white digestive gland; rhinophores elongate, translucent white with brown bands.

Doto sp. 18
Size: 10 mm — Indonesia
ID: Translucent white with large, dense cerata; cerata with regular rows of opaque white tubercles; rhinophores brown with opaque white markings.

Doto sp. 19
Size: 12 mm   Papua New Guinea
ID: Cerata with rows of apically flattened tubercles, densely packed obscuring body; each tubercle with a yellow-orange marginal ring and dark grey center.

Kabeiro Shipman & Gosliner, 2015
Species of *Kabeiro*, previously included in *Doto*, have very elongated bodies. Most species are several times longer than wide. This shape probably helps these species to become camouflaged on the branches of the hydroids they eat.

Kabeiro sp. 1
Size: 25 mm   Papua New Guinea
ID: Brown; digitiform cerata widely spaced and held parallel to the body; cerata with low whitish tubercles and a terminal yellowish tubercle. In 15 m on a plumularid hydroid, remarkably cryptic by resembling the rachis of the hydroid.

Kabeiro sp. 2
Size: 20 mm   Saudi Arabian Red Sea
ID: Translucent brownish-grey, lacking any distinctive pigment except for a few opaque white dots; digestive gland visible thought the body and cerata as a cream area; body very elongate. On hydroids on shallow reefs, 9 m.

Kabeiro orcha (Yonow, 2000)
Size: 8 mm   Red Sea
ID: White with a black spot at the base of each ceras; cerata papillate, also white. On the thecate hydroid, *Dynamena disticha* in about 6 m.

Kabeiro rubroreticulata Shipman & Gosliner, 2015
Size: 20 mm   Philippines
ID: Light brownish with reticulations of darker brown on the notum and on the cerata; cerata irregularly shaped with a few opaque white tubercles; extremely elongate rhinophores. On campanularid hydroids growing on the sea grass *Enhalus acoroides* in 1-5 m; its pink egg mass is also on the hydroids.

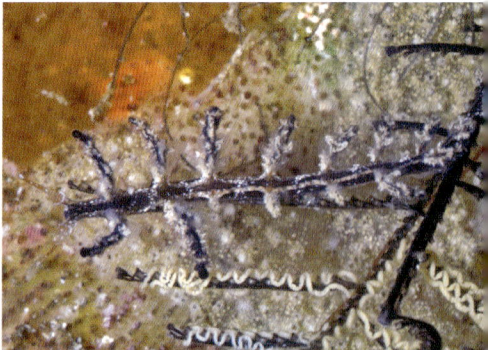

Kabeiro christianae Shipman & Gosliner, 2015
Size: 25 mm   Indonesia, Philippines
ID: Dark brown with opaque white along the margins; cerata with transparent and opaque white tubercles that resemble hydroid polyps; rhinophores much longer than their sheath. Feeds on plumularid hydroids on which is highly cryptic by matching the rachis the hydroid; egg mass deposited parallel to the axis of the hydroid colony as seen in the photo.

Kabeiro phasmida Shipman & Gosliner, 2015
Size: 20 mm   Philippines
ID: Uniformly light brownish with a series of opaque white conical tubercles along the margins of the notum; cerata with numerous acutely pointed conical tubercles; elongate rhinophores within narrow sheaths. On highly pinnate thecate hydroids on mixed and sand rubble slopes; the egg mass consists of tightly coiled ribbons along the edges of the primary branches of the hydroid colony.

Kabeiro sp. 3
Size: 15 mm   Philippines, Indonesia
ID: Body brown with curved cerata having a white base and purple apex, with yellow and white tubercles; Rhinophoral sheath brown with translucent white rhinophores.

Embletoniidae Pruvot-Fol, 1954

This group was considered to be a member of the Aeolidina, but new morphological and molecular evidence confirms that it is a dendronotid although it lacks rhinophoral sheaths. Embletonids are characterized by having a bilobed oral veil, a single row of cerata, and lacking oral tentacles. It appears that these animals feed on hydroids although some instances of egg feeding have been reported.

Embletonia gracilis Risbec, 1928
Size: 30 mm   Indo-Pacific and eastern Pacific
ID: Translucent white with white to pink cerata; oral tentacles short, forming a bilobed veil; body elongate with wedge-shaped, deeply divided cerata. Under coral rubble in shallow water; probably feeds on hydroids.

Aeolidina - "aeolids"

Aeolid nudibranchs are a natural group (Goodheart *et al.* 2015, 2017), which lack distinct gills and utilize cerata for respiration and defense. The cerata contain branches of the digestive tract that transport undeveloped nematocysts acquired from their coelenterate prey, and they are stored at the ceratal tips. The nematocysts are then utilized for the aeolid's defense.

Flabellinidae Bergh, 1889

This is one of the most basal groups of aeolids. Flabellinids have a radula with three teeth across, while most aeolids have only a single tooth. The majority of Flabellinidae are found in polar and temperate waters. Members of the Flabellinidae feed on hydroids. Most species display bright external coloration. The Indo-Pacific species of *Flabellina* have been reviewed by Gosliner & Willan (1991).

Kurshunova *et al.* (2017) divided *Flabellina* into numerous small genera based on examination of a handful of species. We feel many of these genera intergrade into each other without clear divisions. Thus, we prefer to retain most of these species in *Flabellina* until such time that a comprehensive review of the family and genera is undertaken. However, we follow Kurshunova *et al.* (2017) in regarding the families Samlidae and Unidentiidae as distinct from Flabellinidae.

Flabellina exoptata Gosliner & Willan, 1991
Size: 20 mm   Widespread in the Indo-Pacific
ID: Translucent purple-red; cerata thick, each with a purple subapical ring and a cream apex; rhinophores orange with yellow spots. On reefs and slopes on hydroids of the genus *Eudendrium* in 1-20 m.

Species with papillate rhinophores
The next five species can be distinguished by having numerous papillae on the posterior side of the rhinophores.

Nudibranchia - "nudibranchs"

Flabellina rubrolineata (O'Donoghue, 1929)
Size: 25 mm   Red Sea, Arabian Sea
ID: Body pinkish yellow, with a series of three longitudinal violet lines along the length of the body; cerata pink basally with subapical red-violet ring and yellow apex. Feeds on the hydroid, *Eudendrium* sp. on shallow reefs and walls. Introduced to the Mediterranean via the Suez Canal.

Flabellina lotos (Korshunova *et al.*, 2017)
Size: 25 mm   Western Pacific Ocean
ID: Translucent pink with interrupted purple lines on midline and sides of the body; each ceras with a purple subapical ring. Feeds on *Eudendrium* on shallow to deep reefs and walls.

Flabellina sp. 1
Size: 20 mm   Western Pacific Ocean
ID: Opaque white pigment on the sides of notal margin; cerata shorter than in *Flabellina rubrolineata* or *F. lotos* and with white and red ceratal bands, lacking purple subapical rings. Feeds on *Eudendrium* on shallow to deep reefs and walls.

Flabellina sp. 2
Size: 30 mm   Philippines
ID: Translucent orange, digestive gland visible; rhinophores and oral tentacles purple with white tips; cerata translucent purple, with white branches of the digestive gland, subapical dark purple rings and white tips. On coral rubble; feeds on the hydroid, *Eudendrium* sp., 20 m.

Flabellina delicata Gosliner & Willan, 1991
Size: 20 mm   Indian and western Pacific oceans
ID: Purple; each ceras with a subapical band of orange and a purple apex. In 10-20 m on reef slopes and walls where it feeds on hydroids of the genus *Eudendrium*.

Flabellina sp. 3
Size: 20 mm   Malaysia, Philippines
ID: Opaque yellowish white; each ceras with a purple cast and a diffuse subapical purple ring; oral tentacles bright purple; rhinophores yellowish-white with purple apices. On reef slopes on the hydroid, *Eudendrium* sp. in 25 m.

272

Species with smooth rhinophores
The following species have smooth rhinophores.

Flabellina sp. 4
Size: 21 mm   Western Australia
ID: Purple with opaque lines along the notal margin; cerata brick red; rhinophores and oral tentacles purple.

Flabellina sp. 5
Size: 30 mm   Indonesia
ID: Translucent orange with a mid dorsal dark red longitudinal line; oral tentacles almost completely covered with opaque white pigment and few dark red spots; rhinophores translucent orange with subapical dark red rings; cerata covered with opaque white pigment, each with a single dark red spot.

Flabellina sp. 6
Size: 15 mm   Okinawa (Japan)
ID: Red with opaque white oral tentacles; rhinophores mainly red with white pigment mid-length and apically; cerata translucent white, with purple bases and red tips.

Flabellina sp. 7
Size: 20 mm   Indonesia
ID: Opaque white; each ceras with a red subapical band and a purple apex; the white digestive gland visible through the cerata; rhinophores reddish, each with a medial white band.

Flabellina sp. 8
Size: 7 mm   Indonesia
ID: Translucent white with numerous opaque white spots; oral tentacles with translucent grey bases and opaque white apices; rhinophores brown with yellow apices; cerata translucent with purple and yellow subapical bands and white apices.

Flabellina sp. 9
Size: 12 mm   Western Pacific Ocean
ID: Translucent white with opaque white along the edges of the notum; yellow pigment forming a continuous line along the undulating notal margin; black viscera visible through the notum; most of the rhinophores and oral tentacles frosted white. Under coral rubble in 7-8 m on barrier reefs.

Nudibranchia - "nudibranchs"

Family Samlidae Korshunova *et al.*, 2017

Both Carmona *et al.* (2013) and Cella *et al.* (2016) demonstrated that this group of species, formerly included in *Flabellina*, represented a separate evolutionary line. Kurshunova *et al.* (2017) suggested that this group should be be placed in a separate family and included these species in the genus *Samla* Bergh, 1900. We agree with this aspect of their systematic revision. Species of *Samla* are characterized by having perfoliate rhinophores, bearing a series of lamellae.

Samla rubropurpurata (Gosliner & Willan, 1991)
Size: 10 mm   Widespread in the Indo-Pacific
ID: Purple, often with encrusting opaque white; rhinophores and cerata red. On shallow reefs under coral rubble.

Samla bicolor (Kelaart, 1858)
Size: 15 mm   Widespread in the Indo-Pacific
ID: Translucent purple, often with opaque white encrusting pigment; cerata with subapical orange bands. This is probably a species complex of at least two species with similar external morphology but different egg masses (see photos above). From the intertidal zone under coral rubble to reef slopes and walls in 20 m; feeds on the hydroid, *Eudendrium* sp.

Samla riwo (Gosliner & Willan, 1991)
Size: 25 mm   Indian and western Pacific oceans
ID: Opaque white with numerous irregular dark lines forming a complex network; cerata with subapical blue or purple bands. On reef slopes and walls feeding on the hydroid, *Eudendrium*.

274

Samla sp. 1
Size: 25 mm   Indonesia
ID: Cream with brownish rhinophores; oral tentacles and cerata pink with purple tips. Crawling on volcanic sand.

Samla macassarana (Bergh, 1905)
Size: 30 mm   Indian and western Pacific oceans
ID: Pinkish to purplish white, with burnt orange ceratal tips; cerata with subapical orange bands. On hydroids of the genus *Eudendrium* on relatively deep reef slopes and walls in 25-30 m.

Samla sp. 2
Size: 10 mm   Maldives Is.
ID: Deep purple with opaque white pigment on the dorsum; oral tentacles with white tips; rhinophores perfoliate, white with orange tips; cerata orange, bright red basally and apically.

Samla sp. 3
Size: 12 mm   French Polynesia
ID: Deep purple with red oral tentacles; rhinophores perfoliate, each with a white base and red club; cerata white with red tips.

Samla bilas (Gosliner & Willan, 1991)
Size: 25 mm   Widespread in the Indo-Pacific
ID: Orange-brown with a series of medial opaque pale blue diamond-shaped markings; cerata orange-brown with blood-red rings, surrounded by narrower bands of opaque white. On *Eudendrium* hydroids on steep reef slopes and walls in 20-30 m.

Samla sp. 4
Size: 18 mm   Midway Atoll
ID: Translucent pinkish-orange with opaque white spots on the surface; cerata with subapical white bands and orange apical bands. On outer reefs of atolls under coral rubble in 15 m.

Nudibranchia - "nudibranchs"

Samla sp. 5
Size: 10 mm   Okinawa (Japan)
ID: Opaque white; cerata opaque white with orange rings; oral tentacles orange; rhinophores purple with well-separated annulae. In 5 m.

Undetermined family

Myja longicornis Bergh, 1896
Size: 12 mm   Papua New Guinea and Japan
ID: Translucent white with opaque white spots; cerata translucent with the branches of the digestive gland visible; cerata narrow in their basal two-thirds, expanded into a bulbous subapical portion that resembles the athecate polyps of its prey. On the hydroid, _Eudendrium_ sp. on shallow reefs.

Fionidae Odhner, 1934

Fionidae was recently revised by Cella et al. 2016, to combine several families that were previously separated based on updated molecular studies.   More recently, Kurshunova, Martynov & Picton (2017) split this group into several different families with numerous genera. We suggest that these changes created unnecessary splitting of these groups into non-monoplyetic groups based on characters that exhibit more variation than they suggested. Therefore we retain the classification of Cella et al. (2016), until a more comprehensive study is undertaken.

Eubranchus Forbes, 1838
Species in this genus have a triseriate radula and swollen cerata.

Eubranchus inabai Baba, 1964
Size: 12 mm   Western Pacific Ocean
ID: Orange with opaque white patches; cerata inflated, opaque white; widest subapically and tapering into a narrower apex. On hydroids on the brown alga _Sargassum_.

Eubranchus sp. 1
Size: 5 mm   Indonesia
ID: One of the few species of _Eubranchus_ with annulate rhinophores; cerata swollen, rounded with narrow digestive gland duct and blue subapical ring.

Eubranchus ocellatus (Alder & Hancock, 1864)
Size: 20 mm   Indian and western Pacific oceans
ID: Translucent with small brown spots and opaque white markings; cerata translucent with red-brown rings on their surface; cerata inflated, each with a narrow digestive gland duct; rhinophores smooth. On sea grasses and in lagoons; feeds on hydroids.

Eubranchus sp. 2
Size: 10 mm   Indonesia
ID: Translucent with brown and opaque white dots all over the body; cerata inflated, with narrow yellow digestive gland ducts and opaque white apices; rhinophores smooth with opaque white and brown spots.

Eubranchus sp. 3
Size: 8 mm   Papua New Guinea
ID: Translucent white with numerous opaque white spots on the body and cerata; yellow markings on the swollen cerata; rhinophores smooth. On hydroids under coral rubble in 7-8 m.

Eubranchus sp. 4
Size: 7 mm   Indonesia
ID: Translucent with fine brown flecks; cerata bulbous, translucent, with the branching of the digestive gland highly visible.

Eubranchus mandapamensis (Rao, 1968)
Size: 15 mm   Widespread in the Indo-Pacific
ID: Light brown with opaque white spots; cerata with pairs of yellow bands and bright blue bands with red spots in between; cerata and rhinophores densely covered with papillae. *Eubranchus rubropunctatus* is a synonym. On arborescent hydroids on shallow reefs and under rubble.

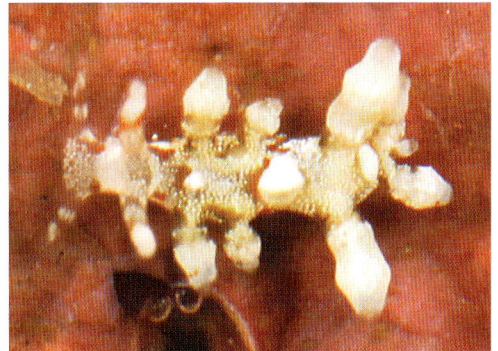

Eubranchus sp. 5
Size: 6 mm   Philippines
ID: Translucent, densely covered with opaque white spots and with some irregular red patches on the dorsum; rhinophores and oral tentacles white with reddish rings; cerata inflated, opaque white. Under coral rubble on shallow reefs, 8 m.

Nudibranchia - "nudibranchs"

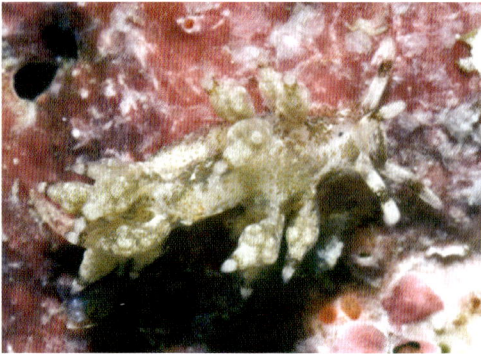

Eubranchus sp. 6
Size: 8 mm   Western and central Pacific Ocean
ID: Opaque white with brown spotting over most of the surface; cerata with a single large swelling near their middle and brown subapical rings; oral tentacles and rhinophores each with a brown ring. On hydroids in shallow water under coral rubble.

Eubranchus sp. 7
Size: 5 mm   Papua New Guinea
ID: Transparent with opaque white pigment; cerata spindle-shaped with opaque white rings in the widest mid-section; rhinophores elongate, much longer than the oral tentacles. On patch reefs in 3-5 m.

Eubranchus sp. 8
Size: 7 mm   Western and central Pacific Ocean
ID: Translucent white with numerous opaque white spots; cerata with two swellings along their length, the outer ones being larger. On shallow patch reefs under coral rubble in 7-10 m.

Eubranchus sp. 9
Size: 10 mm   Japan, Midway Atoll
ID: Opaque white with fine reddish brown spots; cerata with swellings along their length each with a ring of opaque white tubercles; rhinophores and oral tentacles with brown rings. On shallow patch reefs in 8-10 m.

Eubranchus sp. 10
Size: 9 mm   Philippines
ID: Translucent white, completely covered with numerous opaque white spots and some scattered red dots; oral tentacles with the same color, rhinophores translucent, each with a red ring and a white apex; cerata transparent with digestive yellowish gland branches and the white cnidosacs visible. Under coral rubble, among hydroids, in 3 m.

Eubranchus sp. 11
Size: 8 mm   Papua New Guinea
ID: Translucent white with small opaque white and brown spots; cerata translucent with the brown digestive gland visible, covered with scattered black spots and two areas with rings of opaque white tubercles. Under coral rubble on shallow barrier reefs in 7-8 m.

Eubranchus sp. 12
Size: 8 mm   Indonesia
ID: Translucent white with dense covering of brown dots, giving the body, oral tentacles, and rhinophores a brownish appearance; cerata translucent with brown dots and several opaque white rings; yellow digestive gland branches visible.

Eubranchus sp. 13
Size: 6 mm   Saudi Arabian Red Sea
ID: Translucent white with yellow dots and faint black pigment; cerata yellow with brown dots and white apices. On thecate hydroids on floating docks.

Eubranchus sp. 14
Size: 8 mm   Indonesia
ID: Translucent white with abundant opaque white and dark grey pigment; cerata translucent with the digestive gland branches visible, grey and opaque white spots, and numerous papillae; rhinophores with black rings and few papillae.

Eubranchus sp. 15
Size: 7 mm   Indonesia
ID: Translucent white with the red internal organs visible; cerata translucent with branched opaque white tips resembling hydroid polyps; rhinophores elongate; oral tentacles short, tapered.

Eubranchus sp. 16
Size: 7 mm   Philippines
ID: Translucent white with the orange and white digestive gland visible; rhinophores and oral tentacles orange with opaque white tips; cerata bulbous with pointy white tips and scant branching of the digestive gland.

Eubranchus sp. 17
Size: 7 mm   Indonesia
ID: Purple; cerata transparent, bulbous with nipple-like apices and scant branching of the digestive gland; oral tentacles and smooth rhinophores purple.

Nudibranchia - "nudibranchs"

Eubranchus sp. 18
Size: 15 mm Saudi Arabian Red Sea
ID: Translucent with irregular opaque white pigment and minute brown dots on the body, oral tentacles and rhinophores; cerata transparent with the brown branches of the digestive gland visible; ceratal surface with opaque white and brown spots and pink apices. On shallow reefs under coral rubble, 5 m.

Eubranchus sp. 19
Size: 10 mm Indonesia
ID: Translucent with irregular opaque white patches and large reddish spots on the body and cerata; cerata transparent with the pinkish branches of the digestive gland visible; rhinophores and oral tentacles translucent, covered with opaque white pigment and with red rings mid-length.

Eubranchus virginalis (Baba, 1949)
Size: 40 mm Japan, Indonesia
ID: Translucent with numerous black spots; cerata tuberculate, translucent with black spots and the bright orange branches of the digestive gland visible; resembles a species of *Doto*, but lacks rhinophoral sheaths. On hydroids in sandy and silty substrata in shallow water.

Eubranchus sp. 20
Size: 8 mm Widespread in the Indo-Pacific
ID: Dark green with a mid dorsal opaque white line; cerata with subapical opaque white bands and dark blue apices. Commonly on the hydroid, *Sertularia* sp., which grows epibiotically on the green alga *Halimeda* sp. on steep walls in 8-15 m.

Eubranchus sp. 21
Size: 15 mm Papua New Guinea, Mozambique
ID: Bright green with fine opaque white lines on the notum and cerata; each ceras has a bright blue apex. On *Sertularia* sp. hydroids growing on *Halimeda*.

Eubranchus sp. 22
Size: 25 mm Papua New Guinea
ID: Translucent white with small red dots; rhinophores and oral tentacles with subapical brown rings and opaque white tips; cerata transparent with the white branches of the digestive gland visible.

Eubranchus sp. 23
Size: 25 mm   Western Pacific Ocean
ID: Translucent white with the yellowish digestive gland visible through the notum; notum, cerata, rhinophores, and oral tentacles covered with large black spots. On plumularid hydroids on reef slopes in 10-25 m.

Eubranchus sp. 24
Size: 16 mm   Indonesia
ID: Translucent white with reddish tips of the rhinophores and oral tentacles; cerata translucent with the cream branches of the digestive gland visible, an opaque white subapical ring and orange tips.

Eubranchus sp. 25
Size: 17 mm   Indonesia
ID: Translucent white with a dark brown longitudinal dorsal line that branches on the head and penetrates the rhinophores; cerata elongate, translucent with the brown branches of the

digestive gland visible, and opaque white longitudinal lines; ceratal tips rounded or elongate with subapical bluish rings and pale brown tips.

Eubranchus sp. 26
Size: 20 mm   Western Pacific Ocean
ID: Dark brown; cerata with opaque white tubercles in the lower half and a wider smooth whitish bulbous apical portion with orange subapical rings. Feeds on a dark brown plumularid hydroid on which is extremely cryptic.

Eubranchus sp. 27
Size: 15 mm   Indonesia
ID: Brown with white edges of the notum and dense opaque white pigment on the rhinophores; cerata short, rounded, light brown mottled with white. Very cryptic on its hydroid prey.

Nudibranchia - "nudibranchs"

Eubranchus sp. 28
Size: 12 mm   Philippines, Indonesia
ID: Translucent with dark digestive gland branches visible through the notum; cerata slender with brownish cores and bulbous opaque white apices; rhinophores smooth. On branching hydroids in areas of mixed sand and rubble.

Abronica Cella et al., 2016

Species of the genus *Abronica* usually have blue or purple pigment and a curved penial spine. Molecular evidence also support the distinctness of this group from other genera of Fionidae.

Abronica purpureoanulata (Baba, 1961)
Size: 10 mm   Western Pacific Ocean
ID: Translucent white with opaque white and purple spots; cerata with light brown digestive gland branches, each ceras with an opaque white ring and a purple apex; rhinophores with purple bands. Under coral rubble in 5-10 m.

Abronica sp. 1
Size: 7 mm   Western and central Pacific Ocean
ID: Purple with gold pigment on the oral tentacles and rhinophores; cerata pinkish white with yellow rings well below the apices. On shallow water reefs in 5 m under coral rubble.

Abronica sp. 2
Size: 6 mm   Marshall Is.
ID: Dark reddish-brown with yellow spots on the body and cerata; oral tentacles with yellow submarginal rings and translucent apices; cerata opaque bluish-white with reddish-brown bases and subapical yellow rings.

Abronica sp. 3
Size: 9 mm   Western and central Pacific Ocean
ID: Translucent white with opaque white spots covering the notum; cerata translucent white basally and opaque white in the upper halves, each ceras with a yellow and a red subapical band. Under coral rubble in 5-10 m.

Tergipes Cuvier, 1805

Species of the genus *Tergipes* have only single ceras per ceratal row. Species in this group are also characterized by having a short and rounded head. One one species is here reported from the Indo-Pacific tropics.

Tergipes sp.

Size: 15 mm   Kenya
ID: Yellow with opaque white spots on the rhinophores, oral tentacles, cerata and notum; cerata mottled with brown. On drifting debris such as leaves.

Tergiposacca Cella, Carmona, Ekimova, Chichvarkhin, Schepetov & Gosliner, 2016

The single species in this genus is known to lack a penial gland and a penial stylet. Cerata and egg mass elongate.

Tergiposacca longicerata Cella *et al.*, 2016

Size: 15 mm   Western Pacific Ocean
ID: Translucent white; cerata elongate, cylindrical with pink to brick red digestive gland branches becoming dark brown near the cnidosacs; each ceras with a cream subapical band and an opaque white apex. Commonly under rocks in shallow water, in 2-5 m; saccate egg masses also shown in the photo; egg masses expand greatly as the larvae mature.

Fiona Alder & Hancock *in* Forbes & Hanley, 1853

Members of this genus have a sail-like appendage on the hind end of the cerata. Only one species is here recognized, but it probably constitutes a species complex (Trickey *et al.* 2016).

Fiona pinnata (Eschscholtz, 1831)

Size: 25 mm   Widespread in all oceans
ID: Translucent white with opaque white on the head and notum; the brown digestive gland visible through the cerata, which have a characteristic undulating sail on the posterior side. On floating objects; this pelagic species feeds on gooseneck barnacles, *Lepas* sp.

Nudibranchia - "nudibranchs"

Tenellia A. Costa, 1866

Species of *Tenellia* usually have well-spaced cerata arranged in well-defined rows. They used to be regarded as members of *Cuthona*, but recently published molecular evidence indicate they constitute a distinct clade (Cella *et al.* 2016)

Tenellia sibogae (Bergh, 1905)
Size: 35 mm   Widespread in the Indo-Pacific
ID: Pink to purple with yellow ceratal tips; rhinophores slender and acutely pointed. Feeds on hydroids of the genus *Sertularella* on relatively shallow reefs, 5-15 m.

Tenellia sp. 1
Size: 35 mm   South Africa, Mozambique
ID: Pink to purple with orange ceratal tips; rhinophores and oral tentacles purple, slender and acutely pointed. Similar to *Tenellia sibogae*, but with dark blue marking on the cerata below the short yellow apex. On *Sertularella* hydroids.

Tenellia sp. 2
Size: 7 mm   Philippines
ID: Bluish-white with longitudinal yellow lines on the dorsum and sides of the body as well as yellow pigment on the head; oral tentacles and rhinophores brown with opaque white dots; cerata opaque white with series of blue and yellow rings and white apices. Under coral rubble, in 16 m.

Tenellia sp. 3
Size: 8 mm   Eastern Australia
ID: Green with opaque white pigment on the center of the body; bright blue spot near the middle of each ceras and on head in front of the rhinophores; cerata densely crowded and held close to body. On *Aglaophenia* hydroids.

Tenellia sp. 4
Size: 5 mm   Indonesia
ID: Translucent white with orange rhinophores and a y-shaped marking on hthe ead extending on to the oral tentacles; each ceras with a yellow apex and a blue subapical band.

Tenellia ornata **(Baba, 1937)**
Size: 10 mm   Indian and western Pacific oceans
ID: Orange; bright blue cerata with a yellow apices. Feeds on thecate hydroids in 11 m on fringing reefs.

Tenellia **sp. 5**
Size: 9 mm   Tanzania
ID: Orange with light yellow pigment covering most of the head and rhinophores; cerata yellow with dark blue and orange rings and light blue apices. On shallow reefs under coral rubble in 8 m.

Tenellia **sp. 6**
Size: 8 mm   Indian and western Pacific oceans
ID: Orange with bright red bases to the rhinophores; cerata with two yellow bands each, between which the blue digestive gland is visible. Under coral rubble in shallow water in 2-10 m.

Tenellia **sp. 7**
Size: 8 mm   Tahiti
ID: Translucent orange with large patches of opaque white pigment on the head and dorsum; rhinophores opaque white; oral tentacles opaque white with red bases; cerata with bands of black, yellow, blue, orange, yellow and white apices. Reef lagoons in 1 m.

Tenellia **sp. 8**
Size: 9 mm   Western and central Pacific Ocean
ID: Translucent with a cream patch on the head and rhinophores; cerata covered with cream having numerous openings through which the blue digestive gland and black spots are visible; cerata with subapical yellow bands.

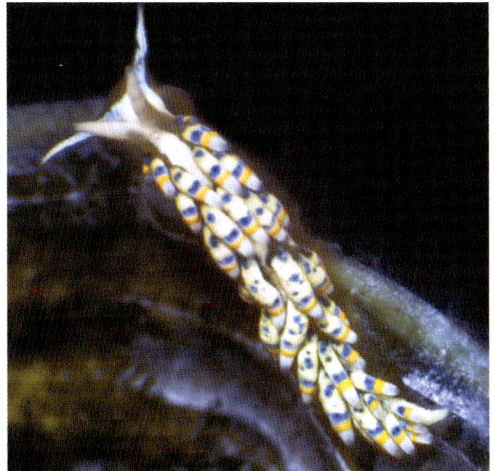

Tenellia sp. 9
Size: 6 mm   Papua New Guinea
ID: Orange; a bluish spot behind the rhinophores with a yellow center; oral tentacles and rhinophores with opaque white pigment; cerata opaque white with yellow and blue rings and white apices.

Tenellia sp. 10
Size: 7 mm   Kenya
ID: Opaque white; oral tentacles red with blue bases; rhinophores white with red tips; cerata white, each having a blue spot with a dark blue center.

Tenellia sp. 11
Size: 10 mm   Western and central Pacific Ocean
ID: Translucent whitish with a patch of blue and cream on the head just behind the rhinophores; cerata covered with opaque cream, each with a bright red spot and a light blue apex. On steep slopes of barrier reefs in 1-15 m.

Tenellia sp. 12
Size: 20 mm   Japan, Marshall Is.
ID: Translucent orange with opaque white pigment on the head, rhinophores and oral tentacles; cerata grey basally with opaque white pustules, each with a subapical blue band, an apical opaque white band, and an orange spot.

Tenellia kanga (Edmunds, 1970)
Size: 14 mm   Western Indian Ocean
ID: Bluish with a white patch on the head and white on the oral tentacles and rhinophores; cerata with blue and yellow bands below the white apices and dark green digestive gland branches. On reefs in 2-4 m; feeds on the hydroid, *Thecocarpus* sp.

Tenellia sp. 13
Size: 7 mm   Philippines
ID: Translucent white, with a "mask" of opaque white around the rhinophores and eyes; oral tentacles and rhinophores translucent white with brown apices; each ceras with a black base covered with irregular yellow spots, followed by a blue ring, then a yellow ring and a white apex.

286

Tenellia diversicolor (Baba, 1975)
Size: 20 mm   Western Pacific Ocean
D: Translucent white; cerata translucent covered with opaque white spots and with bluish and orange subapical bands; digestive gland branches visible through the cerata; tips of the rhinophores and oral tentacles red. On shallow reefs in 7-10 m under coral rubble.

Tenellia sp. 14
Size: 20 mm   Indonesia, Philippines
ID: Translucent with a reddish head including the oral tentacles and rhinophores; opaque white pigment around the rhinophores; cerata translucent with white pigment covering most of their length, apical region of each ceras with a thick blue ring, followed by a yellow ring and a white apex.

Tenellia sp. 15
Size: 50 mm   Indian and western Pacific oceans
ID: Brown with opaque white covering the head; rhinophores wide, dark brown with white apices; cerata with subapical gold rings. Previously thought to be *Cuthona yamasui*, but this species is correctly identified below. Feeds on the hydroid, *Aglaophenia cupressina*; most commonly observed crawling on soft substrate on silty slopes.

Tenellia sp. 16
Size: 40 mm   Western Pacific Ocean
ID: Uniformly bluish; rhinophores wide, black with white apices; oral tentacles black; cerata with subapical gold rings.

Feeds on arborescent hydroids growing on rubble in sandy and silty habitats, 5-40 m.

Nudibranchia - "nudibranchs"

Tenellia sp. 17
Size: 10 mm   United Arab Emirates
ID: Deep brown body with opaque white markings surrounding the rhinophores; each ceras with a blue apex and subapical yellow, blue and white rings.

Tenellia sp. 18
Size: 8 mm   Papua New Guinea, Malaysia
ID: Orange with dense opaque white pigment; anterior faces of the cerata opaque white and posterior sides cream, apices blue; rhinophores and oral tentacles with opaque white pigment and orange apical halves. Under coral rubble on the surface and slopes of barrier reefs in 8-15 m.

Tenellia sp. 19
Size: 10 mm   Western and central Pacific Ocean
ID: Blue with whitish tips on the oral tentacles and rhinophores; cerata having transparent bases with the orange digestive gland visible, above this area opaque white with yellow subapical bands. On the underside of coral rubble in 8 m; feeds on small thecate hydroids.

Tenellia sp. 20
Size: 15 mm   Western and central Pacific Ocean
ID: Translucent purplish-white with opaque white covering most of the body including the cerata; cerata held flat against the notum. On sandy slopes in 5-15 m; appears to feed upon the athecate hydroid *Corymorpha* sp.

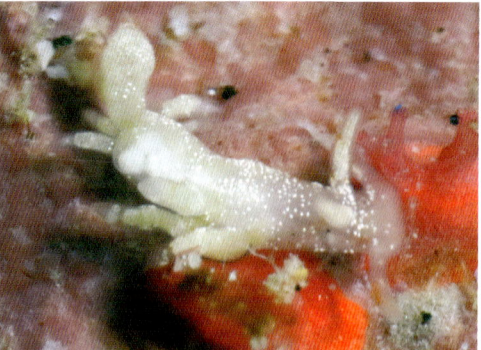

Tenellia sp. 21
Size: 5 mm   Philippines
ID: Translucent pinkish white with scattered opaque white spots over most of the body; cerata cylindrical to slightly bulbous; pink digestive gland visible within cerata; pink on most of the length of the rhinophores. Shallow reefs in 10 m.

Tenellia sp. 22
Size: 5 mm   Hawai'ian Is.
ID: Light purple with a large opaque white marking on the head and notum; cerata purple with an opaque white tips; rhinophores and oral tentacles covered with orange. In 2-3 m under volcanic rocks.

Tenellia yamasui (Hamatani, 1993)
Size: 15 mm — Japan, Philippines, Indonesia
ID: Translucent white with opaque white markings on the head and notum; cerata orange-brown with opaque white spots; rhinophores reddish-orange with opaque white bands and apices; red-orange pigment present on the head and oral tentacles.

Tenellia sp. 23
Size: 8 mm — Indonesia
ID: Translucent white with yellow irregular spots and yellow pigment around the rhinophores; oral tentacles and rhinophores brown with opaque white dots; cerata brownish scattered with black and white spots, each ceras with a subapical yellow ring and a white apex.

Tenellia sp. 24
Size: 7 mm — Philippines
ID: Translucent white with numerous opaque white spots over the entire body including the oral tentacles and rhinophores; oral tentacles with brown bases and white apices; rhinophores with white bases and brown apices; cerata brown with white apices.

Tenellia sp. 25
Size: 8 mm — Tropical Australia
ID: Translucent whitish with scattered opaque white spots; cerata thick and short with brownish digestive gland branches and yellowish spots on the surface.

Tenellia sp. 26
Size: 7 mm — Western and central Pacific Ocean
ID: Translucent yellowish with large opaque white patches on the head and notum; cerata green with gold longitudinal lines; an orange U-shaped marking at the junction of the oral tentacles. Under coral rubble on the outer edge of barrier reef slopes.

Nudibranchia - "nudibranchs"

Tenellia acinosa (Risbec, 1928)
Size: 13 mm   Western Pacific
ID: Opaque white body with orange cerata, which may have opaque white markings; rhinophores and oral tentacles orange. Shallow reefs on rubble and algae.

Tenellia sp. 27
Size: 9 mm   Western Pacific Ocea
ID: Bright cherry-red; cerata may be more purple, with sma yellowish spots and opaque white tips; oral tentacles opaqu white. On shallow barrier reefs in 7-10 m under coral rubble

Tenellia sp. 28
Size: 7 mm   Indonesia
ID: Red with purple oral tentacles and opaque white pigment on the dorsum and sides; rhinophores red; cerata red with opaque white spots, each ceras with a submarginal purple spot and a white apex.

Tenellia sp. 29
Size: 9 mm   Indones
ID: Opaque white pigment covering most of the notum exce for the oral tentacles and rhinophores; cerata red with fe opaque white spots.

Tenellia sp. 30
Size: 7 mm   Marshall Is.
ID: Opaque white with bright red pigment on the head, oral tentacles and the tips of the rhinophores and cerata; a few blue spots on the dorsum. On pier pilings, in 1 m.

Tenellia sp. 31
Size: 7 mm   Western Pacific Ocea
ID: Bright purple with a broad medial opaque white bar that extends on to the lower part of the rhinophores; cera purple, bulbous, with orange-red subapical bands. Unde coral rubble in shallow water, 5-10 m.

Tenellia sp. 32
ze: 7 mm   Indonesia
): Opaque white; rhinophores and oral tentacles orange
ith white apices; cerata dark brown with opaque white spots
nd white apices.

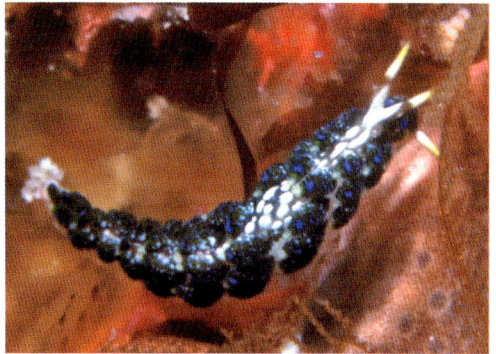

Tenellia sp. 33
Size: 10 mm   Marshall Is.
ID: Black with large opaque white spots on the dorsum; head
with a V-shaped opaque white marking entering the base of
the rhinophores; oral tentacles and rhinophores white, with
brown bases and yellow apices; cerata black with blue spots
and white apices.

Tenellia sp. 34
ize: 7 mm   Indian and western Pacific oceans
): Translucent orange; head pink, with orange pigment on
e oral tentacles and rhinophores; bases of the cerata with
 bluish sheen, apices orange. On the underside of coral
bble in 1-10 m.

Tenellia sp. 35
Size: 12 mm   Papua New Guinea, Palau
ID: Purple to deep maroon including cerata and rhinophores;
oral tentacles purple; tips of the rhinophores opaque white as
the foot and sides of the body; tips of the cerata burnt orange.
On shallow barrier reefs in 7-10 m under coral rubble.

Tenellia sp. 36
ize: 30 mm   South Africa, Madagascar
D: Yellowish with a broad notal patch of opaque white;
e brown digestive gland extends into the cerata and the
nterior part of the head; each ceras with a yellow subapical
and. On thecate hydroids in 20-32 m.

Tenellia sp. 37
Size: 7 mm   Indonesia
ID: Translucent whitish with patches of opaque white and
yellow on the notum; cerata thin and elongate, each filled
with a thin, red digestive gland duct and covered with
scattered opaque white spots on the surface; rhinophores
reddish brown with opaque white apices.

291

Nudibranchia - "nudibranchs"

Tenellia sp. 38
Size: 5 mm   Japan
ID: Body brown with minute white spots over most of the body; cerata transparent basally showing a brown digestive gland; outer half of cerata opaque white; opaque white on rhinophores and oral tentacles.

Tenellia sp. 39
Size: 8 mm   Western Pacific Ocea
ID: Translucent white with a dense covering of opaqu white; cerata covered with opaque white but have interrupte areas of translucence and subapical bands of bright yellow rhinophores and oral tentacles with yellow and red bands. O patch reefs under coral rubble in 5-10 m.

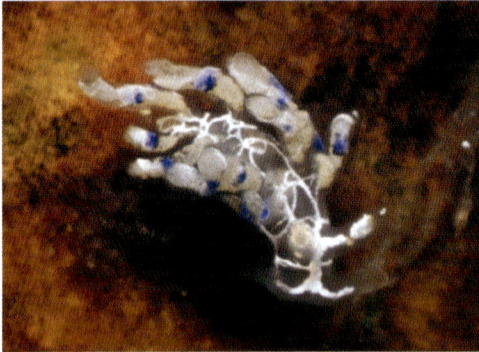

Tenellia sp. 40
Size: 7 mm   Philippines
ID: Translucent white with a network of opaque white lines on the notum; cerata pinkish, each with a bright blue subapical spot. Under coral rubble in 8 m.

Tenellia sp. 41
Size: 8 mm   Papua New Guine
ID: Translucent white with patches of opaque white; cerat translucent white, inflated, each with two opaque white ring and a bright red subapical ring; rhinophores and oral tentacle with red tips. On coral rubble in protected lagoons on th inside of barrier reefs in 3-6 m.

Tenellia sp. 42
Size: 20 mm   Madagascar
ID: Translucent white with opaque white spots; cerata swollen subapically, narrowing into a rounded apex; head broad and rounded. In 1-2 m; feeds on the athecate hydroid, *Pennaria disticha*.

Tenellia sp. 43
Size: 3 mm   Japan
ID: Body white; posterior cerata with dark brown rings; ora tentacles and rhinophores orange. Animal in the photo is likely a juvenile.

Tenellia sp. 44
Size: 14 mm   Indonesia
ID: Translucent whitish; cerata thick and bulbous filled with white, nodular digestive gland branches; ceratal apices orange with acutely pointed tips; digestive gland ducts clearly visible through the notum; rhinophores short and brown.

Tenellia sp. 45
Size: 10 mm   Philippines
ID: Translucent white with an opaque white patch on the head; cerata light blue with a subapical orange ring; oral tentacles and rhinophores orange with white tips. Under coral rubble on shallow reefs in 12 m.

Tenellia sp. 46
Size: 8 mm   Western Pacific Ocean
ID: Translucent grey with opaque white down the middle of the notum and bluish pigment on the head; cerata orange throughout, with brighter orange cnidosacs; oral tentacles and rhinophores mostly orange. Under coral rubble on reefs from 7-15 m.

Tenellia sp. 47
Size: 7 mm   Madagascar, Japan
ID: Translucent white; cerata opaque white, each with a purple subapical ring; rhinophores with orange pigment over most of their surface; brown jaws readily visible through the head. In 0-2 m under volcanic rocks.

Tenellia sp. 48
Size: 6 mm   Papua New Guinea
ID: Opaque white with opaque white cerata; a single dark brown spot below the apex of each ceras; rhinophores and oral tentacles brown. On shallow water reefs in 5 m under coral rubble.

Tenellia sp. 49
Size: 20 mm   Tahiti
ID: Translucent white with the digestive gland visible and some opaque white spots on the notum; rhinophores and oral tentacles translucent with opaque white pigment; rhinophores annulate; cerata translucent, each with a white and a yellow ring and a blue apex. In bays in 5 m.

Nudibranchia - "nudibranchs"

Tenellia sp. 50
Size: 7 mm   Indonesia
ID: Orange with a V-shaped opaque bluish-white marking on the head entering the oral tentacles and surrounded by two yellow short lines; rhinophores white with brownish-orange bases; cerata orange with blue subapical rings and white apices.

Tenellia sp. 51
Size: 3 mm   Tuamotu Archipelago
ID: Uniformly bright yellow to lime green with bright red pigment at the base of the rhinophores and apices of the cerata. In a protected lagoon in 1 m.

Tenellia sp. 52
Size: 12 mm   Vanuatu, Philippines
ID: Translucent white with cream to opaque white pigment on the head and scattered over the center of the notum; each ceras with a single red spot below the apex; rhinophores opaque white basally with red-orange apices; oral tentacles red with orange spots and opaque or translucent white apices. Shallow water on patch reefs.

Tenellia sp. 53
Size: 25 mm   Marshall Is.
ID: Brown with pale areas between the ceratal groups; white oral tentacles; rhinophores white with brown rings midlength; cerata greyish-white with pink bases, subapical red rings and orange apices.

Tenellia sp. 54
Size: 5 mm   Indonesia
ID: Translucent whitish with orange pigment on the head and on the base of the rhinophores; cerata thin and relatively short, each with a wide yellow digestive gland duct and a black subapical spot below the opaque each white cnidosac.

Tenellia sp. 55
Size: 6 mm   Philippines
ID: Translucent white with opaque white dots; oral tentacles with the same color; rhinophores opaque white with red bases; cerata transparent with some opaque white dots on the bases, the brown digestive gland branches and the yellow cinidosacs visible. Under coral heads on top of pinnacle, 5 m.

Tenellia sp. 56
Size: 7 mm   Indian and western Pacific oceans
ID: Translucent white with opaque white and red spots on the notum; cerata with opaque white longitudinal lines; rhinophores and oral tentacles tipped with opaque white. Under coral rubble on shallow reef flats in 1-10 m.

Tenellia sp. 57
Size: 8 mm   Philippines, Indonesia
ID: White with large bright orange spots and opaque white dots on the body; rhinophores brown basally and white apically; cerata translucent grey with black spots at the bases and opaque white longitudinal lines.

Tenellia sp. 58
Size: 7 mm   Philippines
ID: Translucent white with a network of opaque white frosting over much of the notum; cerata translucent white each with an opaque white outer portion and a subapical yellow band; rhinophores and oral tentacles with alternately translucent and opaque white bands. Shallow water on patch reefs under rubble.

Tenellia sp. 59
Size: 11 mm   Philippines
ID: Uniformly orange-brown with lighter tips of the rhinophores and oral tentacles; cerata with dark brown branches of the digestive gland and orange apices. Under rocks on steep slopes of coral reefs, where it feeds on small hydroids, in 12-20 m.

Tenellia sp. 60
Size: 6 mm   Philippines
ID: Opaque white with orange pigment at the base of the oral tentacles; rhinophores translucent basally and opaque white apically; cerata translucent with the grey digestive gland branches visible at the bases and orange and opaque white rings.

Tenellia sp. 61
Size: 15 mm   Madagascar, Tanzania
ID: Translucent white; cerata pinkish red to purple with a fine dusting of opaque white; oral tentacles and rhinophores with opaque white spots. On patch reefs in 2-3 m.

295

Nudibranchia - "nudibranchs"

Tenellia sp. 62
Size: 15 mm   Indonesia
ID: Translucent whitish; cerata thick and elongate, each with a narrow yellowish digestive gland duct; rhinophores and oral tentacles elongate with reddish apices.

Tenellia sp. 63
Size: 10 mm   Philippines
ID: White with opaque white pigment covering the head and dorsum; rhinophores and oral tentacles red; cerata very elongate, opaque white. Under coral rubble on steep slopes of mixed sand and rubble, 22 m.

Tenellia sp. 64
Size: 5 mm   Philippines
ID: Translucent cream with opaque white oral tentacles and rhinophores; cerata translucent with the cream branches of the digestive gland and the white cnidosacs visible; body narrow and elongate with very long oral tentacles and rhinophores.

Tenellia sp. 65
Size: 9 mm   Philippines
ID: Uniformly translucent white with the white digestive gland visible through the body and cerata; rhinophores cream-white; oral tentacles translucent with opaque white apices. Under coral rubble on shallow reefs, 12 m.

Tenellia sp. 66
Size: 5 mm   Philippines, Indonesia
ID: Translucent white with numerous opaque bluish-white spots covering the entire body, including the cerata; rhinophores and oral tentacles same color, also with yellow spots. On coral rubble on steep silty slopes, 18 m.

Tenellia sp. 67
Size: 8 mm   Philippines
ID: Brown with dense covering of yellow and blue dots, and a large opaque white patch on the dorsum; rhinophores and oral tentacles same color but lacking blue dots. Crawling on hydroids in deep areas of rubble, 20-30 m.

Tenellia sp. 68
Size: 6 mm   Philippines
D: Uniformly opaque white with black pigment on the bases of the cerata. On fine sand with many filter feeding organisms on steep slopes, 15 m.

Tenellia sp. 69
Size: 10 mm   Philippines
ID: Bluish with pink cerata, each with a red dot; rhinophores with translucent bases, mid-length opaque cream regions and reddish-brown apices; oral tentacles translucent with reddish-brown pigment. On coral rubble on steep sandy and rocky slopes, 15 m.

Tenellia sp. 70
Size: 7 mm   Indonesia
D: Opaque white; oral tentacles and rhinophores translucent with brown subapical rings; cerata with the cream branches of the digestive gland visible, and yellow-orange apices.

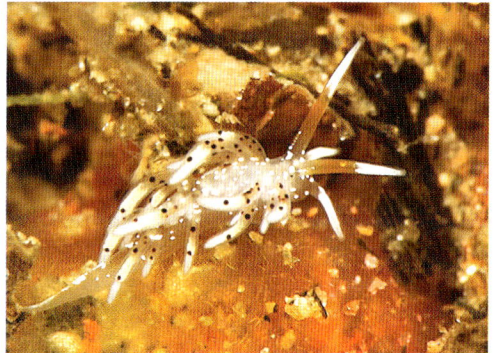

Tenellia sp. 71
Size: 7 mm   Philippines
ID: Translucent white with large opaque white spots; oral tentacles and rhinophores reddish-brown with opaque white apices; cerata translucent with the brown branches of the digestive gland and the white cnidosacs visible, covered with large black spots and with white apices.

Tenellia sp. 72
Size: 11 mm   Philippines
D: Translucent white with opaque white pigment on the head and dorsum; oral tentacles orange; rhinophores with opaque white bases and orange tips; cerata elongate, each with a small orange dot. Under coral rubble on gradually sloping reefs, 15 m.

Tenellia pinnifera (Baba, 1949)
Size: 12 mm   Western and central Pacific Ocean
ID: Opaque white; cerata with opaque white bands; rhinophores with incomplete annulae. On shallow reefs in 1-10 m under coral rubble where hydroids are abundant.

297

Nudibranchia - "nudibranchs"

Tenellia sp. 73
Size: 11 mm   Papua New Guinea, Philippines
ID: Translucent yellow with opaque white spots; tips of the rhinophores bright yellow; cerata translucent with opaque white bands and yellow apices, dark brown digestive gland branches visible. Under coral rubble in 7-10 m.

Tenellia sp. 74
Size: 8 mm   Philippines, Australia
ID: Body light pink with darker pink cerata; outer half of cerata with opaque white markings; rhinophores and oral tentacles with orange and opaque white bands. Shallow reefs, 15 m.

Tenellia sp. 75
Size: 7 mm   Widespread in the Indo-Pacific
ID: Translucent orange with opaque white encrusting on most of the notum; base of each ceras translucent orange followed by a broad band of opaque white and a small subapical band of orange; rhinophores and oral tentacles orange with white tips. Intertidal rock pools at night; presumably feeds on the athecate tubularid hydroid.

Tenellia sp. 76
Size: 6 mm   Papua New Guinea
ID: Yellow with orange rhinophores; cerata with dark green digestive gland branches, opaque white spots and white apices. On arborescent sertularid hydroids on reef slopes.

Tenellia sp. 77
Size: 8 mm   Thailand, Mozambique
ID: Body pink with salmon-colored pigment on the head and in the digestive gland; oral tentacles, rhinophores and tips of cerata dark blue.

Tenellia sp. 78
Size: 12 mm   Philippines
ID: Translucent white with opaque white lines on the notum and cerata; yellow and orange markings on the head extending into the oral tentacles; rhinophores with orange tips. On coral rubble in 20 m.

Coral-eating species

The next several species are members of *Tenellia* that used to be placed the coral-eating nudibranch genus *Phestilla*.

Tenellia lugubris (Bergh, 1870)
Size: 40 mm   Indo-Pacific and eastern Pacific
D: Translucent white with opaque white pigment on the cerata and notum; cerata nodulose with several narrowings and thickenings and opaque white apices; body broad with a wide head. Shallow water (0-10 m), under coral heads of *Porites* spp., on which it exclusively feeds.

Tenellia sp. 79
Size: 60 mm   Widespread in the Indo-Pacific
ID: Brownish with a broad body and transverse wrinkles across the notum; cerata cylindrical, each with a constriction just before the rounded apex. Feeds exclusively upon corals of the genus *Goniopora*, often under coral colonies together with its yellowish egg mass in 1-10 m.

Tenellia minor (Rudman, 1981)
Size: 9 mm   Widespread in the Indo-Pacific
ID: Translucent white with opaque white markings on the notum and cerata; each ceras with two club-like swellings, one near the outer end and the other at the apex. Feeds on *Porites* and produces a white, semicircular egg mass.

Tenellia poritophages (Rudman, 1979)
Size: 15 mm   Indian and western Pacific oceans
ID: Golden brown; cerata with opaque white rings along their lengths, held horizontally away from the body. Feeds upon the scleractinian corals, *Porites* spp. in 1-5 m under loose *Porites* heads.

Tenellia sp. 80
Size: 15 mm   Philippines
ID: Brownish with lines of dark brown pigment. On the underside of *Pavona* corals in 10 m.

Tenellia sp. 81
Size: 18 mm   Philippines
ID: Pale brown with transverse lines across the body. Extremely cryptic on its host coral, *Gardineroseris planulata*; shallow reefs 1-10 m.

Nudibranchia - "nudibranchs"

Tenellia melanobrachia (Bergh, 1874)
Size: 50 mm   Indo-Pacific and eastern Pacif
ID: Color variable, yellow, orange or black, depending upo
the color of its prey. Feeds exclusively on dendrophyllid coral
usually on the underside of detached coral colonies; white eg
masses usually deposited directly on the corals.

Tenellia sp. 82
Size: 10 mm   Western Pacific Ocean
ID: Translucent with the opaque white digestive gland visible;
cerata with brownish pigment and flat apices, each ceras with
two or more opaque white rings. Feeds on *Porites*, under
coral heads; its egg mass is sausage-shaped and is yellow.

Tenellia sp. 83
Size: 30 mm   Indian and western Pacific oceans
ID: Brownish with undulating opaque white patches on the
notum and opaque white lines on the relatively cylindrical
cerata; ceratal apices club-shaped. Shallow water under
coral heads of *Pavona* sp.; extremely cryptic on its host coral.

Babakinidae Roller, 1973

This family appears to be the sister group to the Facelinidae and Aeolidiidae (Gosliner *et al.*, 2007) and is characterized by having perfoliate rhinophores that share a common base and cerata that are arranged densely without having any division into distinct clusters. The anus is situated below the cerata.

Babakina indopacifica Gosliner, González-Duarte & Cervera, 2007
Size: 18 mm   Widespread in the Indo-Pacific
ID: Translucent pinkish purple with opaque white on the notum behind the rhinophores; cerata opaque white with bluish apices; rhinophores sharing a common stalk, red with opaque white pigment on the lamellae. In 1-15 m, on sea grasses and under coral rubble.

Facelinidae Bergh, 1889

Members of this family are characterized by having the anus usually situated within the cerata, behind the inter-hepatic space (cleioproctic) and a radula with a single row of teeth; the teeth have long basal limbs and a large pointed cusp flanked by several denticles. Most facelinids feed on hydroids, except for species of *Phyllodesmium* that feed on alcyonacean soft corals or gorgonians, and species of *Favorinus* that feed on the eggs of other opisthobranchs. *Phyllodesmium* and *Favorinus* are the only two genera in the family that lack cnidosacs. The nematocysts from alcyonaceans are possibly too small to be adequate for defense. When disturbed, several species of facelinids wave their cerata, aggressively pointing the tips containing the cnidosacs at the source of the attack.

Unidentiidae Millen & Hermosillo, 2012

Similar to Flabellinidae but having smooth rhinophores and lacking lateral teeth. Molecular evidence indicates this group is distinct from Flabellindae (Goodheart *et al.* 2017; Korshunova *et al.* 2017). Only one species is present in the Indo-Pacific tropics. *Unidentia angelvaldesi* Millen & Hermosillo, 2012 is restricted to the Eastern Pacific

Unidentia sandramillenae Korshunova *et al.*, 2017
Size: 20 mm   Western Pacific Ocean
ID: Orange, usually with a single medial purple line; cerata pale orange with subapical purple rings and yellow apices. On hydroids on slopes and walls in 10-20 m.

Facelina bourailli (Risbec, 1928)
Size: 15 mm   Indian and western Pacific oceans
ID: Translucent white with red spots; cerata dark brown basally with lighter pigment and opaque white longitudinal lines; rhinophores annulate; specimens from the western Indian Ocean with orange lines rather than spots, lacking opaque white lines on the cerata. Under coral rubble on shallow reefs in 1-10 m; feeds on hydroids, including *Salacia tetracythara* and *Thyroscyphus fruticosus*.

Facelina lineata Eliot, 1905
Size: 20 mm   India, Tanzania
ID: Translucent white with opaque white longitudinal lines and orange patches on the head; rhinophores smooth, black; cerata with an orange subapical ring.

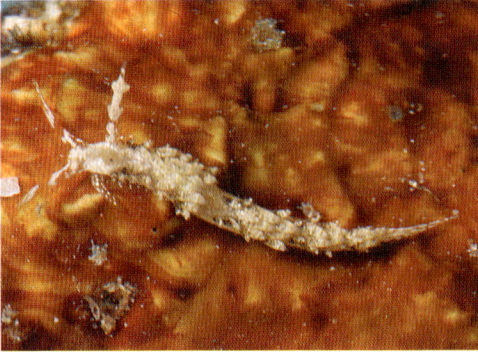

Facelina sp. 1
Size: 15 mm   Philippines, Indonesia
ID: Translucent grey with opaque white, black and yellow spots; rhinophores translucent with white and cream pigment and two bulbous swellings; cerata with opaque white pigment and yellow subapical rings. Under coral rubble on a gradually sloping reefs, 10 m.

Facelina sp. 2
Size: 15 mm   Western and central Pacific Ocean
ID: Light brown; annulate rhinophores brown with opaque white pigment and brown tips; bright red digestive gland branches in the cerata; each ceras with a subapical opaque white band followed by a translucent yellow apex. Under coral rubble in 7-8 m.

Facelina sp. 3
Size: 8 mm   Papua New Guinea
ID: Translucent white with small opaque white spots on the edge of the foot and notum; cerata bright red with yellow tips; rhinophores smooth; oral tentacles orange with opaque white spots. Under coral rubble on shallow water reefs in 3-7 m.

Facelina sp. 4
Size: 10 mm   Philippines
ID: Translucent orange with small opaque white spots; cerata orange with scattered opaque white spots and white apices; rhinophores smooth, orange basally with opaque white apices; oral tentacles orange with opaque white spots, each with an opaque white band just below the apex. Shallow water or rubble patches between sandy areas.

Facelina sp. 5
Size: 15 mm   Philippines, Indonesia
ID: Translucent grey with opaque white pigment on the head and body; oral tentacles opaque white with orange tips; rhinophores smooth with white bases, brown subapical rings and yellow tips; cerata brown and black with opaque white apices; dorsal cerata almost completely white.

Facelina sp. 6
Size: 15 mm   Tuamotu Archipelago
ID: Opaque white with some translucent areas in the oral tentacles and body; rhinophores white with three large annulae; cerata bright red with subapical orange bands and opaque white tips. On shallow reefs in 2 m.

Nudibranchia - "nudibranchs"

Facelina sp. 7
Size: 7 mm   Papua New Guinea
ID: Orange with white rhinophores and oral tentacles; cerata translucent with the brown digestive gland branches visible; ceratal apices white; rhinophores smooth.

Facelina sp. 8
Size: 18 mm   Philippines
ID: Orange-brown; outer cerata each with a small opaque white spot, innermost cerata with the entire distal third opaque white; long oral tentacles with opaque white on the outer half; rhinophores short, smooth, with opaque white bands. On shallow reefs under coral rubble in 8 m.

Facelina sp. 9
Size: 8 mm   Philippines
ID: Translucent orange-brown with a single opaque white line on each oral tentacle, rhinophore and ceras; cerata with brown branches of the digestive gland visible; rhinophores smooth. Crawling on coral rubble on sandy slopes, 15-20 m.

Facelina sp. 10
Size: 15 mm   Papua New Guinea
ID: Golden brown with opaque white spots; rhinophores covered with opaque white, with 1-2 annulae; cerata with black pigment basally and acute apices; opaque white and orange subapical bands on the cerata and oral tentacles. Feeds on hydroids.

Facelina sp. 11
Size: 9 mm   Central Pacific Ocean
ID: Translucent white with opaque white patches and spots on the notum; cerata opaque white with translucent white apices; rhinophores with two large annulae. On shallow reefs in 10-20 m under coral rubble.

Facelina sp. 12
Size: 12 mm   Hawai'ian Is.
ID: Opaque white with grey pigment on the dorsum; oral tentacles with red bases and opaque white apices; rhinophores reddish, smooth; cerata short, with the pale brown digestive gland branches visible at the bases; each ceras with a central opaque white ring, followed by a red ring and an orange apex. Under rocky ledges where it feeds on hydroids, 5-14 m.

303

Facelinella semidecora (Pease, 1860)
Size: 12 mm   Central Pacific Ocean
ID: Translucent white with orange pigment and lines, and opaque white spots; cerata dark basally with orange and opaque white pigment apically; rhinophores with 3-4 low annulae. Under coral rubble in the intertidal zone to 3 m; feeds on thecate hydroids.

Facelinella anulifera Baba, 1949
Size: 15 mm   Western and central Pacific Ocean
ID: Cream with bright red irregular longitudinal lines on the dorsum and sides of the body; oral tentacles and rhinophores with abundant opaque white pigment; cerata brown with black lines on the bases and white apices.

Caloria indica (Bergh, 1896)
Size: 30 mm   Widespread in the Indo-Pacific
ID: Color variable, translucent grey to orange or reddish-brown; dorsum with white or yellow markings, variable in length, in some specimens forming long longitudinal lines; head with two thick white lines running from the bases of the rhinophores to the bases of the oral tentacles; rhinophores with reddish bases, each with a lighter, typically opaque white central region, and red apices; oral tentacles mainly bluish-white with yellow and blue pigment on their bases and bluish-purple apices; cerata with red bases, blue pigment in their central regions and yellow to white apices. The most common species of facelinid in the Indo-Pacific; relatively shallow reefs in 1-15 m; feeds on the hydroids *Eudendrium* sp. and *Pennaria disticha*.

Caloria militaris (Alder & Hancock, 1864)
Size: 25 mm   Indian and western Pacific oceans
ID: Translucent white with orange lines on the head and sides of the body; cerata dark brown basally with orange lines and white apices; rhinophores smooth and shorter than the oral tentacles. Under coral rubble in 10-20 m.

Caloria sp. 1
Size: 15 mm   Widespread in the Indo-Pacific
ID: Reddish with a line of opaque white patches on the medial portion of the notum; cerata with dark brown to black bases and blue and orange subapical bands; rhinophores with 2-3 oblique annulae. From the intertidal zone to 9 m under coral rubble.

Caloria sp. 2
Size: 12 mm   Widespread in the Indo-Pacific
ID: Translucent orange with opaque white patches on the notum and head; cerata orange basally and opaque white in the apical half; largest cerata with curved apices; rhinophores smooth. Under coral rubble on shallow reefs in 1-10 m.

Caloria sp. 3
Size: 40 mm   Hawai'ian Is.
ID: Translucent orange with bluish pigment on the cerata and orange apices; rhinophores smooth with a lighter orange apices. In 20 m, under coral rubble on outer reefs.

Caloria sp. 4
Size: 22 mm   Philippines
ID: Translucent orange with an opaque line from the anterior end of the head to just behind the rhinophores; cerata straight and opaque white, except for the translucent apices; rhinophores smooth, orange basally with opaque white for most of the length; oral tentacles opaque white. On hydroids along walls in 15-20 m.

Caloria sp. 5
Size: 18 mm   South Africa
ID: Orange with an opaque white line between the rhinophores; cerata opaque white basally transitioning into purple, magenta and orange.

305

Nudibranchia - "nudibranchs"

Favorinus japonicus Baba, 1949
Size: 20 mm   Widespread in the Indo-Pacific
ID: Translucent white with opaque white markings and diamonds on the notum; cerata nodular with the digestive gland branches adopting the color of the food ingested; rhinophores with 2-3 bulbous swellings. Feeds on the eggs of other opisthobranchs, especially *Hexabranchus sanguineus*, *Aplysia* spp. and *Dolabella auricularia*.

Favorinus sp. 1
Size: 10 mm   Indonesia
ID: Brownish-orange; cerata cream with purple tips; rhinophores dark brown with numerous crowded lamellae; oral tentacles brownish-orange. On the egg masses of other opisthobranchs.

Favorinus tsuruganus Baba & Abe, 1964
Size: 30 mm   Indian and western Pacific oceans
ID: Translucent white with opaque white covering most of the body; digestive gland branches within the cerata orange with black apices; rhinophores with 3 lamellae. Feeds on the eggs of *Hexabranchus sanguineus*, *Goniodoris felis* and *Hypselodoris* spp.

Favorinus mirabilis Baba, 1955
Size: 12 mm   Widespread in the Indo-Pacific
ID: Translucent whitish with an opaque white and yellow diamond on the head just behind the brown, perfoliate rhinophores; cerata usually pink to red with opaque white

spots, each with a dark bluish spot below the apex. Feeds on egg masses of opisthobranchs, especially *Hexabranchus sanguineus*.

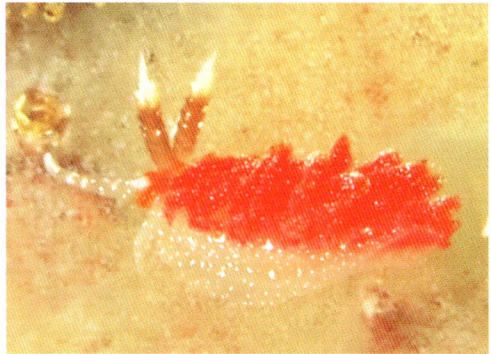

Favorinus sp. 2
Size: 15 mm   Philippines
ID: Orange-red with orange lines on the oral tentacles; cerata brown with conspicuous lamellae and black apices; cerata orange with white subapical rings and purple tips. Coral rubble in 20 m.

Favorinus sp. 3
Size: 8 mm   Kenya
ID: Translucent white with numerous opaque white dots; rhinophores perfoliate, brown with white apices; cerata bright red with opaque white dots.

Favorinus sp. 4
Size: 5 mm   Philippines
ID: Translucent white with opaque white dots and orange pigment on the head; rhinophores black with white tips; oral tentacles translucent with white dots, each with a black line; cerata translucent with brownish branches of the digestive gland and surface opaque white pigment; each ceras with a reddish-brown dot. Clean sandy areas, nocturnally active, 6 m.

Favorinus sp. 5
Size: 15 mm   Tuamotu Archipelago
ID: Cream with opaque white pigment on the dorsum and oral tentacles; rhinophores brownish with white spots and black tips; cerata white with purple subapical pigment and white tips. On shallow reefs, in 3 m.

Favorinus sp. 6
Size: 7 mm   Philippines
ID: Translucent white with yellow spots on the dorsum, head, oral tentacles and rhinophores; cerata with short, black branches of the digestive gland; cerata short and smooth. Clean sandy areas, nocturnally active, 6 m.

Favorinus sp. 7
Size: 9 mm   Papua New Guinea
ID: Translucent white with a pink digestive gland visible through the cerata, which have yellow apices; smooth rhinophores and oral tentacles with opaque white bands. Under coral rubble in 8 m on fore-reefs.

Favorinus sp. 8
Size: 18 mm   Papua New Guinea, Palau
ID: Translucent brownish with opaque white spots on the notum, cerata, oral tentacles, and rhinophores; dark brown digestive gland branches visible through the transparent cerata; rhinophores with single bulbous swellings situated just below the acute apices. In a marine lab sea water system, feeding on the eggs of *Stylocheilus striatus*.

Favorinus sp. 9
Size: 10 mm   Papua New Guinea, Guam
ID: Translucent with opaque white spots on the head and pericardium; cerata translucent, inflated with thick digestive gland branches; each ceras with an opaque white ring in the outer third and an opaque white apex; rhinophores short, smooth with opaque white tips. On the eggs of *Diniatys dubius* on shallow sandy habitats.

Favorinus sp. 10
Size: 15 mm   Red Sea, western Pacific Ocean
ID: Translucent white with opaque white spots on the notum and cerata; digestive gland branches narrow, dark brown, visible through the cerata; rhinophores smooth, short. On silty, sandy slopes; feeds on the egg masses of *Diniatys dubius*; it crawls into the egg mass and "swims" through the mucus of the mass feeding on the eggs.

Favorinus sp. 11
Size: 12 mm   Papua New Guinea
ID: Translucent white with opaque white over most of the body; cerata light brown encrusted with opaque white; rhinophores smooth, long, dark grey to black. Under coral rubble on patch reefs in 10 m; feeds on an unidentified dorid egg mass.

Favorinus sp. 12
Size: 6 mm   Philippines
ID: Translucent white; cerata light yellow-brown, short; rhinophores elongate, black, each with three swollen bulbs and some yellow spots near the apex. On shallow water reefs; feeds on the egg masses of *Hexabranchus sanguineus*.

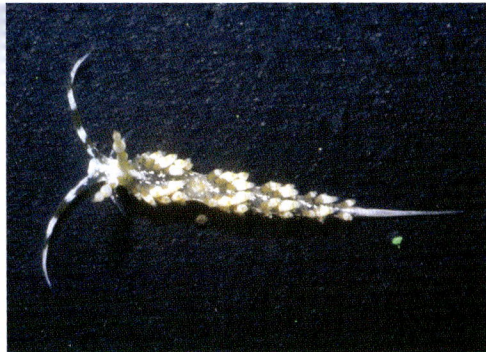

Favorinus sp. 13
Size: 8 mm   Philippines
ID: Translucent whitish with brown pigment in the digestive gland branches below the white ceratal apex; rhinophores opaque white with two rounded knobs; oral tentacles elongate, with several bands of opaque white. On the egg masses of other opisthobranchs.

Favorinus sp. 14
Size: 4 mm   Indonesia
ID: Translucent grey with opaque white pigment on the dorsum and head, penetrating into the oral tentacles; rhinophores brownish with opaque white tips; cerata transparent with the whitish and purple branches of the digestive gland visible, and white subapical rings.

Favorinus sp. 15
Size: 12 mm   Philippines
ID: Opaque white; translucent white cerata with brown apices; rhinophores brown, each with three bulbous swellings. In coral rubble areas, 20 m.

Protaeolidia juliae (Burn, 1966)
Size: 30 mm   Indian and western Pacific oceans
ID: Black with a longitudinal opaque white line; cerata sparsely arranged with white apices; smooth rhinophores with small opaque white spots. Feeds on the black hydroid, *Solanderia* sp.; the egg mass consists of several pinkish coils deposited on the hydroid axis.

Antonietta sp. 1
Size: 7 mm   Indonesia
ID: Orange head, oral tentacles and rhinophores; dorsum with a longitudinal broad band of opaque white pigment; rhinophores with characteristic lighter rings mid-length; cerata short, purple.

Antonietta sp. 2
Size: 3 mm   Mozambique
ID: Opaque white with purple digestive gland in cerata; rhinophores smooth with two orange bands.

Noumeaella rehderi Er. Marcus, 1965
Size: 12 mm   Widespread in the Indo-Pacific
ID: Translucent white with patches of opaque white on the notum, cerata, rhinophores and oral tentacles; inwardly curved cerata usually pale brown, often with a dark brown spot near the apices; rhinophores papillate with a dense covering of papillae on the posterior side. Under coral rubble; feeds on small thecate hydroids in 3-15 m.

Noumeaella isa Ev. Marcus & Er. Marcus, 1970
Size: 10 mm   Indian and western Pacific oceans
ID: Translucent white with a fine network of opaque white lines on the head, notum and cerata; cerata curved inwardly; rhinophores papillate. Under coral rubble on shallow reefs in 3-15 m.

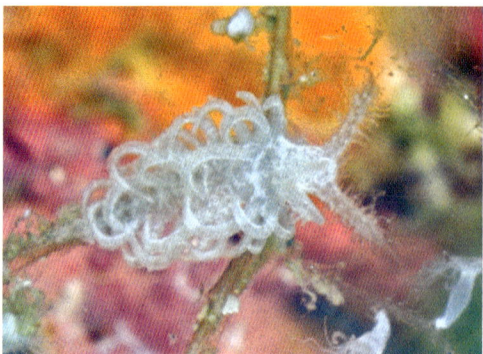

Noumeaella sp. 1
Size: 8 mm   Philippines
ID: Translucent white with opaque white markings, cerata narrow, curved inwardly; oral tentacles with fine filamentous appendages. Feeds on the hydroid *Eudendrium* sp. on which it is shown in this photo,

Noumeaella sp. 2
Size: 10 mm   Philippines
ID: Translucent with opaque white spots and patches; cerata curved inwardly; outer half of the oral tentacles and tips of the rhinophores with orange pigment. On hydroids growing on the underside of the flattened leaf sponge, *Phyllospongia lamellosa*.

Nudibranchia - "nudibranchs"

Noumeaella sp. 3
Size: 10 mm   Western Pacific Ocean
ID: Translucent white with opaque white encrustations over most of the body, and some areas of transparence; inwardly curved cerata with the same pattern of coloration; papillate rhinophores and oral tentacles brown with opaque white pigment. On the underside of the flattened leaf sponge, *Phyllospongia lamellosa*, feeding on small hydroids.

Noumeaella sp. 4
Size: 8 mm   Philippines
ID: Translucent white with patches of opaque white on the notum, rhinophores and oral tentacles. Similar to *Noumeaella rehderi*, but with opaque white tubercles on cerata. Under foliose sponges on shallow reefs, 10 m.

Noumeaella sp. 5
Size: 20 mm   Madagascar, Indonesia, Malaysia
ID: Light brown or reddish-orange with fine opaque white markings on the notum and cerata; numerous, thin cerata

arranged in 8-9 distinct clusters; head broad; rhinophores short, sparsely papillate. In 2 m, under volcanic rocks on rocky and sand habitats.

Noumeaella sp. 6
Size: 7 mm   Indonesia
ID: Translucent white with opaque white pigment and a black "mask" on the head around the rhinophores and eyes; oral tentacles, cerata and rhinophores with opaque white and black pigment; rhinophores with elongate papillae on their posterior sides.

Noumeaella sp. 7
Size: 10 mm   Indonesia
ID: Translucent cream with scattered opaque white and brown pigment; cerata curved inward, each ceras with a dark spot; rhinophores with posterior papillae

Nudibranchia - "nudibranchs"

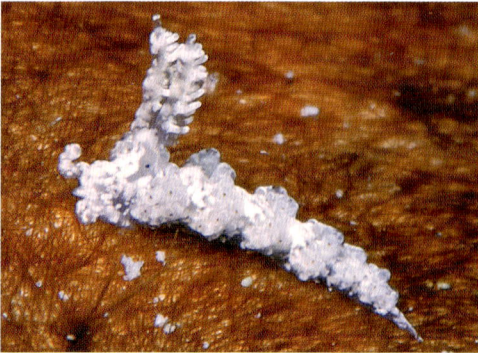

Noumeaella sp. 8
Size: 6 mm   Marshall Is.
ID: Translucent white with opaque white blotches on the head and dorsum; cerata short, translucent white, each with a single brown dot; rhinophores extremely large, with the posterior side covered with large and long papillae.

Noumeaella sp. 9
Size: 7 mm   Philippines
ID: Translucent white with an opaque white patch on the anterior portion of the head and notum; cerata light brown, curved inwardly; translucent white oral tentacles with opaque white spots; rhinophores dark brown. Under volcanic rocks on shallow reefs in 7 m.

Noumeaella sp. 10
Size: 8 mm   Marquesas Is.
ID: Translucent white with opaque white pigment on the dorsum, rhinophores and oral tentacles; rhinophores with elongate papillae on their posterior side; cerata relatively short, smooth, curved inwardly.

Noumeaella sp. 11
Size: 4.5 mm   Guam
ID: Translucent greyish-white; a longitudinal opaque white medial line with branches extending to the base of each ceratal cluster; cerata less curved than other species, each with an opaque white line along the edge; rhinophores with opaque white on the papillae; oral tentacles covered with opaque white.

Noumeaella sp. 12
Size: 7 mm   Philippines
ID: Uniformly cream-white with translucent oral tentacles covered with opaque white spots; cerata curved inwardly with numerous faint papillae; rhinophores relatively short, with few, small papillae on their posterior side.

Noumeaella sp. 13
Size: 5 mm   Western Pacific Ocean
ID: Dark grey with opaque white spots on the notum, cerata, rhinophores and oral tentacles; dark grey cerata curved inwardly. On the underside of the flattened leaf sponge, *Phyllospongia lamellosa*, feeding on small hydroids.

312

Noumeaella sp. 14
Size: 12 mm — Indonesia
ID: Brown with fine opaque white spots; cerata elongate and curved only near their apex; opaque white pigment concentrated on the posterior side of the rhinophores; oral tentacles long, grey with opaque white spots.

Godiva sp. 1
Size: 30 mm — Western and central Pacific
ID: Translucent orange with opaque white patches on the head, separated by lines of translucent orange; blue and opaque white on the rhinophores and oral tentacles; cerata covered with opaque white, each with a bright blue band and a yellow apex; rhinophores weakly annulate. In 1-5 m; feeds on hydroids on algae and on Godiva sp. 6.

Godiva rachelae Rudman, 1980
Size: 35 mm — Indian Ocean
ID: Translucent orange with opaque white markings on the head, forming a series of diamonds on the medial region of the notum; orange lines on the head and oral tentacles;

cerata with orange, blue opaque and white bands; annulate rhinophores orange with opaque white markings. Under coral rubble in 1-3 m on shallow reef flats.

Godiva sp. 2
Size: 6 mm — Philippines
ID: Orange with a series of light blue patches on the dorsum forming a mid-dorsal line, surrounded by purple and pinkish pigment; oral tentacles blue with cream apices; cerata translucent orange with the brown branches of the digestive gland visible and purple and white tips.

Godiva sp. 3
Size: 50 mm — Western Pacific Ocean
ID: Orange with large areas of opaque white; an opaque white diamond immediately posterior to the rhinophores and another covering the pericardium, narrowing into a line; cerata bright red with a blue apices; rhinophores burnt orange with pale-yellowish tips.

Nudibranchia - "nudibranchs"

Godiva sp. 4
Size: 25 mm   Indonesia
ID: Uniformly translucent yellowish; rhinophores with brown apices; cerata with a translucent base showing the cream branches of the digestive gland and with opaque white pigment followed by purple, and reddish pigment; ceratal apices white.

Godiva sp. 5
Size: 35 mm   Hawai'ian Is
ID: Translucent orange with opaque white spots forming patches rather than a series of diamonds; cerata with opaque white patches and blue tips. On hydroids on floating docks and under rocks on fore reefs to 20 m.

Godiva sp. 6
Size: 30 mm   Western and central Pacific
ID: Translucent white with opaque white patches on the head and pericardium; blue and opaque white pigment on the rhinophores and oral tentacles; cerata brown to green, with

opaque white spots, each with a bright blue or purple apical band; rhinophores smooth; reddish lines on the head. In 1-5 m; feeds on hydroids on algae.

Phyllodesmium Ehrenberg, 1831
Species of *Phyllodesmium* are found only in the Indo-Pacific tropics and are specialized predators on octocorals. Most species have symbiotic zooxanthellae and are often cryptic on their prey species. These symbiotic zooxanthellae may provide additional nutrition. They also lack sacs for storing nematocysts. The group has been well studied by Rudman (1981, 1991) and several other species have been described more recently.

Phyllodesmium rudmani Burghardt & Gosliner, 2006
Size: 50 mm   Indonesia, Philippines
ID: Brownish white; cerata pale brown with club-shaped tips bearing a series of vertical ridges separated by dark brown areas, resembling the polyps of *Xenia* soft corals; rhinophores smooth and white. On colonies of *Xenia* in shallow water.

314

Phyllodesmium jakobsenae Burghardt & Wägele, 2004
Size: 35 mm   Western Pacific Ocean
ID: Light brownish-white; cerata elongate with recurved apices that are dark brownish along the apical third; rhinophores smooth. On shallow reefs, on colonies of a white species of *Xenia* with brown tentacles; extremely well camouflaged on its prey.

Phyllodesmium sp. 1
Size: 40 mm   Philippines
ID: Opaque white body; rhinophores brown; cerata translucent with numerous ramified digestive gland ducts. Sandy areas, 20 m.

Phyllodesmium pecten Rudman, 1981
Size: 22 mm   Tanzania, Philippines
ID: Translucent white with a series of opaque white patches on the anterior end of the head, at the base of the rhinophores, on the pericardium, and along the posterior sections of the notum; cerata smooth, fairly cylindrical. Feeds on *Xenia* spp. soft corals; on reefs in 2-10 m.

Phyllodesmium hyalinum Ehrenberg, 1831
Size: 45 mm   Indian and western Pacific oceans
ID: Translucent white with opaque white frosting; cerata relatively smooth to nodulose, curved apically; anus quite high dorsally compared to other species. Feeds on soft corals, especially *Xenia* spp.; from the lower intertidal zone to 10 m; the body and curved cerata mimic the soft coral on which it feeds.

315

Nudibranchia - "nudibranchs"

Phyllodesmium tuberculatum Moore & Gosliner, 2009
Size: 30 mm   Philippines
ID: Greyish-white; cerata with rounded tubercles along their length with a concentration near their apices; rhinophores smooth and short. On shallow water reefs in 10 m, in areas with an abundance of soft corals; its specific prey has not been identified.

Phyllodesmium crypticum Rudman, 1981
Size: 50 mm   Indian and western Pacific oceans
ID: Translucent white with opaque white frosting; cerata with translucent areas where the digestive gland branches are visible; cerata with tubercles along the edges. On shallow reefs where it feeds on the soft coral *Xenia* spp.; very cryptic on its host prey species.

Phyllodesmium lizardense Burghardt, Schrödl & Wägele, 2008
Size: 30 mm   Australia, Indonesia, Philippines
ID: Translucent white with light brown cerata having darker brown pigment; cerata curved apically with rounded tubercles. On xeniid soft corals on shallow reefs in 10-15 m.

Phyllodesmium colemani Rudman, 1991
Size: 20 mm   Western Pacific Ocean
ID: Brown with lighter pigment along the edges of the slightly flattened cerata; scattered light pigment on the notum; rhinophores short, smooth. On shallow reefs in 3-10 m, where it feeds upon the organ-pipe coral *Tubipora musica*.

Phyllodesmium magnum Rudman, 1991
Size: 130 mm   Widespread in the Indo-Pacific
ID: Translucent whitish-brown, juveniles (right photo) with purple pigment; cerata brown, curved, flattened, often with

bluish pigment and yellowish apices; rhinophores relatively short. Sandy habitats; feeds upon the soft corals *Sarcophyton* sp. and *Sinularia* sp. in 1-10 m.

Phyllodesmium sp. 2
Size: 130 mm   Indonesia
ID: Translucent whitish-brown, with blue pigment on the head
and anterior cerata; cerata brown, flattened, with yellowish
apices. Similar to _Phyllodesmium magnum_ but with less
curved cerata. On shallow reefs where it feeds on soft corals.

Phyllodesmium sp. 3
Size: 30 mm   Kenya
ID: Translucent grey with opaque white pigment on the
dorsum; oral tentacles and rhinophores with opaque white
apices; cerata curved with highly ramified, cream digestive
gland branches having dark brown tips; ceratal apices white.

Phyllodesmium sp. 4
Size: 65 mm   Western Indian Ocean
ID: Translucent whitish-brown; cerata brownish lacking blue
pigment. Similar to _Phyllodesmium magnum_ but the internal
anatomy is dramatically different. Under coral rubble in 1-2
m.

Phyllodesmium parangatum Ortiz & Gosliner, 2003
Size: 20 mm   Philippines
ID: Translucent white; cerata milky white with the branches
of the digestive gland visible; cerata cylindrical with curved
apices. On shallow reefs in 5-10 m, frequently observed in
the vicinity of xeniid corals, _Xenia_ sp. and _Anthelia_ sp.

Phyllodesmium pinnatum Moore & Gosliner, 2009
Size: 40 mm   Philippines
ID: Translucent white with fine opaque white spots over
its entire surface; brownish cerata with elongate, pinnately
arranged papillae over most of their length; elongate
rhinophores with nodular tubercles along their length. On
shallow water reefs in the vicinity of soft corals, especially
Anthelia spp.

**_Phyllodesmium koehleri_ Burghardt, Schrödl &
Wägele, 2008**
Size: 20 mm   Western Pacific Ocean
ID: Translucent white with fine brown reticulating lines
over the surface of the body; cerata with pointed tubercles
over their surface; digestive gland within each ceras highly
branched. On xeniid soft corals on shallow reefs in 10-30 m.

Phyllodesmium longicirrum (Bergh, 1905)
Size: 120 mm   Western Pacific Ocean
ID: White with golden brown clusters of zooxanthellae. In association with the soft coral, *Sarcophyton* sp., but also seen crawling on sandy bottoms; it derives much of its nutrition from the symbiotic zooxanthellae.

Phyllodesmium lembehense Burghardt, Schrödl & Wägele, 2008
Size: 30 mm   Western Pacific Ocean
ID: Greyish brown with darker pigment along the tuberculate edges of the flattened cerata, resemble pinnations of xeniid soft coral tentacles; cerata tips usually curved inwardly; rhinophores elongate, smooth. On patch reefs in 0.3-10 m; feeds on xeniid soft corals.

Phyllodesmium sp. 5
Size: 25 mm   Indonesia, Marshall Is.
ID: Translucent grey with the orange buccal mass and the white digestive gland visible; oral tentacles and rhinophores

with opaque white apices; cerata curved, arranged in distinct rows, with highly ramified, cream digestive gland branches having dark brown tips; ceratal apices white; body elongate.

Phyllodesmium sp. 6
Size: 45 mm   Kenya
ID: Uniformly brownish cream; rhinophores with inconspicuous papillae; cerata densely arranged, covered by numerous papillae, some with brown apices.

Phyllodesmium kabiranum Baba, 1991
Size: 40 mm   Western Pacific Ocean
ID: Reddish with a white mid-dorsal line; cerata inflated, corrugated, with white tips. Feeds upon the rust orange soft coral, *Heteroxenia* sp. on large rocky outcrops at 15-20 m.

Phyllodesmium sp. 7
Size: 10 mm   Indonesia
D: Translucent grey with blue oral tentacles; dorsum with several large patches of opaque white; rhinophores translucent with opaque white tips; cerata long, translucent, with the cream branches of the digestive gland visible at the bases, but covered by opaque white pigment and subapical blue rings on the distal halves.

Phyllodesmium sp. 8
Size: 6 mm   Japan, Philippines
ID: Translucent white with patches of blue and yellow on the notum; cerata transparent, blue in the middle, showing the yellow digestive gland, and faint orange subapical bands; distinguishable by its relatively few cerata. In 23 m on mixed sand and rubble near reef forefronts.

Phyllodesmium macphersonae (Burn, 1962)
Size: 20 mm   Western Pacific Ocean
ID: Translucent grey, with small brownish dots that extend on to the basal portion of the cerata and oral tentacles as well as all over the rhinophores; curved cerata, each with a large blue band and a whitish-yellow apex; rhinophores may have opaque white spots. On reefs in 5-15 m; feeds on unidentified soft corals.

Phyllodesmium sp. 9
Size: 20 mm   India
ID: Translucent cream with a network of opaque white lines on the dorsum; oral tentacles with bluish bases and cream apices; rhinophores with short papillae, translucent at the base and opaque cream apically; cerata sinuous, transparent, with orange branches of the digestive gland.

Phyllodesmium briareum (Bergh, 1896)
Size: 30 mm   Western Pacific Ocean
ID: Light brown; cerata and oral tentacles with yellow apices; cerata long and cylindrical. Feeds on the mat-forming soft coral *Pachyclavularia violacea* in moderately shallow water (5-20 m); the cerata closely resemble the tentacles of their prey.

Phyllodesmium iriomotense Baba, 1991
Size: 44 mm   Indonesia, southern Japan
ID: Translucent pinkish; delicately branched digestive gland visible through the cerata; cerata with curved apices. On finely branched octocorals in 10-67 m.

Nudibranchia - "nudibranchs"

Phyllodesmium sp. 10
Size: 25 mm   Philippines
ID: Reddish-orange to orange; cerata yellowish with white apices, slightly curved apically, each with a subapical red spot on the inner curved side; rhinophores and oral tentacles mostly white with yellow bases; foot extremely wide, yellow. On shallow reefs in 15 m.

Phyllodesmium poindimiei (Risbec, 1928)
Size: 40 mm   Widespread in the Indo-Pacific
ID: Translucent pink with numerous opaque white spots on the surface of the notum, cerata, rhinophores and oral tentacles; purple markings on the cerata, oral tentacles and rhinophores; cerata curved, with the lateral branches of the digestive gland visible; rhinophores smooth. On shallow water reefs where it feeds on the octocoral, *Carijoa* sp.

Phyllodesmium undulatum Moore & Gosliner, 2014
Size: 40 mm   Western Pacific Ocean
ID: Translucent pink with purple pigment and a white medial longitudinal line on the notum; digestive gland duct unbranched and highly undulated within the cerata; cerata with yellow apices. On red and orange gorgonians, such as *Melithaea flabellifera*, in 5-10 m.

Phyllodesmium acanthorhinum Moore & Gosliner, 2014
Size: 32 mm   Mozambique, India, southern Japan
ID: Translucent whitish with an opaque white medial line that branches into the base of each ceratal group; cerata with undulate digestive gland branches having dark brown bases and yellowish apices; rhinophores papillate. Surge channels among coral rubble in 3 m.

320

Phyllodesmium karenae Moore & Gosliner, 2009
Size: 20 mm   Indonesia, Philippines
ID: Bluish purple with opaque white on the tips of the cerata, rhinophores and oral tentacles; digestive gland unbranched within each cylindrical ceras; cerata with curved apices. On sandy substrate on slopes in 15 m.

Phyllodesmium opalescens Rudman, 1991
Size: 20 mm   Western Pacific Ocean
ID: Translucent with a series of bluish diamonds in the center of the notum; cerata elongate with thin, slightly undulating, digestive gland ducts; bluish purple pigment near the apex of each ceras with an opaque white apex. Crawling on mixed sand and rubble in 3-12 m; the prey of this species is unknown.

Phyllodesmium sp. 11
Size: 20 mm   Indonesia
ID: Translucent reddish with red rhinophores and orange oral tentacles; cerata long, sinuous, with reddish branches of the digestive gland and opaque bluish-white pigment of the surface.

Phyllodesmium serratum (Baba, 1949)
Size: 35 mm   Australia, Japan
ID: Translucent purplish pink with a narrow longitudinal bluish band down the center of the notum; digestive gland within each ceras reddish brown. On soft corals such as *Clavularia* and *Carijoa* spp., and on gorgonians such as *Junceella* and the octocoral *Stereonephthya* sp.

Phyllodesmium sp. 12
Size: 20 mm   Indonesia
ID: Reddish pink with red cerata and an opaque white line along the edge of each ceras; apices of the cerata highly coiled; rhinophores moderately long and smooth.

Phyllodesmium sp. 13
Size: 12 mm   Hawai'ian Is.
ID: Translucent white with opaque white markings on the notum; tips of the cerata, rhinophores and oral tentacles opaque white. Crawling on reef flats at night in less than 1 m.

321

Nudibranchia - "nudibranchs"

***Phyllodesmium* sp. 14**
Size: 13 mm   Hawai'ian Is.
ID: Translucent brown with opaque white spots over most of the body; ceratal apices, rhinophores, and oral tentacles opaque white; a few black specks on the cerata. Under rocks in 1 m, on reefs.

***Phyllodesmium guamense* Avila, Ballesteros, Slattery, Starmer & Paul, 1998**
Size: 40 mm   Guam
ID: Translucent bluish; cerata curved, flattened, with brown digestive gland branches and yellowish apices; similar to *Phyllodesmium magnum*, but has distinctive radular teeth. On shallow water reefs; appears to feed on large soft corals such as *Sarcophytum*.

***Moridilla brockii* Bergh, 1888**
Size: 40 mm   Indian and western Pacific oceans
ID: White to orange; cerata orange with yellowish apices; rhinophores white or orange, papillate; cerata arranged in distinct clusters leaving areas of the notum bare; some of the longest cerata recurved and erected when the animal is disturbed. On shallow water reefs; feeds on hydroids.

***Moridilla* sp. 1**
Size: 40 mm   Western Pacific
ID: Deep orange body with dark red digestive gland; rhinophores pale orange with darker orange apex. On shallow reefs, under coral rubble, 10-15 m.

***Moridilla* sp. 2**
Size: 35 mm   Western Australia
ID: Translucent white with red rhinophores and oral tentacles; smaller cerata with opaque white tips; longer, curved cerata bright red orange. Further study is needed to determine whether this species is distinct from *Moridilla brockii*.

***Moridilla* sp. 3**
Size: 7 mm   Indonesia
ID: Translucent orange with opaque white pigment on the head, dorsum and rhinophores; cerata with the brown digestive gland branches visible and opaque white apices; most dorsal cerata almost completely covered with opaque white.

322

Pruvotfolia rhodopos (Yonow, 2000)
Size: 20 mm   Widespread in the Indo-Pacific
ID: Translucent white or orange; cerata with yellowish white apices; rhinophores perfoliate. Originally described as a *Facelina*, it has specialized cerata modified for copulation as a *Pruvotfolia*. Under rocks and coral rubble in 1-10 m.

Pruvotfolia sp. 1
Size: 20 mm   Papua New Guinea
ID: Translucent with dense opaque white pigment on the notum; cerata translucent with visible digestive gland ducts, which vary in width. On shallow barrier reefs under coral rubble.

Pruvotfolia sp. 2
Size: 15 mm   Papua New Guinea
ID: Translucent white with opaque white spots on the notum and cerata; each ceras with an iridescent blue ring between two areas of opaque white. On shallow barrier reefs under coral rubble.

Pruvotfolia sp. 3
Size: 15 mm   Philippines
ID: Uniformly translucent grey to yellowish-brown, with the white and brown digestive gland visible; dark brown branches of the digestive gland visible in the transparent cerata; cnidosacs opaque white and elongate; rhinophores with numerous lamellae. On hydroids under coral rubble in 5 m.

Pruvotfolia sp. 4
Size: 14 mm   Philippines, Indonesia
ID: Translucent brown with yellow spots between the rhinophores and pink pigment on the apices of the oral tentacles and rhinophores; some specimens with pink and

opaque bluish-white pigment on the head and dorsum; cerata transparent with white apices and the dark brown digestive gland visible, and in some specimens pink subapical rings.

Nudibranchia - "nudibranchs"

Pruvotfolia sp. 5
Size: 32 mm   Marshall Is.
ID: Translucent brownish with bluish and opaque white pigment on the head, oral tentacles and rhinophores, and an opaque white longitudinal line on the dorsum; cerata with pinkish rings and white apices.

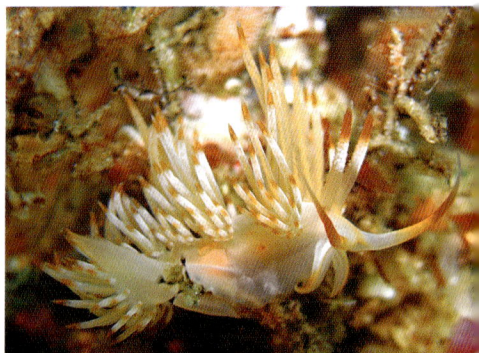

Sakuraeolis nungunoides Rudman, 1980
Size: 35 mm   Western Pacific Ocea
ID: Translucent white with an orange triangular patch on th head; orange pigment on the tips of the rhinophores, or tentacles, and foot corners; cerata opaque white, numerou and congested, each with a bright red subapical band. C shallow reefs; feeds on athecate hydroids such as *Tubularia* s

Sakuraeolis gujaratica Rudman, 1980
Size: 30 mm   Indian Ocean
ID: Pale orange; oral tentacles and smooth rhinophores white basally with orange outer halves; cerata slender with purple digestive gland branches and orange apices.

Sakuraeolis sp. 1
Size: 18 mm   Indones
ID: Opaque white with two large yellowish orange patche on the sides of the head; rhinophores translucent brown wi yellow apices; cerata brown with opaque white dots; "ta long and opaque white.

Sakuraeolis kirembosa Rudman, 1980
Size: 40 mm   Indian Ocean
ID: Pale translucent orange including the tips of the rhinophores and oral tentacles; digestive gland black; cerata

slender, green basally, each with a bright blue outer portio and an orange apex. On the athecate hydroid, *Eudendriu* sp., in shallow water.

Sakuraeolis sp. 2
Size: 35 mm   Indonesia
ID: Cream with pale brown tips of the rhinophores and oral tentacles; cerata brown basally, with opaque white and purple subapical rings and a brown apex each.

Sakuraeolis sp. 3
Size: 20 mm   Philippines, Hawai'ian Is.
ID: Pinkish-grey; cerata with the same color, cylindrical, curved apically, with opaque white tips; oral tentacles and rhinophores red with opaque white spots. On shallow water reefs under coral rubble in 10-15 m.

Sakuraeolis sp. 4
Size: 30 mm   South Africa, Papua New Guinea
ID: Deep orange with translucent cerata having grey cores and opaque white spots on their outer surface; rhinophores and oral tentacles tipped in opaque white.

***Phidiana salaamica* Rudman, 1980**
Size: 13 mm   Tanzania, Japan
ID: Orange with the pinkish digestive gland visible within the cerata; each ceratal row with elongate, curved inner cerata; rhinophores smooth, same size as the oral tentacles. On hydroids on the sea grass *Syringodium* sp.; it erects its curved cerata when disturbed to defend itself.

***Cratena* Bergh, 1864**
Species of *Cratena* have the first group of cerata arranged in an arch followed by posterior simple rows. Many species have red or orange "cheek patches" on the head.

Species with smooth rhinophores
This informal group of species has smooth rhinophores.

***Cratena simba* Edmunds, 1970**
Size: 8 mm   Indian and western Pacific oceans
ID: Translucent white with abundant opaque white pigment and undulating red lines on the notum; cerata translucent, club-shaped with white pigment and abrupt acute apices; rhinophores smooth. From tidal pools to 10 m, under coral rubble.

***Cratena* sp. 1**
Size: 20 mm   Papua New Guinea
ID: Translucent white with opaque white spots; an orange line bifurcates into a series of ovals along the notum; cerata narrow basally, expanding into a wide club-shaped portion below the elongate, acutely pointed cnidosacs and apices; two small red spots on either side of the head. In clam rearing tanks where hydroids are abundant.

Cratena sp. 2
Size: 20 mm   Western Pacific Ocean
ID: Translucent white with opaque spots on the notum and cerata; two orange patches on the side of the head; rhinophores smooth. Additional study is needed to determine whether individuals without lines on the notum represent a distinct species from *Cratena lineata*. On reefs in 10-20; observed feeding upon unidentified hydroids.

Cratena lineata (Eliot, 1905)
Size: 20 mm   Indian and western Pacific ocean
ID: Translucent white with opaque white longitudinal lines on the notum and cerata; two red patches on the side of the head; rhinophores smooth. On shallow water reefs in 2-3 under volcanic boulders.

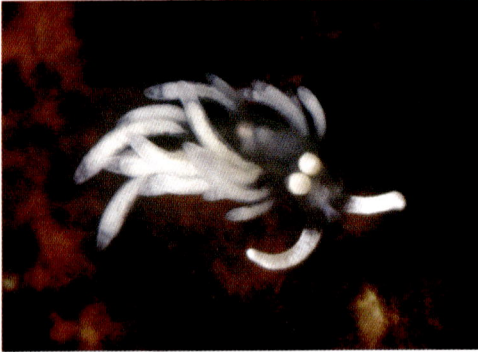

Cratena sp. 3
Size: 10 mm   Papua New Guinea
ID: Translucent white with opaque white cerata; rhinophores and oral tentacles opaque white. Under coral rubble in harbors, in 12 m.

Cratena sp. 4
Size: 22 mm   Indones
ID: Translucent brown, completely covered with opaque white, irregular lines; bluish-white oral tentacles and rhinophoral apices; cerata ochre with white apices.

Species with annulate rhinophores
Members of this informal group have annulate rhinophores.

Cratena affinis (Baba, 1949)
Size: 10 mm   Philippines, Japan
ID: Translucent white with opaque white spots; a red-orange patch on either side of the head; cerata with opaque white longitudinal lines; rhinophores with two distinctive large annulae. Under coral rubble in 1-2 m, on near shore reefs.

Cratena sp. 5
Size: 10 mm   Widespread in the Indo-Pacif
ID: Translucent with numerous opaque white and orang spots; opaque white covers the cerata, except for th transparent bases, with visible dark brown digestive glan branches; rhinophores with two large annulae; rounde corners of the foot. Commonly under coral rubble in 1-10 m

Cratena sp. 6
Size: 7 mm   Indonesia
ID: Translucent white with a network of orange lines on the dorsum; cerata brown with longitudinal white lines; rhinophores annulate, white with brown bases.

Herviella albida Baba, 1966
Size: 20 mm   Widespread in the Indo-Pacific
ID: Translucent brownish-white with opaque white markings; purplish brown lines on the head behind the rhinophores and between the oral tentacles; translucent cerata, each with an opaque white ring and apex; rhinophores translucent basally, each with a brownish purple band and an opaque white tip. Under coral rubble in 0-1 m.

Herviella claror Burn, 1963
Size: 12 mm   Eastern Australia
ID: Translucent white, covered with dark brown spotting; each ceras with a subapical orange ring and a yellowish white apex; rhinophores and oral tentacles tipped with pale yellow. Intertidal zone under small stones.

Herviella mietta Er. Marcus & Burch, 1965
Size: 40 mm   Western and central Pacific Ocean
ID: Dark brown or black; a translucent white patch immediately behind each rhinophore; opaque white pigment on the base of some of the cerata. Intertidal zone; feeds on the black sea anemone *Anthopleura nigrescens*.

Herviella yatsui (Baba, 1930)
Size: 18 mm   Malaysia, Japan
ID: Translucent white with dense patches of dark brown and a few opaque white markings; cerata brown with opaque white apices. Intertidal zone under small volcanic rocks in silty areas.

Herviella sp. 1
Size: 12 mm   Philippines
ID: Translucent white with brown spotting over most of the body; each ceras with a bluish base, a narrow yellow ring and white apex; rhinophores brown with white spots and white apices. On coral rubble, 15 m.

Herviella cloaca Rudman, 1980
Size: 12 mm   Indian Ocean
ID: Opaque white with dark brown to black spots over most of the body; cerata with opaque white tips. The name derives from the fact that it was first found near a sewage outfall. Under rocks in 1-2 m.

Herviella sp. 2
Size: 9 mm   Indonesia
ID: Translucent grey with abundant black pigment on the dorsum; oral tentacles and rhinophores black with white pigment mid-length and white apices; cerata black with white apices.

Herviella sp. 3
Size: 50 mm   Tahiti, Panama
ID: Brown with translucent white branches of the digestive system and opaque white spots on the notum, head, oral tentacles, rhinophores, and cerata; body very long and narrow; cerata short with white apices; "tail" extremely long and sticky. On floating objects, probably disperses long distance by rafting.

Herviella sp. 4
Size: 15 mm   Tuamotu Archipelago
ID: Translucent greyish-brown with abundant white spots, particularly on the pericardium, head and tips of the oral tentacles; cerata with brown branches of the digestive system and white tips; rhinophores smooth.

Facelinid sp. 1
Size: 10 mm   Japan, Hawai'ian Is.
ID: Opaque white with a yellow orange Y-shaped mark on the head; cerata club-shaped with yellow-orange bases; oral tentacles and annulate rhinophores reddish with opaque white spots. On shallow reefs in 10-20 m under coral rubble.

Facelinid sp. 2
Size: 20 mm   Western and central Pacific Ocean
ID: Translucent white with a network of opaque white frosting over much of the notum; cerata translucent brownish, each with a cream subapical band; a pair of dark brown spots near the base of each ceras; rhinophores and basal portion of the oral tentacles deep purple; rhinophores with small, incomplete annulae. On shallow patch reefs under rubble.

Facelinid sp. 3
Size: 35 mm   Malaysia, Philippines
ID: Opaque white with a network of orange patches and lines; cerata translucent brownish, each with a purple spot and a subapical opaque white band; a pair of dark brown spots near the base of each ceras; opaque white rhinophores with 8 annulae and red extended apices. On shallow reefs; feeds on small thecate hydroids.

Facelinid sp. 4
Size: 25 mm   Marshall Is.
ID: Light purple with a white longitudinal line on the head; oral tentacles light purple with white pigment; rhinophores smooth, light purple; cerata brown with white pigment and greyish orange tips.

Facelinid sp. 5
Size: 30 mm   Indonesia
ID: Uniformly greyish-orange; each ceras with a purple submarginal spot; rhinophores annulate with brown pigment; oral tentacles brownish-orange.

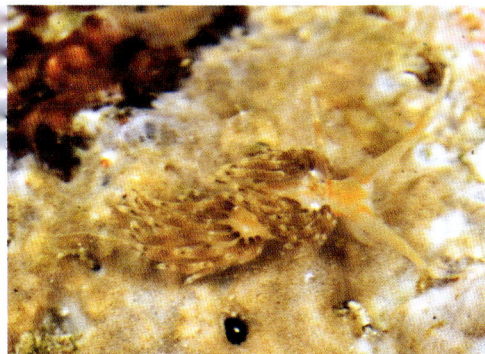

Facelinid sp. 6
Size: 10 mm   Indonesia, Philippines
ID: Pale brown with orange lines and white dots on the dorsum, head, rhinophores and oral tentacles; cerata dark brown with opaque white dots, subapical darker brown patches and white apices. Crawling on clean sand at night, 6 m.

Facelinid sp. 7
Size: 20 mm   Indonesia
ID: Opaque white with purple oral tentacles and rhinophores; cerata greyish purple with subapical purple bands and orange apices; rhinophores annulate. On coarse volcanic sand, 10-15 m.

Nudibranchia - "nudibranchs"

Glaucus Forster, 1777

Species of *Glaucus* are adapted to pelagic environments feeding on floating colonial hydrozoans such as the portuguese man-of-war, the blue button and the by-the-wind sailor. They spend their life floating upside down on the water surface (as seen on the photo on the right), and maintain buoyancy by swallowing air into their stomachs. Because of the highly venomous stinging cells of their prey, species of *Glaucus* can produce painful stings to humans. The systematics of this group has been recently reviewed by Churchill *et al.* (2014).

Glaucus atlanticus Forster, 1777

Size: 40 mm   Worldwide in tropical oceans
ID: Bright dark blue and silver; cerata elevated on three cushions per side of the body; rhinophores and oral tentacles short. Pelagic, feeds on the floating colonial hydroids, *Porpita* and *Physalia*; occasionally washes up on beaches or floating in tide pools.

Glaucus marginatus (Reinhardt *in* Bergh, 1864) species complex

Size: 20 mm

G. marginatus - Indo-Pacific
G. bennettae - South Pacific
G. thompsoni - North Pacific
G. mcfarlanei - North Pacific

ID: Similar to *Glaucus atlanticus*, but has multiple rows of cerata in each cluster. Molecular data indicates that this is a complex of four indistinguishable species: *Glaucus*

marginatus (Reinhardt *in* Bergh, 1864), *Glaucus bennettae* Churchill, Valdés & Ó Foighil, 2014, *Glaucus thompsoni* Churchill, Valdés & Ó Foighil, 2014, and *Glaucus mcfarlanei* Churchill, Valdés & Ó Foighil, 2014. Floating in the open ocean; feeds on the colonial hydrozoans, *Porpita* and *Physalia*; it may wash up on beaches when strong onshore winds occur.

330

Pteraeolidia semperi (Bergh, 1870)
Size: 100 mm   Widespread in the Indo-Pacific
ID: Variable in color with different shades of green, blue, and brown, but consistently with bright blue bands on the oral tentacles. Dragon-like aeolid, easily recognized by its elongate shape and perfoliate rhinophores. Commonly in shallow water (1-10 m), often just below the low tide mark on walls; may be in the open or feeding on hydroids; adults tend to receive most of their nutrition from symbiotic zooxanthellae. The systematics of this group was clarified by Wilson & Burghardt (2015), *Pteraeolidia ianthina* is a temperate Australian species.

Nudibranchia - "nudibranchs"

Aeolidiidae J. E. Gray, 1827

Most members of this group feed on sea anemones and close relatives. The body tends to be wide with numerous cerata. Many species sequester unicellular plant-like dinoflagellates (called zooxanthellae) from their prey. Zooxanthellae are common symbionts of cnidarians that are ingested by the aeolid while feeding on anemones. Instead of being digested with the cnidarian tissue, they are transported to specialized branches of the digestive gland. The zooxanthellae are maintained alive in the aeolid tissue and photosynthetic products are utilized by the aeolid for its own nutrition. Species with zooxanthellae are usually recognizable by having brown reticulations in the body wall. This group has been recently reviewed by a series of papers by Carmona *et al.* (2013; 2014a; 2014b; 2014c; 2014d).

Anteaeolidiella cacaotica (Stimpson, 1855)
Size: 30 mm western and central Pacific Ocean
ID: Orange, usually with opaque white spots on the notum that vary in width; cerata orange, each with an opaque white ring and apex; rhinophores orange, smooth. On shallow water reefs; feeds upon small sea anemones.

Anteaeolidiella sp. 1
Size: 15 mm Tuamotu Archipelago
ID: Translucent brownish-grey, with bright red pigment on the head and anterior cerata; dorsum with a thick longitudinal line of opaque white pigment, completely covering the pericardium; cerata mainly white, with brown bases.

Anteaeolidiella sp. 2
Size: 30 mm Indonesia
ID: Uniformly orange with reddish pigment around the pericardium; rhinophores, oral tentacles and cerata translucent orange with white apices.

Anteaeolidiella sp. 3
Size: 12 mm Tuamotu Archipelago
ID: Translucent with opaque white pigment on the dorsum, pericardium, tips of the rhinophores, and oral tentacles; cerata with white subapical areas. On rocky intertidal bottoms, 0.1-0.5 m.

Bulbaeolidia alba (Risbec, 1928)
Size: 15 mm   Circumtropical
ID: Translucent white with a dense covering of opaque white; rhinophores with two bulbous swellings and a distinctive red half circle at their base. Shallow water from the intertidal zone to 10 m; feeds on small sea anemones.

Bulbaeolidia paulae Carmona, Paula, Gosliner & Cervera, 2017
Size: 5 mm   Hawaiian Is., South Africa
ID: Translucent white with opaque white pigment on the dorsum; cerata with a brown digestive gland and opaque white spots. Similar to *Bulbaeolidia alba*, but with more elongate body and narrower cerata.

Bulbaeolidia sp. 1
Size: 5 mm   South Africa
ID: Translucent white with scattered broad patches of opaque white; cerata short, curved; rhinophores with three bulbous swellings.

Baeolidia moebii Bergh, 1888
Size: 70 mm   Widespread in the Indo-Pacific
ID: Usually grey or brown; cerata curved and flattened, often with blue and yellow markings; a brown circle usually at the base of the oral tentacles; rhinophores papillate. Shallow water, 1-5 m, on grass beds and algal mats; feeds upon sea anemones, *Aiptasia* sp. and *Boloceroides* sp.

Baeolidia salaamica (Rudman, 1982)
Size: 20 mm   Widespread in the Indo-Pacific
ID: Translucent grey with opaque white patches on the head, the pericardium and more posteriorly; cerata relatively cylindrical, with opaque white markings along their length. On shallow water reefs under rocks; feeds on sea anemones.

Baeolidia chaka (Gosliner, 1985)
Size: 8 mm   South Africa, possibly Japan
ID: Brownish with opaque white on the head and notum; anterior ends of the foot rounded; rhinophores and oral tentacles brownish with opaque white apices. Intertidal rock pools at night.

Baeolidia japonica Baba, 1933
Size: 8 mm   Western Pacific Ocean
ID: Dark brown with opaque white pigment on the notum and blue pigment on the inside of the cerata; ceratal tips with nipple-like protuberances; rhinophores and oral tentacles dark brown with white apices. Under coral rubble on reefs in 10 m.

Baeolidia gracilis Carmona, Pola, Gosliner & Cervera, 2014
Size: 12 mm   Philippines
ID: Light brown with a dark brown head and pericardium, as well as the short rhinophores and oral tentacles; cerata lighter brown, each with an opaque white line on its inner margin; rhinophores with only a few short papillae; anterior end of the foot rounded. Under coral rubble in 10 m on fringing reefs.

Baeolidia sp. 1
Size: 50 mm   South Africa, Mozambique
ID: Bright pinkish red with flat, curved cerata; cerata with red pigment basally, opaque white spots and blue and red apically; blue spot surrounded by opaque white present on the head anterior to the rhinophores.

Baeolidia palythoae Gosliner, 1985
Size: 13 mm   South Africa, possibly Japan
ID: Light brown with a network of darker brown reticulations on the notum and cerata; cerata flattened and leaf-like; anterior foot corners rounded. Feeds on zoanthids, especially *Palythoa nelliae* in the lower intertidal zone.

Baeolidia ransoni (Pruvot-Fol, 1956)
Size: 20 mm   Widespread in the Indo-Pacific
ID: Variable from white to brown with numerous opaque white dots; cerata flattened and leaf-like arranged along to entire length of the body; rhinophores smooth; anus dorsal. Feeds on the zoanthid, *Palythoa* sp. by scraping away tissue and leaving a depression that the slug occupies, making it even more cryptic on its prey; common, but easily overlooked.

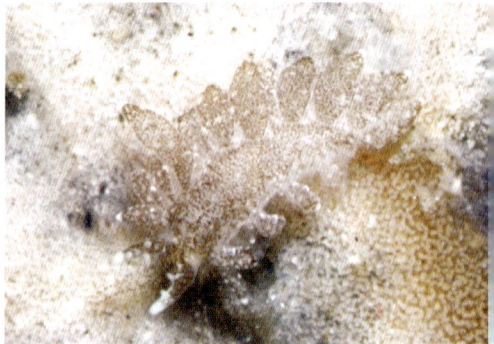

Baeolidia harrietae (Rudman, 1982)
Size: 40 mm   Western Pacific Ocean
ID: Light brown with brown and opaque white spots densely arranged over the entire body; cerata flattened and leaf-like; rhinophores and oral tentacles with the same color as the rest of the body and white apices. On species of the zoanthid *Palythoa*, in the intertidal zone to 10 m.

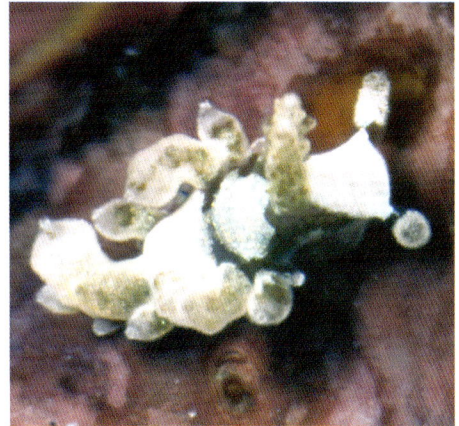

Baeolidia variabilis Carmona, Pola, Gosliner & Cervera, 2014
Size: 10 mm   Western and central Pacific Ocean
ID: Color variable, some animals translucent white with patches of opaque white on the head and notum; other animals brown with opaque white pigment on the posterior side of the basal portion of the cerata and on the tips of the rhinophores; cerata recurved inwardly and with scattered papillae over their surface; rhinophores and oral tentacles white or brown. On reefs in 7 m under coral rubble.

Baeolidia rieae Carmona, Pola, Gosliner & Cervera, 2014
Size: 5 mm   Tropical Japan
ID: Pale brown, scattered with dark brown pigment all over the body and some opaque white on the tips of the rhinophores and cerata; cerata with the dark brown branches of the digestive gland visible. In 7 m, near green zoanthids.

Baeolidia lunaris Carmona, Pola, Gosliner & Cervera, 2014
Size: 10 mm   Tanzania
ID: Brown with fine iridescent opaque white spots; cerata broadest basally tapering to rounded apices, with the same color as the rest of the body. Feeds on zoanthids in 1-3 m on shallow patch reefs.

335

Nudibranchia - "nudibranchs"

Baeolidia scottjohnsoni Carmona, Pola, Gosliner & Cervera, 2014
Size: 12 mm   Marshall Is., Hawai'ian Is.
ID: Brown with opaque white and pale brown pigment on the dorsum, rhinophores and oral tentacles; cerata short, brown, with opaque white and blue pigment; rhinophores with numerous long papillae. On *Caulerpa*, probably feeding on sea anemones, in 10 m.

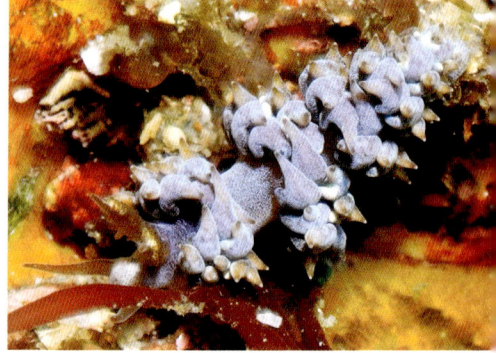

Baeolidia sp. 2
Size: 15 mm   Indonesia
ID: Blue with opaque white spots; cerata flat, curved with narrow apices; head, rhinophores and oral tentacles brown with white pigment.

Limenandra confusa Carmona, Pola, Gosliner & Cervera, 2014
Size: 8 mm   Western and eastern Pacific Ocean
ID: Translucent brownish white with of a series of opaque white spots surrounded by purple and yellow concentric rings; cerata with highly papillate surfaces. Under coral rubble in 3-10 m; it appears to feed upon small sea anemones.

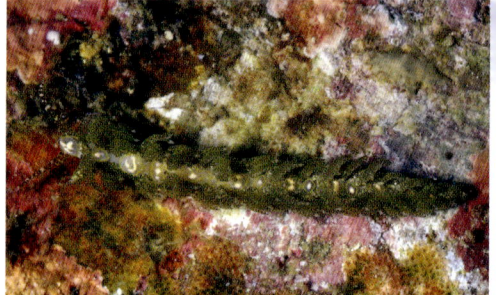

Limenandra rosanae Carmona, Pola, Gosliner & Cervera, 2014
Size: 40 mm   Philippines, Hawai'ian Is.
ID: Pale brown with a series of opaque white rings; cerata dark brown, smooth, densely arranged along the body. On shallow patch reefs crawling in the open in the vicinity of sea anemones.

Limenandra fusiformis (Baba, 1949)
Size: 20 mm   Indian and western Pacific oceans
ID: Pale brown with bright yellow spots including the cerata; dorsum with concentric circles of bright yellow, pale brown and white; rhinophores ashy brown with small bright yellow spots and white apices, densely papillate posteriorly; oral tentacles brownish with opaque yellow patches.

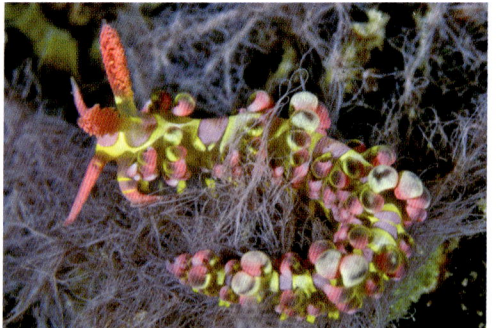

Limenandra barnosii Carmona, Pola, Gosliner & Cervera, 2014
Size: 60 mm   United Arab Emirates, western Pacific
ID: Pinkish brown with purple ovals on the notum, surrounded by areas of bright yellow pigment; cerata smooth and curved, with yellow, pink, white and brown pigment; rhinophores pink with orange on the posterior papillae; body highly elongate. Areas of mixed rubble and sand; feeds on the nocturnally active sea anemone, *Alicia sansibarensis*.

336

Spurilla braziliana MacFarland, 1909
Size: 70 mm   Circumtropical
ID: Orange with numerous opaque white spots on the notum, head and cerata; cerata elongate with opaque white

curved apices; rhinophores orange, perfoliate. Feeds on sea anemones on shallow reefs and in the intertidal zone.

Cerberilla Bergh, 1873
Species of *Cerberilla* are found in sandy habitats where they feed on burrowing coelenterates such as cerianthids. The broad foot is an adaptation for crawling on sandy substrate.

Cerberilla affinis Bergh, 1888
Size: 90 mm   Widespread in Indo-Pacific
ID: Translucent grey with a black "mask" around the rhinophores; cerata with black rings and yellow apices; oral tentacles and rhinophores with black and bright blue tinges; foot wide. On sandy substrates in 3-30 m; feeds on cerianthids; nocturnally active.

Cerberilla africana Eliot, 1903
Size: 35 mm   Tanzania
ID: Translucent white with dark grey to black pigment on the notum, head and cerata; cerata with black and yellow bands and light blue pigment near their midlines; oral tentacles black; rhinophores tipped in blue. On sandy flats in 1-2 m; active during the day.

Cerberilla ambonensis Bergh, 1905
Size: 50 mm   Western Pacific Ocean
ID: Opaque white with black horizontal lines along the edge of the foot; cerata black, each with a subapical yellow ring and a grey apex; oral tentacles with black, yellow and blue pigment. On sandy slopes in 12-15 m.

337

Nudibranchia - "nudibranchs"

Cerberilla annulata (Quoy & Gaimard, 1832)
Size: 70 mm   Widespread in the Indo-Pacific
ID: Translucent bluish-white with a black "mask" around the rhinophores; cerata with black rings and yellow apices; oral tentacles opaque white; foot wide. On shallow water sandy slopes; active at night.

Cerberilla sp. 1
Size: 25 mm   Tahiti
ID: Translucent bluish-white with a black and yellow "mask" around the rhinophores; cerata with black and yellow rings and light blue apices; oral tentacles dark blue; foot wide. Sandy areas in 5 m.

Cerberilla sp. 2
Size: 70 mm   Philippines
ID: White with blue markings on the foot corners, oral tentacles and rhinophores; a yellow orange mark on the head at the base of the rhinophores; cerata white with yellow, blue and black pigment. On shallow sandy slopes at night; it appears to feed on cerianthids.

Cerberilla sp. 3
Size: 30 mm   Western and central Pacific
ID: Translucent white with a black "mask" around the rhinophores; tips of the oral tentacles and cerata opaque white; cerata with subapical black spots. On coarse sandy slopes at night.

Cerberilla sp. 4
Size: 14 mm   Indonesia
ID: Blue with a yellow marginal line around the foot; head with yellow and black pigment; oral tentacles blue, black and yellow; cerata with yellow-orange longitudinal lines. Sandy areas.

Cerberilla sp. 5
Size: 8 mm   Indonesia
ID: Bluish-white; cerata brown with yellow spots and white apices, held close to the body; head, rhinophores and oral tentacles with dark brown pigment forming a mask around the eyes.

Cerberilla sp. 6
Size: 7 mm   Vanuatu, New Caledonia
ID: Grey with light blue pigment on the head and notum; yellow markings also present on the head; cerata mostly black, each with an opaque white longitudinal line and a yellow base; some inner cerata mostly white with yellow pigment. Sandy areas in 10 m.

Cerberilla sp. 7
Size: 25 mm   United Arab Emirates
ID: Pink; cerata short, pink, with yellow apices; short rhinophores and longer oral tentacles with yellow pigment, projecting foot corners also yellow, with orange tips; foot edged in yellow.

Cerberilla sp. 8
Size: 15 mm   Philippines
ID: Brownish-grey with golden rhinophores and anterior end of the body; oral tentacles and foot corners white, apices of the oral tentacles golden; cerata brown, posterior ones with black pigment and longitudinal bluish and golden lines. On clean sand where it is nocturnally active, 6 m.

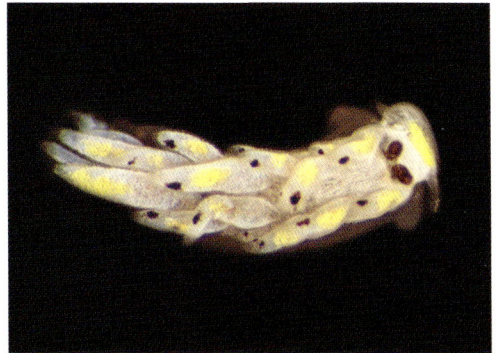

Cerberilla sp. 9
Size: 4 mm   Papua New Guinea
ID: Pale grey with a transversal yellow line on the head; rhinophores brown; cerata mainly grey with yellow pigment at their bases, each with a brown spot subapically; body narrow, oral tentacle short. Fine sand, 6 m.

Cerberilla sp. 10
Size: 30 mm   Reunion Is.
ID: Brown with some white spots on the oral tentacles; cerata brown with white tips and subapical black spots. On sandy substrates in 8-10 m.

Cerberilla sp. 11
Size: 6 mm   Hawai'ian Is.
ID: Grey with a yellow marking on the head between the rhinophores and at the junction of the oral tentacles. Sandy areas in 10 m.

Cerberilla asamusiensis Baba, 1940
Size: 9 mm   Japan, Indonesia
ID: White with brown pigment on the dorsum; rhinophores brown; oral tentacles bluish with brown apices; cerata yellow with white apices, larger cerata with brown bases and subapical brown pigment.

Cerberilla sp. 12
Size: 40 mm   Tahiti
ID: Translucent grey with orange transverse lines on the head and opaque white spots; dorsum brown with white dots; cerata brown with yellow rings, white spots and brown apices. On sandy bottoms in 3 m.

Cerberilla albopunctata Baba, 1976
Size: 40 mm   Indonesia, Japan
ID: Black with numerous white spots; cerata with yellow subapical bands and white apices; blue, black and yellow pigment usually present on the oral tentacles. On shallow water sandy slopes; active at night.

Umbraculoidea - "umbrella shells"

Members of this group have a gill situated on the right side of the body and an external shell. They were formerly united with the Pleurobranchoidea in the Notaspidea but evidence shows them to be distinct (Wägele & Willan, 2000; Wägele & Klussmann-Kolb, 2005).

Umbraculidae Dall, 1889

Umbraculidae probably includes a single species with a world-wide distribution in tropical and temperate areas. It is characterized by having a flat, limpet-like shell covering only the central part of the body and the gill situated on the right hand side of the body.

***Umbraculum umbraculum* (Lightfoot, 1786)**
Size: 120 mm   Possibly circumtropical
ID: Body yellow with large white rounded papillae; shell white, typically covered with algal growth. Seems to feed on sponges; frequently in shallow pools or on subtidal reefs to 120 m.

Tylodinidae J. E. Gray, 1847

This group, closely related to Umbraculidae, includes species with an elevated limpet-like shell that is much higher than *Umbraculum* and covers the body completely. Most Tylodinidae are found in temperate regions although there are a few tropical species.

***Tylodina* sp. 1**
Size: 20 mm   Japan
ID: Body pale yellow; shell white, semi-translucent. On sponges of the genus *Aplysina* in moderate depths on rocky reefs.

***Tylodina* sp. 2**
Size: 20 mm   Philippines
ID: Body yellow; cap-shaped shell with brown radiating bands near the margins; rhinophores and oral tentacles yellow, elongate. Rocky reefs on yellow or brownish sponges.

Cephalaspidea - "head-shielded slugs"

Cephalaspideans are a group of opisthobranchs which usually have a bubble shell, an internal shell or may entirely lack a shell. They are easy to recognize by the presence of a cephalic shield, or a thick layer of skin covering the head and the lack of conspicuous tentacles or rhinophores. The evolutionary relationships within this group are poorly known and the current classification is based on anatomical as well as shell characteristics. Recent studies (Mikkelsen, 1996; Wägele & Klussmann-Kolb, 2005; Malaquias *et al.*, 2009) confirm that Cephalaspidea *sensu stricto* appears to be a natural group once the Acteonoidea are excluded.

Members of the Cephalaspidea occupy different marine habitats, many species are burrowers, commonly found in muddy and sandy areas, whereas other groups are inhabitants of rocky or hard substrates. Burrowers normally lack the bright external coloration present in many other sea slugs. There are also different diets among members of this group, with herbivorous and carnivorous species, including species that feed on other sea slugs. There is a rich diversity of poorly known deep-sea species not covered in this book.

Colinatydidae Oskars, Bouchet & Malaquias, 2015

Colinatydidae constitutes a group of cephalaspideans that have an inflated, well-developed, quadrangular shell, wider anteriorly, with a reticulate pattern of whitish squares.

Colinatys sp.
Size: 4 mm — Western and central Pacific Ocean
ID: Body translucent white; shell rounded with a blunt apex, ornamented with a network of opaque white markings. Under rocks and coral rubble in 2-12 m.

Cylichnidae H. Adams & A. Adams, 1854

The Cylichnidae are family of cephalaspideans with a well calcified shell and bulloid spire. The shells are usually whitish but may have a darker periostracum on the outside of the calcareous portion. Species of Cylichnidae probably feed on a variety of marine organisms such as foraminiferans, annelids, crustaceans and other mollusks. They are found from intertidal mudflats to the deep-sea down to 5,000 m depth.

Cylichna labiata Watson, 1883
Size: 18 mm — Guam, Indonesia
ID: Body white with brown spots on the headshield; shell oval, translucent, with spiral bands near the anterior and posterior ends.

Cylichna sp. 1
Size: 10 mm — Papua New Guinea
ID: Body white with an elongate headshield, indented anteriorly; shell cylindrical, white, with spiral lines at the anterior and posterior ends. Under the surface of sandy substrate in 20-25 m.

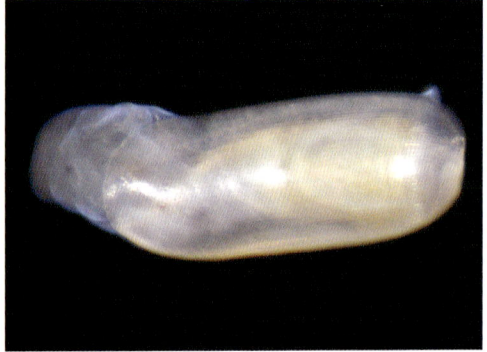

Cylichna sp. 2
Size: 5 mm — Papua New Guinea
ID: Body white with a short headshield; shell similar to the preceding species but lacking spiral lines. Under the surface of sandy substrate in 1-8 m.

Cylichna biplicata (A. Adams in Sowerby, 1850)
Size: 25 mm   Western and central Pacific
ID: Body white; shell with numerous brown spiral bands; shell cylindrical, bulloid, covered by a brownish periostracum.

Cylichna braunsi is a synonym. In dredged material in 10-250 m.

Cylichna sp. 3
Size: 7 mm   Papua New Guinea
ID: Body and shell white; headshield elongate; an elongate filamentous "tail" extending from the posterior end of the body that can equal the length of the shell. Under the surface of sandy substrate in 5-6 m.

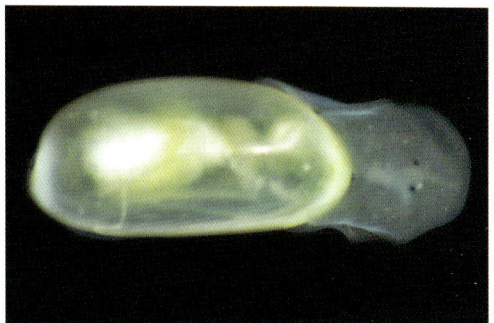

Cylichna sp. 4
Size: 10 mm   Papua New Guinea
ID: Body white; headshield elongate with two deep posterior lobes; shell oval, translucent, smooth; similar to *Cylichna labiata*, but shell less globular and headshield lacking small black flecks. Under the surface of sandy substrates in 1-4 m.

Mnestiidae Oskars, Bouchet & Malaquias, 2015

Members of this family have unique characteristics such as the presence of small, thick, cylindrical and white and brown colored shells with spiral striations. They have a radula, ridged gizzard plates.

Mnestia villica (Gould, 1859)
Size: 6 mm   Widespread in the Indo-Pacific
ID: Body brown with small opaque white spots; shell white with highly variable banding of brown. Sandy habitats in shallow water to 10 m.

Mnestia girardi (Audouin, 1826)
Size: 10 mm   Indian and western Pacific oceans
ID: Body translucent white with small opaque brownish spots on the mantle, head and parapodia; shell whitish, cylindrical with faint spiral lines on the anterior and posterior ends. Crawling on the surface of coarse, silty sand in 10-12 m. Introduced into the Mediterranean.

Cephalaspidea - "head-shielded slugs"

Haminoeidae Pilsbry, 1895

Members of this family are also herbivorous and are characterized by having a thinly calcified bulloid shell, with some exceptions. They have three ridged gizzard plates to shred their algal prey. Most species are cryptic and infaunal under sand or mud, but some are found crawling in the open and are often brightly colored.

Atys multistriatus Schepmann, 1913
Size: 10 mm   Indian and western Pacific oceans
ID: Body brownish with opaque white pigment; shell shiny white with yellow pigment on the posterior end and often along the margin of the lip. Active at night, crawling on the surface of sand in mixed rocky and sandy habitats, in 1-5 m.

Atys semistriatus Pease, 1860
Size: 8 mm   Widespread in the Indo-Pacific
ID: Body translucent with black dots on the head and mantle; shell translucent, fairly squat, with striations at the anterior and posterior ends; red spots from the visceral mass visible through the shell. During the day actively crawling on the surface of coral rubble or sand in a few meters.

Atys ukelele Too, Carlson, Hoff & Malaquias, 2014
Size: 5 mm   Western and Central Pacific Ocean
ID: Body translucent white with opaque white spots on the head and parapodia; light yellowish spots present on the mantle, visible through the translucent white shell; shell glossy white with fine spiral incised lines at both ends. Sandy habitats in 6-17 m.

Atys naucum (Linnaeus, 1758)
Size: 40 mm   Indian and western Pacific oceans
ID: Body white, with a brownish headshield and translucent white areas around the eyes and a black spot between them; adult specimens (left photo) with white patches on the edges of the parapodia and black and white markings along the

posterior edge of the mantle; shell brown, broad, with dark striations throughout; juvenile specimens (right photo) with brown longitudinal lines on the shell. *Atys kuhnsi* is a synonym. Under sand during the day or cruising on the surface at night, in 1-25 m.

Atys sp. 1
Size: 11 mm   Philippines
ID: Body translucent to opaque white with brown and opaque white spots; headshield short, rounded and undivided posteriorly; parapodia elongate; shell smooth with white and brown spots visible through. On sand with Cyanobacteria in 2 m.

Atys pittmani Too, Carlson, Hoff & Malaquias, 2014
Size: 12 mm   Western and central Pacific Ocean
ID: Body translucent white with opaque white spots; body and shell elongate; relatively small parapodia; posterior end of the head shield notched; small opaque white and red spots visible below the surface of the translucent shell. Sandy habitats on reef slopes in 10 m.

Atys sp. 2
Size: 10 mm   Philippines, Indonesia
ID: Body brown with dark brown dots and opaque white patches; shell cylindrical with many striations and white patches visible through. Under sand on slopes in 5-10 m; it can also swim.

Atys sp. 3
Size: 20 mm   Palau, Guam
ID: Body white with opaque white and dark brown pigment; shell similar to *Liloa curta* but more elongate. Under fine sand; appears to feed on Cyanobacteria; also capable of swimming.

Atys sp. 4
Size: 15 mm   Papua New Guinea
ID: Body white with brown spots; shell even more elongate than the preceding species; head shield elongate rather than triangular. Under fine sand in 5-8 m; also capable of swimming.

Atys sp. 5
Size: 8 mm   Philippines
ID: Body translucent to opaque white with orange and white spots; headshield short, acute with short cleft posteriorly; parapodia short; shell cylindrical with spiral lines along entire shell. On sand with mixed algae in 7 m.

Cephalaspidea - "head-shielded slugs"

Atys sp. 6
Size: 15 mm   Philippines, Vanuatu, Indonesia
ID: Body translucent white with black pigment; shell translucent, cylindrical with prominent striations; opaque white and brown spots visible below the surface of the shell. Burrows in fine sandy substrates in 1-3 m.

Atys sp. 7
Size: 6 mm   Papua New Guinea, Philippines
ID: Body white with brown spots; shell very glossy and thickly calcified without obvious striations; shell apex blunt. Under clean, coarse sand in 3-10 m.

Atys sp. 8
Size: 10 mm   Vanuatu
ID: Body translucent white with black and opaque white spots on the head; shell translucent with a prominent incised spiral sculpture that covers most of the shell except for the central portion; dark pigment visible through the shell.

Atys sp. 9
Size: 8 mm   Philippines
ID: Body translucent white with orange brown and opaque white dots; shell glossy white with fine spiral incised lines at both ends and smooth in the middle. In fine silty sand in 8 m.

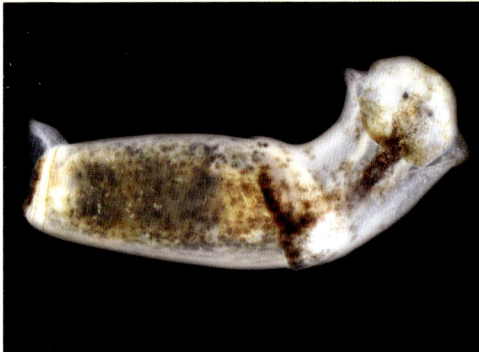

Atys sp. 10
Size: 10 mm   Papua New Guinea
ID: Body translucent white with brown and opaque white dots; a dark brown line on the body behind head and at the posterior end of the parapodial lobes; shell elongate, smooth or with faint spiral lines. In 20 m.

Atys sp. 11
Size: 8 mm   Papua New Guinea
ID: Body translucent white with scattered black dots; shell translucent with reddish-brown pigment visible through and fine spiral incised lines at both ends, smooth in the middle; Similar to *Atys semistriatus* but with a more globular shell and less prominent spiral striations. In 12 m.

Cephalaspidea - "head-shielded slugs"

Atys sp. 12
Size: 7 mm   Papua New Guinea
ID: Similar to the preceding species but with narrow elongate lobes at the posterior end of the head shield rather than rounded, blunt lobes; shell with more prominent spiral striations on the anterior and posterior ends of the shell. In 20-25 m.

Atys sp. 13
Size: 9 mm   Papua New Guinea
ID: Body with black spots on the mantle, head and parapodia; a black mid-dorsal line present on the headshield; shell elongate, smooth, without striations. Mangrove and seagrass flats in 2 m.

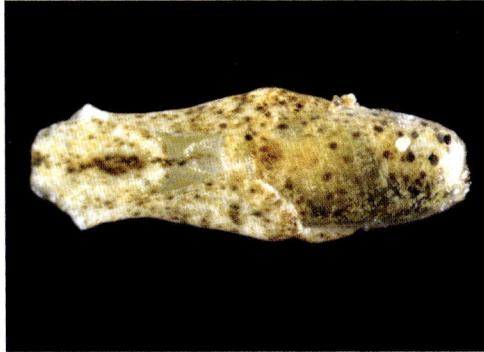

Atys sp. 14
Size: 8 mm   Papua New Guinea
ID: Body translucent white with small opaque white and brown spots on the mantle, head and parapodia; headshield short, oval with a rounded posterior end; parapodia with angular projections near the head; shell shiny, transparent. In 8 m.

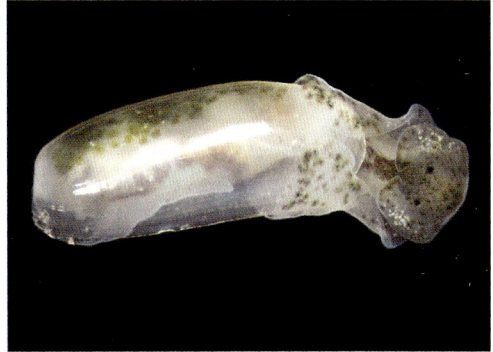

Atys sp. 15
Size: 8 mm   Papua New Guinea
ID: Body translucent white with small brown spots on the mantle, head and parapodia; shell shiny white, cylindrical, smooth; headshield short, bilobed; parapodia short. In 2 m.

Atys sp. 16
Size: 15 mm   Philippines
ID: Body translucent without spots; headshield and parapodia short; shell shiny white, cylindrical with prominent spiral lines on the anterior and posterior ends. Sand with dense algal cover in 7 m.

Atys sp. 17
Size: 15 mm   Philippines
ID: Body translucent white with dense covering of dark brown spots on the mantle, head and parapodia; headshield and parapodia short; shell shiny white, cylindrical; faint spiral lines on the entire shell. Sand with dense algal cover in 7 m.

347

Cephalaspidea - "head-shielded slugs"

Atys sp. 18
Size: 10 mm   Tuamotu Archipelago
ID: Body translucent white with dark spots on the head and mantle; brown pigment just below the eyes and posterior end of the headshield; headshield and parapodia short; shell shiny white, cylindrical with prominent spiral and axial lines. Sand with dense algal cover in 7 m.

Aliculastrum debilis (Pease, 1860)
Size: 20 mm   Hawai'ian Is., possibly more widespread
ID: Body translucent white with opaque white pigment; shell white, narrower posteriorly and anteriorly, with striations only at the ends. Under sand in shallow water.

Aliculastrum cylindricum (Helbling, 1779)
Size: 30 mm   Indian and western Pacific oceans
ID: Body white with greenish pigment; shell white, long, cylindrical with prominent opaque striations at both ends, but without striations in the middle of the shell. Commonly just below the surface of fine to coarse sand in 1-15 m; feeds on filamentous algae.

Aliculastrum parallelum (Gould, 1847)
Size: 13 mm   Western and central Pacific Ocean
ID: Body translucent white with reddish spots on the mantle visible through the translucent white shell; shell glossy white with fine spiral incised lines at both ends. Fine silty sand in 5-18 m.

Aliculastrum sp. 1
Size: 8 mm   Papua New Guinea
ID: Body translucent white with small opaque white spots on the mantle, head and parapodia; shell shiny white, cylindrical with faint spiral lines on the anterior and posterior ends. In 2-10 m.

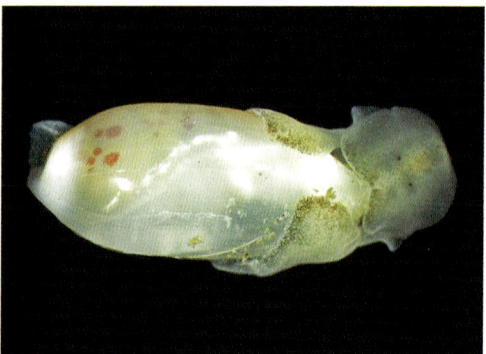

Aliculastrum sp. 2
Size: 8 mm   Papua New Guinea
ID: Body translucent white with small brownish spots on the mantle, head and parapodia; headshield short; parapodia moderately large; shell shiny white, cylindrical, without visible lines. In 1-4 m.

Aliculastrum sp. 3
Size: 20 mm   Philippines
ID: Headshield broad, brownish, with deeply bilobed posterior end; shell with incised spiral lines anteriorly and posteriorly. Silty sand, 7 m.

Liloa curta (A. Adams, 1850)
Size: 25 mm   Widespread in the Indo-Pacific
ID: Body translucent white with opaque white spots; shell translucent with the dark pigmented visceral mass having opaque white and red spots visible underneath; shell long, cylindrical with evenly spaced striations over the entire surface. On fine sand in shallow water; capable of swimming by flapping its parapodia.

Liloa porcellana (Gould, 1859)
Size: 20 mm   Western and central Pacific
ID: Body translucent white with small opaque white spots on the mantle, head and parapodia; headshield and parapodia short; shell shiny white, cylindrical, with faint spiral lines on the entire surface. Sandy areas in 8-300 m.

Liloa sp. 1
Size: 8 mm   Papua New Guinea
ID: Body translucent white with small black spots on the foot, head and parapodia; headshield small; shell whitish, cylindrical with prominent spiral lines on the anterior and posterior ends. In 8-13 m.

Liloa sp. 2
Size: 15 mm   Papua New Guinea
ID: Body translucent white with dense brown spots on the mantle, head and parapodia; short headshield with a dark brown medial line; shell translucent, cylindrical with faint spiral lines on the entire surface. In 5 m.

Liloa sp. 3
Size: 15 mm   Philippines
ID: Headshield dark brown, shallowly divided posteriorly; shell cylindrical, elongate with incised spiral lines over the entire surface. Shallow silty sand, 10 m.

Cephalaspidea - "head-shielded slugs"

Haminoea cymbalum (Quoy & Gaimard, 1832)
Size: 15 mm   Widespread in the Indo-Pacific
ID: Body green with large orange spots and larger pale orange patches outlined in white under the shell; shell translucent so the body color is visible through. Feeds on filamentous algae.

Haminoea ovalis Pease, 1868
Size: 10 mm   Western, central and eastern Pacific
ID: Body pale green with numerous scattered yellow and purple spots and areas of opaque white pigment; shell translucent so the body color is visible through; similar to *Haminoea cymbalum* but lacks the broad orange bands surrounded by opaque white under the shell. Shallow water on the surface of coral rubble covered with green algae.

Haminoea sp. 1
Size: 8 mm   Saudi Arabia
ID: Body greenish with purple and orange spots on the headshield and mantle; distinct purple margins on the parapodia and mantle; shell translucent so the body color is visible through. Crawls on the surface of rocks covered with green algae in 4-6 m.

Haminoea sp. 2
Size: 10 mm   Western Pacific Ocean
ID: Body green with large orange spots surrounded by opaque white but lacking purple spots; shell translucent so the body color is visible through. In relatively shallow water on the surface of coral rubble; active during the day.

Haminoea cyanomarginata Heller & Thompson, 1983
Size: 7 mm   Western Indian Ocean
ID: Body white with purple lines along the margins of the headshield, parapodia, posterior shield, and foot; yellow spots may also be present; shell translucent, almost entirely covered by body tissue. On shallow reefs in the open in 3-15 m. Introduced into the Mediterranean.

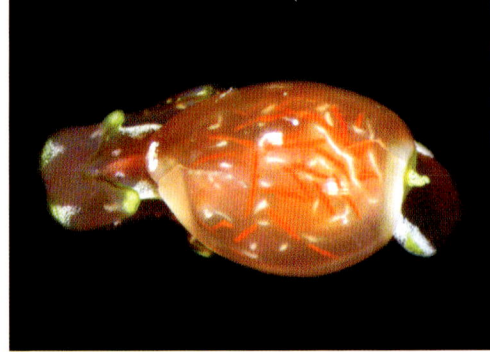

Haminoea sp. 3
Size: 8 mm   Philippines, Papua New Guinea
ID: Body translucent white with orange, yellow and opaque white markings; orange and opaque white lines visible on mantle through shell; short posterior tail behind shell. Crawling on the surface of rocks covered with green algae in 3-8 m.

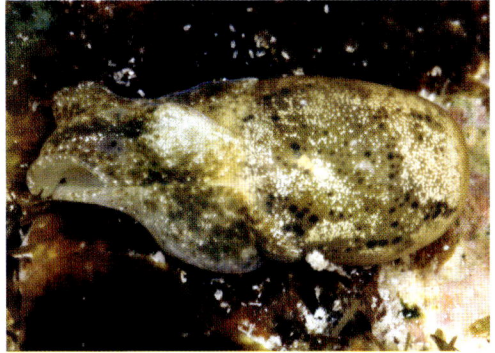

Haminoea natalensis (Krauss, 1848)
Size: 15 mm   Widespread in the Indo-Pacific
ID: Greenish with dark brown to black and white spots; shell semi-translucent so the body color is visible through but slightly darker. *Haminoea crocata* is a synonym. On the surface of sandy intertidal pools and sea grass beds in 0-3 m.

Haminoea sp. 4
Size: 15 mm   Mauritius
ID: Body translucent white with dense brown and opaque white spots; similar to *Haminoea natalensis*, but with far more opaque white pigment. Crawling on the surface of rocks covered with green algae in 1 m.

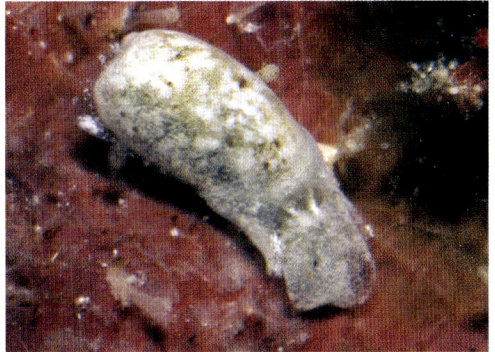

Haminoea cf. fusca (Pease, 1863)
Size: 12 mm   Philippines, Australia
ID: Body orange with black pigment and white spots; shell white, semi-translucent, allowing some of the orange body pigment to be visible; head broad and shell wide. Intertidally in mixed sand and mud habitats.

Haminoea sp. 5
Size: 8 mm   Philippines
ID: Body translucent whitish with dense opaque white spots and a few scattered large black spots; shell translucent so the body color is visible through. Sandy slopes in 12 m, crawling in the open.

Haminoea sp. 6
Size: 7 mm   Western Pacific Ocean
ID: Body brownish with opaque white spot concentrations, particularly on the head; shell translucent so the body color is visible through; short siphon extending from the posterior end of the shell. On clumps of Cyanobacteria such as *Lyngbya* on patch reefs in shallow water.

Haminoea sp. 7
Size: 8 mm   Papua New Guinea
ID: Body translucent white with opaque white spots; dark grey spots present on the middle of the headshield; yellow and black spots visible on the mantle through the globular shell. Crawling on the surface in 2-3 m.

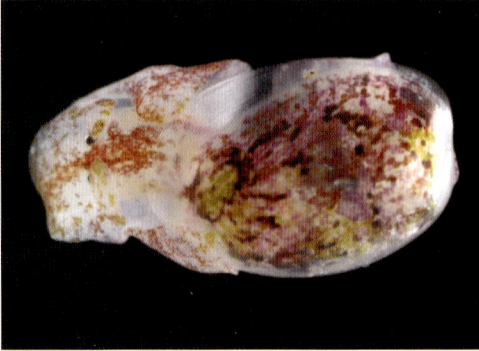

Haminoea sp. 8
Size: 8 mm   Papua New Guinea
ID: Body translucent white with a variable pattern of dark brown pigment on the head, parapodia and mantle; shell globular, smooth. Crawling in 15 m.

Haminoea sp. 9
Size: 8 mm   Papua New Guinea
ID: Body brown with opaque white spots on the headshield parapodia and foot; dark grey spots on the middle of the headshield; dark brown blotches visible on the mantle through the globular shell. Crawling on the surface of green algae, where they may form dense aggregations.

Diniatys dubius (Schepman, 1913)
Size: 12 mm   Western Pacific Ocean
ID: Body brown with a network of orange to brown lines and opaque white spots; head with an elongate opaque white patch; shell translucent so the body color is visible through. Below the surface of sand on reef slopes; appears to feed on the cyanobacterium, *Microcoleus*.

Diniatys dentifer (A. Adams, 1850)
Size: 5 mm   Widespread in the Indo-Pacific
ID: Body color highly variable; characterized by a darker patch on the middle of the head; shell with a columellar tooth on the edge of the aperture. A common but rarely seen species associated with Cyanobacteria, especially *Lyngbya*, on rock reef flats and shallows.

Smaragdinella calyculata (Broderip & Sowerby I, 1829)
Size: 20 mm   Widespread in the Indo-Pacific
ID: Green with opaque white spots; body stout with a brownish, well-calcified external shell. Intertidal zone along wave-swept marine benches; it has a broad foot to be able to withstand wave shock.

Phanerophthalmus luteus (Quoy & Gaimard, 1833)
Size: 50 mm   Western and central Pacific
ID: Uniformly yellowish green to dark green with no opaque white markings on the body. Mixed coral and sandy patch reefs in shallow water, 2-10 m.

Phanerophthalmus olivaceus (Ehrenberg, 1828)
Size: 20 mm   Red Sea
ID: Uniformly green with sparse white spots on the overlapping parapodial lobes. Shallow water on patch reefs, active at night.

Phanerophthalmus minikoiensis (Smith, 1903)
Size: 25 mm   Indian Ocean
ID: Uniformly light green. Commonly in shallow water, 1 m; feeds on algae growing on small volcanic rocks.

Phanerophthalmus sp. 1 "paulayi"
Size: 10 mm   Widespread in the Indo-Pacific
ID: Greenish body with lighter margins of the parapodia and posterior part of the head shield. Common in intertidal pools, nocturnally active.

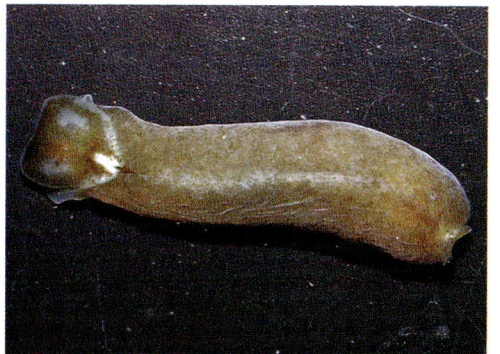

Phanerophthalmus cylindricus (Pease, 1861)
Size: 10 mm   Widespread in the Indo-Pacific
ID: Greenish body with lighter margins of the parapodia and posterior part of the head shield. Common in intertidal pools, nocturnally active.

Phanerophthalmus engeli Labbé, 1934
Size: 18 mm   New Guinea
ID: Uniformly dark brown body. The only Pacific species with this coloration. Shallow reefs, 3-5 m.

Phanerophthalmus albocollaris Heller & Thompson, 1983
Size: 14 mm   Red Sea
ID: Dark green to brown with white pigment only along the posterior margin of the headshield; shell covered by the parapodia. Crawling on the surface of sandy substrate at night, 10-15 m.

Cephalaspidea - "head-shielded slugs"

Phanerophthalmus sp. 2 "abotriangulatum"
Size: 6 mm   Western Pacific Ocean
ID: Greenish brown with an opaque white triangular patch on the posterior end of the headshield and at the posterior end of the body. Under coral rubble in protected lagoons.

Phanerophthalmus sp. 3 "cerverai"
Size: 20 mm   Western Pacific Ocean
ID: Purplish brown with opaque white on the anterior and posterior ends of the headshield. Shallow water in coral rubble, 1-5 m.

Phanerophthalmus sp. 4 "tibiricae"
Size: 32 mm   Mozambique
ID: Uniformly dark brown with a bluish glow around the margins. The only Indian Ocean species with this color pattern. Shallow reefs 0-2 m, nocturnally active.

Phanerophthalmus sp. 5 "batangas"
Size: 8 mm   Philippines
ID: Uniformly purple brown with lighter pigment present on the posterior end of the triangular headshield; shell visible posteriorly. Crawling on the surface of coarse sand on silty slopes in 12 m.

Phanerophthalmus perpallidus Risbec, 1928
Size: 8 mm   Widespread in the Indo-Pacific
ID: Predominantly white with scattered darks spots; distinctive opaque white mark extending to the anterior end of the headshield. Under coral rubble in shallow water.

354

Phanerophthalmus sp. 6 "boucheti"
Size: 8 mm   Philippines
ID: Light green with green-brown spots; lighter areas present around eyes and at posterior end of the headshield.

Phanerophtalmus sp. 7 "lentigines"
Size: 9 mm   Widespread in the Indo-Pacific
ID: Translucent white with golden brown spots on the headshield, parapodia and mantle; similar to *Phaneropthalmus cylindricus*, but with a less elongate body; shell visible posteriorly. Crawling on the surface of sand in 5-6 m.

Phanerophthalmus sp. 8 "rudmani"
Size: 50 mm   Vanuatu
ID: Translucent greenish white, with darker green brown spots; areas around eyes lighter; inner margins of parapodia darker. Shallow reefs.

Phanerophtalmus sp. 9 "anetteae"
Size: 20 mm   Central and western Pacific Ocean
ID: Body spotted, purple to red; end of the posterior headshield lobes tipped in white. Shallow reefs under rubble.

Phanerophthalmus sp. 10 "purpureus"
Size: 25 mm   Japan, Philippines, Indonesia
ID: Body elongate, purple with overlapping parapodial lobes. Thinner and more elongate than *Phanerophthalmus anettae*. Under coral rubble in 18-21 m.

Haminoeid sp. 1
Size: 5 mm   Western and central Pacific Ocean
ID: Translucent white with concentrations of opaque white spots and black short lines; "tail" relatively long. Members of this unnamed group of haminoeids are characterized by having a long posterior end of the foot that can be adhesive and strongly retractile. Sandy habitats in association with cyanobacteria.

Cephalaspidea - "head-shielded slugs"

Haminoeid sp. 2
Size: 3 mm   Western Pacific Ocean
ID: Translucent with opaque white pigment and characteristic black rings; an extremely long "tail" that is two to three times as long as the rest of the animal. On the undersides of coral rubble; feeds on Cyanobacteria.

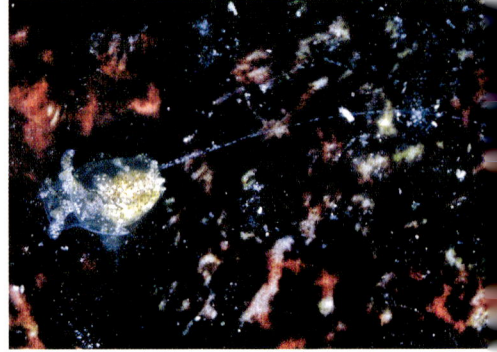

Haminoeid sp. 3
Size: 3 mm   Guam, Papua New Guinea
ID: Translucent white with opaque white spots on the surface; brown viscera visible through the skin; a ring of short tubercles along the posterior margin of the mantle; "tail" relatively long. Mangrove lagoons in shallow water.

Haminoeid sp. 4
Size: 5 mm   Philippines
ID: Orange-brown with opaque white spots on the mantle; shell translucent; "tail" long and black; head triangular. Crawling on the surface of coarse, clean sand in 7 m.

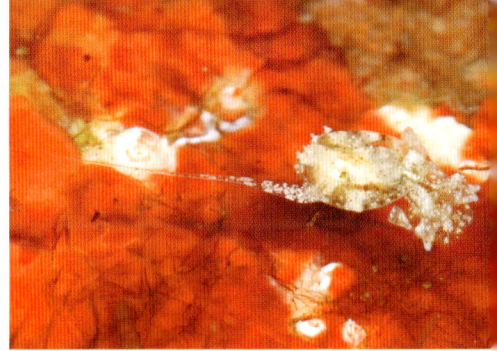

Haminoeid sp. 5
Size: 8 mm   Philippines
ID: Translucent grey with abundant opaque white pigment and small brown dots; "tail" long and thin; anterior end of the head bilobed; conical tubercles present behind shell. Crawling on the surface of coarse, clean sand in 7 m.

Haminoeid sp. 6
Size: 8 mm   Indonesia
ID: White with brown speckling on the head and mantle; anterior margin of the head bilobed; "tail" extremely long. Crawling on the surface of fine, silty sand in 10 m.

Haminoeid sp. 7
Size: 3 mm   Indonesia, Philippines, Guam
ID: Greenish-brown with white spots; tubercles along the posterior margin; "tail" short compared to other related species. In clumps of the cyanobacterium *Lyngbya* in 3-15 m.

Haminoeid sp. 8
Size: 8 mm   Philippines
ID: Uniform cream with two brownish lines posterior to the eyes; head triangular rather than bilobed. Crawling on the surface of sandy substrates during the day in 10-15 m.

Haminoeid sp. 9
Size: 4 mm   Philippines
ID: Body with reddish lines over the surface; row of tubercles present on the posterior end of shell; "tail" medium in length. Found on filamentous cyanobacteria in 10 m.

Bullidae J. E. Gray, 1827

The Bullidae are a group of herbivorous bubble snails that have mottled, well-calcified shells. They are found worldwide in temperate and tropical oceans. Most species are nocturnal and feed on algae during the hours of darkness, burrowing or hiding away during the day. They are shallow water animals, often found in estuarine or lagoonal environments, and prefer areas of soft sandy mud. This group has been recently reviewed by Malaquias & Reid (2008).

Bulla are herbivorous and have been observed eating filamentous algae. Animal material has also been found in the stomachs of some species. Species burrow in soft muddy sand, but sometimes emerge at night from the substrate where they may form breeding aggregations.

Bulla orientalis Habe, 1950
Size: 20 mm   Indian and western Pacific oceans
ID: Body brown with opaque white spots; shell brown with dark spots and opaque white over the mottled surface; often misidentified as *Bulla punctulata*. On shallow reef and sand flats; nocturnally active.

Bulla ampulla Linnaeus, 1758
Size: 50 mm   Indian and western Pacific oceans
ID: Body orange with white spots and brown pigment; shell light brown, globose, usually with white spots and blotches of darker brown pigment. It is the largest of the Indo-Pacific species of *Bulla*. Nocturnally active; often in tidal pools and offshore soft-bottom habitats.

Bulla vernicosa Gould, 1859
Size: 30 mm   Western and central Pacific oceans
ID: Body yellowish with dark brown pigment and opaque white spots; shell globose, brownish with many translucent white spots.

Bulla arabica Malaquias & Reid, 2008
Size: 50 mm   Western Indian Ocean
ID: Body orange with white spots but lacks brown pigment; shell similar to *Bulla ampulla*, but is smaller, lighter, and more squarely shaped. From the intertidal zone to 25 m; often associated with sea grasses; nocturnally active.

Bulla peasiana Pilsbry, 1895
Size: 25 mm   Hawai'ian Is.
ID: Body brownish red with white spots; shell light brown with opaque white spots. It has been considered a synonym of *Bulla vernicosa*, but its shell is more slender and thinner and lacks brown pigment. On shallow reef flats when considerable sand is present; nocturnally active.

Hamineobulla kawamurai Habe, 1950
Size: 8 mm   Western and central Pacific
ID: Body white with dense brown spots; shell white with characteristic brown bands. On the surface of rubble on shallow water reefs in about 10 m.

Tornatinidae P. Fischer, 1883

This family is characterized by having shiny white shells, with a spire that extends posteriorly beyond the main body whorl or may be almost bulloid. Internally, these animals have a radula and three flat gizzard plates present. Tornatinidae used to be considered a synonym of Cylichnidae, but it was recently placed in its own family by Oskars et al. (2015). Animals reside in clean sand where they feed on foraminerans.

Acteocina hawaiensis Pilsbry, 1921
Size: 4 mm   Hawai'ian Is.
ID: Body white; shell milky white with a series of interrupted clear bands; spire moderately elongate. In clean sand.

Acteocina sandwicensis Pease, 1860
Size: 6 mm   Hawai'ian Is.
ID: Body white; shell white, glossy, with a well-elevated spire. Under clean white sand in 1-5 m.

Acteocina sp. 1
Size: 7 mm   Indian and western Pacific oceans
ID: Body white; shell white, glossy with a spire that has channeled, stair-step whorls. Under the surface of clean white sand in 3-5 m.

Acteocina sp. 2
Size: 6 mm   Madagascar
ID: Body white; shell white, glossy, elongate with a canaliculate spire. Clean white sand, on slopes in 1-3 m.

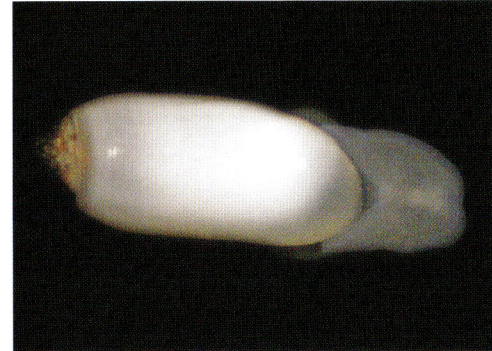

Acteocina sp. 3
Size: 10 mm   Papua New Guinea
ID: Body white, with a moderately long headshield having long posterior lobes; shell white, shiny with a relatively short spire consisting of several whorls. Under the surface of sandy substrates in 12-20 m.

Acteocina sp. 4
Size: 7 mm   Papua New Guinea
ID: Body white; headshield elongate without posterior lobes; shell white globular, with a very short spire. Under the surface of clean sand in 2-6 m.

Acteocina sp. 5
Size: 12 mm   Philippines, Papua New Guinea
ID: Body white with clear openings of the mantle arranged in a linear fashion, which are visible through the shell; headshield elongate with two deep posterior lobes; shell with a relatively elongate spire. Under the surface of sandy substrates in 5 m.

Acteocina sp. 6
Size: 10 mm   Papua New Guinea
ID: Body white; headshield elongate with two elongate posterior lobes; shell white with a relatively low spire; shallow spiral lines present along entire length of the shell. Under the surface of sandy substrates in 3-6 m.

Cephalaspidea - "head-shielded slugs"

Retusidae Thiele, 1925

Members of this family lack a radula and use three papillate gizzard plates to crush their prey. They are infaunal species (animals that live buried in sediment), found from shallow intertidal sand and mud flats to abyssal depths greater than 5,000 m. Retusids appear to feed on diatoms, foraminiferans and small mollusks. There appear to be numerous Indo-Pacific species but the systematics of these taxa remain poorly known.

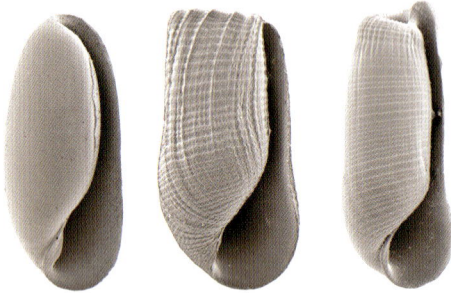

Retusa concentrica (A. Adams, 1850)
Size: 5 mm   Guam, Philippines
ID: Body translucent white with opaque white spots; shell white with transverse lines crossed by growth lines; shell elongate; dark gizzard plates visible through the anterior portion of the shell. Clean fine sand in shallow water.

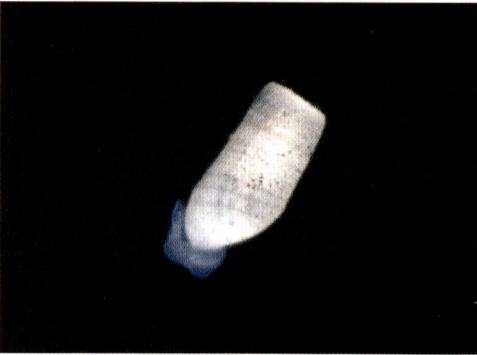

Retusa sp. 1
Size: 2 mm   Aldabra Atoll, western Indian Ocean
ID: Body white; shell white with transverse dark lines, relatively short, cylindrical. On intertidal reef flats in fine, clean sand; feeds on minute foraminiferans.

Retusa sp. 2
Size: 6 mm   Vanuatu
ID: Body translucent white with opaque white spots; shell white, elongate, with faint transverse lines. Clean fine sand in shallow water.

Retusa sp. 3
Size: 4 mm   Philippines
ID: Body translucent white with opaque white spots; shell white with transverse lines crossed by growth lines; similar to *Retusa concentrica*, but shell more elongate with an expanded anterior portion. Crawling on the surface of sandy substrates in 5 m.

Retusa sp. 4
Size: 5 mm   Papua New Guinea
ID: Body white with an elongate headshield; shell white with irregular translucent bands. Under the surface of sandy substrate in seagrass beds in 2 m.

360

Scaphandridae G. O. Sars, 1878

Scaphandridae includes large bulloid shells with an englared, headshield with no visible eyes. The shell has spiral bands along its entire length. Gizzard plates large and flattened. Radula present. Generally, found in deep water in soft sediment where it feeds on bivalves and foraminiferans.

Scaphander mundus Watson, 1883
Size: 30 mm   Western and central Pacific
ID: Body uniformly yellow with deep posterior lobes; shell large, globular, white, often with a yellowish membrane; shell with distinct spiral grooves along its entire length. Dredged from muddy and sandy habitats in deep water, 900-2,300 m.

Scaphander japonicus A. Adams, 1862
Size: 25 mm   Western and central Pacific Ocean
ID: Body white; shell well developed, with alternating brown and white lines. In trawls in 40-450 m.

Philinorbidae Oskars, Bouchet & Malaquias, 2015

Body large, white with large internal shell. Deep-water species with a broad flat, shell. Three small gizzard plates present. Radula present. Found in soft substrate by dredging.

***Philinorbis acutacauda* (Gonzales and Gosliner, 2014)**
Size: 65 mm   Philippines
ID: Uniformly white with an acute posterior end of the body; headshield elongate with a rounded posterior end; shell broad, white without sculpture. Dredged from muddy and sandy habitats in deep water, 459-636 m.

***Philinorbis hearstorum* (Gonzales & Gosliner, 2014)**
Size: 25 mm   Philippines
ID: Uniformly white with an acute posterior end of the body; headshield elongate with a rounded posterior end; shell broad, white with prominent spiral sculpture. Dredged from muddy and sandy habitats in deep water, 397-439 m; feeds on mytilid bivalves.

Philinidae J. E. Gray, 1850

The Philinidae is a family of Cephalaspidea that is well represented around the world from polar regions to the tropics and from shallow water to the deep sea. In the tropics the diversity of species is not well known, but there appear to be relatively few species. Members of this genus are usually white in color, but some tropical species such as *Philine orca* and *P. rubrata* may be brightly colored.

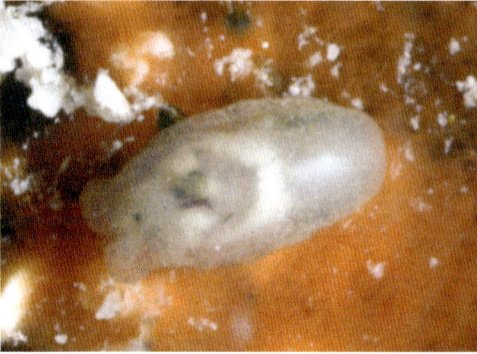

Spiniphiline kensleyi Gosliner, 1988
Size: 4 mm   Aldabra Atoll, western Indian Ocean
ID: Uniformly white; shell with a series of elongate spines that emanate from the posterior end. Among coral rubble in shallow water lagoon habitats.

Philine orientalis A. Adams, 1855
Size: 60 mm   Western Pacific Ocean
ID: Uniformly white. The precise identity of *Philine orientalis* is open to question, based on an incomplete original description and a vague designation of the type locality as "eastern seas." *Philine japonica* and *P. argentata* are likely synonyms. Sand channels in 1-2 m, in protected embayments.

Philine elegans Bergh, 1905
Size: 30 mm   Indonesia, Papua New Guinea
ID: Translucent white with the brown digestive gland and the opaque white gizzard visible through the skin; body long and slender with a proportionately large headshield relative to the posterior shield; very distinctive gizzard plates with long spines extending outwards. Under sand in 5-10 m in protected habitats.

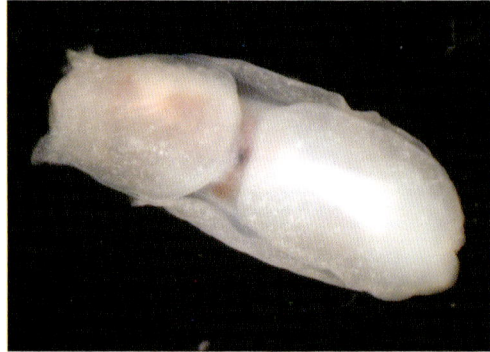

Philine multipapillata Gonzales & Gosliner, 2014
Size: 20 mm   Philippines
ID: Uniformly white with the pink digestive gland and the opaque white gizzard visible through the skin; superficially similar to *Philine orientalis* but has large pores in the gizzard plates and a penis covered with papillae. Trawled from 30-50 m.

Philine orca Gosliner, 1988
Size: 5 mm   Indo-Pacific and eastern Pacific
ID: White with brown or black markings on the dorsal surface, similar to the markings in killer whales; unusual among *Philine* species in that it lacks gizzard plates. Common inhabitant of rocky reefs and coral rubble areas from the intertidal zone to 20 m.

Philine rubrata Gosliner, 1988
Size: 5 mm   Widespread in the Indo-Pacific
ID: Orange to red; body elongate with the posterior lobes forming a long "skirt" that covers the mantle. Coral rubble in shallow water habitats, 1-5 m.

Philine sp. 1
Size: 4 mm   Papua New Guinea
ID: Off-white with small opaque white spots covering the body surface; a characteristic black spot visible in the center of the posterior shield. Among coral rubble on shallow reefs from 5-15 m.

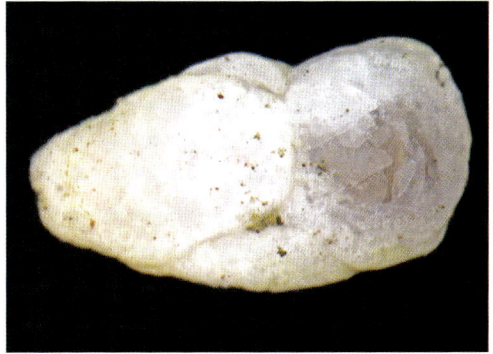

Philine dentiphallus Gonzales & Gosliner, 2014
Size: 9 mm   Philippines
ID: Uniformly white; headshield elongate, quadrangular with a flat posterior end; shell broad, white, smooth except for the base. Dredged from muddy and sandy habitats in 541-636 m.

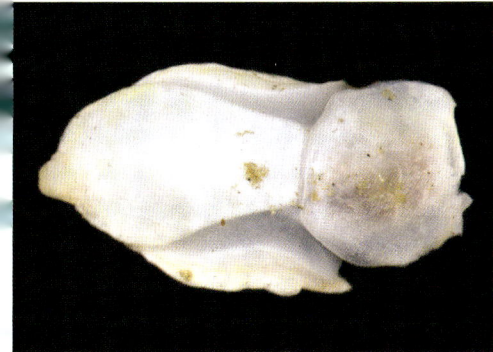

Philine verdensis Gonzales & Gosliner, 2014
Size: 17 mm   Philippines
ID: Uniformly white; headshield elongate, quadrangular with a flat posterior end; shell broad, white, smooth. Dredged from muddy and sandy habitats in 132-172 m.

Philine pittmani Gonzales & Gosliner, 2014
Size: 14 mm   Hawai'ian Is.
ID: Uniformly white with an acute posterior end of the body; headshield elongate with a rounded posterior end; shell broad, white with a prominent spiral sculpture. Fine sand basins, burrowed in *Halimeda kanalona* beds in 3-17 m.

Philine sp. 2
Size: 3 mm   Papua New Guinea
ID: Uniformly white; body minute, elongate with an expanded posterior end; headshield elongate with a flat posterior end. Coarse sand in 1-2 m.

Philine sp. 3
Size: 5 mm   Papua New Guinea
ID: Uniformly yellowish white; body with a rounded posterior end; headshield elongate with a flat posterior end. Coarse sand in 8 m.

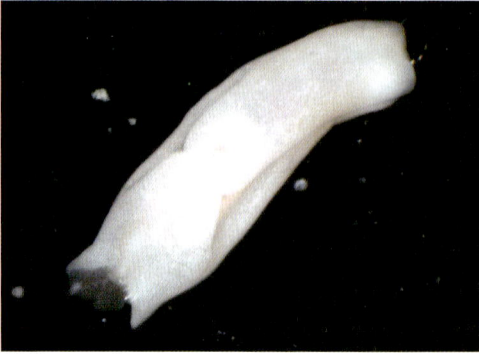

Philine sp. 4
Size: 6 mm   Philippines
ID: Uniformly off-white with small opaque white spots covering the body surface; pointed elements of the shell visible at the posterior end of the animal; headshield much longer than the posterior shield. Among coral rubble on shallow reefs from 0-2 m.

Philine sp. 5
Size: 4 mm   Philippines
ID: Translucent white; the sculpture of the shell and the three equal-sized, lozenge-shaped gizzard plates visible through the notum. Among coral rubble on shallow reefs, 0-2 m.

Aglajidae Pilsbry, 1895

Aglajids are often distinguished from other cephalaspideans by having a broad headshield with clusters of elongate sensory cilia, used for tracking prey. The posterior end of the body has a pair of blunt or elongate "tails" that generally provide protection for the posteriorly situated gill. The shell is internal and is wholly or partially calcified. Members of this family are carnivorous and generally lack a radula; a vestigial radula is present in a few species. The systematics of the Aglajidae has been recently investigated by Camacho-García *et al.* (2014) and Zamora-Silva & Malaquias (2017).

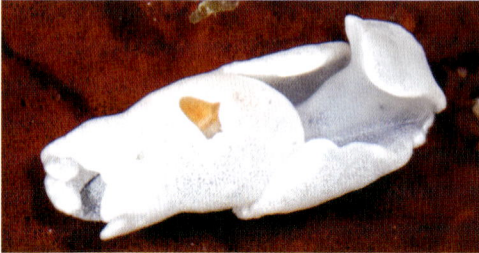

Noalda sp. 1
Size: 7 mm   Red Sea, Indonesia, Papua New Guinea
ID: Uniformly white; relatively short "tails" at the posterior end of the mantle; posterior shield with an opening through which the shell is visible. Crawling on the surface of coral rubble in 10-20 m.

Noalda sp. 2
Size: 4 mm   Papua New Guinea
ID: Uniformly white; a characteristic opening in the posterior shield with a black line across; "tails" elongate. Under coral rubble on reef flats in 7 m.

Noalda sp. 3
Size: 60 mm   Indonesia, Philippines, Malaysia
ID: Lavender with purple or black margins around the headshield, posterior shield and parapodia; a round opening in the middle of the posterior shield through which the shell is visible. Sandy reef flats in 15-20 m.

Noalda sp. 4
Size: 7 mm   Philippines
ID: Uniformly charcoal grey to black with opaque white margins of the headshield, parapodia and mantle; posterior end of the body with two triangular, acutely pointed lobes; headshield triangular with a long posterior lobe. Silty sand in 5-12 m.

Noalda sp. 5
Size: 7 mm   Kenya
ID: Uniformly reddish brown with opaque white margins of the headshield, parapodia, mantle and mantle opening; posterior end of the body with two elongate, triangular, acutely pointed lobes; headshield triangular with a long posterior lobe.

Noalda sp. 6
Size: 5 mm   Indonesia
ID: White with yellow spots; posterior end of the body with two elongate, pointed lobes; headshield triangular with a short posterior lobe; two dark lines on the shell at the opening of the mantle. Silty sand in 5-12 m.

Noalda sp. 7
Size: 4 mm   Indonesia
ID: White with dark pigment along the border of the head-shield and on the papillae on posterior shield.

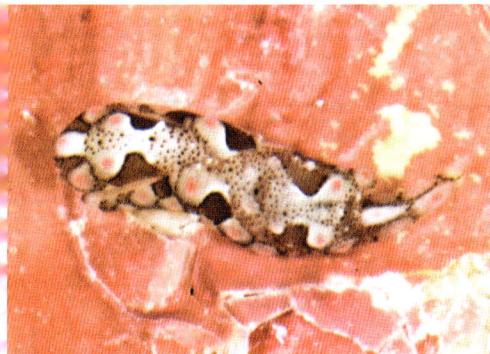

Odontoglaja guamensis Rudman, 1978
Size: 15 mm   Western Pacific Ocean
ID: White with brown patches and a series of rust-brown spots with larger rounded tubercles; the first aglajid that was known to retain a vestigial radula. Under coral rubble on reef flats in 3-20 m.

Odontoglaja mosaica Gosliner, 2011
Size: 15 mm   Western Indian Ocean
ID: Cream with numerous orange-red dots and a series of orange-red reticulations on the body and parapodia. On the surfaces of reef platforms in 13-20 m; isopods have been found in the crop of this aglajid indicating that it is a predator upon small crustaceans.

Cephalaspidea - "head-shielded slugs"

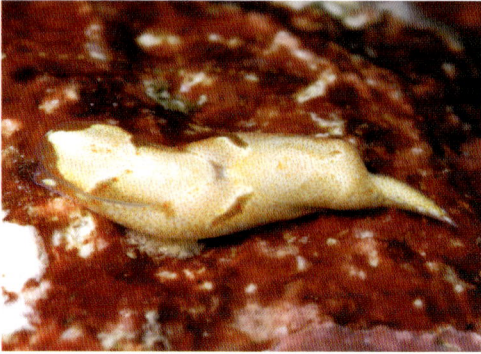

Odontoglaja sp. 1
Size: 8 mm · Philippines
ID: Uniformly yellowish white with brown spots and dashes; body smooth, lacking the rounded tubercles found in *Odontoglaja guamensis*. On small coral rubble pieces in 30 m.

Odontoglaja sp. 2
Size: 10 mm · Western and central Pacific Ocean
ID: Reddish-brown with irregular white pigment in the center and blue or purple spots; considered a color form of *Odontoglaja guamensis*, could be distinct species that requires further study. Under coral rubble in 1-10 m.

Odontoglaja sp. 3
Size: 10 mm · Philippines
ID: Greenish with white pigment occupying most of the dorsum; red spots of varying sizes surrounded by white pigment, mainly on the sides of the body. On small coral rubble pieces in 10-15 m.

Niparaya regiscorona (Bertsch, 1972)
Size: 5 mm · Indo-Pacific and eastern Pacific
ID: Dirty white with scattered tubercles and small black spots. Sandy habitats associated with algae.

Niparaya sp. 1
Size: 7 mm · Papua New Guinea
ID: White with small black dots and orange spots on the head; notum covered with tubercles; body elongate with long "tails." Crawling in sea water tanks at the Christensen Research Institute, feeding on small flatworms.

Niparaya sp. 2
Size: 6 mm · Papua New Guinea
ID: Black with white pigment and orange stripes. Feeding on small acoel flatworms in sea water tanks at the Christensen Research Institute.

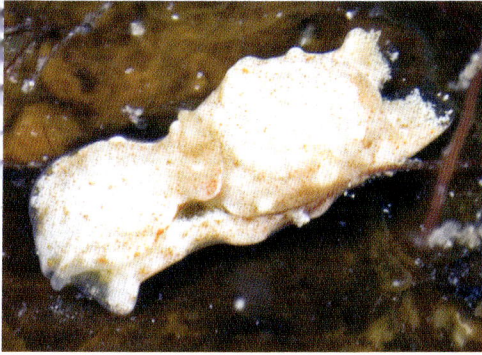

Niparaya sp. 3
Size: 5 mm   East Malaysia
ID: White with numerous small red dots; notum covered with scattered tubercles; posterior end of the headshield not divided into lobes. Usually in the rocky intertidal zone or in coral rubble on shallow reefs.

Niparaya sp. 4
Size: 5 mm   Indonesia
ID: Opaque tan with darker irregular lines over the surface of the parapodia, headshield and posterior shield; posterior end of headshield held upright.

Niparaya sp. 5
Size: 5 mm   Indonesia
ID: Opaque white with brownish markings on the headshield and posterior shield; parapodia with dark brown spots; posterior end of headshield held upright.

Niparaya sp. 6
Size: 5 mm   Indonesia, Philippines
ID: Uniformly reddish with opaque white markings on the tubercles covering the headshield, the posterior shield and the surfaces of the parapodia; posterior end of headshield held upright with a distinct apical tubercle.

Nakamigawaia sp.
Size: 25 mm   Western Pacific Ocean
ID: Uniform black or black with opaque white longitudinal stripes. Usually crawling rapidly on the surface of clean white sand, often on the edge of slopes.

Cephalaspidea - "head-shielded slugs"

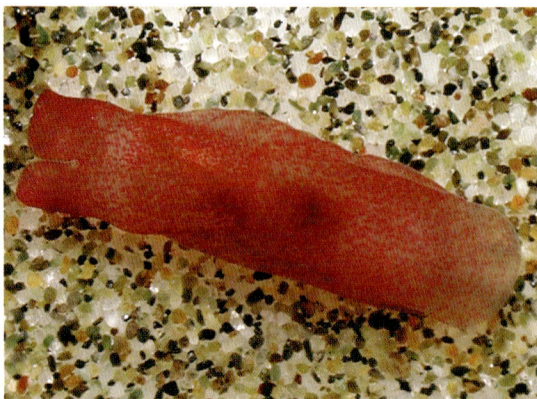

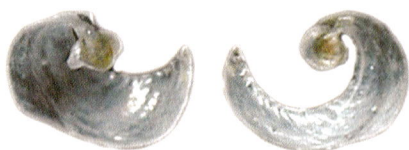

Nakamigawaia spiralis Kuroda & Habe, 1961
Size: 15 mm   Western Pacific Ocean
ID: Body reddish to purple with a quadrangular headshield longer than posterior shield; posterior shield bilobed posteriorly with two short equal lobes.

Philinopsis speciosa Pease, 1860
Size: 35 mm   Indo-Pacific and eastern Pacific
ID: Color extremely variable, whitish, brown or black, with or without yellow and blue markings; body truncate with an extended posterior portion of the headshield. *Philinopsis cyanea* is a synonym. Predator of opisthobranchs, especially bubble snails; emerges at night to track prey by chemical means.

Philinopsis ctenophoraphaga Gosliner, 2011
Size: 20 mm   Philippines, Indonesia, Japan
ID: Maroon with opaque white spots; head quadrangular; an elevated flap on the posterior end of the headshield. Crawling on the surface of fine silt at night in 1-47 m; feeds upon the benthic ctenophore, *Coeloplana meteoris*.

368

Philinopsis gardineri (Eliot, 1903)
Size: 35 mm   Widespread in the Indo-Pacific
ID: Black with a bright blue submarginal band; posterior end
of the headshield with an opaque white line; anterior end of
the body rounded; head bubble-shaped, like a Boeing 747.
Belongs to a species complex whose members probably feed
upon polychaete worms rather than opisthobranchs. Crawling
on the surface of soft substrate.

Philinopsis reticulata (Eliot, 1903)
Size: 30 mm   Indian Ocean, possibly western Pacific
ID: Reticulate brown with blue markings; similar to other
species of *Philinopsis* with a round rather than a quadrangular
anterior end of the head. Buried under clean sand during the
day in 1-5 m.

Philinopsis lineolata (H. Adams & A. Adams, 1854)
Size: 25 mm   Japan, Philippines, Australia
ID: Light with transverse dark lines; belongs to the "bubble-
headed" group of *Philinopsis*. Under sand in relatively
shallow water.

Philinopsis sp. 1
Size: 30 mm   Western Pacific Ocean
ID: White with a black reticulation and some blue markings;
specimens with this color pattern have been identified as
Philinopsis reticulata, but we treat it as a separate Pacific
species. Under and on top of clean sand in 1-15 m; appears
to feed upon polychaete worms.

Philinopsis sp. 2
Size: 30 mm   Papua New Guinea, Philippines
ID: Entirely black; another species of "bubble headed"
Philinopsis. On the surface of mixed sand and patch reefs
in 10 m.

369

Philinopsis pilsbryi (Eliot, 1900)
Size: 40 mm   Widespread in the Indo-Pacific
ID: White to yellowish with irregular black lines forming a reticulate pattern; the width of the black lines varies

considerably; another species of "bubble headed" _Philinopsis_. Either buried or crawling on the surface of sand.

Philinopsis sp. 3
Size: 35 mm   Australia, New Caledonia
ID: White with dense brown spots on the dorsum; external surface of the parapodia dark brown with large white to pale brown spots. Shallow sandy areas, often crawling on the surface.

Philinopsis falciphallus Gosliner, 2011
Size: 9 mm   Indonesia, Philippines
ID: Magenta with black margins and numerous yellow and orange spots over the surface; hind end of the posterior shield blunt with a long rounded lobe. On shallow water silty habitats were is active at night.

Philinopsis coronata Gosliner, 2011
Size: 28 mm   Indonesia
ID: Translucent white with numerous yellow spots on the headshield, parpodia and mantle; reddish spots on the margin of the parapodia and headshield; a rounded lobe at the posterior end of the mantle. On coral rubble in 12 m.

Philinopsis buntot Gosliner, 2015
Size: 30 mm   Philippines
ID: White with irregular brown pigment and numerous yellow spots along the notal margin; similar to lightly colored animals of _Philinopsis speciosa_, but with a distinctive elongate "tail" at the posterior end of the body. Crawling at night on clean sandy bottoms in 3-7 m.

Philinopsis aliciae Gosliner, 2015
Size: 30 mm   Philippines
ID: Translucent yellowish white with a dense pattern of brown mottling; headshield elongate with an expanded posterior lobe; posterior "tails" short and abbreviated; parapodia extending to the posterior end of the mantle. On sand in 3 m at night.

Philinopsis orientalis (Baba, 1949)
Size: 25 mm   Indian and western Pacific oceans
ID: Green with small opaque white spots; transverse bars of opaque white with smaller areas of yellow pigment. On reefs and under coral rubble in 1-15 m.

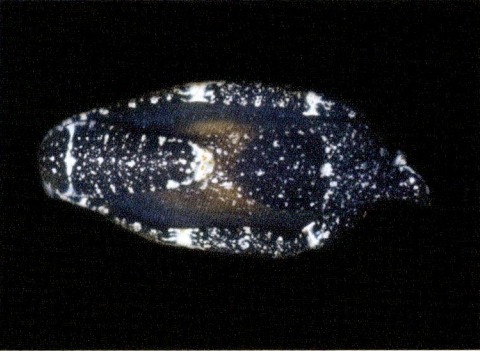

Philinopsis sp. 4
Size: 20 mm   Hawai'ian Is.
ID: Black with white pigment and some orange spots; similar to *Philinopsis orientalis* but is not as elongate, lacks the broad transverse opaque white bands and has more elongate, pointed "tails." In association with mixed sand and algae in 1 m.

Philinopsis sp. 5
Size: 15 mm   Indonesia, Japan
ID: Brownish-green with conspicuous red markings and fine white punctuations with a series of lines between them forming reticulations; notum covered with tubercles.

Philinopsis sp. 6
Size: 10 mm   Vanuatu, Palau
ID: Black with irregular white patches and small yellow dots; notum covered with tubercles.

Philinopsis sp. 7
Size: 5 mm   Papua New Guinea
ID: White with dark brown pigment on the notum; head with red and yellow markings. Similar to *Philinopsis falciphallus* and *P. coronata* but with an elongate extension of the posterior shield.

Mariaglaja sandrana (Rudman, 1973)

Size: 20 mm   Indian and western Pacific oceans
ID: Color highly variable, usually black with scattered or concentrated opaque white pigment and orange spots that may be surrounded by opaque white, forming a floral pattern. *Chelidonura babai* and *Chelidonura tsurugensis* are synonyms as they are genetically indistinguishable. Commonly on sand down to 15 m; feeds on acoel flatworms.

Mariaglaja inornata (Baba, 1949)
Size: 50 mm   Western and central Pacific Ocean
ID: Black with small white spots and a broad white band on the head; also red-orange spots on the head and additional

orange spots may be present on the headshield and posterior shield. Often in large breeding associations on shallow living reefs; feeds upon small flatworms.

Mariaglaja mandraroa (Gosliner, 2011)
Size: 30 mm   Indian and western Pacific oceans
ID: Black with burnt orange markings outlined in yellow. Crawling in the open on reef flats in rubble areas, 4-10 m.

Mariaglaja alexisi (Gosliner, 2015)
Size: 30 mm   Philippines
ID: Black, with or without white spots; head with four lobes anteriorly; posterior left "tail" broad and elongate, right one much shorter. On silty sand in 20 m, active at night.

Aglaja fulvipunctata (Baba, 1938)
Size: 30 mm   Widespread in the Indo-Pacific
ID: Black with yellow or white spots; an opaque white W-

shaped marking on the head. Crawling on the surface of sand in shallow water in 1-10 m; feeds on acoel flatworms.

Aglaja sp.
Size: 30 mm   Maui, Hawai'ian Is.
ID: Translucent grey with numerous opaque white markings and yellow pigment on the anterior and posterior ends. Shallow water among rubble.

Chelidonura electra Rudman, 1970
Size: 80 mm   Indian and western Pacific oceans
ID: White with yellow lines on the margins of the parapodia. Frequently in silty or sandy habitats inside bays; feeds on acoel flatworms.

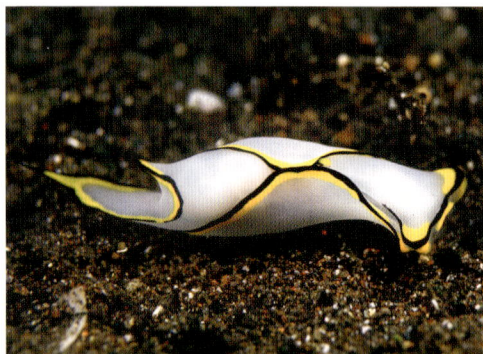

Chelidonura pallida Risbec, 1951
Size: 50 mm   Eastern Indian and western Pacific oceans
ID: White with yellow and black lines around the edges. On shallow patch reefs; presumably feeds on small flatworms.

Chelidonura varians Eliot, 1903
Size: 70 mm   Western Pacific Ocean
ID: Black with electric blue marginal and mid-dorsal lines and elongate "tails;" one of the largest species of *Chelidonura*. Commonly in 1-20 m crawling over the surface of clean, white sand; presumably feeds on acoel flatworms.

Chelidonura castanea Yonow, 1994
Size: 25 mm   Indian Ocean
ID: Brownish with yellow spots and white margins of the parapodia.

Chelidonura punctata Eliot, 1903
Size: 40 mm   Indian Ocean
ID: Black with yellow spots; white pigment may be present along the margins of the parapodia and along the posterior end of the headshield. Crawling over the surface of coral reefs.

Chelidonura flavolobata Heller & Thompson, 1983
Size: 60 mm   Red Sea
ID: Black with two whitish or yellowish lobes on the anterior sides of the head. Crawling in the open of living reefs and in sandy areas.

Chelidonura sp.
Size: 15 mm   Subtropical South Africa
ID: Uniformly white; as in *Odontoglaja*, this species has a vestigial radula. Under rocks and sand in the intertidal zone.

Chelidonura hirundinina (Quoy & Gaimard, 1833)
Size: 30 mm   Widespread in the Indo-Pacific
ID: Black with a variable pattern of blue, orange, and white markings, always with a T-shaped marking on the head. *Chelidonura philinopsis* is a synonym. Currently considered one of the most common and widespread species of *Chelidonura*, but molecular data suggest it could be a species complex; common on rocky or sandy substrates in shallow water; feeds upon small acoel flatworms like *Convoluta* and swallows them whole with the aid of a muscular pharynx.

Chelidonura alisonae Gosliner, 2011
Size: 30 mm   Central Pacific, Easter Is.
ID: Black with a network of orange pigment and bright blue spots, mainly on the mantle edge and anterior and posterior ends of the body; similar to *Chelidonura hirundinina* but lacks the T-shaped marking. On intertidal reef platforms and in rubble areas, 1-5 m.

***Chelidonura amoena* Bergh, 1905**
Size: 55 mm   Western Pacific Ocean
ID: Whitish with yellow marginal lines on the parapodia, headshield and posterior shield, with varying amounts of

grey pigment. In 10-20 m crawling in the open on living reefs; feeds on acoel flatworms.

***Chelidonura livida* Yonow, 1994**
Size: 80 mm   Western Indian Ocean
ID: Brown to black with bright blue spots rather than continuous lines, concentrated near the edge of the parapodia, but also on the cephalic shield; some specimens

with opaque white spots on the dorsum and sides. Sandy habitats in shallow water from 2-20 m. Possibly also present in northern Australia, the Philippines, and Indonesia

***Melanochlamys* sp.**
Size: 30 mm   Indonesia
ID: Shades of brown with no distinctive markings; inflated rounded body with twin "tails" very short and of nearly equal length.

Colpodaspidae Oskars, Bouchet & Malaquias, 2015

Animal with a small internal shell and elongate, acutely pointed appedange on the right side of the animal. The posterior end of the foot is elongate and tapered. Some species have an opening in the mantle through which the shell is visible. Nothing is known about the biology of the members of this family. Recent phylogenetic studies (Oskars et al. 2015) have shown that this family is most closely related to Gastropteridae

Colpodaspis thompsoni Brown, 1979
Size: 3 mm   Widespread in the Indo-Pacific
D: Body black with white and yellow patches that
resemble fried eggs; head with two pale grey dorso-
lateral channels that enter the rhinophores; notum
covering the shell. Generally on the underside of
coral rubble.

Colpodaspis sp. 1
Size: 5 mm   Madagascar
ID: Body black; notum covering the shell, also black with
white opaque white spots. Crawls on the surface of clean
white sand in about 10 m.

Colpodaspis sp. 2
Size: 5 mm   Philippines, Indonesia
ID: Body blue to black with small opaque white spots on the
visceral mass; head orange with a black margin; visceral
appendage elongate, opaque white. On silty slopes in 5-15 m.

Colpodaspis sp. 3
Size: 5 mm   Indonesia
ID: Body opaque white with brown to black markings on
the head, visceral mass and visceral appendage; visceral
appendage long.

Colpodaspis sp. 4
Size: 5 mm   Papua New Guinea
ID: Body reddish with small opaque white spots; visceral
appendage elongate, same color as body; like the preceding
species, has a distinct opening in the mantle. Silty slopes on
sea grass in shallow water.

Colpodaspis sp. 5
Size: 5 mm   Kenya
ID: Body black with yellow spots all over the body; visceral appendage and foot short.

Colpodaspis sp. 6
Size: 4 mm   Japan
ID: Black with opaque white spots and large white pustules; visceral appendage of medium length, white with purple tip.

Gastropteridae Swainson, 1840

Relatively small cephalaspideans with a small internal shell. They lack a gizzard, but have a radula. They are capable of swimming by flapping their large parapodia. Some species feed on sponges whereas others are probably generalist carnivores. They have been reviewed by Gosliner (1989).

Sagaminopteron is characterized by having a funnel shaped siphon with an internal crest and a relatively broad body, *Siphopteron* and *Gastropteron* also have a siphon with a medial ridge but the former has a smaller body size and a rounded visceral mass and the latter a reduced number of teeth. Finally, *Enotepteron* has large spheres in the parapodia.

Gastropteron bicornutum Baba & Tokioka, 1965
Size: 15 mm   Western Pacific Ocean
ID: Whitish with black or yellow pigment; two conical appendages on the posterior shield and an elongate filament on the posterior end of the foot. Crawling on sand in 3-10 m.

Gastropteron viride Tokioka & Baba, 1964
Size: 5 mm   Japan
ID: Translucent yellowish green with bright orange spots on the posterior end of the headshield, the middle of the mantle and the posterior extension, as well as on the sides of the parapodia; parapodia with opaque white margins. In 26-70 m.

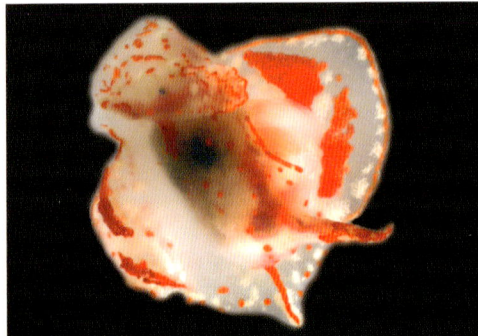

Gastropteron sp. 1
Size: 6 mm   Indonesia
ID: Bright orange with scattered opaque white spots.

Gastropteron sp. 2
Size: 5 mm   Philippines
ID: Off-white with red pigment all over the body; flagellum elongate; foot with a posterior extension. Shallow water under coral rubble.

Gastropteron multo Ong & Gosliner *in* **Ong, Hallas & Gosliner, 2017**
Size: 20 mm   Philippines
ID: Translucent white with bright orange spots on the posterior headshield, mantle, posterior extension, and sides of the parapodia; posterior end of mantle with a rounded medial bump and an elongate lobe. On silty or sand in 5-15 m.

Gastropteron sp. 3
Size: 10 mm   Indonesia
ID: Translucent bluish with irregular bright red patches on the headshield, parapodia and posterior extension.

Gastropteron minutum Ong & Gosliner *in* **Ong, Hallas & Gosliner, 2017**
Size: 3 mm   Western and central Pacific Ocean
ID: White with flecks of brown; body minute, covered in irregular rounded tubercles; long, thin posterior extension at end of the mantle; foot tapering into a thin, elongate extension posteriorly. Rocky or sandy habitats in 1-15 m.

Gastropteron sp. 4
Size: 6 mm   Philippines
ID: Red, with lighter mottling over the surface and minute white spots evenly scattered.

Sagaminopteron ornatum Tokioka & Baba, 1964
Size: 15 mm   Western Pacific Ocean
ID: Uniformly bright purple with yellowish orange on the siphon, posterior appendage and posterior end of the visceral mass; white on siphonal ridge. Coral rubble, 20-25 m.

Sagaminopteron sp. 1
Size: 15 mm   Philippines
ID: Bright purple with orange pigment; white lines on the margins of the parapodia, posterior shield and tail; flagellum very conspicuous, reddish to orange. Feeds on sponges of the genus *Dysidea* in 10-25 m.

Sagaminopteron psychedelicum Carlson & Hoff, 1974
Size: 20 mm   Widespread in the Indo-Pacific
ID: Cream with a series of blue and green irregular markings.
At 1-3 m depth feeds upon the rubbery green sponge,
Dysidea cf. *herbacea*, in deeper water, down to 25 m,
feeds upon the grey sponge, *Dysidea* sp., together with
Sagaminopteron nigropunctatum.

Sagaminopteron nigropunctatum Carlson & Hoff,
1973
Size: 8 mm   Indian and western Pacific oceans
ID: Greyish, usually with orange spots. Subtidal reef habitats
on its prey, the grey sponge *Dysidea* sp., in 0-40 m; cryptic
on the sponge.

Sagaminopteron bilealbum Carlson & Hoff, 1973
Size: 15 mm   Philippines, Guam
ID: Opaque white with scattered orange spots; a series
of tubercles over the surface of the body. Intertidally on a
greenish white sponge, *Dysidea* cf. *herbacea*.

Sagaminopteron sp. 2
Size: 8 mm   Western Pacific Ocean
ID: Purplish with yellow markings around the short siphon. In
2-3 m on an unidentified sponge in a protected lagoon.

Sagaminopteron pohnpei (Hoff & Carlson, 1983)
Size: 5 mm   Western and central Pacific Ocean
ID: Brown, reddish or orange, with opaque white spots;
flagellum absent. On sea grasses of the genus *Enhalus* or on
sand flats in protected bays.

Sagaminopteron multimaculatum Ong & Gosliner in Ong, Hallas & Gosliner, 2017
Size: 5 mm   Philippines
D: Green with opaque white patches, scattered yellow spots, and lighter green flecks; parapodial margins orange; posterior extension of mantle absent; posterior end of headshield short with a dark apex. Clean sandy habitats in 7 m.

Siphopteron sp. 1
Size: 5 mm   Vanuatu
ID: White with yellow parapodial margins; a large brown spot with opaque white and black concentric rings on both parapodial lobes; apex of the posterior extension of the headshield black.

Siphopteron brunneomarginatum (Carlson & Hoff, 1974)
Size: 5 mm   Western and central Pacific Ocean
ID: Yellow with brown margins; a short flagellum with a line of brown extending laterally to it. Under coral rubble in shallow water. Records of this species from the Indian Ocean need confirmation.

Siphopteron citrinum (Carlson & Hoff, 1974)
Size: 4 mm   Guam, Japan
ID: Pinkish or yellowish with black pigment on the tip of the siphon and flagellum, but absent from the parapodial margin. Shallow water on coral rubble.

Siphopteron flavum (Tokioka & Baba, 1964)
Size: 6 mm   Western and central Pacific Ocean
ID: Yellow and black with an elongate visceral bump; lacks a distinctly elongate flagellum; some specimens may have black pigment on the posterior shield. On shallow reefs from 10-20 m.

Siphopteron fuscum (Baba & Tokioka, 1965)
Size: 10 mm   Tropical Japan
ID: Brown with white spots and red pigment on the tip of the siphon and flagellum. On shallow reefs.

Siphopteron nigromarginatum Gosliner, 1989
Size: 5 mm   Western Pacific Ocean
ID: Bluish with yellow irregular markings and orange pigment on the visceral mass; parapodial margin thin and black; black

pigment on the flagellum but not extending laterally to it parapodia not overlapping. On shallow reefs to 20 m under coral rubble.

Siphopteron michaeli (Gosliner & Williams, 1988)
Size: 5 mm   Western Indian Ocean
ID: Yellow-orange with purple spots of varying sizes; black pigment on the siphon and flagellum. Intertidally and on shallow fringing reefs under rocks and coral rubble.

Siphopteron quadrispinosum Gosliner, 1989
Size: 5 mm   Hawai'ian Is.
ID: Yellow with a red siphon and flagellum. *Siphopteron leah* is a synonym. On sandy slopes and in areas of coral rubble in 3-15 m.

Siphopteron leah Klussman-Klob & Klussman, 2013
Size: 5 mm   Western Pacific Ocean
ID: Yellow with red markings on the siphon, headshield, flagellum and posterior shield; white often present on the anterior end of posterior shield; parapodial marginal bands absent. Shallow water under coral rubble, 10 m.

Siphopteron sp. 2
Size: 5 mm   Indonesia
ID: Uniformly chocolate brown with yellow spots and opaque white patches; posterior end of headshield elongate; posterior extension of mantle absent. Sandy habitats in 1-15 m.

Siphopteron tigrinum Gosliner, 1989
Size: 10 mm   Indian and western Pacific oceans
ID: Orange with elongate bluish purple markings over the body; black pigment on the siphon and flagellum. On the undersurface of coral rubble in 1-10 m.

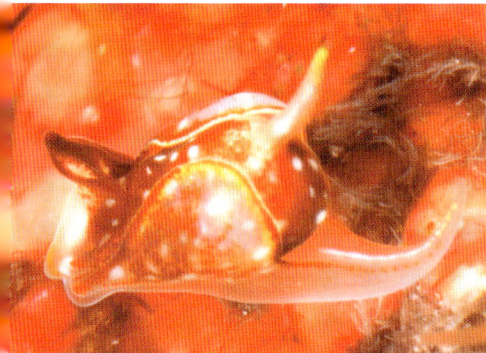

Siphopteron vermiculum Ong & Gosliner *in* Ong, Hallas & Gosliner, 2017
Size: 4 mm   Philippines
ID: Translucent white with dense areas of vermilion red; opaque white and orange spots scattered over the body; parapodial margin opaque white; posterior end of the headshield elongate; posterior extension of the mantle elongate with an orange and vermilion apex. Clean sandy habitats in 7 m.

Siphopteron makisig Ong & Gosliner *in* Ong, Hallas & Gosliner, 2017
Size: 5 mm   Philippines, Indonesia, Australia
ID: White with yellow and orange parapodial and headshield margins; an orange ring surrounding the short posterior extension of mantle; posterior end of headshield elongate; foot with a medial yellow line. In 10 m on shallow reefs.

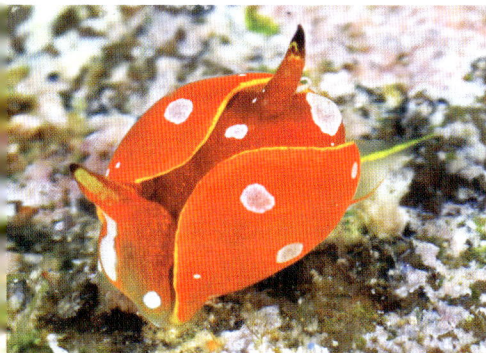

Siphopteron flavolineatum Ong & Gosliner *in* Ong, Hallas & Gosliner, 2017
Size: 7 mm   Philippines, Malaysia
ID: Ochre with a yellow parapodial margin; large opaque white spots on the body; posterior extension of the mantle

elongate, tip brown; posterior end of the headshield elongate with a yellow and brown apex; foot with a medial yellow line. Clean sandy habitats in 7 m.

Cephalaspidea - "head-shielded slugs"

Siphopteron nakakatuwa Ong & Gosliner *in* Ong, Hallas & Gosliner, 2017
Size: 8 mm   Philippines, Indonesia
ID: Orange with opaque white patches and orange parapodial margins; posterior extension of the mantle elongate, brown

with pigment extending below the base; posterior end of the headshield elongate, brown; foot with a medial white line. Clean sandy habitats in 7 m.

Siphopteron dumbo Ong & Gosliner *in* Ong, Hallas & Gosliner, 2017
Size: 3 mm   Philippines, Japan
ID: Pale yellow with pale blue on the margins of the parapodia, headshield, visceral mass and foot; black on siphon and flagellum. Moderately deep reefs, 20 m.

Siphopteron sp. 3
Size: 4 mm   Mozambique
ID: White with patches of orange over the entire body; dark brown pigment on the siphon and on the posterior shield, where it extends on to the short flagellum. Under small rocks, 1 m.

Siphopteron sp. 4
Size: 5 mm   Indonesia
ID: Yellow orange with opaque white patches on the head, visceral mass and foot; reddish lines on the headshield and visceral mass; visceral appendage short, same color as the body; posterior end of the headshield with an elongate reddish appendage.

Siphopteron ladrones (Carlson & Hoff, 1974)
Size: 5 mm   Indian and western Pacific oceans
ID: Opaque white with a medial orange line on the head and a network of orange pigment surrounding white spots. Under coral rubble in 1-16 m.

Siphopteron sp. 5
Size: 5 mm   Indian Ocean
ID: Lemon-yellow with dark brown margins and lines on the headshield, parapodia, and visceral mass; visceral mass with an opaque white central region; posterior extension of the mantle elongate, apex brown; posterior end of the headshield elongate, brown. On shallow rocky reefs in 9 m.

Siphopteron sp. 6
Size: 8 mm   Indonesia
ID: White with yellow parapodial margins and lines; headshield edged in crimson; visceral mass with concentric rings of yellow and crimson; posterior extension of the mantle elongate, with a crimson apex; posterior end of headshield elongate, crimson; foot with a medial yellow line.

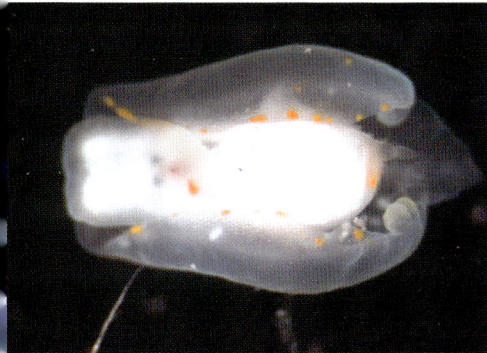

Enotepteron rosewateri Gosliner, 1988
Size: 4 mm   Indian and western Pacific oceans
ID: White with scattered orange spots; two minute rounded structures at the posterior margin of the parapodia. Among coral rubble in intertidal and shallow reefs to 4 m.

Enotepteron cf. rubropunctatum Hamatani, 2013
Size: 10 mm   Japan
ID: Dark brown with opaque white spots, red lines and large spots on the surface. Shallow water, from tidepools to the subtidal of 10 m.

Philinoglossidae Hertling, 1932

This family includes colorless, very elongate, worm-like cephalaspideans adapted to interstitial life (between sand grains). They are normally very small, less than 3 mm in length, have a small vestigial shell on the posterior part of the body or lack a shell completely. These animals are very difficult to find and collecting requires the use specialized techniques.

Philinoglossa sp.
Size: 1 mm   Vanuatu
ID: Translucent, with the internal organs visible through the skin; body very elongate. Between sand grains.

Pteropoda - "pteropods"

This is a group of pelagic opisthobranchs with heavily modified bodies, adapted to live in the water column. Molecular studies suggest pteropods are closely related to cephalaspideans and sea hares (Klussmann-Kolb & Dinapoli 2006). In this section a few examples of Indo-Pacific pteropods are illustrated to show their morphological diversity, but not as an attempt to provide a comprehensive guide for identification. The taxonomy of Pteropoda needs a substantial amount of revisionary work, some species appear to constitute complexes of several species with restricted ranges, whereas other species have broad ranges including several oceans (Jennings et al., 2010).

Pneumoderma cf. peroni (Cuvier, 1817)
Size: 15 mm   Tropical oceans
ID: Transparent body with two anterior lateral wings, short rhinophores, and a lateral appendage near the posterior end; shell absent. Feeds on zooplankton.

Styliola subula (Quoy & Gaimard, 1827)
Size: 13 mm   Cosmopolitan
ID: Transparent body and shell; shell needle-like, long and narrow, tapering into a distal narrow end. Feeds on phytoplankton in the epipelagic.

Cuvierina columnella (Rang, 1827)
Size: 10 mm   Cosmopolitan
ID: Transparent body and shell; shell bottle-shaped. Several subspecies have been described for regional forms but their validity is unclear. Feeds on phytoplankton in the epipelagic.

Diacria trispinosa (Blainville, 1821)
Size: 10 mm   Cosmopolitan
ID: Transparent body and shell; shell flat with three elongate posterior spines, the central one much longer than the rest. Feeds on phytoplankton in the epipelagic.

Cavolinia uncinata (d'Orbigny, 1834)
Size: 8 mm   Cosmopolitan
ID: Transparent body and shell; shell globose, with three triangular posterior spines, the central one larger than the two elongate lateral ones. Indo-Pacific animals are genetically distinct from the Atlantic and likely constitute a different species. Feeds on phytoplankton in the epipelagic.

Cavolinia tridentata (Forsskål *in* Niebuhr, 1775)
Size: 20 mm   Cosmopolitan
ID: Transparent body and shell; shell globose, with three triangular posterior spines, the two lateral ones very short. Three subspecies are currently recognized but their validity is uncertain. Feeds on phytoplankton in the epipelagic.

Clio pyramidata Linnaeus, 1767
Size: 20 mm   Cosmopolitan
ID: Transparent body and shell; shell flat, rhomboid, tapering into a elongate posterior end. Feeds on phytoplankton and protozoa in the epipelagic.

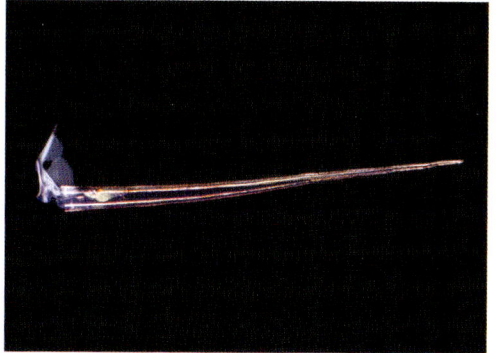

Creseis clava (Rang, 1828)
Size: 6 mm   Cosmopolitan
ID: Transparent body and shell; shell straight, needle-like, long and narrow. Feeds on phytoplankton in the epipelagic.

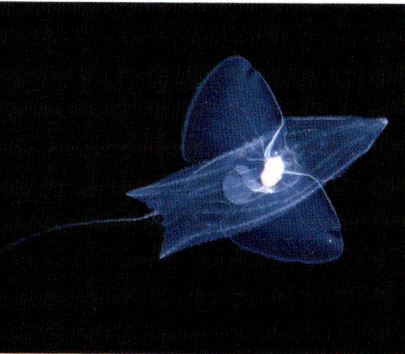

Cymbulia peronii Blainville, 1818
Size: 20 mm   Cosmopolitan
ID: Transparent body, with a cartilaginous pseudoconch having spines arranged in rows; sides of the body with two large separate "wings" and posterior end with an elongate filament; shell absent.

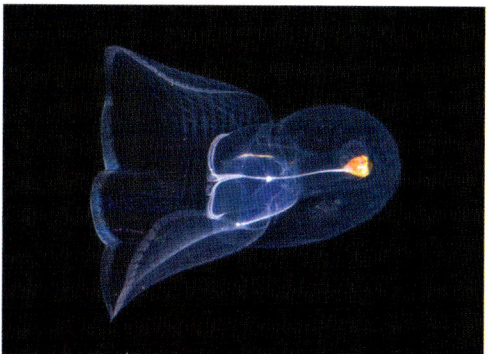

Corolla spectabilis Dall, 1871
Size: 20 mm   Cosmopolitan
ID: Transparent body, with a cartilaginous pseudoconch having numerous small tubercles; two large "wings" fused together posteriorly; shell absent.

Runcinida - "runcinids"

Recent studies (Malaquias *et al.*, 2008; Oskars *et al.*, 2015) clearly show that this group represents a distinct, basal lineage that is quite distinct from other heterobranch sea slugs that have gizzard plates.

Runcinidae H. Adams & A. Adams, 1854

The Runcinidae includes many species of small sea slugs with an internal shell. They generally are less than 5 mm in length and have four striated gizzard plates. Most runcinids look like very small, worm-like slugs, probably the smallest species overall. They can be seasonally and locally extremely abundant, with population explosions that last a few days or weeks. Very little is known on their habits and food source, although they are probably herbivorous animals.

Very few species have been found in the Indo-Pacific and they appear to be more diverse in temperate regions. The species from the tropical areas of the Indian and Pacific oceans are in need of far more detailed study.

***Metaruncina setoensis* (Baba, 1954)**
Size: 15 mm   South Africa, Japan, Marshall Is
ID: Uniformly dark; one of the longest species of runcinid
Commonly in intertidal and shallow subtidal areas; feeds on
filamentous algae.

***Runcina* sp. 1**
Size: 3 mm   Western Indian Ocean
ID: Uniformly reddish-brown with minute darker spots. It may be the same as other similarly colored species found throughout the Indo-Pacific, the systematics of this group is poorly understood. Among filamentous green algae in shallow intertidal pools.

***Runcina* sp. 2**
Size: 4 mm   Philippines
ID: Brownish with black marginal lines around the mantle and foot; foot with an elongate posterior extension. On the surface of sandy substrates.

***Ilbia mariana* Hoff & Carlson, 1990**
Size: 3 mm   Western and central Pacific
ID: White pigment with a series of yellow spots over the notum. On shallow reefs in association with filamentous algae.

Anaspidea - "sea hares"

Sea hares are a group of herbivorous sea slugs that often have widespread distributions. Most species have an internal shell and secrete purple ink as a defense mechanism. Although these animals are normally large and many species are abundant, there are problems with the taxonomy of the group and it is often difficult to identify and distinguish species. The phylogeny of this group has been studied by Medina & Walsh (2000) and Klussmann-Kolb (2004).

Akeridae Mazzarelli, 1891

Members of this family have an external shell and a well developed headshield. They retain many cephalaspidean characteristics, but also have several features of their internal anatomy that they share with other anaspideans.

Akera soluta (Gmelin, 1791)
Size: 70 mm   Indian and western Pacific ocean
ID: Body pale brown with white spots; shell semi-translucent so that the tissue below is visible. Burrows in silty to muddy habitats. Appears to feed on Cyanobacteria and algae.

Akera sp.
Size: 20 mm   Vanuatu
ID: Body grey with black spots; shell translucent; body more elongate and shell more compact than in *Akera soluta*. Burrows in sandy to muddy habitats from the intertidal to 5 m.

Aplysiidae Lamarck, 1809

Sea hares with internal shells are included in the Aplysiidae. Species may have large or reduced parapodia and may be dorso-ventrally flattened. This is not a highly diverse group of herbivorous sea slugs and many species are widely distributed. Sea hares feed primarily on red algae, but will feed on a variety of algal species when their preferred food is not present. Most species live in shallow waters, where algal diversity is highest.

The last attempt to review this group was published by Eales (1960) and it did not include descriptions of living animals. A new world-wide revision of *Aplysia* is necessary to determine species boundaries and guidelines for identification of species.

Aplysia juliana Quoy & Gaimard, 1832
Size: 200 mm   Circumtropical
ID: Color variable, light with dark spots or uniformly dark brown; posterior portion of the foot used as a sucker to adhere to the substrate. It does not secrete purple ink.

Aplysia sp.
Size: 70 mm   Western and central Pacific Ocean
ID: Mottled white and brown; margins of the parapodia highly convoluted. Shallow water rocky substrates; feeds on red algae. Previously confused with *Aplysia pulmonica*, which is a synonym of *A. argus*.

Aplysia argus Rüppell & Leuckart, 1830
Size: 200 mm   Indo-Pacific, tropical eastern Pacific
ID: Color variable, often with large black rings present on the mantle; margins of the parapodia usually highly convoluted.

Aplysia oculifera A. Adams & Reeve, 1850
Size: 80 mm   Widespread in the Indo-Pacific
ID: Color variable with small black rings and abundant opaque white spots. Shallow reef and rubble habitats in 1-10 m; capable of swimming by flapping its parapodia.

Aplysia extraordinaria (Allan, 1932)
Size: 400 mm   New Zealand, eastern Australia
ID: Brownish with darker brown lines on the head; parapodia large and thin. Shallow water bays; it produces large amounts of purple ink when disturbed and swims by flapping its parapodia.

Aplysia parvula Mörch, 1863
Size: 70 mm   Circumtropical
ID: Variable in color from light brown with spots to uniformly dark brown; shell visible through a large round opening in the mantle. Shallow water rocky substrates where it feeds on red algae. Molecular evidence suggest this is a species complex and a new name may be needed for the Indo-Pacific species.

Syphonota geographica (A. Adams & Reeve, 1850)
Size: 100 mm   Circumtropical
ID: Elaborate patterns of green and white; distinguishable by its high parapodia and short "neck." Nocturnal, lives in sandy habitats where it feeds on brown algae; capable of swimming by flapping its parapodia.

Dolabella auricularia (Lightfoot, 1786)
Size: 500 mm   Indo-Pacific and eastern Pacific
ID: Greenish-grey; it can be immediately distinguished by its discoidal hind end that makes it look like the posterior of the animal was chopped off. During the day under coral heads or stones, emerges at night to forage.

Stylocheilus striatus (Quoy & Gaimard, 1832)
Size: 50 mm   Circumtropical
D: Brownish with longitudinal lines and blue spots. Sometimes misidentified as *Stylocheilus longicaudus*. Often feeding on filamentous Cyanobacteria in sandy and rocky habitats.

Stylocheilus longicaudus (Quoy & Gaimard, 1825)
Size: 30 mm   Circumtropical
ID: Yellowish with large blue spots and no lines. On floating algae such as *Sargassum* where presumably feeds on epiphytic Cyanobacteria. *Stylocheilus citrinus* is a synonym.

Bursatella leachii leachii de Blainville, 1817
Size: 150 mm   Widespread in the Indo-Pacific
D: Grey with blue ocelli; recognized by its elongate papillae. Shallow water environments usually on soft substrate; feeds on Cyanobacteria.

Notarchus indicus Schweigger, 1820
Size: 35 mm   Indo-Pacific and eastern Pacific
ID: Greenish or brown with scattered black spots and smaller opaque white and yellow dots. Characterized by a squat body and fused parapodia. Among *Sargassum* algae; swims by jet propulsion, expelling water from its siphon between the fused parapodia.

Petalifera lafonti (Fisher, 1870)
Size: 25 mm   Circumtropical
D: Grey with concentric rings of fine opaque white lines. Often misidentified as *Petalifera petalifera*, which is restricted to the Mediterranean. On the brown alga *Padina* feeding on epiphytic diatoms.

Petalifera ramosa Baba, 1959
Size: 70 mm   Circumtropical
ID: Greenish-grey with white ocelli; the elongate branched papillae at the tips of the rounded tubercles are distinctive. On *Sargassum*; capable of swimming by contracting its body dorso-ventrally.

Anaspidea - "sea hares"

Petalifera cf. edmundsi (Bebbington, 1974)
Size: 35 mm   Tanzania, Reunion Is., Philippines
ID: Green with opaque white and brown conical branched papillae; a much rougher body surface than *Petalifera ramosa*. On *Sargassum*.

Petalifera sp.
Size: 25 mm   Western Pacific Ocean
ID: Mottled greenish with a few opaque white spots. Under rocks on shallow reefs, in less than 3 m.

Phyllaplysia sp.
Size: 60 mm   Western Pacific Ocean
ID: Green with a series of green longitudinal lines and opaque white spots. Exclusively on the sea grass *Enhalus acoroides* during the day deep at the base of sea grass blades, emerges at night.

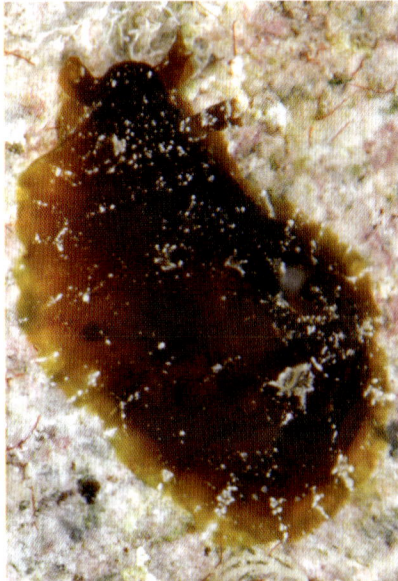

Dolabrifera dolabrifera (Rang, 1828)
Size: 60 mm   Widespread in the Indo-Pacific
ID: Color variable from pink to brown; always with short conical papillae that may have branched apices. Usually under rocks in areas dominated by coralline algae; appears to feed on Cyanobacteria and/or diatoms.

392

Sacoglossa - "sapsucking slugs"

This is a highly specialized group of herbivorous sea slugs They have a well-developed radula and mouth parts to pierce algal cells and suck out the contents. Representatives of most groups of sacoglossans are associated with species of the green algal genus *Caulerpa*. It has therefore been suggested that much of the initial evolution occurred in association with this alga. Primitive members have a shell, while more derived ones entirely lack a shell as adults. Molecular evidence suggest sacoglossans are closely related to marine pulmonate snails (Kocot *et al.*, 2013). The systematics of sacoglossans has been reviewed by Jensen (1996) and Maeda *et al.* (2010). Krug *et al.* (2015) produced a comprehensive phylogeny for this group.

Cylindrobullidae Thiele, 1931

Members of this group are among the most primitive sacoglossans with a well-developed shell. Some workers have placed them in the Cephalaspidea (Jensen, 1996), but other studies show that they share several derived features with the Sacoglossa (Mikkelsen, 1998).

Cylindrobulla sp. 1
Size: 10 mm   Hawai'ian Is.
ID: Body greyish-white; elongate headshield with two distinct lobes; shell translucent. Associated with the green alga *Halimeda* sp. in sandy habitats.

Cylindrobulla sp. 2
Size: 7 mm   Aldabra Atoll (western Indian Ocean)
ID: Body greyish-white; elongate headshield lobes; shell globose posteriorly, translucent white. Associated with algae and rubble in 1 m.

Cylindrobulla sp. 3
Size: 9 mm   Philippines
ID: Body greyish-white; headshield much longer than the shell; shell cylindrical and brownish. Associated with algae and rubble in 1 m.

Cylindrobulla sp. 4
Size: 5 mm   Papua New Guinea
ID: Body white with opaque white spots; shell thin and elongate, largely transparent; headshield broad, as long as the shell with flattened lobes. In 2 m, in sea grass and mangroves.

Cylindrobulla sp. 5
Size: 5 mm   Papua New Guinea
ID: Body white with opaque white spots; shell thin and elongate, largely transparent; shell apex elongate; headshield broad, much shorter than the shell, with flattened lobes. In 2 m, in sea grass and mangroves.

393

Sacoglossa - "sapsucking slugs"

Ascobulla fischeri (A. Adams & Angas, 1864)
Size: 12 mm   Widespread in the Indo-Pacific
ID: Body greyish-white; extensions of the headshield rounded and extending posteriorly; shell translucent greenish-white. Associated with *Caulerpa racemosa*.

Ascobulla sp. 1
Size: 15 mm   Papua New Guinea
ID: Body greyish-white; shell translucent; it appears to have a more elongate shell than *Ascobulla fischeri*. Among clumps of *Caulerpa racemosa* in mangrove lagoons.

Ascobulla sp. 2
Size: 8 mm   Philippines
ID: Body greyish-white; shell translucent greenish and much more rounded than the other species illustrated here. A thorough review of Indo-Pacific species is needed to establish variability. On shallow reefs among algae and coral rubble.

Volvatella vigourouxi (Montrouzier, 1861)
Size: 25 mm   New Caledonia, Hawai'ian Is.
ID: Body yellow orange; shell translucent, posteriorly swollen. *Volvatella fragilis* is probably a synonym. Associated with *Caulerpa taxifolia* in tidal pools.

Volvatella angeliniana Ichikawa, 1993
Size: 8 mm   Western Pacific Ocean
ID: Body white with cephalic shield lobes having orange tips; shell translucent, with opaque white spots. In 0-3 m.

Volvatella ventricosa Jensen & Wells, 1990
Size: 15 mm   Western and central Pacific Ocean
ID: Body white; shell green with a short posterior siphon. Associated with *Caulerpa racemosa* on shallow patch reefs.

Sacoglossa - "sapsucking slugs"

Volvatella sp. 1
Size: 12 mm   Widespread in the Indo-Pacific
ID: Body white; shell bright green with an elongate siphon. Feeds on *Caulerpa cupressina* in sandy habitats between reefs.

Volvatella sp. 2
Size: 8 mm   Papua New Guinea
ID: Body grey; shell white with a few orange spots and an elongate siphon. Shallow water in protected lagoons.

Volvatella sp. 3
Size: 10 mm   Western and central Pacific Ocean
ID: Body greyish white; shell lightly colored with a moderately long posterior end. Only on *Caulerpa racemosa*, in 10 m.

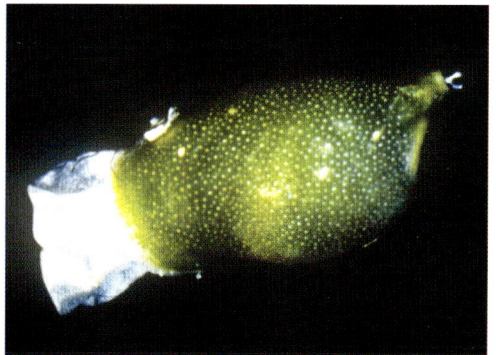

Volvatella sp. 4
Size: 10 mm   Okinawa (Japan)
ID: Body white; shell green with lighter green punctuations on the mantle visible through the shell. In 3 m.

Volvatella maculata Jensen, 2015
Size: 9 mm   Singapore, Philippines, Marshall Is.
ID: Body white; shell elongate with a narrow, elongate posterior siphon; shell and mantle white with rounded clear areas; headshield broad, much shorter than the shell, with short rounded lobes. In 8-20 m in areas with diverse green algal cover on patch reefs.

Volvatella sp. 5
Size: 8 mm   Philippines
ID: Body whitish-cream; shell elongate, whitish-cream; posterior end of the shell bulbous, posterior apex elongate; headshield broad, much shorter than shell, with short triangular lobes. In 14 m in association with *Caulerpa racemosa*.

Volvatella sp. 6
Size: 9 mm   French Polynesia
ID: Body white; shell yellowish with opaque white patches; similar to *Volvatella vigourouxi*, but with a more elongate shell and siphon.

Volvatella sp. 7
Size: 9 mm   Marshall Is.
ID: Body white; shell cream-white with yellowish spots; shell elongate, with a long posterior siphon; headshield broad much shorter than the shell with pointed triangular lobes. In association with *Caulerpa racemosa* in in 23 m.

Juliidae E. A. Smith, 1885

Members of this family have the unique characteristic of having two shell halves, like a clam. At one time they were thought to be a "missing link" between snails and clams, but this has been shown not to be the case and that their bivalved shell is derived secondarily from a coiled shell that splits during development. Juliids are tropical and temperate animals distributed throughout the world except for the eastern Atlantic and Mediterranean, where they are present only in the fossil record. They specialize in and are restricted to species of the lower intertidal and subtidal green alga *Caulerpa*. They may be locally common but extremely difficult to find because of their cryptic coloration.

Julia exquisita Gould, 1862
Size: 8 mm   Widespread in the Indo-Pacific
ID: Body green to brown with dark spots and white diffuse patches; shell green with radiating lines of spots on its surface. On moderately exposed rocky habitats in 1-15 m.

Sacoglossa - "sapsucking slugs"

Julia sp. 1
Size: 2 mm   Western and central Pacific Oceans
ID: Body brown with small white spots; shell with diffuse dark spots and larger white patches. Similar to *J. exquisita* but much smaller and the dark spots on the shell are larger and more diffuse.

Julia zebra Kawaguchi, 1981
Size: 5 mm   Widespread in the Indo-Pacific
ID: Body light brown with white and reddish spots; anterior portion of the shell with narrow, continuous brown bands, and broader, fainter bands on the posterior portion.

Julia sp. 2
Size: 4 mm   Widespread in the Indo-Pacific
ID: Body pale green with dark green mottling and numerous minute white dots except for two bands on the rhinophores;

shell light green with brownish radiating streaks containing oval white patches, and a larger red, triangular patch near the apex. On coral rubble in 30 m.

Julia sp. 3
Size: 2 mm   Western and central Pacific Oceans
ID: Body green with some opaque white patches; shell uniformly green, more oval than in other species of *Julia*.

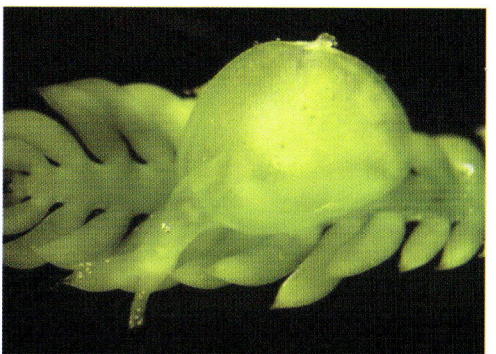

Berthelinia sp.
Size: 30 mm   Indian and western Pacific oceans
ID: Body green with some opaque white dots on the rhinophores and around the eyes; shell translucent with the green mantle visible through. In association with *Caulerpa*.

Berthelinia pseudochloris Kay, 1964
Size: 8 mm   Widespread in the Indo-Pacific
ID: Body green with opaque white dots more concentrated on the rhinophoral tips; shell translucent with the greenish mantle showing through, often with radiating bluish white lines and scattered, irregular, opaque white patches. In 1-3 m in association with *Caulerpa*.

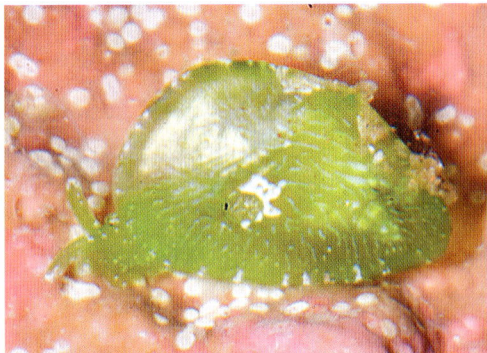

Oxynoidae Stoliczka, 1868

Members of this family have an oval shell, partially covering the center of the body. They also have a very elongate, thick "tail" that often use as a propeller to swim away from danger. Some species have lateral papillae around the shell that can also be used for swimming. Both the tail and the lateral papillae can be detached from the body in case of attack, and remain moving for a few minutes to attract the attention of potential predators, while the animal crawls away. The head has a pair of rolled rhinophores and lateral anterior prolongations of the foot. Species of Oxynoidae are associated with algae of the genus *Caulerpa* on which they feed and remain cryptic for long periods of time. Most species display various defensive behaviors, including secretion of white chemicals.

Oxynoe viridis (Pease, 1861)
Size: 20 mm   Widespread in the Indo-Pacific
ID: Green with yellowish areas; scattered blue spots surrounded by yellow and lacking black in the center; tail elongate. Associated with *Caulerpa racemosa*.

Oxynoe sp. 1 "kylei"
Size: 15 mm   Western and central Pacific Ocean
ID: Cream with a reticulate black pattern, some specimens with blue spots; body with large papillae. In association with *Caulerpa filicoides* in Guam and *Caulerpa fastigiata* in Palau; also found in the famed Jellyfish Lake of Palau.

Oxynoe sp. 2
Size: 20 mm   Western Pacific Ocean
ID: Green with scattered yellow blue spots having darker centers; parapodia covering the shell; foot elongate, thick. In association with *Caulerpa* sp.

Oxynoe sp. 3
Size: 50 mm   Tuamotu Archipelago
ID: Light green with elongate finger-like papillae some of which have opaque white tips; parapodia covering the shell; foot elongate. In association with *Caulerpa taxifolia* in 2 m.

Oxynoe sp. 4
Size: 7 mm   Philippines, Papua New Guinea
ID: Light green with blue spots; body with small conical papillae. It could be a color variety of *Oxynoe viridis*, further study is required. Shallow water in association with *Caulerpa racemosa*.

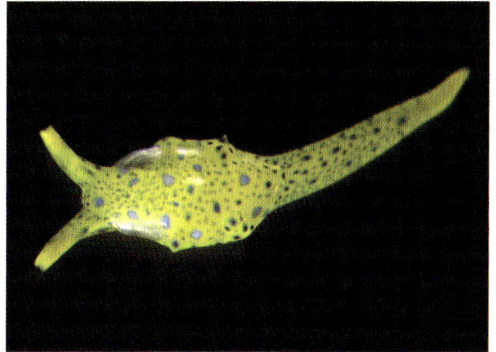

Oxynoe sp. 5 "jacksoni"
Size: 3 mm   Lord Howe Island (Australia)
ID: Pale white to bright yellow, with large blue ocelli surrounded by small blue spots, covering much of the body. Associated with *Caulerpa* sp.

Oxynoe sp. 6 "jordani"
Size: 22 mm   Philippines, Australia
ID: Pale green with abundant opaque white pigment on the body, parapodia, and "tail"; body covered with black spots surrounded by blue circles. Similar to *Oxynoe* sp. 2, could be the same species. Associated with *Caulerpa* sp.

Oxynoe sp. 7 "neridae"
Size: 9 mm   Lord Howe Island (Australia)
ID: Green with white, red and bright green spots; parapodial margin lined with dark green patches; parapodia with scattered white or blue papillae. Associated with *Caulerpa* sp.

Sacoglossa - "sapsucking slugs"

***Oxynoe* cf. *natalensis* E. A. Smith, 1903**
Size: 15 mm   South Africa, Madagascar
ID: Light green; rhinophores and margins of the parapodia yellowish, with scattered blue spots; parapodia scalloped, partially covering the shell; lobes very short, irregular; foot short.

***Lobiger* sp. 1**
Size: 15 mm   Widespread in the Indo-Pacific
ID: Green with white spots; shell lacking blue lines; lobes with elongate internal branches. Often confused with *Lobiger viridis*, it is distinguishable by the absence of blue lines on the shell, which are mentioned in the original description of *L. viridis*. Feeds on *Caulerpa racemosa* on shallow reefs; when disturbed, it erects its lobes that can also be shed.

***Lobiger viridis* Pease, 1863**
Size: 20 mm   Widespread in the Indo-Pacific
ID: Dark green with bright blue lines on the tissue below the reduced shell; lobes elongate. The Caribbean species *Lobiger souverbii* also has blue lines but it is genetically distinct. Feeds on *Caulerpa racemosa*; when disturbed, it erects its lobes, if disturbed further it can shed the lobes.

Caliphyllidae Tiberi, 1881

Members of this family have deeply divided and flattened rhinophores and leaf-like cerata. Caliphyllidiids feed on a large range of green algae including *Bryopsis*, *Udotea*, *Penicillus*, *Halimeda*, *Chlorodesmis*, *Valonia* and *Cladophora*. Most species shed the cerata when disturbed.

Cyerce nigricans (Pease, 1866)
Size: 40 mm   Indian and western Pacific oceans
ID: Black, with orange and bluish pigment; body with numerous flat cerata. On the filamentous green alga, *Chlorodesmis* sp.

Cyerce nigra Bergh, 1871
Size: 15 mm   Western Pacific Ocean
ID: Orange with a series of black and white lines on the head and the outer surface of the cerata. Feeds on the calcareous green alga *Udotea geppii* on sandy slopes in less than 10 m.

Cyerce kikutarobabai Hamatani, 1976
Size: 15 mm   Western Pacific Ocean
ID: Translucent grey, with dark pigment on the distal half of the cerata and an orange line along the apex. Among mixed rock and rubble, possibly in association with *Padina*.

Cyerce pavonina Bergh, 1888
Size: 30 mm   Widespread in the Indo-Pacific
ID: Color variable from translucent white to cream and pale brown; cerata papillate with a network of brown pigment. Among mixed rock and rubble usually in association with the green alga *Halimeda*.

Cyerce bourbonica Yonow, 2012
Size: 20 mm   Widespread in the Indo-Pacific
ID: Greyish with black and orange pigment; cerata opaque white with yellow pigment and smaller black spots; rhinophores with brown and white spots. Under coral rubble in shallow water on mixed sand and coral environments.

401

Sacoglossa - "sapsucking slugs"

Cyerce sp. 1
Size: 25 mm   Papua New Guinea
ID: Translucent white with dark green pigment on the notum; cerata transparent with opaque white markings on the apices. Under rubble on shallow patch reefs.

Cyerce sp. 2
Size: 30 mm   Western Pacific Ocean
ID: Translucent grey with dark and white pigment; cerata large, transparent, with black or brown reticulations surrounding yellow tubercles. On shallow patch reefs.

Cyerce sp. 3
Size: 20 mm   Philippines
ID: Cerata large, rounded and inflated, each with a red line and opaque white spots along outer margin. On shallow reefs, nocturnally active.

Cyerce sp. 4
Size: 18 mm   Philippines
ID: Body, head and cerata with network of fine brown lines; cerata large, rounded, with opaque white and yellowish spots; a yellow spot present anterior to eyes. Coral rubble, shallow reefs, 5 m.

Cyerce elegans Bergh, 1870
Size: 50 mm   Widespread in the Indo-Pacific
ID: Translucent white with radiating bands of opaque white on the cerata. Relatively shallow water in 1-10 m; it appears to feed on the alga, *Halimeda* sp.

Cyerce sp. 5
Size: 35 mm   Marshall Is.
ID: Translucent white with very broad, flat cerata; cerata with yellow spots and a series of opaque white spots just below the margins; head with reddish brown markings and fine lines. Under coral rubble in 8-10 m.

Mourgona sp. 1
Size: 20 mm   Hawai'ian Is.
ID: Translucent whitish with opaque white, purple and orange markings; clusters of dark purple immediately behind the eyes; cerata relatively wide with numerous papillae over the surface. Cerata move rhythmically when crawling. Active at night in 1-9 m.

Mourgona sp. 2
Size: 20 mm   Guam, Philippines
ID: Translucent grey; cerata translucent white with yellow pigment and smaller black spots; it lacks the brown and white spots present on the rhinophores of *Cyerce bourbonica*. Under coral rubble in shallow water on mixed sand and coral environments.

Mourgona sp. 3
Size: 15 mm   Philippines
ID: Translucent white with opaque white on the notum; brown spots on the head and rhinophores; margin of the cerata with scalloped appendages having opaque white spots. On filamentous green algae.

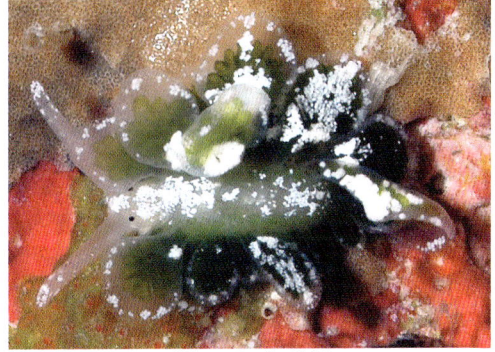

Mourgona osumi Hamatani, 1994
Size: 20 mm   Japan, Vanuatu
ID: Greenish-grey with white spots; cerata with few thick digestive gland branches readily visible. In association with the green alga *Penicillus* sp. in shallow water.

Mourgona sp. 4
Size: 20 mm   Philippines
ID: Cerata large, flattened, with a branched green digestive gland and opaque white lines along the outer edges. On large bubble algae colonies, 15 m.

Sohgenia palauensis Hamatani, 1991
Size: 15 mm   Indian and western Pacific oceans
ID: Green with encrusting white pigment behind the head and on the pericardium; cerata bulbous with opaque white pigment and small black spots. On coral rubble on shallow reefs.

Sacoglossa - "sapsucking slugs"

***Caliphylla* sp. 1**
Size: 40 mm   Hawai'ian Is.
ID: Green with dark pigment; cerata numerous, thin, flat, and green. The only described species of *Caliphylla* is *C. mediterranea*, but this one appears to be distinct. In association with the green alga, *Bryopsis* sp.

***Caliphylla* sp. 2**
Size: 30 mm   Indonesia
ID: White with fine light green spoting; cerata large, flat with highly branched digestive gland; eyes small, at the base of the rhinophores.

***Polybranchia orientalis* (Kelaart, 1858)**
Size: 70 mm   Indian and western Pacific Oceans
ID: Translucent brown with minute dark brown spots; cerata fan shaped, translucent and speckled with cinnamon brown throughout, with two dorso-medial yellowish patches, some specimens with single black dot; pericardium white. On *Caulerpa peltata*.

***Polybranchia jannae* Medrano, Krug, Gosliner, Kumar & Valdés, 2018**
Size: 20 mm   Western Pacific Ocean
ID: Translucent golden yellow with purple and orange spots on the body; white or yellow lines resembling cobweb present on the entire surface of the cerata; pericardium white.

***Polybranchia jensenae* Medrano, Krug, Gosliner, Kumar & Valdés, 2018**
Size: 20 mm   Widespread in the Indo-Pacific
ID: Translucent dark grey or completely translucent in juveniles, with small white papillae throughout body; cerata translucent olive green, fan shaped, with yellow or white pigment on the 2–3 larger papillae and white web-like network on the dorsal surface. Under rocks, feeds on *Caulerpa racemosa*.

***Polybranchia* sp. 1**
Size: 90 mm   Marshall Is.
ID: Translucent white with grey pigment on the broad, leafy cerata with irregular margins, bearing numerous small papillae. Under dead coral in 6 m.

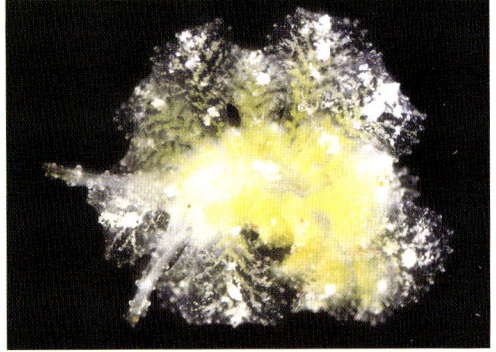

Sacoglossa - "sapsucking slugs"

Polybranchia samanthae Medrano, Krug, Gosliner, **Kumar & Valdés, 2018**
Size: 40 mm　　　　　　Widespread in the Indo-Pacific
ID: Pale olive-green to tan or brown, with evenly distributed small white papillae on dorsum; cerata translucent, olive green or dark tan; dorso-medial surface of the cerata with large green patch enclosed by dense white pigment on the dorsal surface. Found under rocks.

Polybranchia burni Medrano, Krug, Gosliner, Kumar **& Valdés, 2018**
Size: 10 mm　　　　　　　　Lord Howe Is. (Australia)
ID: Translucent with white patches formed of congregated dots between oral tentacles, below base of rhinophores, and on the pericardium; cerata with a single, large, white papillate knob on the dorso-medial surface. On the alga *Caulerpa sertularioides*.

***Polybranchia* sp. 2**
Size: 18 mm　　　　　　　　　　　　　Philippines
ID: Cerata large, flattened with golden brown digestive gland branches; fine black lines present along edge of cerata.

Limapontiidae J. E. Gray, 1847

Members of this family have long, simple rhinophores, sometimes with a lateral groove at the base. The eyes are normally visible behind the rhinophores. The cerata are variable in shape from globular to slender, absent in some species, internally with branches of the digestive gland. Members of *Costasiella* are characterized by having their eyes very close together.

Limapontiids feed and live on several green algae, although some species feed on eggs. Several species vary considerably in color, from black to green forms, depending on the depth at which they are found. A number of limapontiids can tolerate reduced salinities.

Placida barackobamai McCarthy, Krug & Valdés, **2017**
Size: 10 mm　　　　Western and central Pacific Oceans
ID: Rhinophores black with posterior white stripes from base to tip; oral tentacles black; foot corners yellow with black intrusions; proximal half of cerata yellow-orange, distal half black; foot yellow-orange from head to tail ventrally. In association with *Derbesia* sp.

Placida* cf. *kevinleei McCarthy, Krug & Valdés, **2017**
Size: 10 mm　　　　　　Widespread in the Indo-Pacific
ID: Rhinophores black with posterior white stripes from base to half-way up, apices completely black; oral tentacles black; foot corners yellow; proximal half of cerata yellow-orange, distal half black; foot yellow-orange from head to tail ventrally. In association with *Derbesia* sp.

Sacoglossa - "sapsucking slugs"

Placida sp. 1
Size: 8 mm   Philippines, Hawai'ian Is.
ID: Light green with dense dark green branches of the digestive gland and white spots. Many *Placida* species have been lumped under the name *Placida dendritica*, but they have distinctive branching patterns of the digestive gland and probably represent a complex of species. In association with the green alga, *Codium* sp.

Placida sp. 2
Size: 12 mm   Madagascar
ID: Light green with dark green branches of the digestive gland but less dense than in the previous species; cerata more sparse. In association with the green alga *Bryopsis* sp. on which it feeds.

Placida sp. 3
Size: 10 mm   Philippines
ID: Translucent light green with dark green branches of the digestive gland that completely fill the cerata; cerata with pointy white apices; branches in the rhinophores sparse.

Placida sp. 4
Size: 10 mm   Vanuatu, Mariana Is.
ID: Light green with dark green branches of the digestive gland that do not completely fill the cerata; branches in the rhinophores sparse. In association with green algae.

Placida sp. 5
Size: 8 mm   Philippines
ID: Translucent white; cerata translucent with opaque white spots and apices; a narrow opaque white patch on the center of the body with bright reddish markings; green digestive gland extends into the middle of the rhinophores. On filamentous green algae.

Placida sp. 6
Size: 15 mm   Saudi Arabian Red Sea
ID: Light green with opaque white pigment on the head and cerata; cerata elongate with white apices and green branches of the digestive gland; broad rounded foot, indented in the front end of the head.

Placida sp. 7
Size: 5 mm   Philippines
ID: Translucent white with branches of the digestive gland; cerata with opaque white dots; body broad with large part

of notum without cerata; slightly branched digestive gland extending into head. Shallow reefs on the green alga *Boodlea*.

Caulerpa mimic "Stiliger"
The following species constitute an undescribed genus that is genetically distinct from Stiliger. These animals live in close association with *Caulerpa* and most are remarkably camouflaged on it.

Placida sp. 8
Size: 8 mm   Philippines
ID: Short rounded cerata with acute apices; digestive gland extending into the rhinophores for their entire length. Shallow reefs on the green alga *Boodlea*.

Caulerpa mimic "Stiliger" sp. 1
Size: 5 mm   Guam and Midway Atoll
ID: Translucent with opaque white spots on the notum and rhinophores; brown branches of the digestive gland visible in the head; cerata covered with opaque white pigment. On patch reefs in lagoon environments.

Caulerpa mimic "Stiliger" smaragdinus Baba, 1949
Size: 30 mm   Central and western Pacific Ocean
ID: Uniform pale green; cerata green, spherical, resembling a clump of *Caulerpa racemosa*. Feeds on the green alga, *C. racemosa* on which it is well camouflaged.

Caulerpa mimic "Stiliger" sp. 2
Size: 30 mm   Malaysia, Marshall Is., Hawai'ian Is.
ID: With only a single bulbous swelling on cerata, "mushroom-shaped." Feeds on *Caulerpa racemosa*.

Sacoglossa - "sapsucking slugs"

Stiliger Ehrenberg, 1828

The following species are currently considered members of the genus *Stiliger,* which is not a natural group (Krug *et al.,* 2015) and probably will have to be synonymized with *Placida.*

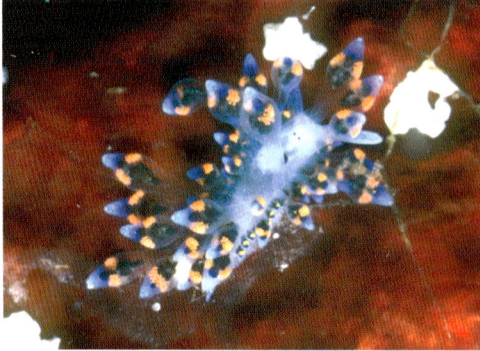

Stiliger sp. 1
Size: 8 mm   Western and central Pacific Ocean
ID: Bluish; cerata with yellow and blue; digestive gland dark. This species has been listed as a *Costasiella* since it eyes are relatively close together, but it appears to be an undescribed *Stiliger.*

Stiliger sp. 2
Size: 7 mm   Papua New Guinea
ID: Green with opaque white dots on the oral tentacles; cerata greenish with opaque white spots on the edges, widest near the base and narrowing to an acute tip. Under coral rubble in 10 m.

Stiliger sp. 3
Size: 5 mm   Papua New Guinea
ID: Light green with the reticulated digestive gland visible in the head; cerata with opaque white lines along the margins. Under coral rubble in 10 m.

Stiliger sp. 4
Size: 8 mm   Hawai'ian Is., tropical Japan
ID: Translucent with fine brown ducts visible through the body and cerata; rhinophores very elongate. On sandy substrate in 5 m.

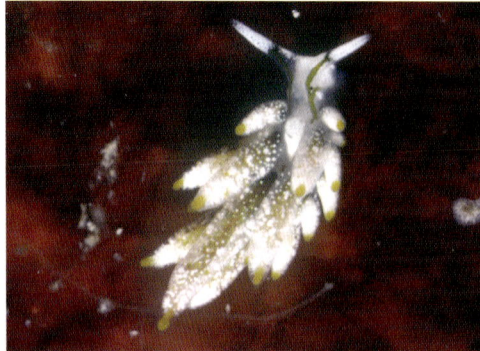

Stiliger sp. 5
Size: 10 mm   Papua New Guinea
ID: Opaque white; green branches of the digestive gland visible in the head; cerata translucent with abundant opaque white spots and orange tips. Under coral rubble in 8 m.

Stiliger sp. 6
Size: 10 mm   Philippines
ID: Translucent white with light green digestive gland branches within the cerata; cerata tips opaque white; a dark brown line on the head between the eyes; rhinophores contain branched digestive gland. On filamentous algae on sand in 7 m.

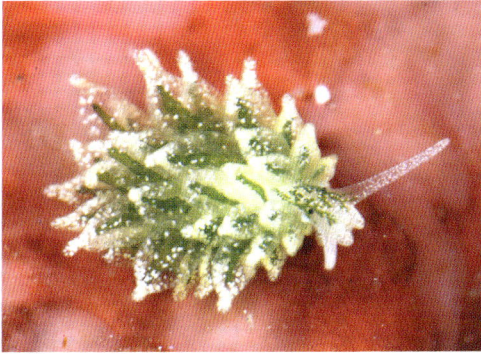

Stiliger sp. 7
Size: 6 mm   Philippines
ID: Translucent white with light green digestive gland branches within the cerata; cerata with elongate apices and scattered opaque white spots; branched digestive gland pigment on the head not extending into the rhinophores.

Stiliger sp. 8
Size: 25 mm   Philippines
ID: Translucent white with light green digestive gland branches; elongate cerata with apices densely packed with white pigment; a brownish longitudinal band present on the head. On filamentous algae on sand in 7 m.

Stiliger ornatus Ehrenberg, 1828
Size: 10 mm   Indian and western Pacific oceans
ID: Yellow with opaque white and black pigment; cerata yellow with black, blue and yellow subapical and apical bands; head with a yellow band; rhinophores black, each with yellow stripe. Feeds on *Codium* sp. in shallow water on patch reefs.

Stiliger sp. 9
Size: 10 mm   Philippines, Taiwan
ID: Orange-green with opaque white and black pigment; cerata green to orange with less prominent black, blue and yellow subapical and apical bands. Rhinophores dark without yellow stripes; head with blue spots. Feeds on *Codium* on shallow patch reefs.

Stiliger aureomarginatus Jensen, 1993
Size: 15 mm   Indian and western Pacific oceans
ID: Black with opaque white rhinophores at the base, and blue for most of their length; cerata black, bulbous with rounded yellow apices. Feeds on *Codium intricatum*.

Stiliger sp. 10
Size: 25 mm   Philippines
ID: Transparent with greenish yellow digestive gland branches in the center of the bulbous cerata; cerata with opaque white tips; rhinophores black on the apices; foot corners elongate, curved; posterior end of foot elongate. On rubble on shallow patch reefs.

Sacoglossa - "sapsucking slugs"

Stiliger sp. 11
Size: 7 mm   French Polynesia
ID: Translucent white with the light green branched digestive gland visible within the cerata; cerata elongate and wide; rhinophores with branches of the digestive gland. Feeds on green filamentous algae.

Stiliger sp. 12
Size: 5 mm   Tahiti
ID: Translucent white with opaque white patches on the body and surface of the cerata; cerata with light green branches of the digestive gland within. On filamentous green algae in 3 m.

Stiliger sp. 13
Size: 4 mm   Philippines
ID: Cerata short, brownish; head with darker brown pigment; rhinophores translucent white.

Stiliger sp. 14
Size: 8 mm   Philippines
ID: Body green with scattered opaque white spots; cerata with several parallel lines around the margin; digestive gland extending anteriorly into the entire rhinophore. On the green alga *Boodlea*.

Stiliger sp. 15
Size: 6 mm   Philippines
ID: Cerata with light bright pink digestive gland and opaque white tips; rhinophores short, each with a yellow-green subapical band.

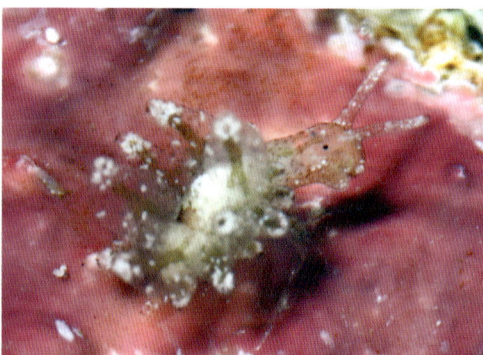

Stiliger sp. 16
Size: 5 mm   Philippines
ID: Body with sparse cerata, each with a white tip and white spots; rhinophores short, white. On shallow sand on filamentous green algae, 7 m.

Stiliger sp. 17
Size: 20 mm   Philippines
ID: Cerata smooth, swollen with numerous greenish lines converging at apex; rhinophores long, with diffuse digestive gland. Intertidal sea grass beds, nocturnally active.

Ercolania endophytophaga Jensen, 1999
Size: 13 mm   Australia, Philippines
ID: White with dark green digestive gland in the cerata and extending into most of the length of the rhinophores. Lives inside large algal cell of *Struvea plumosa* and *Valonia ventricosa*.

Ercolania annelyleorum Wägele, Stemmer, Burghardt & Händeler, 2010
Size: 5 mm   Australia
ID: Translucent white with opaque white spots; cerata with pale green branches of the digestive gland and white apices; rhinophores with branches of the digestive gland. Feeds on the alga *Boodlea composita*.

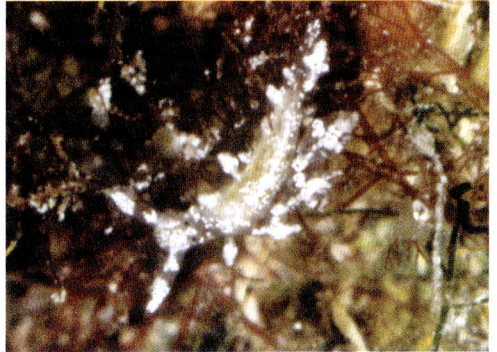

Ercolania sp. 1
Size: 5 mm   Hawai'ian Is.
ID: Translucent with fine brown digestive ducts visible and an opaque white marking on the pericardium; cerata bulbous with an opaque white apices. On shallow patch reefs.

Ercolania cf. coerulea Trinchese, 1892
Size: 12 mm   Tanzania, Hong Kong, Philippines
ID: Greenish; cerata rounded, each with an opaque white apex and white and blue spots. Similar to *Ercolania coerulea* from the Mediterranean but appears to have subtle differences. Feeds on the bubble alga *Dictyosphaeria cavernosa* in shallow water.

Ercolania kencolesi Grzymbowski, Stemmer & Wägele, 2007
Size: 6 mm   Australia, Guam
ID: Uniformly light green with opaque white bands on the rhinophores and cerata; body often elongate; foot broad. Feeds on the giant cells of the lobed green alga *Boergesenia forbesii*, often seen inside the alga.

411

Sacoglossa - "sapsucking slugs"

Ercolania sp. 2
Size: 4 mm   Madagascar
ID: Translucent white with black markings on the head; cerata short and bulbous, black with white apices. Among filamentous green algae in 1 m.

Ercolania sp. 3
Size: 10 mm   Vanuatu
ID: Translucent white with black markings on the head and rhinophores; cerata elongate and cylindrical, green with black apices. Oral tentacles shorter and body much stockier than in the previous species.

Costasiella kuroshimae Ichikawa, 1993
Size: 7 mm   Indian and western Pacific oceans
ID: Color variable, but always with a greenish diamond-shaped patch behind the eyes. In association with

Avrainvillea sp. in sandy patches between reefs. Shown here with its egg mass.

Costasiella usagi Ichikawa, 1993
Size: 10 mm   Western Pacific Ocean
ID: White with black rhinophores; cerata black with longitudinal white lines. In association with *Avrainvillea* sp. on sandy patches between reefs.

Costasiella sp. 1
Size: 12 mm   Widespread in the tropical Indo-Pacific
ID: Grey with opaque white pigment on the head and rhinophores and a black oval area situated immediately behind the rhinophores. In association with *Avrainvillea* sp.

Costasiella sp. 2
Size: 10 mm   Tahiti
ID: Greyish-green with two black lines on the head that converge behind the eyes; cerata greenish with scattered opaque white spots and a few brown spots; apices of the cerata white; rhinophores elongate. Shallow lagoons, in 3 m.

Costasiella sp. 3
Size: 8 mm   Tahiti
ID: Translucent white with green cerata having scattered opaque white spots; a brown patch behind the eyes; rhinophores short with black tips. On the green algae *Avrainvillea* spp.

Costasiella sp. 4
Size: 12 mm   Indonesia, Philippines
ID: White, with a black spot on the pericardium; head with two black lines extending anterior to the rhinophores; rhinophores short, black; cerata elongate, yellow, each with a black central line and a white apex. On the green algae *Avrainvillea* spp.

Costasiella sp. 5
Size: 10 mm   Indonesia
ID: White with a yellow longitudinal line on the head; rhinophores elongate with black tips and yellow lines at the bases, connected by a black line; pericardium opaque white outlined with yellow-green; cerata green with scattered opaque white spots and each with a yellow subapical spot.

Costasiella formicaria (Baba, 1959)
Size: 15 mm   Hawai'ian Is., Japan
ID: Translucent grey with black edging on the head and rhinophores; cerata green with numerous opaque white spots. Unlike other *Costasiella*, this species appears to feed on Cyanobacteria; often seen crawling on the surface of sandy slopes.

Costasiella sp. 6
Size: 5 mm   Papua New Guinea
ID: Translucent white with black rhinophores and an opaque white patch behind the rhinophores; cerata green with black spots. In association with *Avrainvillea* sp. on sandy areas between reefs.

Sacoglossa - "sapsucking slugs"

Costasiella sp. 7
Size: 12 mm   Papua New Guinea
ID: Translucent white with blue rhinophores; cerata green with blue tips. In association with *Avrainvillea* sp. on sandy patches between reefs.

Costasiella sp. 8
Size: 10 mm   Saudi Arabian Red Sea
ID: Translucent green; head with black pigment in front and behind the rhinophores; rhinophores short with black tips and white bases; cerata crowded, elongate, green with scattered opaque white spots and white apices. On the green algae *Avrainvillea* spp.

Hermaeidae H. Adams & A. Adams, 1854

Hermaeids are characterized by having the anterior edge of the foot rounded or with two oral lobes projecting laterally above the mouth. Cerata vary from elongate to fusiform, sometimes irregular, with visible branches of the digestive gland. Feed on green and red algae.

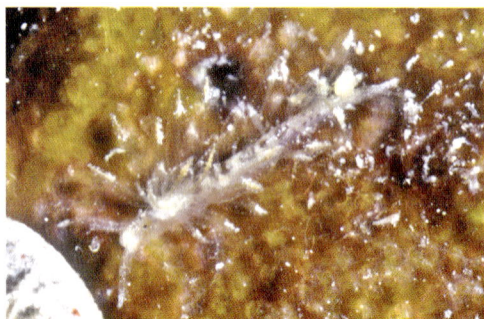

Hermaea noto (Baba, 1959)
Size: 10 mm   Japan
ID: White, with thick brownish rhinophores and four black lines on the head; cerata brownish-purple with black lines.

Hermaea sp. 1
Size: 12 mm   Papua New Guinea
ID: Translucent grey with numerous white spots; cerata semi-transparent with opaque white apices. Feeds on filamentous green algae.

Hermaea sp. 2
Size: 10 mm   Thailand
ID: Light purple with darker pigment on the ear-shaped rhinophores and two darker purple longitudinal lines on the head; cerata few, bright orange with purple apices.

Hermaea sp. 3
Size: 10 mm   Indonesia, Philippines
ID: Translucent white with fine purple lines on the head and purple on the tips of the rhinophores; cerata orange with a subapical opaque white line and purple tips.

414

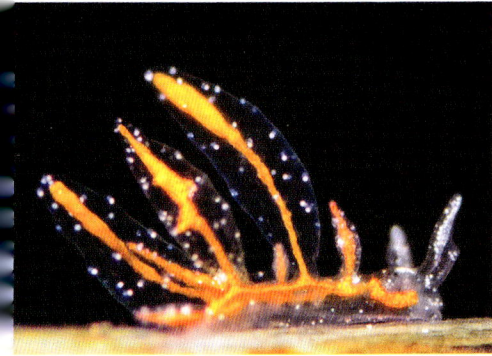

Hermaea sp. 4
Size: 10 mm   Indonesia
ID: Translucent white with brown and opaque white spots; cerata transparent with the orange branched digestive gland

readily visible; outer surface of the cerata with brown and opaque white spots; rhinophores elongate, ear-shaped.

Hermaea sp 5
Size: 4 mm   Philippines
ID: Translucent white with fine white opaque white speckles; digestive gland branched in the cerata; rhinophores long, each with a yellow-green band.

Plakobranchidae J. E. Gray, 1840

Members of this family lack cerata and have paired elongate parapodia. *Elysia* is the largest genus with dozens of species recorded from the Indo-Pacific, the majority of which are undescribed. Species of *Thuridilla* are usually brightly colored while species of *Plakobranchus* have a flattened body and are found in sandy areas.

Plakobranchids feed primarily on green algae, but also on diatoms. Many species sequester live chloroplasts from the algae they eat, and keep them functional in their tissue (kleptoplasty).

Elysia rufescens (Pease, 1871)
Size: 60 mm   Indian and Pacific oceans
ID: Mottled green and white with an inner orange and an outer bluish parapodial marginal bands. Feeds on the filamentous alga *Bryopsis* sp.

Sacoglossa - "sapsucking slugs"

Elysia punctata Kelaart, 1858
Size: 30 mm   Indian Ocean
ID: Green with large black spots and lacking orange pigment; parapodia forming only two undulations. On the green alga *Bryopsis* sp.

Elysia sp. 1
Size: 60 mm   Palau, Papua New Guinea, Philippines
ID: Grey with two opaque white lines on the head and rhinophores; differs from *Elysia marginata* in having a white rather than orange line along the margin of the parapodia. On the blades of the large green seagrass *Enhalus acoroides* in shallow water lagoons.

Elysia marginata (Pease, 1871)
Size: 50 mm   Widespread in the Indo-Pacific
ID: Color variable, typically green with black spots and orange and black parapodial margins. Molecular evidence suggests this is a complex of four cryptic species and the Caribbean species *Elysia ornata* is distinct. In association with the green alga *Bryopsis*.

Elysia sp. 2
Size: 30 mm
Widespread in the Indo-Pacific
ID: Grey with black pigment, rhinophores brown; parapodia thicker than in *Elysia marginata*, forming three rounded undulations lined with orange. In association with *Bryopsis* on shallow reefs.

Elysia sp. 3
Size: 30 mm
Saudi Arabian Red Sea
ID: Green with rows of opaque white dashes; parapodia with orange submarginal and black marginal lines; head with two black lines that extend to the base of the rhinophores; two opaque white lines on the head and rhinophores; rhinophores with additional parallel white lines. On filamentous green algae.

Elysia sp. 4
Size: 15 mm
Fiji
ID: Greenish-red with scattered yellow spots; parapodia large, undulate, each with a broad submarginal purplish band and thin opaque white margin.

Elysia nigropunctata (Pease, 1871)
Size: 30 mm
Tahiti
ID: Green with large opaque white and smaller black spots; parapodia large with two large convoluted openings; no lines on the parapodial margins; rhinophores moderately long with white tips and dense spotting of black. Shallow lagoons, in 2 m.

Elysia nealae Ostergaard, 1955
Size: 15 mm
Western and central Pacific Ocean
ID: Green with a greenish-orange area along the margin of the highly convoluted parapodia; white spots present on the body, head and rhinophores. Feeds on the green alga, *Udotea* sp. in shallow water to 8 m.

Elysia yaeyamana Baba, 1936
Size: 70 mm
Southern Japan
ID: Green with white mottling; parapodia highly convoluted, each with an orange terminal band; body elongate. From the intertidal zone to 13 m.

Sacoglossa - "sapsucking slugs"

Elysia sp. 5
Size: 20 mm   Papua New Guinea
ID: Mottled green with large yellow spots; parapodia highly convoluted with red terminal bands. On patch reefs where it feeds on *Caulerpa racemosa*, in 3 m.

Elysia lobata Gould, 1852
Size: 10 mm   Western and central Pacific Ocean
ID: Pale green with small papillae and black spots; parapodial margins yellowish, each with an outer pink band and three undulations. Under rocks in shallow water; its food is unknown.

Elysia thompsoni Jensen, 1993
Size: 10 mm   Madagascar, Western Australia, Indonesia
ID: Green with numerous black spots and tips of the rhinophores purple; parapodia forming three distinct undulations that are lined in purple; body papillate. On filamentous green algae.

Elysia sp. 6
Size: 8 mm   Western and central Pacific Ocean
ID: Pale green with a series of darker green longitudinal lines; parapodia with three undulations as in *Elysia lobata*. On the green alga *Chlorodesmis fastigiata* on shallow reef flats.

Elysia sp. 7
Size: 10 mm   Great Barrier Reef (Australia)
ID: Green with a series of white and black parapodial lines. On turtle weed, *Chlorodesmis* sp. in 2-3 m.

Elysia sp. 8
Size: 10 mm   Philippines
ID: Yellowish green with longitudinal opaque white lines that bear tubercles; opaque white pigment present on the head and rhinophores.

Elysia sp. 9
Size: 6 mm   South Africa
ID: Pale green with yellow, black and green spots; rhinophores with distinctive green markings. Similar to *Elysia trilobata* from the Red Sea. Intertidal rock pools at night.

Elysia cf. *trilobata* Heller & Thompson, 1983
Size: 10 mm   Philippines
ID: Greyish green with lighter green scattered pustules; parapodia irregular possibly due to damage, covered with tiny yellow and black spots; rhinophores with darker green diagonal bands. In 7 m.

Elysia sp. 10
Size: 18 mm   South Africa
ID: Mottled green with light green papillae, large yellow spots with smaller black ones. In 1 m; feeds on the green alga, *Caulerpa racemosa*.

Elysia sp. 11
Size: 30 mm   Tahiti
ID: Green with numerous small yellow spots; highly developed elongate papillae on the sides of the body; head and tips of the rhinophores covered with lighter green. Shallow bays, in 2 m.

Elysia sp. 12
Size: 8 mm   Philippines
ID: Mottled green with yellow spots and white tubercles; rhinophores darker below apex with white tips. Shallow patch reefs on sand.

Elysia sp. 13
Size: 10 mm   Philippines
ID: Greenish brown with opaque white flecks and yellow spots; parapodia smooth, short; rhinophores with black tips. Areas of mixed algae and sand in 7 m.

Sacoglossa - "sapsucking slugs"

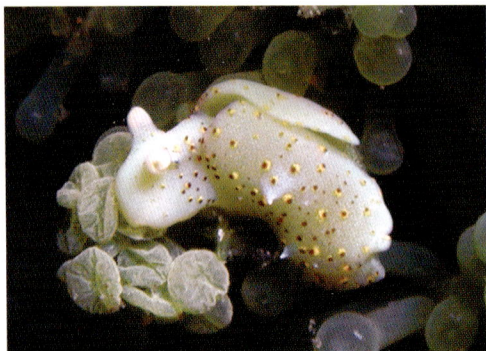

Elysia sp. 14
Size: 12 mm   Southern Japan
ID: Light green body with golden yellow and brown spots and a few white papillae on the sides; rhinophores pink. Feeds on *Caulerpa* sp.

Elysia sp. 15
Size: 5 mm   South Africa, Papua New Guinea
ID: Uniformly light green, body and rhinophores papillate as in *Elysia mercieri*, but with dark green rhinophores. In intertidal pools, active at night.

Elysia sp. 16
Size: 20 mm   Oman
ID: Brownish-green with lighter pustules; parapodia with scattered small black spots; posterior end of the foot and head with opaque white and dark blue; tips of the rhinophores blue.

Elysia sp. 17
Size: 20 mm   Tahiti
ID: Uniformly bright green with a few scatted opaque white spots; parapodial margin reddish, highly convoluted. In lagoons at night in 3 m.

Elysia tomentosa Jensen, 1997
Size: 30 mm   Widespread in the Indo-Pacific
ID: Grassy green with black and whitish parapodial marginal bands; body with numerous papillae on the surface. Feeds exclusively on *Caulerpa racemosa* and *C. taxifolia*.

Elysia sp. 18
Size: 18 mm   Western Pacific Ocean
ID: Parapodia with two pairs of expanded extensions; body covered with elongate papillae; parapodial margin light; a blue spot on head. Feeds on *Caulerpa*.

Elysia sp. 19
Size: 60 mm   Tuamotu Archipelago
ID: Bright grassy green with numerous small black spots and dense covering of opaque white papillae, some of which are branched; parapodia short, without distinct marginal bands; rhinophores with the same papillae as the body. In lagoons on *Codium* sp., in 3 m.

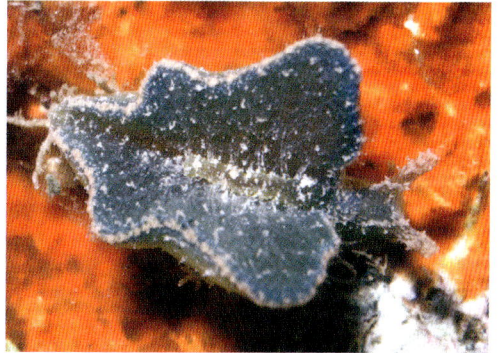

Elysia sp. 20
Size: 20 mm   Indian and western Pacific oceans
ID: Greyish-green with numerous greyish-brown papillae and parapodial edges. Similar to *Elysia tomentosa* but lacks black or white bands on the parapodial margin, which is distinctly lobed. On *Caulerpa racemosa* on shallow reef flats.

Elysia sp. 21
Size: 15 mm   Western Pacific Ocean
ID: Green with white spots and longitudinal lines as well as yellow patches along the parapodial margins; body elongate and highly papillate. Feeds exclusively on the green alga *Tydemania expeditionis* on which it is shown crawling in the photo.

Elysia sp. 22
Size: 12 mm   Indonesia
ID: Green with opaque white lines and papillae; lacks yellow tubercles along the margin of the parapodia. It appears to feed on the green alga *Tydemania expeditionis* on which it is shown crawling in the photo.

Elysia sp. 23
Size: 8 mm   French Polynesia
ID: Green but densely covered with opaque white markings and irregular short papillae; white lines on the head and rhinophores. A cryptic and nondescript species. Shallow water lagoons in 1 m.

Elysia arena Carlson & Hoff, 1978
Size: 20 mm   Palau, Guam
ID: Mottled green with white and black pigment; body papillate; a series of transverse lamellae inside of the parapodia. Shallow sandy areas where it feeds on *Caulerpa racemosa*.

Sacoglossa - "sapsucking slugs"

Elysia sp. 24
Size: 15 mm   Western and central Pacific Ocean
ID: Uniformly light green with numerous small opaque white spots; body texture relatively smooth; rhinophores short. Exclusively on the green calcareous alga, *Udotea geppii* on shallow sandy slopes.

Elysia sp. 25
Size: 4 mm   Philippine
ID: Translucent light green with cream pigment and minut reddish-brown spots. Shown here crawling on its foo *Caulerpa racemosa*.

Elysia sp. 26
Size: 30 mm   Marshall Is.
ID: Green with a dense covering of opaque white spots giving it a frosted appearance.

Elysia asbecki Wägele, Stemmer, Burghardt Händeler, 2010
Size: 5 mm   Western and central Pacific Ocea
ID: Green with pink markings on the side; rhinophores wit yellow rings; body papillate. On the underside of coral rubbl on shallow reef flats.

Elysia sp. 27
Size: 20 mm   Philippines
ID: Thin narrow body with low parapodia; parapodial margin lighter than the rest of the parapodia. Shallow patch reefs on *Codium* sp.

Elysia sp. 28
Size: 25 mm   Western and central Pacific Ocea
ID: Green with numerous opaque white spots; body papillate elongate with extremely short rhinophores. On the branchin green alga, *Codium* sp. in shallow water and mixed sand an coral.

Elysia sp. 29
Size: 10 mm   Papua New Guinea
ID: Bright green with dense covering of short papillae;
parapodial margin and head lighter than the rest of the body;
rhinophores papillate, thin, acutely pointed.

Elysia sp. 30
Size: 7 mm   Papua New Guinea, Japan
ID: Greenish orange with elevated opaque white punctuations
and a black transverse line immediately anterior to the
parapodia. Under coral rubble in 3-4 m.

Elysia degeneri Ostergaard, 1955
Size: 10 mm   Hawai'ian Is., Society Is.
ID: Light green; short parapodia with irregular folds and an
orange submarginal line; body elongate with short irregular
papillae over its surface. Common in shallow lagoons on the
alga Udotea sp. in 3 m.

Elysia cf. degeneri Ostergaard, 1955
Size: 10 mm   Philippines
ID: Grassy green with opaque white spots on the body
and parapodia; each parapodium with a yellowish orange
marginal line. On the alga Turbinakia sp., in 2 m.

Elysia sp. 31
Size: 15 mm   Vanuatu
ID: Translucent grey with fine green stippling and dense
opaque white pigment on the parapodia and head.

Elysia sp. 32
Size: 20 mm   Reunion, Mayotte
ID: Light green with numerous opaque white spots, often at
the tip of the short papillae; a distinctive orange line on the
anterior margin of the foot. On shallow rocky reefs in 1 m.

Sacoglossa - "sapsucking slugs"

***Elysia* sp. 33**
Size: 15 mm   Indonesia
ID: Bright green with opaque white markings and bright blue on the parapodia, rhinophores, and foot. Crawling on sand in shallow water.

***Elysia* sp. 34**
Size: 6 mm   Tah[i]
ID: Uniform light green with extensive patches of opaqu[e] white; rhinophores held horizontally. In shallow water o[n] sandy substrate.

***Elysia* sp. 35**
Size: 10 mm   Indonesia
ID: Greenish-white with opaque pustules and yellowish-orange spots; parapodia open anteriorly, with two elevated open areas at the margins having lighter pigment; rhinophores short.

***Elysia* sp. 36**
Size: 10 mm   Philippine[s]
ID: Light green with opaque white mottling and darker green; large blue spots present on the sides of the body; rhinophore[s] acutely pointed and curved, resembling bull horns, with dar[k] blue tips. Sandy habitats.

***Elysia* sp. 37**
Size: 6 mm   Indonesia, Philippines
ID: Light green with opaque white patches on the head and posterior part of the foot, blue pigment also present, rhinophores with black tips. Crawling on the surface of sandy substrate on slopes in 10-20 m.

***Elysia* sp. 38**
Size: 5 mm   Philippines
ID: Light green with large yellow spots and more numerous small white dots; blue pigment present on the rhinophores and posterior end of the foot. In 1-2 m on the sea grass *Enhalus acoroides*.

Elysia sp. 39
Size: 6 mm — Saudi Arabian Red Sea
ID: Light green with dense encrustations of opaque white; body smooth with rounded tubercles; blue pigment on the tips of the short rhinophores and at the posterior end of foot. On shallow reefs.

Elysia sp. 40
Size: 6 mm — Philippines
ID: Bright green with isolated blue spots on the parapodia and the tips of the rhinophores; parapodial margin and head with opaque white pigment; parapodia with a single opening surrounded by opaque white. In areas with microscopic green algae in 6 m.

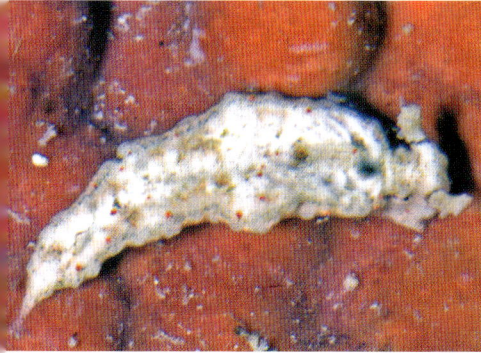

Elysia sp. 41
Size: 20 mm — Vanuatu
ID: Green with a dense covering of opaque white and a few green markings; a green band near the middle of each rhinophore.

Elysia mercieri (Pruvot-Fol, 1930)
Size: 7 mm — Indian and Pacific oceans
ID: Mottled green and white; parapodia with elongate appendages; entire body, including the rhinophores, covered with small papillae. On shallow patch reefs in 1-5 m.

Elysia sp. 42
Size: 12 mm — Philippines
ID: White with greenish pigment throughout the body; parapodia extremely short, undulate, incapable of overlapping; rhinophores black except at the base. On shallow patch reefs in 12 m.

Elysia sp. 43
Size: 7 mm — Madagascar
ID: Whitish with pinkish patches on the sides of the head and brown tips on the rhinophores; parapodia forming two distinct undulations; body covered with papillae. On shallow reef slopes.

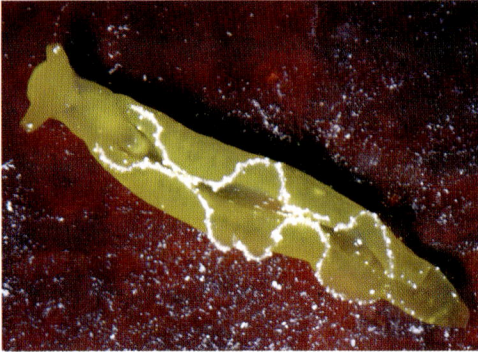

Elysia obtusa Baba, 1938
Size: 20 mm   Indian and Pacific oceans
ID: Pale yellowish green with opaque white parapodial margin. *Elysia flava* from the Caribbean is genetically distinct.

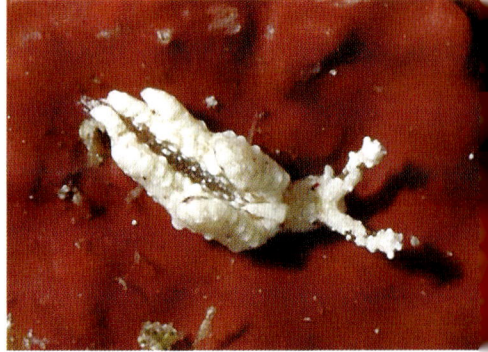

Elysia sp. 44
Size: 12 mm   Vanuat
ID: Opaque white; body covered with prominent tubercle over most of the surface; parapodia with four expande portions.

Elysia sp. 45
Size: 6 mm   Marshall Is.
ID: Dark brown to black with a few low papillae having opaque white pigment; rhinophores opaque white with conical papillae.

Elysia sp. 46
Size: 20 mm   Philippines, Marshall Is
ID: Light green with irregular pink and white pigmen rhinophores dark brown with white spots; parapodia elevatec On shallow reefs; feeds on the green alga *Halimeda* sp.

Elysia pusilla (Bergh, 1871)
Size: 35 mm   Indo-Pacific and eastern Pacific
ID: Uniformly green; rhinophores with opaque white on their outer half; body flattened with smooth texture and short parapodia. *Elysia halimedae* is a synonym. Extremely cryptic on its algal host *Halimeda* spp.; on sandy and rocky habitats to 30 m.

Elysia sp. 47
Size: 6 mm   Philippines
ID: Body short, rich green with a few opaque spots; tips of the rinophores black. Shallow sandy areas, 20 m.

426

Elysia sp. 48
Size: 5 mm   Indonesia
ID: Light green with dense patches of opaque white and scatted small yellow spots; rhinophores short, conical, translucent white.

Elysia cf. trisinuata Baba, 1949
Size: 20 mm   Reunion Is.
ID: Dark green with orange spots and opaque white on the numerous papillae; rhinophores papillate with opaque white tips. Similar to *Elysia trisinuata* from temperate Japan but with the body covered with dense papillae rather than smooth. On *Codium* sp. in 1 m.

Thuridilla hoffae Gosliner, 1995
Size: 20 mm   Western Pacific Ocean
ID: Black with bright blue patches on the parapodia and orange parapodial margins; rhinophores with blue tips. Under coral rubble on shallow reefs.

Thuridilla lineolata (Bergh, 1905)
Size: 30 mm   Philippines, Indonesia
ID: Bright blue with distinctive orange and black areas on the parapodia and head. Shallow water fringing reefs where filamentous algae are abundant.

Sacoglossa - "sapsucking slugs"

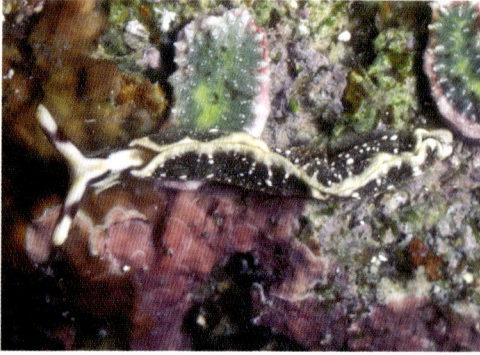

Thuridilla kathae Gosliner, 1995
Size: 15 mm   Widespread in the Indo-Pacific
ID: Green with opaque white spots and opaque white and green pigment on the head and rhinophores; parapodia with cream marginal lines. On shallow water reefs in 1-5 m.

Thuridilla moebii (Bergh, 1888)
Size: 10 mm   Southern Indian Ocean
ID: Light bluish green; parapodial margin undulating, dark brown to black, with scattered opaque white dots. On fringing reefs near the shoreline in 1-2 m.

Thuridilla carlsoni Gosliner, 1995
Size: 30 mm   Western and central Pacific Ocean
ID: Pale green with scattered dark green spots and yellow parapodial marginal bands; each rhinophore with a subapical

band and a burnt orange apex. Crawling in the open on shallow reefs.

Thuridilla splendens (Baba, 1949)
Size: 30 mm   Japan
ID: Greenish with yellow spots and lines; parapodial margin with a series of blue or greenish spots below alternating black and yellow lines. In 2-12 m.

Thuridilla flavomaculata Gosliner, 1995
Size: 22 mm   Western Pacific Ocean
ID: Green with scattered yellow and white spots and cream edges of the parapodia; rhinophores opaque white with black tips. On shallow water reefs where it feeds on unspecified algae.

Thuridilla gracilis (Risbec, 1928)
Size: 25 mm   Indian and western Pacific oceans
ID: Greenish black with white or cream longitudinal lines, blue patches and red pigment may also be present. _Thuridilla bayeri_ and _Thuridilla ratna_ are synonyms. Crawling in the open or under coral rubble in shallow water, not in association with specific algae.

Thuridilla vatae (Risbec, 1928)
Size: 10 mm   Widespread in the Indo-Pacific
ID: Bluish green with diffuse black and yellow spots; head and rhinophores opaque white, tips of the rhinophores orange. On shallow fringing and patch reefs.

Sacoglossa - "sapsucking slugs"

Thuridilla albopustulosa Gosliner, 1995
Size: 25 mm   Indian and western Pacific oceans
ID: Bluish with white pustules and black and orange pigment.
On shallow reefs usually under coral rubble.

Thuridilla virgata (Bergh, 1888)
Size: 30 mm   Western Indian Ocean
ID: Pale blue with a series of longitudinal black stripes and
orange pigment on the rhinophores. On shallow fringing
reefs.

Thuridilla indopacifica Gosliner, 1995
Size: 15 mm   Indian Ocean
ID: Greenish-blue with blue patches on the upper part of the
parapodia; edges of the parapodia with submarginal black
and marginal orange lines; head with white, black and blue
pigment. Crawling on shallow fringing reefs on coral mounds
with filamentous algae.

Thuridilla sp. 1
Size: 18 mm   Reunion Is.
ID: Greenish; edge of the parapodia undulating, with
submarginal black and marginal orange lines; head white
with blue, black and orange marking on the tips of the
rhinophores; sides of the body with white dots. On shallow
fringing reefs in 1 m.

Thuridilla sp. 2
Size: 18 mm   Reunion Is.
ID: Greenish brown; edge of the parapodia with undulating
submarginal black and marginal orange lines; rhinophores
with blue, black and orange markings. On shallow fringing
reefs in 1 m.

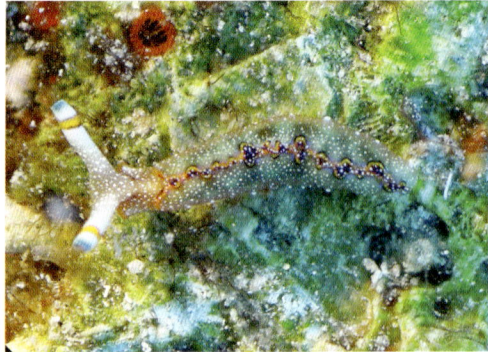

Thuridilla sp. 3
Size: 60 mm   Red Sea, Gulf of Oman
ID: Green with numerous white spots; edges of the parapodia
with thin, undulating submarginal black and marginal orange
lines; rhinophores with black rings on either side of orange
rings. On shallow reefs in 8 m.

Thuridilla livida (Baba, 1955)
Size: 20 mm   Indian and western Pacific oceans
ID: Black with blue, black and orange marginal lines; white pigment present on the tips of the rhinophores. Crawling out in the open on shallow reef flats in 1-5 m.

Thuridilla undula Gosliner, 1995
Size: 15 mm   Indian and western Pacific oceans
ID: Blue with undulating black and orange pigment on the margins of the parapodia and on the rhinophores. On shallow reefs.

Thuridilla decorata (Heller & Thompson, 1983)
Size: 15 mm   Red Sea
ID: Greenish brown with undulating bands of creamy white near the parapodial margins; head and rhinophores white, each with a brownish band near the middle. On filamentous algae on shallow reefs.

***Thuridilla* sp. 4**
Size: 5 mm   Tuamotu Archipelago
ID: Body and head white, with isolated burnt orange patches surrounded by lighter orange and black lines; rhinophores with transverse blue, black, orange and burnt orange bands; apices black. On reefs in 1 m.

Sacoglossa - "sapsucking slugs"

Thuridilla multimarginata Gosliner, 1995
Size: 9 mm   South Africa, Hawai'ian Is.
ID: Orange with white pigment on the head and blue rhinophores; edge of the parapodia with undulating orange, blue, black and yellow marginal lines. In 1-2 m on fringing reefs.

Thuridilla neona Gosliner, 1995
Size: 15 mm   Hawai'ian Is., probably Australia
ID: Bluish green to orange with undulating blue, black, and orange parapodial lines; edge of the foot and rhinophores with the same color bands. On shallow patch reefs. Egg masses with extra-capsular yolk.

Thuridilla sp. 5
Size: 30 mm   Northern Australia
ID: Yellowish orange with a series of alternating yellow and black longitudinal bands; parapodia with a series of submarginal light blue semicircles; rhinophores orange. Often considered as an Australian form of *Thuridilla splendens* is here regarded as a distinct species.

Thuridilla sp. 6
Size: 20 mm   Malaysia
ID: Blue with an undulating pattern of orange to brown along the parapodial margins; orange-brown area punctuated by yellow spots and surrounded ventrally by black edging; each rhinophore with a black subapical band and apex as same color as the parapodial margin.

Thuridilla sp. 7
Size: 15 mm   Marquesas Is.
ID: Light green with lighter parapodial margins; rhinophores and head with white patches; rhinophores with diagonal red-orange lines. Shallow reefs in 3 m.

Plakobranchus sp. 1
Size: 70 mm   Western Pacific Ocean
ID: Brown with blue and black pigment on the parapodia and rhinophores; body with spots rather than ocelli. Of all of the variants of *Plakobranchus* this one appears to be consistently distinct from *P. ocellatus*. On shallow sandy habitats; capable of burrowing under the sand.

432

Plakobranchus ocellatus van Hasselt, 1824
Size: 60 mm   Widespread in the Indo-Pacific
ID: Color highly variable throughout its range (several of those variants are shown here); almost all variations have ocelli on the dorsal surface of the parapodia. Molecular data indicates this is probably a species complex. Sandy habitats where it can survive almost all its life without feeding since it derives most of its nutrition from symbiotic chloroplasts; a truly solar powered opisthobranch.

Plakobranchus sp. 2
Size: 30 mm   Papua New Guinea
ID: Yellow with a dense concentration of green rings having lighter green centers; rings near the base of the parapodia darker, almost black. On fine sand in 2-6 m.

Plakobranchus sp. 3
Size: 26 mm   Papua New Guinea, Philippines
ID: Complex, irregular pattern of green and white mottling over the entire body; a few ocelli present on the head, but otherwise absent. On sand in 6 m.

Plakobranchus sp. 4
Size: 30 mm   Philippines
ID: Light yellow with numerous pustules and reddish rings and spots; rings with bright yellow centers. Shallow sandy and mixed coral habitats in 1-2 m.

Plakobranchus sp. 5
Size: 20 mm   Vanuatu, Indonesia
ID: Dark green with black shades and blue spots. This appears to be another distinct species of *Plakobranchus*. On shallow sandy habitats.

Sacoglossa - "sapsucking slugs"

Plakobranchus sp. 6
Size: 30 mm   Philippines
ID: Opaque white concentrated in areas near the center of the body; ocelli becoming larger towards the basal portion of the parapodia. Sandy habitats in 10-15 m.

Plakobranchus sp. 7
Size: 15 mm   Philippines
ID: Dark green to black with opaque white patches on the posterior half of the parapodia. On fine silty slopes 15-20 m.

Plakobranchus papua Meyers-Muñoz & van der Velde *in* Meyers-Muñoz *et al.*, 2016
Size: 40 mm   Indonesia
ID: Light green with mottled cream pigment; parapodial margins with cream colored rectangles; tips of the rhinophores black. Shallow silty habitats.

Plakobranchus sp. 8
Size: 25 mm   Papua New Guinea
ID: Light green with dense opaque white spots and scattered black spots; posterior end of the parapodia and tips of the rhinophores with blue pigment.

Bosellia sp. 1
Size: 6 mm   Amami Archipelago (Japan)
ID: Uniform green with dark rhinophores; body flattened, lacking parapodia. On *Halimeda* sp. on shallow reefs.

Bosellia sp. 2
Size: 8 mm   Saudi Arabian Red Sea
ID: Bright green with scattered opaque white papillae over the entire body; rhinophores short with opaque white apices. On *Halimeda* sp. on shallow reefs.

Acochlidia

This group is largely composed of interstitial species (living between sand grains), many of which are very small, usually less than a few millimeters. It also contains the only known freshwater sea slugs They lack a shell in the adult state and some species are covered with spicules. They probably feed on microorganisms, especially algae. Recent molecular studies suggest this group is closely related to sacoglossans and marine pulmonate snails (Zapata *et al.*, 2014) whereas previous studies placed them among terrestrial and freshwater snails (Jörger *et al.*, 2010). The systematics of Acochlidia has been reviewed in Schrödl & Neusser (2010) and other papers.

Marine species

The following is a small representation of the diversity of marine Acochlidia in the tropical Indo-Pacific to illustrate their morphology. Most species are extremely small, less than 1 mm and live in between sand grains. Specialized collecting techniques are necessary to study these organisms.

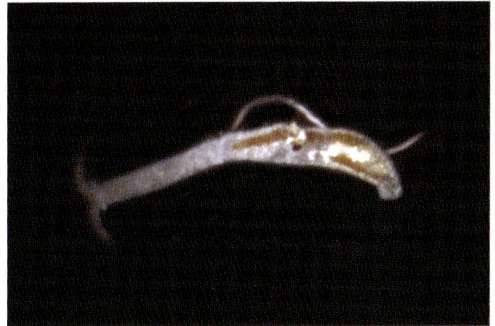

Acochlidium sp.
Size: 8 mm   Philippines
ID: Yellow; oral tentacles and rhinophores with black and opaque white pigment; body elongate. Under coral rubble in a stream opening into mangroves, in 1-2 m.

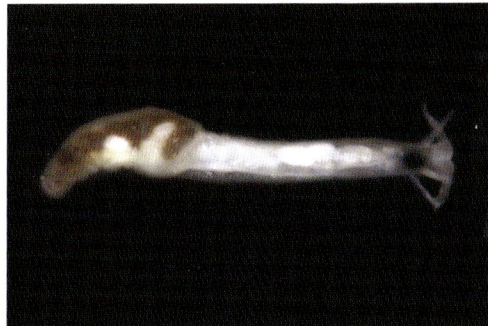

Pseudunela cornuta (Challis, 1970)
Size: 2 mm   Western Pacific
ID: Translucent with the internal organs visible through the skin; visceral mass elongate, digestive gland brown. Between sand grains.

Microhedyle sp.
Size: 1 mm   Vanuatu
ID: Pale grey; visceral mass elongate with the digestive gland visible as a light brown patch. Between sand grains.

Freshwater species

Acochlidia are the only sea slugs that have colonized freshwater. Several species are found high in rivers of the tropical Indo-Pacific, in environments that are completely separated from the ocean. Very little is known about the biology and evolution of these organisms.

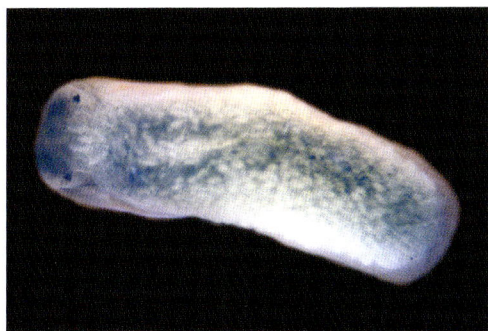

Aiteng sp.
Size: 8 mm   Philippines
ID: Pale green with brown pigment; eyes conspicuous. Intertidal, in embayments around mangrove roots; probably feeds on insects.

Strubellia paradoxa (Strubell, 1892)
Size: 30 mm   Western Pacific Is.
ID: Brown; body large with an elongate visceral mass. Upstream under rocks in freshwater environments.

435

References

REFERENCES

Behrens, D.W. 2005. *Nudibranch Behavior*. New World Publications Inc., Jacksonville, Florida. 176 pp.

Brodie, G.D. & Calado, G. 2006. *Dendrodoris arborescens* (Collingwood, 1881) (Mollusca: Nudibranchia): Larval characteristics reveal a masked porostome species. *Records of the Western Australian Museum*, Supplement 69: 119-126.

Brodie, G.D., Willan, R.C., & Collins, J.D. 1997. Taxonomy and occurrence of *Dendrodoris nigra* and *Dendrodoris fumata* (Nudibranchia: Dendrodorididae) in the Indo-West Pacific region. *Journal of Molluscan Studies* 63: 411-427.

Brunckhorst, D.J. 1993. The systematics and phylogeny of phyllidiid nudibranchs (Doridoidea). *Records of the Australian Museum* Supplement 16: 1-107.

Carmona, L., Pola, M., Gosliner, T.M., & Cervera, J.L. 2013. A tale that morphology fails to tell: A molecular phylogeny of Aeolidiidae (Aeolidida, Nudibranchia, Gastropoda). *PLoS one* 8(5): e63000.

Carmona, L., Bhave, V., Salunkhe, R., Pola, M., Gosliner, T.M., & Cervera, J.L. 2014a. Systematic review of *Anteaeolidiella* (Mollusca, Nudibranchia, Aeolidiidae) based on morphological and molecular data, with a description of three new species. *Zoological Journal of the Linnean Society* 171: 108-132.

Carmona, L., Lei, B.R., Pola, M., Gosliner, T.M., Valdés, A., & Cervera, J.L. 2014b. Untangling the *Spurilla neapolitana* (Delle Chiaje, 1841) species complex: A review of the genus *Spurilla* Bergh, 1864 (Mollusca: Nudibranchia: Aeolidiidae). *Zoological Journal of the Linnean Society* 170: 132-154.

Carmona, L., Pola, M., Gosliner, T.M., & Cervera, J.L. 2014c. The end of a long controversy: Systematics of the genus *Limenandra* (Mollusca: Nudibranchia: Aeolidiidae). *Helgoland Marine Research* 68: 37-48.

Carmona, L., Pola, M., Gosliner, T.M., & Cervera, J.L. 2014d. Review of *Baeolidia*, the largest genus of Aeolidiidae (Mollusca: Nudibranchia), with the description of five new species. *Zootaxa* 3802: 477-514.

Carpenter, K.E. & Springer, V.G. 2005. The center of the center of marine shore fish biodiversity: The Philippine Islands. *Environmental Biology of Fishes* 72: 467-480.

Cella, K., Carmona, L., Ekimova, I., Chichvarkhin, A., Schepetov, D. and Gosliner, T.M., 2016. A radical solution: the phylogeny of the nudibranch family Fionidae. *PLoS one*, 11: p.e0167800.

Churchill, C.K., Valdés, A., & Ó Foighil, D. 2014. Molecular and morphological systematics of neustonic nudibranchs (Mollusca: Gastropoda: Glaucidae: *Glaucus*), with descriptions of three new cryptic species. *Invertebrate Systematics* 28: 174-195.

Coleman, N. 2001. *1001 Nudibranchs - Catalogue of Indo-Pacific Sea Slugs*. Neville Coleman's Underwater Geographic Pty Ltd., Springwood, Australia. 144 pp.

Coleman, N. 2008. *Nudibranchs Encyclopedia - Catalogue of Asia/Indo-Pacific Sea Slugs*. Neville Coleman's Underwater Geographic Pty Ltd., Springwood, Australia. 416 pp.

Dayrat, B. 2010. A monograph of basal discodorid sea slugs (Mollusca: Gastropoda: Nudibranchia: Doridina: Discodorididae): Infra-specific character variation, taxonomy, and phylogenetic relationships. *Proceedings of the California Academy of Sciences* 61(supplement 1): 1-403.

Debelius, H. 1996. *Nudibranchs & Sea Snails - Indo-Pacific Field Guide*. IKAN, Frankfurt, Germany. 320 pp.

Debelius, H. & Kuiter, R.H. 2008. *Nudibranchs of the World*. IKAN, Frankfurt, Germany. 360 pp.

Eales, N.B. 1960. Revision of the world species of *Aplysia* (Gastropoda, Opisthobranchia). *Bulletin of the British Museum (Natural History)* 5: 269-404.

Fahey, S.J. & Gosliner, T.M. 2004. A phylogenetic analysis of the Aegiridae Fischer, 1883 (Mollusca, Nudibranchia, Phanerobranchia) with descriptions of eight new species and reassessment of phanerobranch relationships. *Proceedings of the California Academy of Sciences* 55: 613-689.

Goodheart, J.A., Camacho-García, Y., Padula, V., Schrödl, M., Cervera, J.L., Gosliner, T.M., Valdés, A. 2015. Systematics and biogeography of *Pleurobranchus* Cuvier, 1804 sea slugs (Heterobranchia: Nudipleura: Pleurobranchidae). *Zoological Journal of the Linnean Society* 174: 322-362.

Goodheart, J.A., Bazinet, A.L., Collins, A.G., & Cummings, M.P. 2015. Relationships within Cladobranchia (Gastropoda: Nudibranchia) based on RNA-Seq data: An initial investigation. *Royal Society Open Science* 2: 150196.

Goodheart, J.A., Bazinet, A.L., Valdés, A., Collins, A.G., & Cummings, M.P. 2017. Prey preference follows phylogeny: evolutionary dietary patterns within the marine gastropod group Cladobranchia (Gastropoda: Heterobranchia: Nudibranchia). *BMC Evolutionary Biology*, 17: 221.

Gosliner, T.M. 1989. Revision of the Gastropteridae (Opisthobranchia: Cephalaspidea) with descriptions of a new genus and six new species. *The Veliger* 32: 333-381.

Gosliner, T.M. 2001. Aposematic coloration and mimicry in opisthobranch mollusks: New phylogenetic and experimental data. *Bollettino Malacologico* 37: 163-170.

Gosliner, T.M. 2004. Phylogenetic systematics of *Okenia*, *Sakishmaia*, *Hopkinsiella* and *Hopkinsia* (Nudibranchia: Goniodorididae) with descriptions of new species from the tropical Indo-Pacific. *Proceedings of the California Academy of Sciences* 55: 125-161.

Gosliner, T.M. & Behrens, D.W. 1990. Special resemblance, aposematic coloration, and mimicry in opisthobranch gastropods. In: M. Wicksten (ed.), *Adaptive Coloration in Invertebrates*. Texas A & M University Sea Grant Program: College Station, Texas, USA. Pp. 127-138.

Gosliner, T.M. & Fahey, S. 2008. Systematics of *Trapania* (Mollusca: Nudibranchia: Goniodorididae) with descriptions of 16 new species. *Systematics and Biodiversity* 6: 1-46.

Gosliner, T.M. & Johnson, R.F. 1999. Phylogeny of *Hypselodoris* (Nudibranchia: Chromodorididae) with a review of the monophyletic clade of Indo-Pacific species, including descriptions of twelve new species. *Zoological Journal of the Linnean Society* 125: 1-114.

Gosliner, T.M. & Johnson, S. 1994. Review of the genus *Hallaxa* (Nudibranchia: Actinocyclidae) with descriptions of nine new species. *The Veliger* 37: 155-191.

Gosliner, T.M. & Pola, M. 2012. Diversification of filter-feeding nudibranchs: Two remarkable new species of *Melibe* (Opisthobranchia: Tethyiidae) from the tropical western Pacific. *Systematics and Biodiversity* 10: 333-349.

Gosliner, T.M. & Willan, R.C. 1991. Review of the Flabellinidae (Nudibranchia: Aeolidacea) from the tropical Indo-Pacific, with the descriptions of five new species. *The Veliger* 34: 97-133.

Gosliner, T.M, González-Duarte, M.M., & Cervera J.L. 2007. Revision of the systematics of *Babakina* Roller, 1973 (Mollusca: Opisthobranchia) with the description of a new species and a phylogenetic analysis. *Zoological Journal of the Linnean Society* 151: 671-689.

Hallas, J.M., Chichvarkhin, A. & Gosliner, T.M. 2017. Aligning evidence: concerns regarding multiple sequence alignments in estimating the phylogeny of the Nudibranchia suborder Doridina. *Royal Society Open Science* 4: 171095.

Jennings, R.M., Bucklin, A., Ossenbrügger, H., & Hopcroft, R.R. 2010. Species diversity of planktonic gastropods (Pteropoda and Heteropoda) from six ocean regions based on DNA barcode analysis. *Deep-Sea Research II* 57: 2199-2210.

Jensen, K.R. 1996. Phylogenetic systematics and classification of the Sacoglossa (Mollusca, Gastropoda, Opisthobranchia). *Philosophical Transactions of the Royal Society of London Biological Sciences* 351: 91-122.

References

Johnson, R.F. 2011. Breaking family ties: taxon sampling and molecular phylogeny of chromodorid nudibranchs (Mollusca, Gastropoda). *Zoologica Scripta* 40: 137-157.

Johnson, R.F. & Gosliner, T.M. 2012. Traditional taxonomic groupings mask evolutionary history: A molecular phylogeny and new classification of the chromodorid nudibranchs. *PLoS one* 7(4): e33479.

Jörger, K.M., Stöger, I., Kano, Y., Fukuda, H., Knebelsberger, T., & Schrödl, M. 2010. On the origin of Acochlidia and other enigmatic euthyneuran gastropods, with implications for the systematics of Heterobranchia. *BMC Evolutionary Biology* 10: 323.

Kano, Y., Brenzinger, B., Nützel, A., Wilson, N. G., & Schrödl, M. 2016. Ringiculid bubble snails recovered as the sister group to sea slugs (Nudipleura). *Scientific Reports* 6: 30908.

Klussmann-Kolb, A. 2004. Phylogeny of the Aplysiidae (Mollusca, Gastropoda) with new aspects of the evolution of seahares. *Zoologica Scripta* 33: 439-462.

Klussmann-Kolb, A. & Dinapoli, A. 2006. Systematic position of the pelagic Thecosomata and Gymnosomata within Opisthobranchia (Mollusca, Gastropoda): Revival of the Pteropoda. *Journal of Zoological Systematics and Evolutionary Research* 44: 118-129.

Knutson, V. & Gosliner, T.M. 2014. Three new species of *Gymnodoris* nudibranchs from the Philippines. In: G.C. Williams & T.M Gosliner (eds.), *The Coral Triangle: The 2011 Hearst Biodiversity Expedition.* California Academy of Sciences, San Francisco. Pp. 129-143.

Kocot, K.M., Halanych, K.M., & Krug, P.J. 2013. Phylogenomics supports Panpulmonata: Opisthobranch paraphyly and key evolutionary steps in a major radiation of gastropod molluscs. *Molecular Phylogenetics and Evolution* 69: 764-771.

Korshunova, T., Martynov, A., & Picton, B. 2017. Ontogeny as an important part of integrative taxonomy in tergipedid aeolidaceans (Gastropoda: Nudibranchia) with a description of a new genus and species from the Barents Sea. *Zootaxa* 4324: 1-22.

Korshunova, T., Martynov, A., Bakken, T., Evertsen, J., Fletcher, K., Mudianta, W., Saito, H., Lundin, K., Schrödl, M., Picton, B. 2017. Polyphyly of the traditional family Flabellinidae affects a major group of Nudibranchia: aeolidacean taxonomic reassessment with descriptions of several new families, genera, and species (Mollusca, Gastropoda). *ZooKeys* 717: 1-139.

Krug, P.J., Vendetti, J.E., Ellingson, R.A., Trowbridge, C.D., Hirano, Y.M., Trathen, D. Y., Rodriguez, A.K., Swennen, C., Wilson, N.G. & Valdés, Á. 2015. Species selection favors dispersive life histories in sea slugs, but higher per-offspring investment drives shifts to short-lived larvae. *Systematic Biology* 64: 983-999.

Layton, K.K., Gosliner, T.M. & Wilson, N.G. 2018. Flexible colour patterns obscure identification and mimicry in Indo-Pacific *Chromodoris* nudibranchs (Gastropoda: Chromodorididae). *Molecular Phylogenetics and Evolution* 124: 27-36.

Maeda, T., Kajita, T., Maruyama, T., & Hirano, Y. 2010. Molecular phylogeny of the Sacoglossa, with a discussion of gain and loss of kleptoplasty in the evolution of the group. *Biological Bulletin* 219: 17-26.

Malaquias, M.A.E. & Reid, D.G. 2008. Systematic revision of the Recent species of Bullidae (Mollusca: Gastropoda: Cephalaspidea), with a molecular phylogenetic analysis. *Zoological Journal of the Linnean Society* 153: 453-543.

Malaquias, M.A.E., Mackenzie-Dodds, J., Gosliner, T.M., Bouchet, P., & Reid, D.G. 2009. A molecular phylogeny of the Cephalaspidea *sensu lato* (Gastropoda: Euthyneura): Architectibranchia redefined and Runcinacea reinstated. *Zoologica Scripta* 38: 23-41.

Mikkelsen, P.M. 1996. The evolutionary relationships of Cephalaspidea *s.l.* (Gastropoda: Opisthobranchia): A phylogenetic analysis. *Malacologia* 37: 375-442.

Mikkelsen, P.M. 1998. *Cylindrobulla* and *Ascobulla* in the western Atlantic (Gastropoda, Opisthobranchia, Sacoglossa): Systematic review, description of a new species, and phylogenetic reanalysis. *Zoologica Scripta* 27: 49-71.

Oskars, T. R., Bouchet, P., & Malaquias, M.A.E. 2015. A new phylogeny of the Cephalaspidea (Gastropoda: Heterobranchia) based on expanded taxon sampling and gene markers. *Molecular Phylogenetics and Evolution* 89: 130-150.

Pola, M., Cervera, J.L., & Gosliner, T.M. 2005a. Review of the systematics of the genus *Roboastra* Bergh, 1877 (Nudibranchia, Polyceridae, Nembrothinae) with the description of a new species from the Galapagos Islands. *Zoological Journal of the Linnean Society* 144: 167-189.

Pola, M., Cervera, J.L., & Gosliner, T.M. 2005b. Four new species of *Tambja* Burn, 1962 (Nudibranchia: Polyceridae) from the Indo-Pacific. *Journal of Molluscan Studies* 71: 257-267.

Pola, M., Cervera, J.L., & Gosliner, T.M. 2006a. Description of two new phanerobranch nembrothid species (Nudibranchia: Polyceridae: Doridacea). *Journal of the Marine Biological Association of the United Kingdom* 86: 403-409.

Pola, M., Cervera, J.L., & Gosliner, T.M. 2006b. Taxonomic revision and phylogenetic analysis of the genus *Tambja* Burn, 1962 (Mollusca, Nudibranchia, Polyceridae). *Zoologica Scripta* 35: 491-530.

Pola, M., Cervera, J.L., & Gosliner, T.M. 2007. Phylogenetic relationships of Nembrothinae (Mollusca: Doridacea: Polyceridae) inferred from morphology and mitochondrial DNA. *Molecular Phylogenetics and Evolution* 43: 726-742.

Pola, M., Cervera, J.L., & Gosliner, T.M. 2008a. Revision of the Indo-Pacific genus *Nembrotha* (Nudibranchia: Dorididae: Polyceridae), with a description of two new species. *Scientia Marina* 72: 145-183.

Pola, M. & Gosliner, T.M. 2010. The first molecular phylogeny of cladobranchian opisthobranchs (Mollusca, Gastropoda, Nudibranchia). *Molecular Phylogenetics and Evolution* 56: 931-941.

Rudman, W.B. 1981. The anatomy and biology of alcyonarian feeding aeolid opisthobranch molluscs and their development of symbiosis with zooxanthellae. *Zoological Journal of the Linnean Society* 72: 219-262.

Rudman, W.B. 1984. The Chromodorididae (Opisthobranchia: Mollusca) of the Indo-West Pacific: A review of the genera. *Zoological Journal of the Linnean Society* 81: 115-273.

Rudman, W.B. 1991. Further studies on the taxonomy and biology of the octocoral-feeding genus *Phyllodesmium* Ehrenberg, 1831 (Nudibranchia: Aeolidoidea). *Journal of Molluscan Studies* 57: 167-203.

Rudman, W.B. 2004. Further species of the opisthobranch genus *Okenia* (Nudibranchia: Goniodorididae) from the Indo-West Pacific. *Zootaxa* 695: 1-70.

Rudman, W.B. 2007. Two new species of *Okenia* (Gastropoda: Nudibranchia: Goniodorididae) from eastern Australia and Tanzania. *Zootaxa* 1657: 57-67.

Rudman, W.B & Bergquist, P.R. 2007. A review of feeding specificity in the sponge-feeding Chromodorididae (Nudibranchia: Mollusca). *Molluscan Research* 27: 60-88.

Schrödl, M. & Neusser, T.P. 2010. Towards a phylogeny and evolution of Acochlidia (Mollusca: Gastropoda: Opisthobranchia). *Zoological Journal of the Linnean Society* 158: 124-154.

Shipman, C. & Gosliner, T.M. 2015. Molecular and morphological systematics of *Doto* Oken, 1851 (Gastropoda: Heterobranchia), with descriptions of five new species and a new genus. *Zootaxa* 3973: 57-101.

Trickey, J.S., Thiel, M., & Waters, J.M. 2016. Transoceanic dispersal and cryptic diversity in a cosmopolitan rafting nudibranch. *Invertebrate Systematics* 30: 290-301.

Turner, L.M. & Wilson, N.G. 2008. Polyphyly across oceans: A molecular phylogeny of the Chromodorididae (Mollusca, Nudibranchia). *Zoologica Scripta* 37: 23-42.

References

Valdés, A. 2002a. A phylogenetic analysis and systematic revision of the cryptobranch dorids (Mollusca, Nudibranchia, Anthobranchia). *Zoological Journal of the Linnean Society* 136: 535-636.

Valdés, A. 2002b. Review of the genus *Actinocyclus* Ehrenberg, 1831 (Opisthobranchia: Doridoidea). *The Veliger* 45: 193-202.

Valdés, A. & Gosliner, T.M. 1999. Phylogeny of the radula-less dorids (Mollusca, Nudibranchia), with the description of a new genus and a new family. *Zoologica Scripta* 28: 315-360.

Valdés, A. & Gosliner, T.M. 2001. Systematics and phylogeny of the caryophyllidia-bearing dorids (Mollusca, Nudibranchia), with the description of a new genus and four new species from Indo-Pacific deep waters. *Zoological Journal of the Linnean Society* 133: 103-198.

Vallès, Y. 2002. *Taxonomy and Phylogeny of* Kaloplocamus *and* Plocamopherus *and their Relationships with other Phanerobranchs*. M.A. Dissertation, San Francisco State University. 266 pp.

Vallès, Y. & Gosliner, T.M. 2006. Shedding light onto the genera *Kaloplocamus* and *Plocamopherus* (Mollusca: Nudibranchia) with description of new species belonging to these unique bioluminescent dorids. *The Veliger* 48: 178-205.

Wägele, H. & Klussmann-Kolb, A. 2005. Opisthobranchia (Mollusca, Gastropoda) - more than just slimy slugs. Shell reduction and its implications on defence and foraging. *Frontiers in Zoology* 2 [pages unnumbered].

Wägele, H. & Willan, R.C. 2000. Phylogeny of the Nudibranchia. *Zoological Journal of the Linnean Society* 130: 83-181.

Willan, R.C. 1987. Phylogenetic systematics of the Notaspidea (Opisthobranchia) with reappraisal of families and genera. *American Malacological Bulletin* 5: 215-241.

Willan R.C. & Chang Y.-W. 2017. Description of three new species of *Tambja* (Gastropoda, Nudibranchia, Polyceridae) from the western Pacific Ocean reveals morphological characters with taxonomic and phylogenetic significance for traditional Polyceridae and related 'phaneorobranch' nudibranchs. *Basteria* 81: 1-23.

Wilson, N.G. & Burghardt, I. 2015. Here be dragons - Phylogeography of *Pteraeolidia ianthina* (Angas, 1864) reveals multiple species of photosynthetic nudibranchs (Aeolidina: Nudibranchia). *Zoological Journal of the Linnean Society* doi:10.1111/zoj.12266

Wilson, N.G. & Lee, M.S.Y. 2005. Molecular phylogeny of *Chromodoris* (Mollusca, Nudibranchia) and the identification of a planar spawning clade. *Molecular Phylogenetics and Evolution* 36: 722-727.

Yonow, N. 2008. Sea slugs of the Red Sea. Pensoft Publishers, Sofia. 304 pp.

Zapata, F., Wilson, N.G., Howison, M., Andrade, S.C., Jörger, K.M., Schrödl, M., Goetz, F.E., Giribet, G. & Dunn, C.W. 2014. Phylogenomic analyses of deep gastropod relationships reject Orthogastropoda. *Proceedings of the Royal Society Biological Sciences* 28: 20141739.

Index

Index

Index

Index

Index

Index

Index

Index

Index

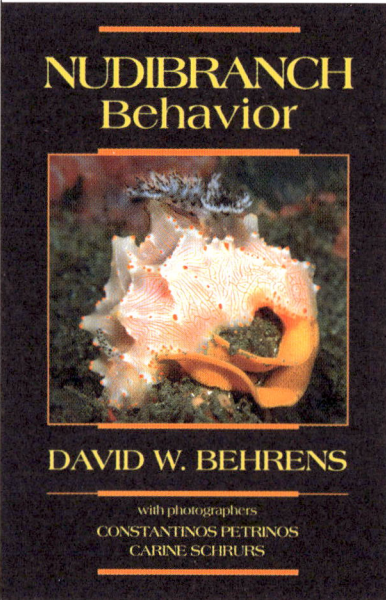

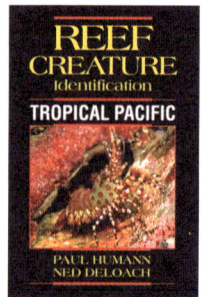

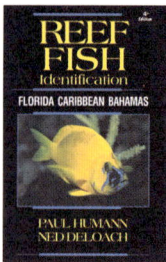

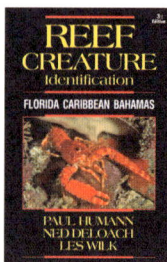

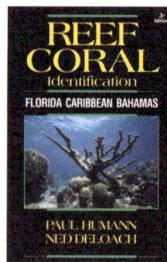

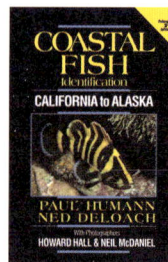